THE
OPEN
LEARNING
FOUNDATION

An Active Learning Approach

Principles of Human Resource Management

THE
OPEN
LEARNING
FOUNDATION

An Active Learning Approach

PRINCIPLES OF HUMAN RESOURCE MANAGEMENT

Alan Price

First published 2000

Blackwell Publishers Ltd
108 Cowley Road
Oxford OX4 1JF
UK

Blackwell Publishers Inc.
350 Main Street
Malden, Massachusetts 02148
USA

British Library Cataloguing in Publication Data

A CIP catalogue record for this book is available from the British Library

Library of Congress Cataloging-in-Publication Data

Library of Congress data has been applied for.

The ISBN for this title is 0-631-20178-5

Typeset in 10 on 12pt Times New Roman

Printed in Great Britain by MPG Books, Bodmin, Cornwall

This book is printed on acid-free paper

Acknowledgements

For the Open Learning Foundation

Martin Gibson (University of Central Lancashire), *Series Editor*

Maurice Benington, *Open Learning Editor*

Trevor Bolton (Anglia Polytechnic University), *Reviewer*

Leslie Mapp, *Director of Programmes*

Stephen Moulds (DSM Partnership), *Production Manager*

Caroline Pelletier, *Publishing Manager*

Julia Peart, *Programmes Assistant*

Copyright acknowledgements

Contents

GUIDE FOR STUDENTS

Course introduction

Welcome to *Principles of Human Resource Management*. The objectives of this student guide are:

- to explain why it is important to study human resource management as part of your degree
- to give you an outline of the subject of human resource management
- to describe the nature of the material on which this workbook is based
- to outline the programme which you will be following
- to offer practical hints and advice on how to study human resource management using the open learning approach
- to point out some of the advantages of studying human resource management by the methods used in this book.

Why study human resource management?

Every business is made up of people, the human resources of the business. How effectively those human resources are managed will have a major impact on how successful the business becomes. Indeed in many industries, the quality of the human resources, how effectively they work together and how well they are trained and developed, can be the major factor in maintaining the competitiveness and profitability of the business.

It follows then that the study of human resource management (HRM) is a vital part of the business studies curriculum and the ability to manage people effectively is a key skill requirement for the effective business manager. The process is a complex one. Partly this complexity stems from the fact that one is dealing with people, with all the inevitable variation in skills, personalities, attitudes and behaviours which this implies. HRM is further complicated by the major changes we are experiencing in technologies, in patterns of trade and business and the need for businesses and their employees to respond quickly if they are to remain competitive. This module is designed to help you understand these issues and begin to acquire some of the knowledge and skills required for effective management of people.

In recent years there has been a major debate amongst academics and practitioners about the significance of HRM and in particular whether there it offers anything new compared to more traditional approaches to personnel management. This module will explore such issues as well developing an understanding of some of the techniques which can support a professional approach to the management of people.

Some students take an interest in HRM because they intend to specialise in people management and perhaps work towards membership of the Institute of Personnel and Development. Indeed this area of specialisation provides a number of career avenues. However, the need for all managers to have competence in HRM is becoming inescapable. Increasingly as organisations become flatter, with fewer layers of management, line managers are playing an increasingly important role in the management of people

What is in this workbook?

Principles of Human Resource Management presents an introductory overview of the study of the management of people in organisations. It covers material one would normally expect to encounter in the second year of an undergraduate business studies degree.

The module is intended to be largely free standing, although it does build on some of the material contained in *Business Functions*, one of the other modules in the Active Learning series. Similarly one of the other level 1 modules, *People in Organisations*, will provide a useful foundation to many of the ideas covered.

Principles of Human Resource Management is part of a series of interactive texts designed to cover the entire curriculum of an undergraduate Business Studies degree. It can be used by itself or in conjunction with the other volumes in the series.

This module is particularly useful for students who may be following a course in which an 'open learning' approach is being used. The features which make it particularly suitable for open learning include:

- very careful sequencing of the materials so that there is a clear and logical progression
- a step-by-step approach so that you will be able to understand each new point thoroughly before proceeding to the next one
- a very clear layout with relatively short sections and paragraphs
- numerous activities and examples which help to illustrate the ideas and provide opportunities for analysis and developing understanding
- lots of opportunities for you to check that you understand what you have just read.

As with many of the other modules in Active Learning Business Studies series, the units are accompanied by a Resources section which provides you with additional learning materials. These have been carefully selected to complement the units and to provide you with an insight into the issues and debates which are covered in the professional practitioner literature. They are also used as the basis for some of the activities which form a central feature of the module

Students on more conventional courses will also find that the workbook provides a useful supplement to other text books which they may have been recommended.

Although the workbook is designed to be complete in itself, your understanding of the subject will be improved by wider reading. Each unit therefore has a list of recommended reading to guide you towards the more important and useful literature. At various points in the module you will be recommended to access information about particular companies, from the internet or elsewhere.

Unit structure

The module begins with an introduction to the study of human resource management. The first unit examines both the theoretical and practical significance of HRM, tracing the origins of the approach and the various ideas which have contributed to it. In particular the unit considers the differences between HRM and more conventional approaches to personnel management. Unit 2 focuses attention on the changing nature of work in contemporary society, examining the changing types and patterns of work and the shifts being seen in the requirements of the labour market. In particular, the unit considers the need for greater flexibility, the growth of part-time and temporary working and the trends in the type of work organisations which are emerging. Unit 3 introduces you to the idea of employee resourcing, in particular to the need for the development of appropriate strategies and plans to ensure that a cost-efficient approach is taken to ensure a suitable staffing base for the organisation. This is followed in Unit 4 with a more detailed consideration of the techniques available for selecting employees.

Unit 5 introduces the idea of performance management and considers the various ways in which individuals and teams can managed in order to improve organisational effectiveness. This includes practices such as performance appraisal as well as payment and other reward systems. The following unit explores the issue of discrimination in the workplace and argues the business case (as well as the ethical case) for promoting equality of opportunity. Unit 7 looks at the changing nature of employee relations and Unit 8 develops the idea of human resource development, and the ways in which performance can be improved through effective training and development processes

Using the workbook

You will probably find it most effective to work through the units in sequence. You should begin by noting the points which the unit outline identifies as the crucial aspects of the material. This will put the contents of the units into context and guide you through them.

Each unit is based around a number of activities. All of these are intended to be attempted by you as they arise and should be completed before you move on. Commentaries about the activities provide you with suggested answers, and just as importantly, suggest ways for tackling the questions and exercises. These are given immediately after each activity.

The activities are intended to give you the opportunity to reinforce your knowledge and understanding. Avoid the temptation to skip through the activities quickly.

They are there to assist you in developing your knowledge and understanding and your confidence with the material. Often the activities are included in order to develop important learning points and the commentaries which follow provide an important basis for discussing the ideas and techniques being covered. Rather like a question and answer session in a tutorial they are included to help you learn and not just to test your understanding.

Some of the activities will only take you a few minutes to deal with. By contrast, others may take considerably longer to complete. It is important that you discipline yourself to complete each activity before you refer to the answer provided.

Avoid rote learning

You should avoid any attempt at rote learning the material in this workbook. You should aim to understand the underlying logic in the ideas presented by working carefully through all the activities. Simply trying to learn and remember the concepts, ideas and techniques is inappropriate and insufficient. Rather, you should attempt to understand the principles behind the ideas and models, and understand the thinking behind the particular techniques presented.

Set time aside for your studies

At the start of the study period you will not know how long it will take to do the necessary work. It is sensible, therefore, to make a start on the work at an early stage in the study period. Try to discipline yourself to set aside particular times in the week to study, though not necessarily the same times each week. Experiment with different ways of studying the material to find the one which suits you. Try skimming each unit to get a grasp of the ideas covered before you go through it in detail. Alternatively, try reading the unit objectives and the summaries before you settle down to study the unit in any depth. Try to find the most suitable time to study when your concentration is at its highest and interruptions are at a minimum. And do set aside sufficient time to complete all the activities – they are a crucial part of the learning process.

UNIT 1
INTRODUCTION TO HUMAN RESOURCE MANAGEMENT

Introduction

Every business is made up of people: its human resources. Human resource management (HRM) is about managing these people effectively. It is aimed at achieving business objectives through the best use of an organisation's human resources. HRM incorporates the functions of traditional personnel management within a wider, more strategic framework. These functions include essential tasks which must be performed in every effective organisation, such as:

- forecasting and planning the number and type of staff required in the future
- recruiting and selecting suitable people when they are needed
- organising the assessment of employee performance and providing a system for dealing with inadequate performance
- devising and implementing the schemes by which staff are paid for their work
- training and developing new and experienced staff to cope effectively with changes in technology, products and services
- managing employee relations, dealing with controversial and sensitive issues including pay disputes, grievances, discipline and dismissal.

Human resource management is often presented as a proactive approach to managing people (Storey, 1995). By proactive we mean a perspective which emphasises long-term thinking, anticipating changes and requirements before they become critical. In reality, HRM is a mixture of anticipation and reaction. Human resource managers may have to deal with unexpected problems and radical changes in employer policy (Tamkin, Barber and Dench, 1997). They may, for example, have to manage site closures and redundancies because of market changes. They need to react quickly and competently within the bounds of employment law and contractual agreements.

Of necessity, therefore, HRM is both **pragmatic** and **eclectic**:

- it is pragmatic because it aims to achieve practical solutions to real work problems
- it is eclectic because those solutions can be drawn from a variety of theoretical and practical managerial traditions.

This module takes a realistic approach, mixing practical techniques with critical analysis as appropriate.

THE PURPOSE OF THIS MODULE

Why should you study human resource management? For students intending to specialise in human resource management as a business function, it is obviously essential to gain a broad but critical overview of the subject at an early stage. If, on the other hand, your interests lie in general management or a non-HR discipline you may wonder what relevance human resource management has for you. The answer is that all management careers inevitably involve some people management, making a knowledge of HRM important regardless of your specialism. Accountants, marketers, production engineers and sales managers all benefit from understanding the basic principles of recruitment, selection, performance management, training and employee relations.

The module is designed to provide you with a thorough grounding in the key areas of human resource management. This first unit sets the scene for later parts of the module by addressing some fundamental questions.

- Where does the term human resource management come from? Its origins are complex. We analyse the various strands which have contributed to its development.

- Is HRM simply another name for personnel management or a significantly different approach to managing people? This is a controversial issue, reflected by the continuing use of both terms to describe the people management function. We consider recent evidence on the adoption and influence of HRM.

- Should we approach the subject from a management point of view or focus on its implications for ordinary workers? In this unit we take a balanced approach, taking account of both sides of the employment equation.

Objectives

By the end of this unit you should be able to:

- explain the basic concepts underpinning the study and practice of human resource management

- provide a critical analysis of the practicality and effectiveness of the HRM approach for any organisation

- compare and contrast the characteristics of human resource management and earlier perspectives on people management

- discriminate between the rhetoric and reality of human resource management

- outline two influential models of HRM

- approach the remainder of this module with confidence.

SECTION 1

The Theoretical Basis of Human Resource Management

Introduction

Where do the fundamental concepts of human resource management come from? Human resource management incorporates ideas from different strands of management thinking which have developed throughout the twentieth century. In this section we trace some of the varied and sometimes contradictory origins of the subject. In doing so, we identify the main theoretical basis for the practice and philosophy of human resource management. Additionally, we assess the prevailing economic and ideological circumstances which led to the adoption of HRM. This discussion provides a foundation for a detailed examination of the functions and implications of HRM in section 2.

The aim of this section is to help you to:

- define human resource management

- compare and contrast some of the key management theories which underpin HRM

- describe the economic circumstances and ideological influences which encouraged the adoption of the HRM approach.

1.1   Defining HRM

What is human resource management? In essence, HRM is about managing people. It includes 'all management decisions and actions that affect the relationship between the organisation and employees – its human resources' (Beer et al., 1984). In the USA, the term was used for many years as an alternative label for **personnel management**. In the UK and other predominantly English-speaking countries, HRM and personnel management are still used interchangeably by many people in business. As we will see in section 2, however, since the 1980s management theorists and academics have attempted to draw clear distinctions between the two terms.

Writers on HRM emphasise a stronger link with business strategy than is the case with traditional personnel management but vary a great deal in other respects. Consequently, there is no single, universally accepted definition for the term. Here are some writers' definitions.

A strategic, coherent and comprehensive approach to the management and development of the organisation's human resources in which every aspect of that process is wholly integrated within the overall management of the organisation. HRM is essentially an ideology.

(Armstrong, 1992)

A diverse body of thought and practice, loosely unified by a concern to integrate the management of personnel more closely with the core management activity of organisations.

(Goss, 1994)

Human resource management is a distinctive approach to employment management which seeks to achieve competitive advantage through the strategic development of a highly committed and capable workforce, using an integrated array of cultural, structural and personnel techniques.

(Storey, 1995)

ACTIVITY 1

On the basis of our discussion so far, and the sample definitions given above, make a list of keywords which apply to the concept of HRM. Then write your own definition of human resource management in no more than 25 words.

It is difficult to provide a succinct definition of the subject which reflects reality. Obviously, you must include some element which covers the process of managing people. But your definition should also include the word strategic and convey the holistic (all-embracing) philosophy of human resource management. In later sections of this unit, we emphasise that HRM is not simply a loose collection of activities, such as recruiting new staff and dealing with trade unions. There must be some form of planned integration.

1.2   Origins

Where has HRM come from? Is it a totally modern concept or an adaptation of older ideas about the management of people? Tracing the origins of some of the ideas which underpin the philosophy and techniques of human resource management will help you to understand the subject. People have been organised into workforces for thousands of years: the construction of ancient monuments such as the pyramids, Stonehenge and the Great Wall of China must have involved huge numbers of workers. But modern managerial techniques, as we understand them, date from the late nineteenth century when large manufacturing companies first emerged. As these were predominantly US businesses, it is not surprising, therefore, that many key concepts of human resource management come from the USA (Gallagher et al., 1997).

Take a few minutes to think of some of the major management theories you may have encountered in your earlier studies. Already, you may have realised that human resource management is only one of the many management concepts to have emerged in recent years. For example, you may have come across terms such as total quality management, business process re-engineering, benchmarking and change management. These concepts share a common theme: the improvement of business organisation and performance. They reflect the concerns of management writers whose ideas have travelled the world, drawing on different influences and traditions. Now consider the origins of these ideas by completing activity 2.

ACTIVITY 2

Recall from your previous studies six or so twentieth century management writers such as FW Taylor and Rosabeth Moss Kanter.

1. Briefly describe some of the significant contributions of each of these writers that may have influenced the development of HRM as it is today.

2. Your review will indicate a number of features about the nature of HRM. Write down two or three.

These are some of the many writers that have contributed to or influenced the development of human resource management. (You may have mentioned others.)

- FW Taylor's scientific management ideas continue to influence production techniques and 'hard' (financially-driven) human resource management. He popularised the notion of analysing work performance in order to minimise costs and align employee effort to production needs as closely as possible. His ideas on higher pay for more work continue to be debated in the context of performance-related pay.

- Frank and Lilian Gilbreth developed work study methods which have since been elaborated into performance measurement and job design. These are key elements of strategic HRM.

- Elton Mayo advocated 'human relations' and the study of group behaviour. Mayo's ideas owed a great deal to others but underpin 'soft' (humanistic or people-centred) HRM and today's highly fashionable team-based work practices.

- Kurt Lewin introduced models of change for people and organisations and attempted to explain why change initiatives often fail. HRM is often introduced as a vehicle for change.

- Neo-human relations and socio-technical theorists – based principally in Scandinavia and the UK – developed Mayo's pre-war ideas in the 1950s and 1960s. They experimented with alternatives to Fordist production lines by emphasising the use of work teams. Team organisation has been a feature of human resource management in the 1980s and 1990s.

- Deming promulgated ideas about total quality which were enthusiastically adopted in Japan and later in the West. Many elements of the total quality management (TQM) approach overlap with HRM techniques.

- Pascale and Athos investigated Japanese working practices and transmitted concepts of just-in-time and quality assurance back to the Western world. This coincided with the emergence of HRM in the early 1980s.

- Tom Peters and his collaborators focused on the notion of excellence in organisational performance. Strategic HRM is focused on achieving organisational competitiveness through the development of excellent human resources.

- Charles Handy, Chris Argyris and Edgar Schein extended our ideas on the nature of work and organisation. They provided much of the theoretical underpinning for HRM.

- Henry Mintzberg researched what managers and leaders *really* did and made critical assessments of strategic planning techniques. Mintzberg encouraged human resource and other managers to be realistic in their approach to strategy.

- Rosabeth Moss Kanter focused on organisational change and the role of women in management, drawing on her experience of the difficulties of managing people in numerous US companies. She is one of the few female management theorists to have influenced the way in which HRM is conducted.

These writers are distinguished by the quality and originality of their ideas. Their ideas overlap in many ways. Management ideas come in and out of fashion but, for decades, these theorists, and others, have been convinced that the most successful organisations are those which make best use of their employees. This is the central theme of human resource management.

This activity should have helped you to see that HRM has emerged from many different sources; some writers pulled in one (hard) direction (such as Taylor and the Gilbreths), while others pulled in a different (softer) direction (such as Mayo and Kanter). More recent writers have also introduced new ideas on the nature of organisations which have moved forward thinking about HRM. Three further important points might have emerged from your study:

- HRM is largely a collection of ideas from the twentieth century
- these ideas have many different roots and they do not fit comfortably within one coherent and self-consistent body of knowledge
- the development of HRM continues today.

1.3 The driving forces of human resource management

During the last 20 years or so, many management writers began to develop a consensus on the factors that are important for organisational effectiveness, and their views influenced the directions HRM has taken recently. Four key factors have been identified:

- strong, goal-directed leadership
- high levels of employee motivation and skill
- a holistic approach to people management and organisational change
- a perception of employees as 'human capital' – assets rather than costs to a business.

What circumstances led to an emphasis on these themes? There were two significant influences in the 1970s and 1980s: rising competition from Japan and government action in countries such as the USA, UK and New Zealand to encourage managers to manage (Storey, 1995).

JAPANESE COMPETITION AND HRM

Why was Japanese competition such an important factor in the development of HRM? You may be aware that Japan was the first of the Asian Tigers: the vigorous economies in South-East Asia which challenged the pre-eminence of US and Western European businesses from the 1970s onwards. Japanese business culture was particularly distinctive (Garraghan and Stewart, 1992; Whitehill, 1991). It was different from the free market capitalist culture found in predominantly English-speaking countries, including Australia, the UK and the USA. Free market capitalism is short-termist, emphasising:

- a fast return on risk capital
- organisational growth from deals, mergers and aggressive takeovers
- hard-headed managerial attitudes towards employees, including the ready acceptance of redundancies
- provision of limited employee rights
- little emphasis on research, development or staff training
- minimal acceptance of social responsibilities such as maintaining low levels of unemployment and family-friendly working practices.

Eccles (1989) concludes that free market capitalism is inherently at a disadvantage when compared with the South-East Asian model which emphasises long-term organic growth through developing products and people. In contrast to Western businesses, Japanese management focused on:

- a culture of teamwork rather than individualism
- developing high levels of quality and motivation
- encouraging experiential learning through job rotation 循以
- mutual commitment between the organisation and its staff.

ACTIVITY 3

According to Eccles and other writers, a major difference between the stereotypical characterisation of Japanese and free market approaches has been the Japanese emphasis on long-term thinking in contrast to free market short-termism.

We are not saying here that all Japanese organisations exhibit a long-term perspective and all free market organisations have a short-term attitude, but that each approach is more strongly associated with one region than with the other.

Consider the likely consequences or implications of these different approaches for:

- business organisations
- employees.

In their stereotypical forms, the employment relationship between organisations and employees is more certain and predictable in Japanese business. Expertise is bought and sold in free market countries whereas large Japanese organisations have 'grown' talent within their workforces.

So, for the Japanese business:

- staff are treated as a resource to be developed and exploited, hence skilled employees are 'grown' rather than poached from other firms
- plans are made and resources are invested for the development of employees to fill positions that are forecast to be needed three, five or ten years in the future
- employees are encouraged to work in teams, relying on collective team effort rather than individual flair.

For the individual employee in Japanese business there is:

- a strong sense of belonging to teams which fosters a company-minded attitude – conformity and compliance are encouraged as opposed to entrepreneurial diversity and risk-taking
- paternalism which encourages acceptance of authority and infuses a sense of security but which may fail to stimulate the excitement of individual competitiveness and personal achievement.

In contrast, the individualistic orientation of the free market emphasises immediate, personal rewards as opposed to long-term security from team effort. Conformity is less important in free market businesses, partly because it is easier to change jobs in mid-career and therefore less risky. As a result, there has been freer movement between organisations in the West bringing with it the advantages of cross-fertilisation.

You may have reached some tentative conclusions from your speculations on the differences between Japanese and free market approaches. You will have recognised that Japanese management displays features that you might regard as incompatible with Western cultures. Also, some of its characteristics could lead to rigidities and lethargic development in different circumstances to those faced by Japanese businesses in the 1970s and 1980s.

Partly due to the management methods described above, Japanese industry advanced considerably until the mid-1990s. There were other factors which helped in this success: protected home markets, government co-ordination of industry-wide investment and specialisation in electronic consumer goods and motor vehicles. Nevertheless, Japanese people management techniques were given prominence and studied carefully by Western managers and academics (Pascale and Athos, 1981).

Japanese culture could not be replicated in Australasia, North America and Europe but the notion of strong culture and teamwork found considerable favour as managerial concepts (Deal and Kennedy, 1982). However, managing an organisational culture required a much more extensive and people-centred approach than that used by most free market organisations (Ouchi, 1981; Peters and Waterman, 1982). HRM addressed this need (Legge, 1995).

It is worth noting that the notions of Japanese management developed at that time were excessively stereotypical and based on research into a small number of large corporations (Garraghan and Stewart, 1992). In reality, the much trumpeted concepts of life-long employment and mutual commitment between management and employees were not so common in smaller Japanese businesses. Moreover, the shallowness of this commitment was revealed in the late-1990s when a financial crisis hit East Asian stock markets. Paradoxically, large Japanese businesses began to adopt the practices of the West and made large numbers of employees redundant.

HRM AND WESTERN BUSINESS CULTURE

The development of HRM as a management subject occurred at the time when Japanese competition was having a considerable impact on Western businesses. A significant landmark was reached in 1981 when human resource management was introduced on to the influential Master in Business Administration (MBA) programme at Harvard Business School. Since then, HRM has been taught in many other business schools and universities throughout the world. The Harvard course drew on a number of significant themes:

- **strategic management** – directing people to achieve business objectives
- **leadership** – particularly in developing and inspiring teams of individuals
- **human relations** – making use of the group phenomena which moderate and influence behaviour at work through, for example, social pressure and conformity
- **vocational selection and performance assessment** – psychometric and other techniques which measure desirable individual qualities
- **training and development** – increasing the value of an organisation's human capital by developing employees' skills and expertise
- **motivation** – primarily focused on the individual, through reward schemes and feedback from performance assessment
- **flexibility** – moving away from standard, collectively-negotiated employment conditions towards varied, individual arrangements including part-time work and temporary contracts.

The Harvard approach is further discussed in section 3 of this unit where we consider major models of human resource management.

In the early 1980s, political events in the West became conducive to a philosophy of people management which focused on the relationship between organisations and individual employees rather than that between employers and trade unions (Legge, 1995). Why should politicians have encouraged the adoption of HRM? During the period of increasing Japanese competition, the UK and US governments headed by Margaret Thatcher and Ronald Reagan actively promoted the free market ideal. How did they create a receptive environment for human resource management to develop, given that many of the central themes of Japanese business culture such as state-controlled industrial strategy were not politically acceptable?

As Guest (1991) points out, both Thatcher and Reagan governments valued rugged entrepreneurial individualism. They aimed to create **enterprise cultures** unrestricted by employee protection legislation. Above all, they encouraged managers to be strong leaders by restricting workers' rights to organise and strike. According to their unitarist perspective, workers should not be loyal to another body outside the firm. Dismissal became easier and changes in tax systems encouraged the use of differential forms of remuneration such as performance-related pay and incentive bonuses. State-owned industries were privatised and the civil service mentality was disparaged. As we shall see later in this unit (see section 3), the individualistic and unitarist values expressed in the concept of enterprise culture are consistent with HRM models which emphasise a close match between individual performance, workforce deployment and business strategy (Legge, 1995).

Summary

Human resource management is a subject with complex origins. Its theoretical basis is rooted in a wide range of management ideas and techniques which share a common preoccupation with increasing business competitiveness through effective use of an organisation's employees. The development of HRM owes much to the prevailing economic and ideological conditions of the 1970s and 1980s, particularly the Western reaction to Japanese competition and, in the USA and UK, a political commitment to the enterprise culture.

SECTION 2

HRM and Personnel Management

Introduction

Our exploration of human resource management continues with a consideration of the origins of HRM as a professional and expert activity. Managing people is not simply a theoretical matter, it is also a practical subject concerned with real-life activities. Human resource management incorporates practices developed by practitioners of people management: both specialists in personnel management and generalists in line and senior management.

Proponents of HRM argue that it is a coherent and integrated approach to managing people, distinct from personnel management (Storey, 1995). Others hold that the two are little different and overlap in their techniques and range of interest (Legge, 1995). As we shall see in this section, the continuing use of both terms, often interchangeably, indicates a degree of confusion.

The aim of this section is to help you to:

- analyse further the complex origins of HRM
- outline the main functions of personnel/ human resource managers
- critically evaluate the main arguments about differences between HRM and traditional personnel management
- compare and contrast the activities performed by specialist and generalist managers
- explain the need for specific human resource expertise.

2.1   The personnel management tradition

There is a continuing debate as to whether HRM is a genuinely different management philosophy or simply 'old wine in new bottles'. In other words, there is some doubt as to whether it is significantly different from older forms of people management. Again, we return to the question: what exactly is human resource management? As we saw, the debate is made all the more difficult because there is no consistent view of human resource management. Different writers interpret the concept according to their individual perspectives, interests and audiences. Reading different accounts of the subject, we can identify three contradictory views:

- HRM is **managing people** in the widest sense – an activity for all managers with staff responsibilities
- HRM is really **personnel management** – a new label for specialist activities
- HRM is a **strategic model** for the utilisation of human resources – people are assets to be made use of and valued, in fact they are the most important assets in any organisation.

Some would argue that human resource management embodies all of these ideas. Storey (1995) considers that 'HRM is an amalgam of description, prescription, and logical deduction. It describes the beliefs and assumptions of certain leading-edge practitioners. It prescribes certain priorities. And it deduces certain consequent actions which follow from the series of propositions.'

Human resource management undoubtedly owes many of its most important concepts to practitioners in the personnel profession. Personnel management was first recognised as a business function in the USA during the 1890s when NCR (National Cash Register) opened its personnel office. In the USA, personnel managers have always identified closely with the objectives of their employing organisation: human resource management is a natural continuation of this managerialist tradition.

Elsewhere, human resource management represents a radical departure from previous practice. For instance, in the UK personnel management partly originated with the welfare officers employed by Quaker-owned companies such as Cadburys in the early twentieth century. They acted as intermediaries between management and employees. By the 1970s, this role was enshrined in the function of the industrial relations negotiator – a difficult and thankless role in the frequent industrial disputes of the period. Activity 4 allows you to refresh your memory on the other functions dealt with by personnel managers.

ACTIVITY 4

Based on your previous studies and reading what tasks would you expect personnel managers to perform? List and write brief notes on six tasks undertaken by personnel managers. Can you select one task that is more important than any other? If so, which one, and why do you think it is particularly important?

Table 1 lists tasks undertaken by personnel managers, though the range and nature of tasks obviously varies from one organisation to another. Similarly, individual organisations attach different degrees of importance to each function.

You might have selected any one of these tasks as being more important than the others, depending on the context you have in mind. However, it is important to recognise that many of these tasks are interrelated, so that successful performance of one task – selection, for example – is dependent on another, such as recruitment. Recruitment itself is dependent on other issues such as the image of the company, which in turn, is determined by factors including communication, pay, training and welfare.

Recruitment and selection are part of the process of resourcing – maintaining sufficient people with the right skills for an organisation to function efficiently. Dismissal is also a component of the resourcing process. Equally, pay and performance assessment have obvious connections and both are linked to grading. Welfare and employee relations have some close relationships, as both do with pay and performance assessment – and dismissal.

The key point as far as HRM is concerned is that these are all interrelated and the performance of each task is potentially of equal importance to effective people management.

Function	Task
Recruitment	Advertising for new employees and liaising with employment agencies
Selection	Determining the best candidates from those who apply, arranging interviews, tests, references
Promotion	Running selection procedures to determine progression within the organisation
Pay	Playing a minor or major role in pay negotiation, determination and administration
Performance assessment	Co-ordinating staff appraisal and counselling systems to evaluate individual employee performance
Grading structures	Comparing the relative difficulty and importance of functions as a basis for pay or development
Training and development	Co-ordinating or delivering programmes to fit people for roles required by the organisation now and in the future
Welfare	Providing or organising specialist counselling for people with personal or domestic problems affecting their work
Communication	Providing an internal information service, perhaps through staff newspapers, magazines, handouts, booklets and videos
Employee relations	Handling disputes, grievances and industrial action, often dealing with unions or staff representatives
Dismissal	Handling dismissal and severance on an individual basis as a result of failure to meet requirements or as part of a redundancy or closure exercise involving large numbers of people
Personnel administration	Record-keeping and monitoring legislative requirements related to equal opportunities and, possibly, pensions and tax

Table 1: Specialist personnel functions
Source: Adapted from Price (1997)

CRITICISMS OF PERSONNEL MANAGEMENT

Between 1950 and 1980, the personnel profession expanded its role considerably (Townley, 1994). Personnel directors were appointed in many large organisations and strategic personnel management became a recognised topic of study. In the UK, the Institute of Personnel Management (now the Institute of Personnel and Development) became a recognised and comparatively influential professional body, although it represented fewer than half of personnel practitioners. However, there was dissatisfaction within and outside the profession regarding the role, training and authority of personnel managers. For example, they were criticised (Sisson, 1995) for having a narrow, functional outlook with little appreciation of:

- business strategy
- the competitive business environment
- labour economics
- work of other organisational functions, such as marketing and finance
- balance sheets.

Personnel managers were not often seen as being on the side of senior management. Their 'welfare' orientation placed them as intermediaries between the business and its employees. This positioning meant that personnel managers had comparatively low levels of power within many organisations and consequent disadvantages in terms of salaries, career positions and influence in comparison with other management professionals in, for example, finance or marketing. Sisson (1995) describes personnel management as a Cinderella profession.

Tyson (1989) made a useful distinction between three types of personnel management functions.

- **Clerk of works** – A term applicable to a majority of personnel managers, covering those involved in the routine of administration, record-keeping, letter-writing, setting up interviews and welfare matters. Reports to personnel or senior line manager.

- **Contracts manager** – Likely to be found in large organisations with formal industrial relations structures. Involved in detailed short-term policy-making and resolving problems. A 'fixer' with some degree of influence with trade unions and senior management.

- **Architect** – Probably highly qualified but not necessarily in personnel. Broad portfolio with a significant strategic role. A business manager first and personnel manager second.

2.2   Personnel management and HRM

Human resource management has been adopted, in part, as a response to the criticisms and difficulties of the personnel management profession (Legge, 1995). Can we clarify the essential differences between personnel and human resource managers? In many ways, they perform the same tasks. The activities of traditional personnel managers listed in table 1 continue to be undertaken by staff now increasingly labelled as human resource managers. However, if the rhetoric of HRM is to be believed, there are some crucial differences.

First, personnel activities tended to be disconnected and conducted as independent processes. Decades ago Drucker (1961) dismissed the work of personnel staff as being 'largely a collection of incidental techniques without much internal cohesion'. Tyson (1989) describes this as Balkanisation. For example, people were sent on training courses because training was seen to be 'a good thing'. The HRM perspective stresses that each activity should form part of the whole process of people management. So training should form part of a development programme meeting the needs of the business, and not as a discrete process

Second, within human resource management there is a greater stress on the role of line managers in managing their own people. Traditional personnel management is viewed as a specialist function, whereas HRM is the responsibility of all managers. In keeping with this thinking, Tamkin et al. (1997) found that the human resource function had split into core and peripheral units in many of the organisations they surveyed. The core unit was usually small and strategic, whereas peripheral human resource staff typically provided day-to-day technical support for line managers.

Third, traditional personnel managers had little power or prestige, but human resource management is of strategic interest to the most senior managers (Fowler, 1987). According to the rhetoric, human resource managers are expected to be firmly managerialist in outlook, conducting their activities in line with business objectives. It has been argued that personnel managers have been happy to accept HRM because it means better salaries (Goss, 1994).

Fourth, traditional personnel management is operational, focused on technical skills and functions such as recruitment and selection, training, salary administration and employee relations. The human resource management approach relates all employee matters to business strategy in a comprehensive and organised way (Storey, 1995). For example, recruitment, training and dismissal are planned to meet the strategic objectives of the organisation. Human resource managers are expected to be proactive, constantly looking forward to the needs of the future. This contrasts with the largely reactive or fire-fighting approach of traditional personnel management.

Fifth, human resource management is aimed at achieving competitive advantage for an organisation through the development of a highly committed, skilled workforce. It does so by means of a carefully integrated set of 'cultural, structural and personnel techniques' (Storey, 1995). HRM encompasses these functions and techniques within an approach which emphasises higher-level organisational issues such as strategic planning, competence development programmes and benchmarking.

From this perspective, therefore, human resource management has taken on a wider meaning which can be distinguished from traditional personnel management. In Tyson's terminology, clerks of works are being replaced with architects. Proponents of this view present HRM as a specific approach or philosophy, concerned with the achievement of business objectives through effective use of an organisation's people (Armstrong, 1992; Storey, 1995). They argue that human resource management:

- provides a strategic, coherent and comprehensive framework for acquiring, motivating, developing and managing people
- integrates every aspect of that process within the overall management of the organisation.

Legge (1995) makes the significant point that when we contrast personnel management with human resource management, we are not comparing like with like. In most cases we are contrasting a descriptive, and often stereotyped view, of personnel management, as it has been over recent decades, with a rhetorical or prescriptive account of human resource management which does not necessarily have any basis in commercial reality.

The extent to which traditional personnel management has been replaced by HRM is further debated in Unit 2. The next activity reviews our study of personnel management and its relation to human resource management.

ACTIVITY 5

State which of the following statements are more true than false, and which are more false than true.

1. With the growth of the Institute of Personnel Management during the 1970s, personnel managers in the UK acquired significant status, influence and power within their own organisations.

2. Personnel management is regarded by many managers as a set of mainly administrative activities.

3. Human resource management is only concerned with strategic issues whereas personnel management is entirely focused on operational matters.

4. The essential difference between personnel management and human resource management is said to be the different emphasis on strategic planning and strategic issues.

The first statement is false. Although the Institute of Personnel Management became influential, less than half of personnel managers were members, and their roles continued to be seen as largely administrative or devoted to providing a service to line managers. Thus, the second statement is true.

The third statement is false. Although the emphasis of personnel management might be on day-to-day operational matters such as recruitment and selection, performance assessment and training, this is not the whole story. Personnel managers are also involved in strategic issues such as preparing resourcing plans and making forecasts of future skills requirements in preparation for recruitment and training programmes. Human resource managers may be more concerned with the big picture, taking a broader overview of the links between business plans, future resourcing needs, organisational culture and staff development; however the operational matters of recruitment, assessment, disciplinary issues and training must still be carried out.

The fourth statement in activity 5 is true. Remember, HRM is a different *emphasis*. As we have explained, there is no definitively clear distinction between HRM and personnel management.

INTEGRATION OF PERSONNEL FUNCTIONS WITHIN HRM

Human resource management incorporates the specialist personnel functions described in table 1, which may have been dealt with as separate and unconnected topics, within broader, integrated and strategic areas. These areas include:

- resourcing
- performance management
- developing employees
- rewarding employees.

RESOURCING

This involves providing human resources from within or outside an organisation. The functions of recruitment, selection and dismissal have been integrated within a wider framework which focuses on questions such as:

- do we really need to recruit a new, full-time, permanent member of staff?
- are there other ways of dealing with the work?
- should we consider temporary staffing, reorganisation or subcontracting to an outside specialist firm?

In other words, there is a greater emphasis on *why* a specific course of action should be taken as opposed to *how* it should be undertaken.

PERFORMANCE MANAGEMENT

This links the assessment of knowledge, skills and abilities to job grading, training, promotion opportunities and pay levels. The focus has shifted from appraising individual employees to the creation of a system which informs both the organisation and its employees of the level of necessary competences they possess. Developing employees

This covers training, education and career experiences. Human resource development transcends 'training for its own sake'. It seeks a systematic and integrated process which takes information on competence levels from performance assessments and aims to meet any shortfall in requirements through carefully organised development programmes.

REWARDING EMPLOYEES

This involves designing and implementing payment systems which emphasise and encourage good performance. Pay is increasingly tied to performance assessment and the achievement of job competences. However, it can be just one element of a wider approach designed to reinforce appropriate behaviour through communication strategies, employee relations policies and day-to-day people management.

These are important issues as we shall discover in Unit 2. To understand the topic more clearly we need to consider the way in which HRM takes place in different organisations.

2.3 Generalists and specialists

If HRM is more than a common-sense activity, should managing people be restricted to specialists with human resource expertise? The answer has to be no, because managers in areas such as finance, production, marketing, sales and customer service need other skills which are equally important. Managing people is part of the normal work of every generalist line manager or supervisor. Indeed, as we shall see, various models or theories of human resource management emphasise the importance of line managers in the conduct of HRM. In fact, some theorists consider that ultimately HRM will be done entirely through generalist managers. For example, Sullivan (1998) concludes that:

- line managers are much closer to individual problems and the people involved than centralised HR departments
- managers with appropriate information and systems can make faster and better decisions than remote human resource specialists
- giving line managers the authority to make most human resource decisions allows them to take ownership of their people problems.

Conversely, we can argue that some elements of human resource management are too specialised for the average sales manager, accountant or engineer to handle satisfactorily. Activity 6 gives you the opportunity to analyse the views of five senior human resource managers.

ACTIVITY 6

Read the article *The credible journey* (see Resource 1 in the Resources section). This article presents a range of opinions on the credibility and role of human resource professionals. List three benefits which human resource managers could gain from having had line management experience that are likely to be of value when dealing with people management problems. Explain your selection of each of these benefits in 50–100 words.

You might have concluded that the ability to use line managers' terminology (to speak their language) and understand their concerns are particularly important strengths that are difficult to acquire without direct experience. Similarly people management is made easier if line managers know that a HR professional has direct knowledge of some of the good and bad features of practical management. This bolsters credibility and respect which, in turn, increases the HR manager's influence.

In the long term, it is likely that a wide knowledge of the business can counterbalance a deep specialism in particular areas of human resources such as performance assessment, compensation (pay and benefits) and selection. It is also probable that experience of information technology will be highly relevant as sophisticated personnel management information systems become common.
At this point, consider the question posed by Activity 7.

ACTIVITY 7

Now list three reasons why it is beneficial to employ human resource professionals, based on your reading of Resource 1. Again, write down your conclusions for each reason in 50–100 words.

Non-HR managers are less likely to have been trained in behavioural sciences, employment law and personnel practice (Sisson, 1995). Also, new developments in employee and human resource information systems are demanding even more specialised skills, drawing from both information technology and conventional human resource management. In addition, specialists can make use of corporate intranets (internal information distribution systems, accessed by internet technology) to develop communication, training, resourcing and administration facilities.

ORGANISATION OF HUMAN RESOURCE MANAGEMENT

There are several key organisational factors which help to determine the balance between the provision of specialist and generalist HR management. Organisational size is critical – small businesses, for example, have no choice but to manage most tasks through generalist management. The cultures of small businesses – their characteristics as places to work – are determined by the personalities of the owners. Small businesses tend to be managed directly and informally: bosses hire and fire, decide pay and conditions and often demand flexible working attitudes from their staff. We discuss this issue further in later units.

Conversely, most large organisations tend to have specialist human resource staff. Because of the number of people involved, someone has to keep staff records. A large business has to be organised in a deliberate, systematic way, probably with groups of workers reporting to individual managers or supervisors. Larger firms have formal structures with clearer division into specialist functions. The function designated to look after aspects of people management is usually labelled personnel or human resources.

We have looked briefly at the question of whether human resource management should be carried out by specialists or by general managers. Now we turn to consider how a specialist HRM function might be organised.

According to Werther and Davis (1995) 'a separate (HR) department usually emerges when the expected benefits of a department exceed its costs'. Line managers can take on many human resource management tasks but, if they do, will they have sufficient knowledge of employment law and personnel techniques to deal properly with issues such as dismissals, retirements and grievance procedures. If not – and they probably do not have this knowledge – what are the implications of legal action, employment tribunals, training costs and so on? In this case, you may agree that the best solution is a slimmed-down central human resource function with delegation of day-to-day people management to line managers.

The management of human resources can be organised in a variety of ways. Adams (1991) identifies five main types of HR service.

- The traditional personnel department with a range of specialist human resource services.

- In-house human resource agencies which act as cost centres, charging client departments for activities such as recruitment.

- Internal human resource consultancies, selling their activities to the organisation and possibly competing with outside agencies.

- Business-within-business human resource consultancy, selling services within and outside the company.

- Outsourcing human resource services to external providers.

The following short case study, Fulmar Furnishers, illustrates the dilemma faced by most organisations at some stage in their development.

Fulmar Furnishers

Fulmar Furnishers is a specialist discount furniture company which has been taking orders through a small chain of shops and a mail-order department for over twenty years. These parts of the business are in decline, but its telesales and new internet sales operations are growing quickly. The company is increasingly divided between an old-style furniture company with well-trained, seasoned, full-time sales staff and the newer office-based operation employing a range of part-timers with little experience of furniture retailing.

The management structure is similarly divided into a hierarchical retail operation with a central HR department, and a small team of hands-on managers in the telecentre who do most of their own hiring and firing. The personnel tasks are different in the two parts of the business. There are few changes in staff in the retail outlets other than through retirement. Human resource staff dealing with the retail outlets are employed largely on administration of sick and holiday leave, pension entitlements, staff grievances, union negotiations, and the performance and commission scheme. In contrast, there is a steady turnover of employees in the telecentre. Some staff fail to make the grade and need to be dismissed, and there are frequent recruitment campaigns. There is also a need for the administration of a complicated attendance roster. Telecentre managers try to do these tasks themselves.

To cut costs and focus more investment in the telecentre, the management board is aiming to slim down the retail business. It is questioning the value of the HR department and debating the need for human resource specialists.

ACTIVITY 8

Reflect on the dilemma faced by the board of Fulmar Furnishers.

1. List the advantages and disadvantages of maintaining the specialist HR departments.

2. Outline the consequences of making the HR department redundant.

3. Write down your ideal solution to the problem, with justifications, in no more than 300 words. List some specialist roles which are worth retaining.

In answering these questions, you did well if you realised that the company needs to consider more than just the costs of paying for specialist HR staff. There is a trade off between the short-term benefit of reducing HR costs against the potential disadvantages of devolving the HR function to line managers. Obviously there is no perfect solution to this problem – it comes down to striking a balance between factors. You may have decided to retain specialists to cover some of the roles shown in table 2. Alternatively, you could have considered outsourcing some of these activities to external consultants.

Role	Activity
Human resource director/manager	Head of specialist people management function
Personnel administrator	Formerly a clerical function concerned with maintaining paper records, now requires expertise in creating and developing computer bases of human resource information
Employee relations manager	A long-standing specialist role with responsibility for collective bargaining and liaison with trade union officials, now extends to employee involvement and communication
Recruitment specialist	Trained in interviewing techniques and psychometric testing, may be occupational psychologists in larger organisations – this activity is often outsourced to specialist firms
Training and development specialist	Previously concerned with direct training, now becoming an internal consultancy role, often requires a psychology qualification
Human resource planner	Statistical and planning expert providing projections of human resource requirements for strategists
Employee counsellor	Comparatively new but increasingly common role, requires counselling qualification and knowledge of stress reduction techniques, typically replaces the welfare role of personnel management and may be part-time position or outsourced
Health and safety officer	Ensures compliance with legislation on workplace health and safety, liaises with local authority and other enforcement officials

Table 2: Specialist human resource roles
Source: Adapted from Price (1997)

What happens in practice? An Institute of Employment Studies report (Tamkin, Barber and Dench, 1997) suggests that line managers in most organisations deal with day-to-day staffing matters, such as low-level absences and minor discipline problems, and offer 'counselling' for a variety of problems which affect work performance and work allocation. Specialist HR managers tend to have more of a background role. They organise and administer resourcing, and deal with serious discipline cases and dismissal, the performance assessment process, promotion, and development programmes. They may also be responsible for much of the formal side of employee relations, including union negotiations. However, it is obvious that there is a considerable overlap between generalist and specialist functions and that no two organisations allocate tasks in the same way.

Summary

Businesses are dependent on their people for success. Managing people can be regarded as a matter of common sense but there are elements which require specific expertise. Human resource management offers a comparatively new approach to managing people. It is distinguished from personnel management by a strategic and holistic perspective.

There needs to be a careful balance between the contribution of line managers and HRM specialists. Businesses need to consider how the HRM function can be organised to suit their particular circumstances.

SECTION 3
Models and Theories of Human Resource Management

Introduction

We have already noted that the emergence of human resource management as a separate discipline owes much to the influence of management writers and to MBA programmes at major US business schools. Different models or theories of HRM with hard and soft orientations formed the academic basis of the subject. There are several models of HRM, the two most influential being the Harvard and the Michigan models. They have been described in terms of hard and soft approaches. Hard HRM models focus on employee costs and numbers; soft models take a greater interest in psychological elements such as commitment, skills and empowerment.

The aim of this section is to help you to:

- compare and contrast the classic HRM models from Harvard and Michigan business schools

- distinguish between hard and soft orientations of human resource management
- analyse the links between HRM and other business functions and processes
- outline common features in HRM models and theories.

3.1   The Harvard model

The Harvard model provides a **strategic map** intended to guide all managers in their relations with employees (Beer et al., 1984). It emphasises the human or soft side of human resource management, featuring issues such as:

- **motivating people** by involving them in decision making
- developing an **organisational culture** based on trust and teamwork.

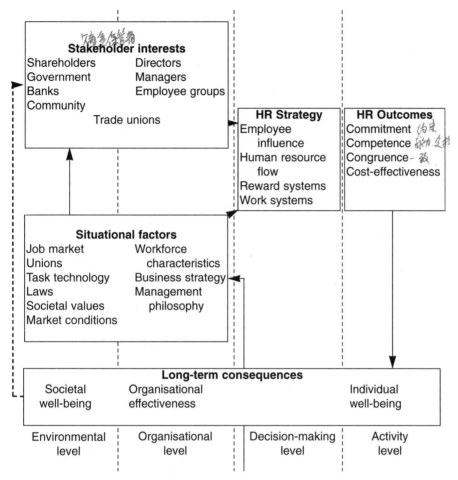

Figure 1: The Harvard perspective on human resource management
Source: Price (1997) adapted from Beer et al. (1984)

The Harvard approach is rooted in the human relations tradition, and supports the view that people can influence the outcomes of strategy. It employs the **multiple** **stakeholder** model. Employees are seen as having interests along with other stakeholders such as shareholders, management, unions and government. HRM has four policy areas which must be addressed:

- human resource flows
- reward systems
- employee influence
- work systems.

Human resource flows involve managing the flow of people:

- into the organisation (recruitment, selection)
- through the organisation (placement, appraisal, promotion)
- out of the organisation (termination) 报酬

HR policy must ensure the right mix and number of staff through resourcing and developing employee competences.

Reward systems cover pay and benefits designed to attract, motivate and keep employees. **Employee influence** is concerned with controlling levels of authority, power and decision-making. **Work systems** involve defining and designing jobs, so that the arrangement of people, information and technology provide the best outcomes.

These policies are designed to achieve the crucial goals of:

- commitment
- congruence
- competence
- cost effectiveness.

The Harvard approach also emphasises a belief in an organisation's people as assets rather than costs. People can be allocated in order to obtain maximum efficiency. Their efforts can be directed towards particular objectives and their competences developed to achieve the highest quality work. Time spent on training and development is an investment in a firm's human capital. Human capital is the body of knowledge, skills and experience possessed by an organisation's people. This is a concept we develop further in later units.

According to this viewpoint, investment in people provides long-term benefits for an organisation. Every business consists of physical, financial and human resources but human resources are particularly important because a firm's competitiveness depends upon its employees' ability to make best use of the physical and monetary resources. Consequently, the success of a business depends ultimately on the people working for it.

For an outsider, however, it is difficult to establish what an organisation or, more specifically, its higher management, feels about its people. Employees in many organisations also find this difficult. The next activity gives you the opportunity to explore these difficulties in interpreting an organisation's official 'line' about the importance of its staff.

HR-Strategy Personnel Development Plan.

Performance Plan -

ACTIVITY 9

Find a selection of annual company reports or company career information packs at your library. Alternatively access a number of corporate websites for familiar organisations such as Ford, Tesco or IBM on the internet. What do these official sources say about employees? Do you think these businesses share a belief in people as assets?

Ford, Tesco and IBM are particularly good examples of the HRM approach, demonstrating considerable commitment to staff development. You may find that some organisations make no reference to their staff, concentrating on financial and marketing information. Many other businesses pay lip service to the notion that 'employees are their greatest assets' in a token paragraph or two. How many of your sources give useful information on career opportunities? Can you tell from these official company sources of information if salaries are competitive?

The media is another source of information about HR policies in companies. Business news sections and journals may reveal that some companies are taking hard decisions about their staffing. In such cases, do companies publicly acknowledge that they are transferring operations to locations overseas where people are poorly paid, instead of investing in skills training and new technology? How many people have they 'unfortunately had to let go' in the past year? From media reports are you able to judge whether or not they are really committed to their staff?

Obviously, references to employee issues through the media and official corporate communication channels provide only a crude measure of the apparent importance attached to human resources by businesses.

3.2   The Michigan model

Another influential model – from Michigan Business School – focuses on the harder 'resource' side of human resource management. This model emphasises that people should be managed like any other resource. They should be:

- obtained cheaply
- used sparingly
- developed and exploited fully.

The model applies to all people who resource the organisation, including contractors and temporary workers. Human resource policies are designed to obtain a tight fit or match between human resources and business strategy. As a result, this is sometimes described as the **matching model** because of its central theme of 'matching available human resources to jobs in the organisation' (Tichy et al.,

1982). The purpose of HRM in this model is to ensure that business strategies are realised, for example, through:

- structural reorganisation
- performance-related pay
- reducing staff numbers.

It embodies a comparatively **low-trust** management approach towards employees, unlike the **high-trust** elements of the Harvard model, such as commitment.

3.3　The purpose of HRM

In considering the appropriateness of these models to organisations, we need to consider what should be the main purpose of HRM? Armstrong (1992) argues that business need should be the main driving force behind the organisation of human resource systems and policies. A universal package, suitable for every organisation, does not exist. Instead, HRM in each organisation should take into account the individual requirements of the business, covering its strategies, culture, structure, environment, resources, processes and traditions. Specialist departments can demonstrate expertise by developing key techniques and levers to meet an organisation's business needs exemplified in these human resource strategies (Lundy and Cowling, 1996).

- **Strategic selection**: making a close link between the strategic requirements of the organisation and the decision criteria used by recruiters, using state-of-the-art selection methods to achieve the best possible results. Lundy and Cowling point to a lack of evidence for this link between strategy and selection in practice.

- **Strategic training and development**: methods of identifying, training and developing the most suitable people for specific jobs. This plays a central role in aligning the competences (knowledge and skills) of an organisation's employees with its strategic needs.

- **Strategic management of motivation and rewards**: developing measures of appropriate performance, pinpointing areas for improvement. Lundy and Cowling demonstrate that this is an area which has been strangely neglected by writers on strategic management.

- **Strategic employee relations**: an area which has gone beyond industrial relations to embrace teamwork, communication strategies, quality compliance, employee involvement and commitment.

3.4 Common features of human resource models

Are the major models of human resource management contradictory? Are there common elements? Take a few moments to reflect on this unit. Clearly there are some key concepts which have arisen several times in different contexts. You may agree with Sisson (1990) that there are four major features which appear to some degree in all HRM models and theories.

- Integration of human resource policies, and alignment with the organisation's business plan. HRM is a key instrument of business strategy, viewing employees as important assets.

- Responsibility for managing people moves from personnel specialists to senior (line) managers. Specialists provide a consultancy service for line managers.

- Employee relations shifts away from collective bargaining (dialogue between management and unions). Instead, direct discussion between management and individual employees is encouraged.

- A stress on commitment to the organisation and personal initiative.

Softer models of HRM, exemplified by the Boral case study in the review activity at the end of this unit, advocate that managers should become:

- **enablers** structuring organisations to allow employees to achieve objectives

- **empowerers** devolving decision-making to the lowest level

- **facilitators** encouraging and assisting employees.

From this perspective, managers are no longer supervisors. The organisations move away from rigid hierarchies and power distinctions towards people taking responsibility for their own work (Price, 1997).

Guest (1987) provides a fusion of various approaches into a theory of human resource management which we can recognise in the Boral case study. It incorporates a number of policy goals:

- aim for a **high level of commitment** from employees, so that workers identify with the organisation's goals and contribute actively to its improvement and success

- obtain a **high quality output** from workers who want to continually improve standards

- expect **flexibility** from workers, a willingness to depart from fixed job definitions, working practices and conditions

● seek **strategic integration** through HR policies directed towards agreed objectives which interact with each other in a cohesive way.

These goals require support from top managers and integration of human resource strategy with business policy. The activities outlined in table 1 (see page 15) are linked and overlaid by HR staff to improve communication and increase involvement, commitment and productivity. They are integrated and match the requirements of the organisation's strategic plans. We cannot take a decision or make a change in one without having repercussions in at least some of the other areas. The essential point of HRM is that the functions should be managed as a whole, and not as stand-alone activities.

The central aim of the HRM approach is to combine all personnel or human resource activities into an organised and integrated programme to meet the strategic objectives of an enterprise. It moves us away from common-sense solutions for day-to-day problems, such as 'get someone to fill that job', towards a conscious attempt to think through the consequences of hiring that 'someone'. Do we want a recruit who is perfect for that particular position right now, or an individual who might require considerable training but shows great adaptability? Do we hire someone for an overworked production department, knowing that the sales unit are forecasting a drop in orders later in the year?

In the next activity you have the chance to review the two models so that the key differences are clear.

ACTIVITY 10

Allocate each of the following sentences or phrases to:

● the Harvard model
● the Michigan model
● both Harvard and Michigan
● neither Harvard nor Michigan

1. HRM integrates the full range of personnel management activities with those of the business as a whole.

2. People are to be used economically and fully utilised.

3. Line managers take responsibility for human resource activities, rather than personnel specialists.

4. HRM ensures that business strategies are realised through devices and actions such as performance-related pay, downsizing and delayering.

5. Employees are trusted to give of their best in return for satisfying and motivating jobs.

6. Close links are made between the recruitment, selection and development of employees and the future needs of the business.

7. Individual employees are encouraged to take their grievances through formal channels, involving trade union or other representatives.

8. Employees are expected to be flexible in the tasks they will undertake.

9. Managers are seen more as leaders, helpers and guides rather than rigorous authority figures.

10. An important feature of HRM is to obtain the commitment of employees.

11. The interests of employees, shareholders, management and unions are all given attention when considering business decisions.

12. Because of globalisation and rapidly changing technology it is inadvisable to try to match human resources and jobs too closely, provided a pool of skilled employees is retained by the company.

Here are our answers.

1. Both models of HRM propose the close integration of personnel management activities with business objectives.

2. While the Harvard approach does not advocate wastage of human resources, the emphasis on using people economically belongs to the Michigan model.

3. Both. The movement from personnel management to human resource management implies that managers take responsibility for their own staff. HR specialists are involved in more strategic aspects of people management and the provision of advice and technical services to line managers.

4. Michigan. Remember that this is a harder, tougher approach which is more ready to dismiss, redeploy and otherwise treat employees as resources to be managed in the interests of the business, rather than to meet the needs of the people.

5. Harvard. Treat people well and you release their potential creativity and efforts.

6. Both. Human resource management (as opposed to personnel management) is concerned with the integration of all human resource activities with the organisation's strategic plan.

7. Neither. Human resource management advocates identification with the firm rather than an outside body such as a trade union.

8. Both. Greater flexibility of employees has become the norm, in contrast to the rigidities and demarcation disputes of earlier periods. This expectation is true of both Harvard and Michigan models, though the basis of this expectation is different. The Harvard approach seeks to achieve flexibility through commitment, whereas the Michigan model makes it an element of the employment contract.

9. Harvard. Emphasis on charismatic leadership is typical of softer models of HRM.

10. Harvard. Commitment to an organisation is desirable according to any model but the Michigan approach would expect this to be obtained through enforcement of the employment contract.

11. Harvard. The Michigan model places greater emphasis on other stakeholders such as shareholders and managers.

12. Neither. Businesses will not survive if they hold on to staff who are unsuitable for their needs.

Summary

There are several models of human resource management. The Harvard model emphasises the soft approach to human resource management, providing a strategic map to guide managers in their relations with employees. It focuses on issues such as motivation and teamwork. The Michigan model takes a harder approach, arguing that people should be managed like any other resource, and advocates HR policies that seek a tight fit between human resources and business strategy. There are some features which appear to some degree in all HRM models. These include the need to integrate and align human resource policy with an organisation's business plan, switching responsibility for managing people to line managers and building employee commitment.

Unit review activity

The case study describes how Boral addressed its human resource problems and, in 1998, won Australia's most important award for HRM by taking a strategic approach to its people management. Read the case study and then answer the questions that follow.

Boral

Boral, the building, construction materials and energy multinational, was founded in Australia in 1946. In 1992, it had no specialist HR staff despite having 22,000 employees worldwide. It outsourced all its non-core functions.

The company decided it needed to develop expertise in human resources. A new HR head was appointed who quickly identified some major problems:

- no systematic salary reviews

- no performance management systems

- no co-ordinated training and development programmes

- no succession planning, and most senior managers would retire in a few years without nominated successors.

A further boost came with a new managing director who made human resource management a key part of Boral's 'Magna Carta' change programme, its corporate values – leadership, respect, focus, performance, persistence – and its mission statement.

Boral now provides a mix of centralised and decentralised human resource management with just 45 HR staff (excluding training, occupational health and payroll) for its current 18,600 employees. A small central team of 11 specialists co-ordinates human resource initiatives, with local HR teams reporting to the group managing directors for each business unit. The main human resources management committee co-ordinates activities across the whole group to ensure consistency. The committee meets every month with a key strategy convention every year. A key project is the introduction of a web-based human resource information system to improve communication and co-ordination. The main guiding principles are:

- strategic rather than administrative HRM

- strong business/commercial focus

- communications through high visibility and face-to-face contact

- building HR expertise in line managers

- values-driven decision-making

- minimalist HR systems and procedures

- speed of delivery

- outsourcing

- key links between core elements

- strong employee involvement.

Boral's human resource strategy focuses on the concept of 'best people'. The best people strategy has six main elements, broken down into sub-strategies and action programmes.

- **Performance management** aimed at fostering and acknowledging excellence within a performance culture which does not tolerate poor standards. Staff set objectives for the year with formal feedback at least once during that time. The company has trialled a 360 degree performance feedback system.

- **Training and development** follows on from performance management which identifies individual development needs. Continuous learning is encouraged to meet the needs of both company and individual employees. Mentoring and 'Boral leader as coach' programmes have been introduced.

- **Succession planning** designed to identify and develop pools of talent from which to draw the next generation of experienced, qualified and motivated people. There are strong links between succession planning and performance management, remuneration and incentives, and training and development processes because people with high potential are rewarded and given the opportunity to learn and develop.

- **Remuneration and incentives** have been improved to attract and keep the best people. The executive pay system links up to 35 per cent of pay to individuals' abilities to add value to the business. The annual Magna Carta awards provide recognition for excellence in eight business categories including human resources.

- **Selection and recruitment** is outsourced to approved consultants, but the aim is to select the best people from inside or outside the company. They are matched with Boral's corporate values and targeted for progression to higher positions.

- **Communication, information, and knowledge sharing**, cutting through organisational boundaries so that Boral's staff share information and learn more quickly than those in competitor companies.

In November 1998 Boral won the national corporate award for leadership and excellence in the human resources industry, given by the Australian Human Resources Institute.

Adapted from Waldon (1997) and Ruzek (1998).

1. To what extent is Boral's human resource function operated (in Tyson's terminology) by 'clerks of works, contracts managers and architects'?

2. Compare the list of personnel functions in table 1 (see page 15) with the key elements of Boral's HR policy as described in the case study. List the organisational benefits you can see in a human resource management approach as opposed to a traditional personnel management approach

3. Reflect back on the Harvard and Michigan models of human resource management. Which model best describes HRM in Boral at present?

4. To what degree is the Boral case study an example of Guest's theory of HRM in action (which we outlined on page 30)?

Unit summary

This unit has introduced you to some of the broader aspects of human resource management. It has explored the origins of HRM and examined some classic models of its role in achieving business objectives. The essential differences between modern human resource management and traditional personnel functions have been discussed. The need for expertise in dealing with specific human resource issues has been introduced.

Human resource management has a variety of definitions. The term is around 50 years old, having been used in the USA as an alternative label for personnel management. It has evolved from a number of different strands of thought and is best described as a loose philosophy of people management rather than a focused methodology. The subject was popularised after its introduction on the Harvard MBA programme in the 1980s. This was a soft (humanistic) map of HRM in contrast to the major alternative model of hard (numbers-driven) HRM developed by Michigan Business School.

HRM was imported into the UK, Australia and other English-speaking countries at the end of the 1980s but there is considerable debate about its prevalence. There is general agreement that it has a closer fit with business strategy than previous personnel management models. It is a topic which continues to attract debate and disagreement. As a consequence, practitioners and textbooks use a diverse and sometimes contradictory range of interpretations.

References

Adams, K (1991) 'Externalisation vs specialisation: what is happening to personnel?', *Human Resource Management Journal*, 1(4)

Armstrong, M (1992) *Human Resource Management: Strategy and Action*, Kogan Page

Beer, M, Spector, B, Lawrence, P R, Quinn-Mills, D and Walton, R G (1984) *Managing Human Assets*, Free Press

Deal, T E and Kennedy, A (1982) Corporate Cultures, Addison-Wesley

Drucker, P (1961) *The Practice of Management*, Mercury Books

Eccles, A (1989) 'Brief case: if we're so smart, why are they winning?', *Long Range Planning,* October

Fowler, A (1987) 'When chief executives discover HRM', *Personnel Management*, 19(1): 3

Gallagher, K, Rose, E, McClelland, B, Reynolds, J and Tombs, S (1997), *People in Organisations: An Active Learning Approach*, Open Learning Foundation/ Blackwell Business

Garraghan, P and Stewart, P (1992), *The Nissan Enigma*, Cassell

Goss, D (1994) *Principles of Human Resource Management*, Routledge

Guest, D (1987) 'Human resource management and industrial relations', *Journal of Management Studies*, 24(5)

Guest, D (1991) 'Personnel management: the end of orthodoxy?', *British Journal of Industrial Relations*, 29(2)

Hollinshead, G and Leat, M (1995) *Human Resource Management: An International and Comparative Perspective*, Pitman

Legge, K (1995) *Human Resource Management: Rhetorics and Realities*, Macmillan Business

Lundy, O and Cowling, A (1996) *Strategic Human Resource Management*, International Thomson Business Press

Ouchi, W (1981) *Theory Z*, Addison-Wesley

Pascale, R T and Athos, A G (1981), *The Art of Japanese Management*, Simon and Schuster

Peters, T J and Waterman, R H jr (1982) *In Search of Excellence, Lessons from America's Best Run Companies*, Harper and Row

Price, A J (1997) *Human Resource Management in a Business Context*, International Thomson Business Press

Ruzek, P (1998) '1998 AHRI national awards for leadership and excellence in the human resources industry', *HR Monthly*, December, Australian Human Resources Institute

Sisson, K (1990) 'Introducing the Human Resource Management Journal', *Human Resource Management Journal*, 1(1)

Sisson, K (1995) 'Human resource management and the personnel function', in Storey. J (ed.) *Human Resource Management: A Critical Text*, Routledge

Storey, J (ed.) (1995) *Human Resource Management: A Critical Text*, Routledge

Sullivan, J (1998) 'Hi-tech HR', *HR Monthly*, November, Australian Human Resources Institute

Tamkin, P, Barber, L and Dench, S (1997) *From Admin to Strategy: the changing face of the HR Function*, IES Report 332, Institute of Employment Studies

Tichy, N M, Fombrun, C J and Devanna, M A (1982) 'Strategic human resource management', *Sloan Management Review*, 23(2)

Townley, B (1994) *Reframing Human Resource Management*, Sage

Tyson, S (1989) 'The management of the personnel function', *Journal of Management Studies,* September

Waldon, S (1997), 'Boral Builds An HR Function', *HR Monthly*, November, Australian Human Resources Institute

Werther, W B jr and Davis, K A (contributor) (1995), *Human Resources and Personnel Management*, McGraw Hill College Div., 5th edn

Whitehill, A (1991), *Japanese Management*, Routledge

Recommended Reading

There are many excellent introductory human resource management textbooks, most of which give consideration to the origins and development of HRM. Among the specialist discussions of the issues debated in this unit, the following books are particularly noteworthy.

Human Resource Management: Rhetorics and Realities (1995) by Karen Legge, Macmillan Business. Karen Legge is one of the foremost analysts of the HRM phenomenon.

Human Resource Management: A Critical Text (1995) edited by John Storey, Routledge. Chapters 1, 2, 4 and 15 are particularly relevant.

The clearest description of Harvard, Michigan and other human resource models is provided by Graham Hollinshead and Mike Leat in *Human Resource Management: An International and Comparative Perspective* (1995), Pitman.

To orientate yourself with the work done by human resource specialists, you should read some practitioner journals such as the Institute of Personnel and Development's *People Management*. Many of these journals are available on the internet: access the author's *Internet Guide to Human Resource Management* for extensive lists to journals, articles and HR-related websites, (currently available at http://www.hrmguide.com).

Answers to Unit Review Activity

1. Boral has switched attention away from lower-level clerk of works aspects of HR towards the more strategic architect function.

2. Boral has addressed its human resource requirements as a whole, rather than dealing with it piecemeal. In other words, Boral's key people management priorities have been thought through systematically. The company has set up a structure of policies, activities and systems within an integrated and co-ordinated human resource management framework. Every key element is linked to the others and fits with overall business objectives.

3. You may have found it difficult to match the description of the organisation in the case study with either of the two major models described in this unit. Models never entirely capture the reality of organisations such as Boral. In fact, Boral can be recognised to some degree in both the Harvard and Michigan approaches. However, the company's approach is focused primarily on soft factors such as commitment and its policies clearly recognise the importance of employees as stakeholders in its future. Less attention is given to the hard matching issues of employee numbers and costs. Boral's determination to attract and keep the best people places the organisation firmly within the Harvard approach to HRM.

4. Boral's approach is a good illustration of a pragmatic form of HRM which addresses commercial reality. In this respect it is an example of Guest's model in action. A high level of commitment is encouraged through the linking of remuneration and performance management to business objectives. Equally, a high quality of output is facilitated by continuous training and development, supported by improved communication and knowledge sharing. This also leads to a flexible attitude from employees. The whole process is strategically integrated at a corporate level.

UNIT 2
THE CHANGING NATURE OF WORK

Introduction

Jobs and employment relationships are changing continuously. The proportion of jobs which can be described as manual or unskilled is steadily decreasing, and the positions requiring knowledge and expertise are often hard to fill (Rothwell, 1995). As a result there is a trend for the job market to polarise between low-skill, low-paid employees and expert 'knowledge workers' who are heavily in demand.

Why are these changes taking place? There are many reasons but the most important is the advent of new technology which is leading to significant changes in the structure of many large organisations and the ways in which work is processed. In manufacturing, advanced production technology has broken down departmental boundaries by integrating design, procurement and manufacturing. Information technology (IT) has opened up the physical boundaries of modern businesses, so that employees can work from any location. As a consequence, teleworking has moved from a fashionable concept to a reality in many industries.

Large businesses have often reacted to new technology and increasing competition by developing flatter, decentralised organisations. IT has affected manufacturing industries, leading to new organisational structures and working relationships, changing (in some cases) a rigid hierarchical structure into something more flexible. Flexible work patterns, including various forms of part-time, temporary and contingent work, are being used – and probably over-used – to cut employee costs and concentrate effort when and where it is required. In some companies, traditional management is being replaced by self-supervision and automatic supervision, empowering some staff and locking others into rigid, prescribed working practices, typified by some call centres.

This unit provides a critical introduction to the changes. It examines these developments as they effect organisational structure and culture and explores some of the consequences on employee commitment and motivation. Flexible and contingent work practices have become a fashionable topic for consultants, with much coverage in the business pages of newspapers. In reality, changes in working life have been less radical and, yet, more complex for most employees. This unit explores such complexities.

As well as looking at the theoretical aspects of the changing nature of work, we will also consider how the changes affect individual employees. So you will be asked to consider your own working experience and aspirations to gain an understanding of the implications of new work patterns. For example:

- what hours would you like to work?
- are you prepared to consider short-term contracts?
- would you take on two or more part-time jobs at the same time?

Objectives

By the end of this unit, you will be able to:

- outline and explain the major changes in work patterns that have taken place during the past 20 years

- examine the meaning of flexibility, flexible firm and flexible specialisation in the context of HRM

- outline the advantages and disadvantages of the main forms of flexible working arrangements.

SECTION 1
Changing Types and Patterns of Work

Introduction

Work has been changing over the past 20 years. Work patterns have become more flexible: there are fewer full-time jobs and a greater proportion of part-time jobs. In 1999, there were 6.8 million part-timers in the 27.4 million UK workforce, with part-time positions accounting for most new jobs (Adams, 1999). A higher proportion of women work. The number of manual jobs has declined, and the demand for higher level skills and education has increased. Many jobs have been altered so that they are simpler, requiring less skills. Some have been broadened to encompass a wider range of skills. Many other jobs, such as telegraphists and telex operators, have vanished. As an example of these kinds of changes consider this case. *disappear*

Lloyds TSB
This major British banking group has experimented with flexible job patterns in order to reduce costs and increase productivity. Its scheme offers the choice to employees of how, when and where they wish to work. They can vary their hours and ease the conflict between work and family life. Job sharing, reduced hours and teleworking are all possible. The bank is hoping to gain from improved employee commitment and reduced staff turnover. There is also scope for providing new services outside normal hours.

Why is the nature of work changing? The purpose of this section is to clarify some of the most significant reasons and to highlight key issues which human resource managers must address. Before continuing with this unit, take some time to think about the reasons and implications of new working patterns by completing this activity.

ACTIVITY 1

The nature of work and the patterns of working have changed over the past 20 years. From your previous studies and knowledge of current events, list what you think are the main factors that have led to these changes.

Now jot down some of your ideas about the consequences of these changes for employees and employers:

- small businesses
- large commercial firms
- large public service organisations.

In exploring the reasons behind the changing nature of work, you could have suggested several factors. These include information technology (computerisation), global competition, technological advances in products and processes, changes in fashion and demand, more rapid transmission of change across the globe, new management techniques (what is everybody else doing?), new communication techniques such as the internet, changes in the position of women in society, different employee expectations in the quality of working life, and political, governmental and international developments such as EU directives and World Trade Organisation rulings (Tailby, 1999).

Established small organisations run the risk of failure if they are unable to react quickly; new entrepreneurial start-ups can spring up to take advantage of the opportunities offered by technological and market changes. Larger businesses may have the financial muscle and market awareness to deal with change in a planned and positive fashion. Many public sector organisations have been placed under market conditions and have adopted similar change strategies (Price, 1997).

The overall impact of these factors is a strong impetus to change for all types of organisation. Competitive pressures lead to employers placing ever greater demands on their employees, emphasising the importance of performance, productivity, quality, initiative and creativity. Staff look to their employers for greater rewards, career opportunities, and the chance to acquire skills.

The aim of this section is to help you to:

- critically assess the rationale behind changes in work patterns
- be able to define and evaluate the concept of flexibility in its various manifestations
- outline the implications of the flexible firm model
- identify key faults in the concepts of the flexible firm and flexible specialisation.

1.1   Knowledge, skills and the job market

As we have noted, low skill jobs are gradually disappearing and expertise is at a premium. More than a decade ago, Handy (1989) predicted that between 70 and 80 per cent of all jobs would be filled by knowledge workers in the early twenty-first century. Knowledge workers are people who perform tasks which require experience, skills or learned techniques. According to Handy, a third of all jobs will require professional qualifications or training at graduate level.

As a consequence business and personal success will depend increasingly on the possession of skills. People with the right talents – such as information technology and customer relations skills – can ask for high rates of pay because they are in demand. From a wider perspective, the development of organisations and national economies can be held back by a lack of such skills.

Support for this argument comes from a survey of major UK businesses: two thirds of respondents felt their organisations would be held back because it was difficult to recruit people with key management skills (Taylor, 1998). There was a shortage of managers at all levels with leadership credentials, strategic awareness and the capacity to be innovative. Half the businesses surveyed said they had trouble acquiring people with skills in managing relationships with customers, or even recruiting people with the expected level of commercial awareness.

The survey showed increasing demand for all employees to have skills which have traditionally been expected only from managers. Businesses need to invest heavily and continuously in knowledge and talent – their human capital.

ACTIVITY 2

An increasing demand for skilled personnel suggests that more people will need to be educated and trained. What methods can the state, and individual companies, use to develop human capital?

1. List some of the ways open to governments and organisations to develop people.

2. Review your list of options and try to pick out any general trends. For example, you might have noticed that in some cases training by the state is compulsory, but training within private enterprises is not. (It might help you to form your answer if you think about the general function of government and private enterprise.)

The training options open to business include:

- in-house training programmes
- supporting employees on college training or education courses
- experiential learning of all kinds – job exchanges, placements, projects, job rotation
- shadowing – where one employee follows a more experienced member of staff around the workplace, learning what is involved in that person's job
- personal self-development programmes in which the employee, with company support, identifies a learning need and then plans and pursues a course of activity and study intended to meet that need.

The options open to government include:

- compelling organisations to contribute to training programmes
- providing a full-time education system for all the nation's young people, together with part-time education for workers
- subsidising education and training for post-school leavers
- using propaganda and information to encourage positive attitudes to life-long learning
- funding (or encourage the funding of) libraries and other sources of information
- allocating research money and awarding contracts to areas of the economy that are believed to be developing, and associating this funding with education and training programmes.

The main point you might have drawn from the study of these lists is that while businesses can operate at the level of the individual employee, and can motivate and support the individual employee, they do not have the power to affect national training. On the other hand, the government has the resources and power to set up a framework of education and training. It can for example:

- provide the resources for schools, colleges, universities and public libraries

- create and maintain a system of qualifications or standards of training, such as National Vocational Qualifications (NVQs) or the Scottish equivalent (SVQs).

1.2 Flexibility

What is flexibility? Flexibility can be defined as the opportunity to vary human resource numbers, types, skills, hours and costs to match closely the requirements of business objectives. But in activity 3 you may find that this definition does not encompass the entire range of meanings implied in press and academic articles on the subject. Often it is difficult to distinguish between prescription – what we would like to do – and description – that which we are doing (Legge, 1995). In fact, there are at least three separate concepts to consider: labour market flexibility, the 'flexible firm' model, and flexible specialisation. We will consider these in turn.

ACTIVITY 3

Read the following extracts from articles about flexibility:

Flexibility is often interpreted in relation to its opposite – that is, as the absence of rigidity and constraint.

Tailby (1999)

Demands for employee flexibility have escalated as organisations seek tighter control of head count, markets and finance. Financial benefits may accrue from the ability to acquire and shed labour 'on demand', but what measurement has there been of the long-term cost in terms of employee performance and commitment?

Corbridge and Pilbeam (1998)

The importance of specialist knowledge for producing good quality work, and of maintaining a personal relationship with industrial customers, was recognised as an inhibitor on full flexibility.

Storey (1995)

Additionally, you could look through a selection of business journals such as *The Economist* or conduct a keyword search for flexibility on your library's newspaper archives. When you come across the word, try to replace it with other words or phrases that could stand for flexibility without changing the meaning of the passage. The word(s) you substituted is (are) the meaning of flexibility in that passage.

In different passages you probably found that the word 'flexibility' has been used in different senses. Write down at least three different meanings of flexibility.

You probably discovered that the term flexibility is used in discussions of topics as diverse as national economies and shift patterns in a local firm. You would have done well if you included some of the following examples of meaning listed by Tailby (1999):

- adaptability of wage payment systems
- versatility of workers within a production process
- ease of engaging and dismissing workers
- adaptable working-time patterns
- mobility of workers between firms, industries and regions
- career paths and expectations of employees.

At its simplest, the flexibility concept fits the Michigan matching model of human resource management described in Unit 1. In practice, as you can see from the activity, the word has a variety of meanings.

LABOUR MARKET FLEXIBILITY

In free market economies such as the UK and USA, there has been a trend since the 1980s towards replacing full-time, long-term jobs with other, flexible employment relationships, typically on a part-time or temporary basis. However, the extent and nature of this trend has been heavily debated (Tailby, 1999).

Flexible working has been encouraged in order to reduce employee costs and so-called rigidity. Rigidity refers to lack of mobility, unwillingness to work unfamiliar and unsociable hours, or reluctance to accept new (worse) working conditions. Many politicians and business leaders argue that competitiveness comes from reducing such rigidities in the employment market, for example (Price, 1997) by:

- eliminating or cutting minimum pay rates
- removing laws which limit employers' rights to hire and fire
- deregulating the job market by removing statutory restrictions on any aspect of the employment relationship, such as limits on working hours, the ability to strike and minimum holiday entitlements.

Its proponents argue that flexibility enables organisations to react quickly and cheaply to environmental changes. The justification comes from a comparison of growth rates, job creation and speed of recovery from recession in different countries. In most instances, the USA has done better than Europe. One argument is that the US employment market is considerably more flexible than its European equivalents.

You may be able to think of other reasons to explain the strength of the US economy. The USA has a common business language and currency; its business methodology has a similar basis from the Atlantic to the Pacific; state legislation varies, but not to the same degree as the legal differences between some European countries; there is a high rate of investment in scientific research; there is a common culture of entrepreneurship. Arguably, these are more important factors than labour market flexibility. It is also the case that the US employment market has rigidities of its own in the shape of extensive federal and state legislation on issues such as equal opportunities, minimum wages and family-friendly working arrangements.

In the UK, Conservative governments of the late-1970s to mid-1990s introduced a variety of labour-market reforms with flexibility in mind. They placed restrictions on industrial action, closed shops, paid time off for union activities and picketing of unrelated work premises (secondary picketing). Other measures introduced by the Conservative government included the abolition of wages councils, which set minimum pay rates for several industries, and narrowing the entitlement for redress against unfair dismissal and maternity rights. To date, the Labour administration which came to power in 1997 has not chosen to revoke the majority of these changes.

What are the consequences of flexibility for employees? Are they likely to be beneficial? Hyman (1991) argues that the language of flexibility hides a debatable value-judgement within a rhetorical slogan:

> *To define certain social realities as rigidities (rather than points of stability) and others as flexibilities (rather than areas of uncertainty) is to impose a particular evaluation, to commend a particular distribution of options and constraints, and hence to propose a particular structure of social power.*

In other words, it may be that the powerful are pushing the powerless away from stable, secure working patterns towards uncertain and insecure forms of employment. Employees may have accepted flexibility out of fear of losing their jobs during periods of high unemployment. Critics such as Hyman argue that the result of flexibility is that workers are being forced to accept:

- reductions in employment rights
- unsociable working hours
- job insecurity
- inferior pay and conditions.

There is an inherent contradiction between flexibility and fairness. On the one hand it is necessary for countries such as the UK to provide employment market conditions which are competitive with those in comparatively deregulated economies such as the USA. On the other hand, employees – particularly those in the European Union – have increasing expectations of family-friendly working lives. An examination of UK newspapers and journals from the late 1990s will give you an indication of the considerable debate about the introduction of legislation to restrict the maximum hours which can be worked (through the EU Working Time Directive) and the extension of various employment benefits to part-time employees.

TYPES OF FLEXIBILITY

You will recall from Unit 1 that flexibility features as an important element in Guest's theory of human resource management. Committed workers are expected to deviate from job definitions, working practices and conditions. At the organisational level, flexibility can take several basic forms (Atkinson, 1984).

- **Numerical**. Human resources are matched closely to requirements. Staffing schemes are designed to have people available only at busy times. Clearly this is easier to achieve with part-time and temporary workers than full-time staff. Numerical flexibility is a direct implementation of the Michigan matching model of human resource management. Activity 4 gives you the opportunity to explore numerical flexibility in a practical situation.

- **Functional**. Employees are selected and trained to be multi-skilled, breaking down restrictions that dictate which employees can perform particular tasks. They can be moved between tasks as required. This category is related to the notion of flexible specialisation described later in this section. Functional flexibility is a feature of Japanese production techniques closely studied in the West during the 1980s and 1990s.

- **Pay**. Different rates of pay are offered for similar work, depending on location and available skilled people. Wages are varied to reflect supply and demand in the local or industrial sector job market. For instance, hospital trusts have been encouraged to set local rates of pay for nursing and ancillary staff who were previously on national pay scales. There is also the opportunity to vary pay rates on the basis of individual performance.

- **Distancing**. Employees are hired on a subcontract basis, so that employment contracts are replaced with contracts of service. For example, doorstep milk deliveries are often serviced by franchisees rather than dairy employees. Most franchisees were previously employed by the dairy companies.

As Tailby (1999) points out, these practices have been used for decades in the UK, but they were not described in terms such as numerical or functional flexibility at the time.

Even if an employer prefers to use traditional patterns of employment – such as 9 a.m. to 5 p.m. five days a week, with a one-hour lunch break – it may be very difficult or impossible to staff some jobs using this pattern alone. In the following activity, use your ingenuity to make the greatest use of traditional forms of employment and the least use of flexible forms to staff the centre.

ACTIVITY 4

Imagine that you are responsible for staffing an insurance company's call centre. The centre is open from 7 a.m. to 10 p.m., Monday to Friday. Operators require a one hour lunch break, and a rest break of 20 minutes after every two hours continuous operation of a VDU.

On an average week day, telephone calls come in to the centre at the following rates.

7 a.m. – 8 a.m.	200 calls per hour
8 a.m. – 9 a.m.	300 calls per hour
9 a.m. – 10 a.m.	200 calls per hour
10 a.m. – 1 p.m.	500 calls per hour
1 p.m. – 2 p.m.	200 calls per hour
2 p.m. – 5 p.m.	400 calls per hour
5 p.m. – 7 p.m.	200 calls per hour
7 p.m. – 9 p.m.	300 calls per hour
9 p.m. – 10 p.m.	200 calls per hour

It takes, on average, three minutes to deal with each call.

How would you staff the call centre? You could mix full and part-time staff if you wish. Take a sheet of paper and try to match staff to requirements.

You will find that it is impossible to staff this unit with full-time staff working a conventional eight-hour shift and an hour's lunch break. The solution demands some pattern of part-time work or split shifts. In reality, the call centre would probably be open at weekends, making the problem even more complex. As call centre work is usually computer-based, regular breaks are essential, thus complicating staffing problems.

The staffing problem reflected in this activity is common: few customer-focused businesses have a steady stream of work arriving through the normal working period, day after day throughout the year. Dealing with the problem requires the application of numerical flexibility: devising staffing patterns which match requirements as closely as possible.

1.3   The flexible firm

Atkinson's (1984) **flexible firm** model develops the concept of flexibility into an organisational structure based on two kinds of workers – core and peripheral – to deal with fluctuating work-levels. Efficient firms obtain the optimum balance between core and peripheral workers.

The **core** workforce consists of permanent or regular staff employed on standard contracts. They are comparatively secure and enjoy the full benefits of the organisation such as training and pensions. Their jobs are involved with the essential and continuous processes of the business. Core staff can benefit from career opportunities in the internal job market of the firm. In return, they are expected to be multi-skilled and willing to work on a variety of activities. The organisation derives its functional flexibility from its core workers.

The **peripheral** workforce is made up of semi-permanent staff, contingent or temporary workers and sub-contractors who are hired and fired as required. They do not share the benefits of core staff. Just-in-time employment and the disposable workforce are US terms describing this part of the flexible firm model. They provide numerical flexibility for the firm. The peripheral workforce is comprised of three separate groups.

- A kind of second-class workforce, directly employed by the business on routine and low-skill work. Their numbers may be large but their career prospects are limited and they are vulnerable to downsizing (redundancy) when there are market or technological changes.

- Contingent workers required intermittently to deal with specialist activities such as computer programming, training, marketing initiatives and surveys. These individuals come from the external job market for prescribed periods and are highly paid.

- Low-skill, low-paid workers, involved in tasks such as cleaning, security and catering, subcontracted to individuals or firms. The actual work may be done by casual staff with little employment security.

ACTIVITY 5

According to Atkinson's model there are two main classes of worker: the core worker and the peripheral worker. Handy has distinguished between knowledge workers and others.

In the following table, provide some examples of the different types of worker and then judge how far these two classifications overlap. Would you agree that peripheral workers are usually unskilled whereas core workers are usually highly skilled? (Don't forget that Atkinson proposes three sub-classes of peripheral workers – and it may not be possible to find examples for each cell of the table.)

	Knowledge work	Unskilled work
Core worker		
Peripheral worker (Directly employed)		
Peripheral worker (Contingent)		
Peripheral worker (Low pay)		

To personalise this activity, ask yourself in which category you would be least happy to be found, and which you would most prefer. You might find it interesting and useful to jot down the characteristics of the two kinds of employment that appeal or disturb you. If possible, compare your results with a friend.

The table below contains a few suggestions; you may have included some of the same examples. Notice that there are a number of jobs that could fall into different categories. For example, the security personnel at many universities are permanent part-time staff. They are regarded as peripheral workers.

	Knowledge work	Unskilled work
Core worker	Chief scientist Part-time lecturer Manager Job-sharing analyst	
Peripheral worker (Directly employed)		Clerical staff
Peripheral worker (Contingent)	Computer programmer Contract scientist Consultant	Window cleaner
Peripheral worker (Low-pay/low-skill)		Cleaner

You will see from our suggestions that it is not necessary to be a full-time employee to be a core worker. However, workers must possess key skills in order to be classified as core. If their work is in any way routine, such as most clerical tasks, they become peripheral since the jobs could be farmed out to a specialist provider or automated in some way.

Obviously, these classifications can be interpreted in different ways. An office cleaner undoubtedly comes into the low-pay, low-skill category of peripheral worker; but a window cleaner can potentially earn substantially more for similar work. Some contingent workers, such as computer programmers and consultants can be highly rewarded, despite the relative lack of security.

In terms of your own career choices, you may feel that contingent work is unappealing with too little security. Alternatively, you may prefer the novelty, change and excitement of frequent changes of assignment and employer.

The idea of the flexible firm has taken root but its theoretical basis has been heavily criticised (Legge, 1995). Legge comments that it is difficult to tell from the literature whether writers are advocating what should be or describing a prevailing situation. Also, concepts such as core and periphery may seem logical on paper but their conceptual boundaries are less than clear in real life. Managers use the terms in varying ways. Some work, such as research and development, may be core in its importance to a company but can be subcontracted to an outside specialist provider.

In fact, there is some doubt about the prevalence of the flexible firm in practice – for example, 70 per cent of people in the UK who have been in employment for 20 years or more have worked in just one organisation during that time (Tamkin et al., 1997). Other surveys show only a small number of deliberate core-peripheral HR strategies being used in reality (Tailby, 1999). Reviewing the evidence, Legge (1995) comes to a number of conclusions.

- There is some evidence of numerical flexibility, but it is mostly pragmatic and opportunistic rather than strategic. Ironically, however, the public sector has provided some of the clearest demonstrations of the flexible firm philosophy.

- Functional flexibility is generally modest and mostly due to the breakdown of rigid job descriptions rather than multi-skilling.

- Financial flexibility follows on logically from numerical flexibility. But, as we see in a later unit, there is no evidence that performance-related pay provides financial benefits to an organisation.

- Flexibility has become part of managerial rhetoric. This may be because the concepts of flexibility provide managers with a language in which to discuss and analyse HR strategy.

In general, as we see in the next section, particular aspects such as distancing or outsourcing (subcontracting) work processes and the use of non-traditional work contracts are far more prevalent than the flexible firm model itself.

ACTIVITY 6

Which of the following statements is more true than false? And which is more false than true?

1. Authors writing about the flexible firm describe the results of their research, rather than advocate a new way of organising.

2. Work that is important to a company is always retained within its core.

3. During the past 20 years the flexible firm model has taken hold and now describes the strategies of upwards of 35 per cent of UK companies.

4. One of the major increases in flexibility has been brought about by multi-skilling.

5. Public sector organisations, as usual, have been slow to adopt any form of flexible organisation.

6. The concept of the flexible firm rests on a clear distinction between core and peripheral workers.

In fact, each of the statements in the activity are more false than true. As we have pointed out, it is not always clear whether writers are describing what they have observed, or what they think should be more common. The flexible firm model has not been adopted widely, rather flexibility has been brought about more by the end of rigid job demarcations and the introduction of new technology. Some public sector organisations (such as hospitals) have taken the lead in introducing flexible working practices and subcontracting. Finally, there is a fuzzy dividing line between important peripheral workers, such as consultants, and more easily replaced core employees, such as managers.

FLEXIBLE SPECIALISATION

What other forces are driving the trend towards flexible working? Piore and Sabel (1984) introduced the concept of flexible specialisation to explain how manufacturers and service providers can respond to consumer requirements. They argued that purchasers are becoming accustomed to ever higher standards of service and want availability on demand. So, for example, more and more organisations are working evenings and weekends to meet demand – some supermarkets are open 24 hours a day; manufacturers give increasingly wide choices in their product ranges; financial and other service providers offer a wide range of investment and insurance products.

Flexible specialisation describes a new set of multi-skill requirements and systems that allow managers to switch staff and equipment from one product or service to another to meet consumer demand. Flexible specialisation requires flexible people. In particular, employees need a broad range of skills and the ability to move between tasks without extra training. Reflecting back on Atkinson's category of functional flexibility, you may have concluded that flexible specialisation is a closely related concept. The requirements of functional flexibility and flexible specialisation have produced new pressures on human resource and line managers to devise appropriate selection, development and performance management procedures to locate, motivate and reward the right kind of staff.

Sunday staffing

A number of UK banks have experimented with Sunday opening. The Halifax deployed 1,000 staff in 200 branches, offering pay rates of up to £22 an hour for staff volunteering to work the extra shifts. Flat-rate incentive payments were also awarded, depending on the number of Sundays worked. Barclays has also tried Sunday opening. If the experiments prove successful, it is likely that separate contracts will be offered for weekend staff.

The concept of flexible specialisation has been criticised extensively (Hyman, 1991). For example, it is sometimes claimed that flexible specialisation means that mass production (Fordism) has been superseded. However, it has been pointed out that manufacturing has never been entirely dependent on the assembly-line: craft and batch production techniques have coexisted with large-scale Fordist factories throughout the twentieth century. A second major criticism is that many apparently different products and services are made up of identical components. Variations in colour, trim and detail may require only minor adjustments at the very end of the production process.

To the extent that flexible specialisation occurs, it does create a demand for multi-skilled employees. But yet another criticism of the theory is that these skills do not necessarily have to be of a high order. In practice, the most dramatic changes in working patterns have been seen in the retail industry. So for example, employees may be switched between opening boxes, stacking shelves, pricing individual items or working on the checkouts depending on customer activity within a store.

Regardless of the nature of flexible specialisation, however, it offers employees some degree of variety in their work. By contrast, the benefits of alternative staffing which we discuss in the next section are more controversial.

Summary

This section introduced the topic of flexibility and its component concepts. Flexibility was considered in relation to the labour market and the organisation. Flexibility can be defined in its numerical, functional, pay and distancing forms. We explored the concept of the flexible firm and the notion of core and peripheral staff. Finally we considered the related topic of flexible specialisation.

SECTION 2

Alternative Staffing

Introduction

The implications of flexibility are best seen in the various forms of alternative or non-standard working arrangements which have proliferated in recent years. Part-time working in its various forms remains the most common arrangement. There is also an extensive range of contingent or temporary working patterns and contracts. In large US corporations, as much as 40 per cent of the workforce have a non-permanent contract (Greble, 1997). The trend started later but is becoming more significant in other free market countries such as Australia, New Zealand and the UK.

The aim of this section is to help you to:

- explain the diverse range of alternative forms of working contract
- be able to evaluate the suitability of different working arrangements for specific business situations
- critically assess the advantages and disadvantages of a range of job patterns for both individuals and organisations.

2.1 Part-time working

What is part-time work? In the UK, government statisticians define part-time jobs as being those involving under 30 hours work per week. The movement towards part-time working has grown consistently since the Second World War (Court, 1995). Just 4 per cent of the UK's labour force worked part-time in 1951, rising to 16.4 per cent in 1979 and exceeding 25 per cent in the mid-1990s. Within Europe, the UK is unusual in having national insurance and other conditions which make non-standard contracts attractive to employers.

Why has there been an increase in part-time jobs? Shortage of suitable full-time workers in the 1970s and 1980s encouraged employers to adopt flexible work patterns. Industries which experienced sharp fluctuations of demand for staff turned to part-timers to reduce costs. For example, catering and retailing firms have both busy and slack times during the week. As we saw in activity 4 (the problem of staffing the call centre), the use of part-timers can be an economical solution to provide adequate cover.

Significantly, the increase in part-time work is most prominent for male employees. Although women have always made up the majority of part-timers (and continue to do so), Labour Force Surveys indicate that men working part-time have doubled in number since the 1970s (IRS, 1997).

Part-time work takes a variety of forms.

- **Classical.** Work which can be done in a few hours per day/week. This category includes office cleaning or making sandwiches for lunch bar.
- **Supplemntary.** Part-timers are used instead of offering full-time employees overtime, for example to provide an extra evening shift.
- **Substitution.** Where two or more part-time workers replace a full-time job. Job-sharing is an example we discuss in more detail shortly.
- **Key-working.** The Burton Group is the most quoted example, having replaced 1,000 full-time jobs with 3,000 'key-time' (busy period) part-time positions.
- **Zero-hour contracts.** Commonly used by call centres geared to television advertising campaigns. Employees are paid only when needed.

ACTIVITY 7

Perhaps most people want full-time jobs, but there are a number of groups of people who look for part-time work. These include, for example, full-time students working their way through higher education. List three or four other groups who want part-time work. What are the advantages offered by part-time workers to employers.

You may have concluded that part-time working offers considerable advantages to:

- **parents with children** – mostly female parents who work while children are at school
- **retired or semi-retired** – gaining supplementary income to top-up pensions or provide more interest to life
- **moonlighters** – people with full-time jobs, adding to their income
- **downshifters** – people who aim for a modest income and appreciate the free time available from part-time work
- **portfolio workers** who mix and match different jobs to provide the equivalent of a full-time income.

Part-time work offers numerous advantages to employers, especially in situations where there are extreme variations of demand for human resources. Service work, such as retailing, is a particular example. Peak activity occurs on days and at times when other workers are at leisure. Peak times may be so short that it is impossible for an employer to use full-time workers effectively. Using the language of the flexible firm model, few core full-timers are required in these circumstances. Correspondingly, a large number of peripheral part-timers work at busy periods. Peripheral numbers can be shrunk or expanded as required. This allows greater flexibility than would be possible with a completely full-time workforce.

Other advantages for employers include:

- more intensive work with less time used for breaks
- lower absenteeism (there is less among part-time workers)
- enthusiasm and commitment can be higher (less opportunity for boredom)
- the likelihood of little unionisation among part-time staff.

ACTIVITY 8

Although part-time work can be advantageous, it also carries disadvantages to both employers and employees. Identify the respective disadvantages of part-time work for employers and employees.

Managers have contradictory beliefs about part-timers, particularly women part-timers. Many question their commitment, seeing them as being primarily home-oriented and likely to take time off to be with children and give precedence to partners' careers (Price, 1997). Others believe them to be reliable, loyal and flexible. Depending on the hours worked and the amount they are paid, part-timers have fewer employment rights and benefits. They are excluded from interesting and senior positions. Part-time workers get few training and promotion opportunities (Tailby, 1999).

How does part-time pay compare with that received by full-time staff? Some professional part-timers are paid more than the equivalent full-time rate. However, this is comparatively rare as most rates are the same and there is a concentration of part-time jobs at the lower end of the employment market. UK employment legislation formerly discriminated against part-timers by giving them fewer rights than full-time workers, but the hours limitations for employment rights have been eliminated and part-time staff are entitled to pro-rata holidays and other benefits.

2.2   Job sharing

Job sharing is a hybrid between part-time and full-time work. Job sharing allows two people to take responsibility for one full-time job, dividing pay and benefits in proportion to the hours worked. Job-sharers may split the week with one working at the beginning, the other at the end or use some other pattern to cover the hours. Some job-sharers work alternate weeks.

ACTIVITY 9

An advantage for some employees, job sharing can also benefit employers. What might these be? List as many as possible. What are the disadvantages?

The benefits of job sharing for employers are not obvious but you may have suggested that:

- sharers can overlap hours so that busy periods receive double cover
- jobs are at least partly covered when one person is away through illness or annual leave
- two individuals can bring greater experience and a broader range of views to a job than a single employee.

Job sharing also allows skilled people to be retained in a part-time capacity if they give up full-time employment. However, disadvantages include the fact that:

- training, induction and administration overheads are higher for two people
- finding a suitable partner with matching skills and availability may prove difficult if one sharer leaves
- communication can be inadequate for tasks which can not be dealt with quickly (hand-over problems)
- responsibility for staff can be problematic – people may find difficulty in working for two supervisors
- in practice it may prove difficult to allocate work fairly between sharers.

2.3 Temporary and contingent employees

Temporary staffing has become a $40 billion industry in the USA (Greble, 1995). Around one in ten US workers are temporary employees and the trend is spreading to other countries, particularly the UK. Obtaining temporary cover for periods of high demand is nothing new. Seasonal workers have long been hired in many industries to cope with fluctuations in the requirement for human resources. For example, the tourist industry has high periods of demand, especially during the summer months; chocolate and other gift manufacturers require extra staff prior to Christmas and other religious holidays; farmers require extra help during the fruit picking seasons.

The key reasons for the growth of temporary staffing in the USA are the tax structures, unemployment insurance and contract law which make overtime and contingency working more attractive to employers than hiring new employees. Overall, it is estimated that temporary workers are 20 to 40 per cent cheaper for employers than permanent staff (Greble, 1997).

ACTIVITY 10

There are a number of different forms of staffing contracts. One of these is permanent full-time employment; another is the traditional 'temp' provided by an agency. Write brief descriptions of two or three other arrangements that you have come across, then compare your answers with the entries in table 1.

Arrangement	Description
1 Traditional temporary assistance	Employee is recruited by temp agency, sometimes with testing and screening. Assigned to work at client's workplace to support permanent workforce, to cover absences or skills shortages, or to staff short-term projects. Some agencies specialise in specific types of personnel.
2. Long-term temporary assignment	Employed as peripheral staff to take care of periods of high demand.
3. Master vendor arrangements	An agency is contracted to deal with all resourcing requirements for a specific function or department within the client's workspace. Similar to outsourcing except that client provides accommodation and systems. Agency deals with all payroll, pension and other employee contractual matters.
4. In-house temporary workers	Employees taken on and paid for by a business on an explicit short-term contract.
5. Payrolling	A business identifies suitable recruits but asks an agency to employ them on its behalf, usually at a lower cost to the business than traditional temporary staff.
6. Part-time employees	Working fewer than 30 full-time hours.
7. Independent contractors	Self-employed individuals who take on all responsibility for an activity, together with their own tax liability, social security, national insurance, etc.
8. Contract technical workers	Highly-skilled specialists provided on fairly lengthy contracts by technical service companies.
9. Employee leasing	Staff are transferred to an agency and then leased back. Legal in some countries, including the USA.
10. Outsourcing	A whole activity, including staff and accommodation is transferred to or replaced by a provider company.
11. Temp-to-permanent	Agency staff are taken on with the understanding that satisfactory performance will result in a permanent job.
12. Temp-to-lease	As above, but the temporary staff member becomes a leased employee.

Table 1: Alternative staffing arrangements
Source: Adapted from Greble (1995)

ACTIVITY 11

Consider table 1 and find common characteristics among different types of arrangement. For example, arrangements 1–5 and 8–11 are each applicable to full-time work. Can you see other characteristics common to groups of items.

There are a number of important features common to groups of different working arrangements. For example:

- employment is largely under the control of the worker in arrangements 7 and, possibly, 8
- employment is controlled by a different company to that which actually uses the worker in arrangements 3, 5 and 8–11
- employment is relatively long-term in arrangements 2, 3, 5, 6, 8–10 and, potentially, in 11 and 12
- employment is effectively 'distanced' or subcontracted in arrangements 3, 5, 7, 9 and 10.

You might have found several more common characteristics.

From this analysis it appears that some forms of staffing arrangements are better in particular circumstances than others. For example, it might be wiser to employ contract workers or temporary staff for a start-up business with an uncertain future than to recruit permanent workers.

What is the difference in meaning between temporary and contingent? The term **contingent employees** is nowadays used for any temporary staff, but originally applied to professional or specialist staff such as 'interim managers'. Interim managers are freelance executives, mostly aged over 40 dealing with assignments averaging 40–80 days. They are particularly suitable for covering short-term projects when employers see no long-term need for committed managers. Their expertise is rated highly in functions such as human resources, finance, information technology, marketing, operations and property.

One of the most important issues – which we are able to touch on briefly – is the effectiveness of contingent workers in comparison to traditional forms of employment. The next case study may help you to identify some of the key benefits of using contingent staffing.

Kaizen team at Perkins

Perkins Engines, a UK-based diesel engine maker, brought in a group of outside people in late-1997 to help the company literally tear itself apart. With a brief to undertake a complete review of the way Perkins organised work on the shopfloor, and to implement their ideas, they were given a selection of large mobile cranes, forklift trucks and other equipment and then left to get on with the job. The outside workers had a variety of backgrounds but no connection with process engineering.

Just four days later, they had radically transformed the efficiency and productivity of the production lines in a 'shopfloor *Kaizen* breakthrough'. *Kaizen* is a Japanese term for continuous improvement. In the four main production areas, the outsiders had been formed into teams each with a mix of permanent staff. In one area they had moved heavy machinery and reduced the floor space needed by 72 per cent. Moreover, work in progress had been cut by 93 per cent and labour had been reduced by 40 per cent.

The results were so impressive that more taskforces were sent into another 150 areas of the plant. Previously these teams had always consisted of Perkins staff from the targeted area, but fresh and unbiased outsiders had produced much better results.

There was no resistance from the workforce because they had been promised that there would be no redundancies from the exercise. This was not a difficult promise to make because one of the main motivations was to obtain extra capacity for expansion to meet demand.

Some improvements were fairly obvious and may have come from the briefing sessions given by managers. But Perkins were confident that the process was more radical.

Adapted from Griffiths (1998).

ACTIVITY 12

Reflect on the case study of the Kaizen team at Perkins Engines.

1. To what extent do you consider that outside workers were essential to the success of the exercise?

2. What motivated the outside people to do well?

The case study shows that the scope for improvement was there all along. So, why had changes not been implemented? There are many possible reasons including staff being too busy with day-to-day work, vested interests in keeping things as they were, not being able to see 'the wood from the trees' – the broad picture over the details, and not recognising the significance of particular aspects of the job. Outsiders would not have these limitations.

Contingent staff rely heavily on reputation to obtain extra work. A job well done can lead to another. Also, contingent staff have often chosen to do specific work which they find interesting and challenging – for them the job is intrinsically motivating.

Unlike other forms of staffing, decisions to employ temporary staff are often taken on a haphazard, departmental basis, rather than as part of the comprehensive strategy used by Perkins (Greble, 1995). Departmental managers faced with an immediate staff shortage may recruit agency staff without thinking about long-term implications on morale, training and development, and team spirit.

Guest (quoted in Donkin, 1998) has argued that contingent staffing in such circumstances may reduce fixed pay costs, but it creates other problems for the employer. He concludes that 'managers spend so much of their time trying to sort out contracts that they can't get on with their proper management job'.

Summary

There is a multiplicity of forms of contingent or temporary working. These different forms of non-traditional working arrangements have attractions for employers – and some groups of employees. A majority of part-time workers are women, but the number of male part-timers has increased considerably in recent years. Job-sharing is an attractive option for some but suitable opportunities may be difficult to find and administer.

SECTION 3

Trends in Work Organisation

Introduction

This section focuses on the relationship between changes in work patterns and developments in business organisation. We examine the management of human resources in new forms of organisation. The implications of developments in management thinking and information technology are considered, particularly on organisational structure and working lives. Finally, we debate the advantages and disadvantages of teleworking for employees and organisations.

This section is intended to help you to:

- provide explanations for the complexity of the human resource function in modern types of organisation
- analyse the impact of information technology on business processes and the employees who deal with them
- evaluate the concept of the virtual organisation
- critically assess the merits and disadvantages of teleworking.

3.1 Managing people in flat and distributed organisations

Since the 1980s, large companies have been pressurised into restructuring initiatives for a variety of reasons, particularly through mergers and acquisitions. Such initiatives (Price, 1997; Legge, 1995) include:

- **delayering**, or cutting out layers of management so that individual managers have much larger numbers of staff, resulting in flat organisational structures
- **downsizing**, or slimming down human resources at all levels within firm in order to cut staffing costs, typically subcontracting non-core activities to outside suppliers.

Both approaches are indicative of a hard HRM attitude in which previously important layers of management or entire departments have been reclassified from resources to 'overheads' (Legge, 1995). Inevitably, there are repercussions on morale and commitment and the transition to new and reduced organisational structures requires careful management.

The UK banking industry

The UK banking industry shed tens of thousands of jobs during the 1990s in order to restructure retail banking and move administrative work from local branches to central processing centres. At the same time, thousands of new employees were taken on to service telephone call centres and to facilitate internet access as customers changed their ways of dealing with banks.

In 1999, Barclays announced it would eliminate 6,000 jobs at a cost of £400 million in redundancy payments (see reports in the *Financial Times*, *The Guardian*, *The Independent*, 21 May 1999). Thereafter, it would save £200 million a year. One in ten of retail and corporate banking staff would be expected to leave, mostly on a voluntary basis. At the same time the bank would recruit up to 2,000 new employees for its internet and telephone-based business.

Shedding staff may preoccupy line and HR managers for lengthy periods of time. As a consequence, many companies experience considerable disruption, often because changes have not been thoroughly evaluated (Kettley, 1995). At this point, consider how restructuring can be made easier by studying Kettley's advice set out below before trying activity 13.

Kettley suggests that HR managers could assist restructuring by actions:

- anticipating likely employee response to restructuring
- identifying specific interventions that impact on morale
- championing cultural and behavioural change by investing in management development – this is an issue explored in the unit on employee development
- working on improved systems for reward, career management and resourcing to demonstrate a positive future in the company
- monitoring and evaluating morale and the impact of actions taken – staff attitudes should be measured and acted on to safeguard performance.

Kettley argues that restructuring unsettles the pattern of skills, roles and relationships. Consequently, the human resource function has a role to play over the years that follow major restructuring in achieving a new equilibrium. He contends that reducing the size and influence of the HR function at this stage would be a false economy.

ACTIVITY 13

Study the advice provided by Kettley. Then turn to Resource 2 in the Resources section and read the article *Rewarding a model merger*. Consider whether human resource managers have implemented Kettley's recommendations adequately and, if not, outline what more they could have done.

You might agree that Lloyds TSB appears to have followed Kettley's pointers reasonably well. However, the article implies that the main focus has been on restructuring human resource activities to fit the merger, rather than using HR to anticipate morale and other problems. It is not clear if the four models which Lloyds TSB considered were, in fact, evaluated in terms of such factors. Nevertheless the merged bank has taken a positive approach to restructuring, rather than taking instant cost-cutting measures.

By the end of the 1990s there was a widespread feeling that cost-cutting had gone too far and that many modern organisations were too thinly resourced or 'anorexic' to cope with business needs (Laabs, 1999). Flat, distributed and under-resourced businesses are difficult to manage. Technology offers new ways of managing such organisations. We now investigate various forms of networked organisation and their HR implications.

3.2   Management through networks

Current management thinking advocates that business units should be 'lean and mean'. They should focus on core activities identified as strategically important and worth developing as areas of expertise (Thompson, 1997). It follows from this logic that all other functions can be subcontracted to specialist providers. These may be different business units within the same organisation or entirely independent firms within a network of contacts. For example, a business unit concentrates on manufacturing and selling widgets but buys in research, marketing and billing services from other companies within the network. Networking extends an organisation's business processes beyond its own physical boundaries. Snow, Miles and Coleman (1992) identify three different types of network.

- **Internal** – consisting of business units owned by a parent organisation with each unit specialising in a particular activity. Units network with each other and may also interact with external providers.

- **Stable** – another way of describing Atkinson's flexible firm model. A small team of specialists and managers provide core facilities, with most activities subcontracted to external providers. Broadcasting companies typically work in this way.

- **Dynamic** – all activities are subcontracted with a few core staff acting as brokers and organisers.

VIRTUAL ORGANISATIONS

Networking is not new. This form of organisation has existed for centuries, but information technology allows networking to become invisible to customers and, often, to staff. Advancing technology allows us to construct enterprises with no permanent structures. These virtual organisations are networks composed of specialists who add value through their knowledge. Microsoft UK, for example, has around 1,000 regular staff but employs 20,000 people indirectly (*Financial Times*, 7 May 1999).

Virtual organisations bring people together for specific projects. Many of these people will never meet each other. Employees – whether in the next office, in their cars, or overseas – communicate through the telephone or e-mail (Avery, 1998). Teams dissolve on completion, to reappear in new combinations for other tasks. Departments, divisions and offices disappear leaving an amorphous mass of people connected electronically and meeting – perhaps through video-conferencing – only when required. Traditional hierarchical structures have no role in this kind of organisational structure.

Truly virtual organisations create new problems for human resource management. A networked company does not require a personnel function but its core management must be adept in managing people at a distance, some of whom may not be 'employees' as such. They are true 'human resource managers' (Thomson and Mabey, 1994). How does performance management or HR development take place in such circumstances? How are people managed on a day-to-day basis? Who resolves conflict and disagreement? These questions are especially relevant in the case of teleworkers, as we discover later in this section.

Managing from a distance

Bradt (1998) cites the case of a manager working for the Bank of Montreal in Toronto, Canada. She and her husband decided to return to England on his retirement. She was reluctant to leave her job and the bank did not want to lose a good manager. The bank arranged for her to manage her group in Toronto by means of teleconferencing, e-mail and voicemail. The experiment was apparently successful, despite a five-hour time difference. According to Bradt (after a visit to her home) 'the image of a little office in the very archetype of English thatched cottage tied to a group of people in a glass building in Toronto is a striking one'.

Avery (1998) points out, however, that in practice most virtual organisations are only partly virtual. Most virtual companies have 'real world' elements which still use offices and have face-to-face meetings. After all, human contact is invaluable for engendering good relationships and sparking off creative ideas. In fact, there may be a continuum of virtuality. Bradt (1998) divides virtual organisations into four types:

- alliance organisations
- displaced organisations
- invisible organisations
- truly virtual organisations.

Alliance organisation

In the alliance organisation functions previously carried out within the boundaries of one organisation are conducted by linked partners which concentrate on their 'core competencies' (best strengths).

Displaced organisations

In displaced organisations individual members are distributed geographically and connected by information technology, but appear to outsiders to be a single unified organisation. One of the most common forms has customer-facing units or corporate headquarters in one country and back office or support activities in another. For example, software companies have made use of the considerable (and comparatively cheap) talents of programmers and data input staff in India. Clerical support for investment and insurance companies can be placed in less expensive locations than cities like London, New York and Tokyo. Businesses can choose to centralise global or regional back offices and call centres or to decentralise them to staff working at home or in rural locations.

Internationally, a virtual shift system may operate – teams around the globe deal with the same project at different times, each group leaving progress reports for the next as they conclude their working day. Virtual shifts operate in circumstances such as global investment or vehicle design.

Invisible organisations

The invisible organisation has no physical structure as such. Bradt cites Direct Line Insurance as a typical example. There are no visible high street branches, simply a network of call centres and back offices. Business is conducted by telephone.

Truly virtual organisations

The truly virtual organisation, such as the on-line Amazon.com bookstore. This is a combination of the first three types. Customers come to the company via internet service providers (ISPs), often from links on the web pages of 'affiliates' who promote particular books and are paid by commission. Orders are processed centrally but relatively few books are held in stock – most are despatched from publishers' warehouses. Delivery is handled by independent agents such as UPS or Parcelforce.

3.3 Teleworking

Virtual organisations allow staff to work at a distance. Increasingly, many people are choosing to work from home or in telecottages – communal locations equipped with computers, modems and fax machines. This form of work introduces significant new challenges to managers, unions and others because it places a question mark over many of the familiar assumptions about managing work performance (Huws, 1997).

Huws (1997) identifies five types of teleworking.

- **Multi-site teleworking** in which employees alternate between work at the firm's premises and elsewhere. The alternative worksite could be at home, at a telecottage or telecentre, or an outpost.

- **Tele-homeworking** where an individual works exclusively at home for a single employer, possibly without formal employee status. As with other more traditional forms of homeworking such as sewing and envelope-filling, this is often low-skill work typically involving those (usually women) who are at home looking after children or other dependants.

- **Freelance teleworking** in which individuals work for a number of clients. Their problems are different from those of homeworkers but equally significant.

- **Mobile teleworking** where travelling employees, such as sales representatives or maintenance engineers, rely on mobile phones, e-mail and fax machines to carry out administrative work 'on the road'.

- **Relocated back office functions**. Teleworking is not necessarily an individual activity. As we noted in our discussion of the virtual organisation, many back office activities have been located at considerable distances from company headquarters. These may be on a small scale, occupying premises which are essentially telecottages.

ACTIVITY 14

Read through Huws' list of the different types of teleworking. For each type write notes on the main implications for human resource managers, line managers and employees. Write about 75 words on each type of teleworking (within the table provided or on plain paper if preferred).

Type of teleworking	Implications for HR department	Implications for line managers	Implications for individuals
Multi-site teleworking			
Tele-homeworking			
Freelance teleworking			
Mobile teleworking			
Back office teleworking			

Each type of teleworking creates its own set of management problems. The fundamental issue is that staff are not located in centralised workplaces under the eyes of managers. Depending on the nature of work involved, there is no necessity for work to be completed in anything resembling a 'normal' working day. Health and safety becomes difficult to manage and employment contracts become radically different from those in traditional organisations.

You might have concluded that some of the implications set out in the table are important.

Type of teleworking	Implications for HR department	Implications for line managers	Implications for individuals
Multi-site teleworking	Communication problems. Difficult to co-ordinate training, appraisal, team briefings.	Keeping control. Difficult to manage performance. Team meetings more difficult to organise.	Highly-favoured by employees: contact plus autonomy. Job security. Promotion prospects.
Tele-homeworking	As above plus substantially different working arrangements. Equal opportunity implications.	As above.	Health and safety. Insurance. More autonomy and personal control. Often low paid and non-unionised.
Freelance teleworking	Subcontracted rather than employed.	Freelancer rather than employee, therefore different forms of control, level of respect and formal relationship.	Not likely to be unionised. No job security. Competing pressures, including work and domestic. Possibility of high income.
Mobile teleworking	As with multi-site but more so.	As with multi-site teleworker but more so. Often line manager is also mobile.	Considerable travelling. Little contact with base. Isolated. Autonomy. Often commission paid.
Back office teleworking	Co-ordination and communication problems. Different regional and national practices, wage rates, etc.	Communication. Possibly dealing with different union branches. Persuading good performers to move.	Possibly in different country. Recognition problems. Lack of promotion.

Table 2: Management implications of teleworking

ACTIVITY 15

Put yourself in the position of a teleworker writing computer manuals at home. What do you think the advantages and disadvantages might be for you over other forms of employment?

Take five minutes to jot down some of your ideas. Compare your thoughts with the findings of the research reported below and Huws' discussion that follows.

Teleworking in practice

Becker et al. (1995) found that the sales force of a large US computer company working from home missed out on two forms of communication: the ability to communicate about work with colleagues or other professionals, and chances to socialise with co-workers.

Three quarters of the respondents in their survey found that professional communication at work had worsened to some extent since they began working from home. Surprisingly, 9 per cent stated that it had improved. A large majority (89 per cent) reported that opportunities to socialise with colleagues were made worse.

Work was more productive at home because of fewer interruptions and better concentration. Over half of the respondents stated that their overall work effectiveness was better at home; 30 per cent felt neutral about this question; 18 per cent stated that their effectiveness was worse. Becker et al. found that employees' satisfaction with teleworking did not seem to be affected by their domestic circumstances such as whether they had children or whether they had a dedicated room in which to work.

The majority of employees found that their most productive work hours fell between the relatively normal working hours of 8 a.m. to 4 p.m. However, nearly 40 per cent preferred to work outside this period.

Huws argues that as teleworking becomes a practical reality for people at a number of levels, ranging from senior manager to clerical assistant, it is no longer valid to refer to all teleworkers as a single category. Their needs are different.

Questions arise about the selection of teleworking staff. Is it important, for example, to make positive selections of employees who do not need the social stimulation and support that many office staff regard as a major feature of working life? Office work is constantly interrupted by telephone calls or visits from colleagues. Many of these interruptions are not work-related and cause significant distractions. Traditionally, supervisors have been employed to police offices and ensure that untimely or non-work interruptions and personal phone calls are kept to the minimum.

Teleworkers do not experience such interruptions but there are other distractions that can interfere with the flow of work. Partners, children and neighbours may ignore the need for quiet concentration – particularly if there is no separate work office.

Summary

Changing work structures are impacting on the conduct of human resource management. The evolution of flat, distributed companies – and the effects of large restructuring programmes – have repercussions on the HR function. Technological advance has led to networked businesses, sometimes taking the form of virtual organisations. Teleworking is increasingly common, providing advantages for companies and employees but posing a different HR challenge.

Unit review activity

Read the case study on Dell Computers and then answer the questions that follow.

Dell Computers

With sales increasing by 59 per cent, 1998 was a brilliantly successful year for Dell Computers. Dell was at the forefront of technological development in desk and laptop personal computers. The company had become the world's largest direct seller of personal computers (PCs). Most of Dell's business comprised making PCs to the individual specifications of customers ordering by mail, telephone and via the internet. To service this growth, the workforce increased by 56 per cent during the year. Dell's HR staff were not simply faced with recruiting a hundred staff a week, but they also had to bear in mind the need to develop employees who could fit into the company's style of organisation.

Dell grows its organisation through a process described as cell division. This is driven by technological advances and a need to address stiff competition from other providers. New developments in computer technology have to be made available as soon as possible, and preferably before these features are offered by competitors. When a business section dealing with a particular product or range reaches a specified size threshold, part is spun off to form a new unit. In turn, this is encouraged to grow until it can be split again. The threshold is not set purely on the number of employees – financial considerations are also taken into account. This method of growth does not suit everyone, so Dell aims to recruit employees with a particular mind-set. As the organisation is flat and distributed, it has no need for grandiose managerial titles and impressive hierarchical charts. The company is not a place for egotists. Employees are expected to take segmentation as a sign of success, although this entails responsibility being taken away.

Managers are rewarded for achieving segmentation thresholds. The company has grown so quickly that units can split and split again within 9–10 months. It has become such a part of the culture that employees regard segmentation as a matter of celebration. In keeping with this culture, Dell seeks to attract people who enjoy constant and rapid change. It is worth noting that Dell paid its staff generously during this period and there was a concern about rising costs.

The HR function at Dell has become a strategic partner in the process of growth. Human resource management is split into operations and management. Through a service centre, the HR operations section co-ordinates transactional functions, including pay and benefits and also employee relations. Operational human resource staff report directly to the top of the organisation through a HR chain of command. There is little contact with business unit managers.

In contrast, the HR management section provides consultants to business units and attends local staff meetings. HR management takes responsibility for 'Dell University' – the education and training function – employee resourcing including recruitment, and a team of HR generalists. The generalists report to the vice-president of specific business units as well as the vice-president of HR. Their function is strategic, focused on developing leadership teams, performance measures and individual business unit HR strategies.

The HR management section is closely involved in growth policy. It is involved in segmentation through designing organisation charts, identifying appropriate people and dealing with training needs. Not surprisingly for a major computer company, Dell makes considerable use of information technology. The company's intranet (internal web-based information system) is used for payroll, administration and appraisals. Line managers conduct their own human resource planning and have the means to calculate the financial consequences of any personnel initiatives.

People are brought into specialist units at appropriate times to help in designing recruitment programmes. For example, IT staff are seconded to advise on the personal qualities and training necessary to perform new jobs.

Adapted from Joinson (1999).

1. To what extent is Dell's organisational structure dependent on technology-driven growth? What would happen if the trend slowed or reversed?
2. How much real power do the HR specialists exercise at Dell?
3. What would happen to the quality of staffing if the HR management functions did not exist?
4. Is this model of HR usable in other organisations?

The commentary on these questions appears at the end of this unit.

Unit summary

This unit has been concerned with relationships between evolving organisational structures and employees' working lives. It examined non-traditional and alternative methods of providing human resources, looked at the competitive pressures that have caused changes in organisational structures and cultures, and considered the effects of new technology with particular regard to the virtual organisation and teleworking.

In terms of the implications for human resource management, these changes in the nature of work can be assessed by considering four main trends.

- The changing **priorities** of HRM – with a move away from full-time, permanent employees to more varied and flexible working practices, HR specialists must focus on different needs. Legal and technical aspects of job sharing, teleworking and other work patterns are more complex than with traditional employment, particularly in terms of equal opportunities, career development and training.

- The changing **power** position of HR practitioners – as line managers take on greater responsibility for day-to-day people management, the influence of HR specialists is determined by their understanding of wider business issues and the legal and technical implications of newer working patterns. Power lies in the quality of analysis and advice they can provide to line managers.

- The changing **processes** which HRM is reliant upon – as with all other forms of management, HR specialists make less use of face-to-face meetings and paperwork. Instead, the range of electronic communication including e-mail, telephone and web-based information systems provide the channels through which information is collected and disseminated.

- The changing **profile** of the profession – there is a need to move away from being an insular profession dominated by the need to fulfil administrative needs. At least a proportion of HR practitioners must be fully adept with modern information technology and familiar with other business specialisms in order to provide quality advice to line managers.

References

Adams, K (1991) 'Externalisation vs specialisation: what is happening to personnel?' *Human Resource Management Journal,* 1(4): 40-54

Adams, C (1999) 'Work: Business wakes up to end of 9-to-5', *Financial Times,* 26 May 1999

Atkinson, J (1984) 'Manpower strategies for flexible organisations', *Personnel Management,* April, Institute of Personnel Management

Avery, G (1998) 'Virtual HR', *HR Monthly,* October, Australian Human Resources Institute

Becker, F, Quinn, K L and Callentine, L U (1995) *The Ecology of the Mobile Worker,* Cornell University International Workplace Studies Program, Ithaca, NY

Bower, M (1966) *The Will to Manage,* McGraw-Hill

Bradt, R (1998) *Virtual Organisations: A Simple Taxonomy,* Infothink

Corbridge, M and Pilbeam, S (1998) *Employment Resourcing,* Financial Times Pitman Publishing

Court, G (1995) *Women in the Labour Market: Two Decades of Change and Continuity,* IES Report 294, Institute for Employment Studies

Donkin, R 'Recruitment: The wrong tools for the job', *Financial Times,* 13 January 1998

Greble, T C (1997) 'A Leading Role for HR in Alternative Staffing', *HR Magazine,* February

Griffiths, J 'Productivity and technology: Lessons in improvement,' *Financial Times,* 23 February 1998

Handy, C (1989) *The Age of Unreason,* Business Books

Handy, C (1993) *Understanding Organisations,* Penguin, 4th edn

Hofstede, G (1994) *Cultures and Organisations,* HarperCollins

Huws, U (1997) *Teleworking: Guidelines for Good Practice,* Institute of Employment Studies

Hyman, R (1991) 'Plus ca change?, The theory of production and the production of theory', in Pollert, A (ed.), *Farewell to Flexibility?*, Blackwell

Joinson, C (1999) 'Moving at the speed of Dell', *HR Monthly*, April 1999

Kettley, P (1995) *Is Flatter Better? Delayering the Management Hierarchy*, Institute of Employment Studies

Laabs, J (1999) 'Has Downsizing Missed Its Mark?', *Workforce*, April 1999, Vol. 78, No. 4

Legge, K (1995) *Human Resource Management: Rhetorics and Realities*, Macmillan Business

Magretta, J (1998) 'The Power of Virtual Integration: An Interview with Dell Computer's Michael Dell', *Harvard Business Review*, 76, 2 March–April 1998

Piore, M and Sabel, C (1984) *The Second Industrial Divide: Possibilities for Prosperity*, Basic Books

Price, A J (1997) *Human Resource Management in a Business Context*, International Thomson Business Press

Rothwell, S (1995) 'Human resource planning' in Storey, J (ed.) *Human Resource Management: A Critical Text*, Routledge

Snow, C C, Miles, R E and Coleman, H J (1992) 'Managing 21st century organizations', *Organizational Dynamics*, Winter

Storey, J (1995) *Human Resource Management: A Critical Text*, Routledge

Tailby, S (1999) 'Flexible Labour Markets, Firms and Workers' in Hollinshead, G, Nicholls, P and Tailby, S (eds) *Employee Relations*, Financial Times Pitman Publishing

Tamkin, P, Barber, L and Dench, S (1997) *From Admin to Strategy: the changing face of the HR Function*, IES Report 332, Institute of Employment Studies

Taylor, R (1998) 'Recruitment: Business leaders fear acute shortage of skills', *Financial Times*, 22 January 1998

Thompson, J L (1997) *Strategic Management: Awareness and Change*, International Thomson Business Press, 3rd edn

Thomson, R and Mabey, C (1994) *Developing Human Resources*, Butterworth-Heinemann

80 UNIT 2

Recommended Reading

Stephanie Tailby's chapter on 'Flexible Labour Markets, Firms and Workers' in *Employee Relations* (Hollinshead et al., 1999) is an excellent summary of the flexibility debate at the end of the 1990s. Chapter 5 of *Human Resource Management: Rhetorics and Realities* by Karen Legge also provides a detailed conceptual debate on the subject of flexibility.

Many of the changes to working practice and organisational structure described in this unit are too new for extensive coverage in book form. You should look to practitioner journals instead, such as the Institute of Personnel and Development's *People Management*, and similar journals around the world. Many of these are available via the worldwide web: access the author's *Internet Guide to Human Resource Management* (currently available at http://www.hrmguide.com) for thematic links to these issues, particularly under the heading Organisational HRM.

Answers to Unit Review Activity

1. Dell Computers is an example of a flat distributed company which networks extensively outside its own business units. Growing organisations present an entirely different set of circumstances to more static companies, or businesses in the process of restructuring. Inevitably, there is a confidence and trust in management not necessarily found in less successful companies. Managers are likely to be happier about relinquishing responsibility for some of their 'territory' if they are more or less certain that fresh growth will bring in more work. In less positive circumstances, there is a greater probability of resistance to this process.

2. Human resource management in Dell clearly has influence but it is arguable that this does not amount to 'power'. The operations aspect of HR plays a valuable, indeed essential, role and is likely to be 'safe', if relatively unexciting, even in more uncertain circumstances. The HR management function has greater influence through its involvement in decision-making, planning and the strategic support given by HR generalists to business sections. However, the HR role is primarily supportive by providing advice and fulfilling basic staffing needs for business managers and the company as a whole.

3. The HR operations function does essential work which would have to be performed by someone, under whatever label or departmental title. Without this work, the company would be unable to fulfil its legal and contractual requirements towards its staff. If cost-cutting became a priority due to less

favourable trading conditions in the future it is possible that the HR management function could be reduced drastically. In the short term this would not create insurmountable problems, but the long-term effect could lead to a terminal decline in the quality of the company's human resources.

4. This is not an uncommon form of HR organisation but the positive atmosphere created by vigorous growth encourages its success at Dell. The particular style of organisational development – evolution would be a more accurate term – is unusual. However, most large businesses are split into definable units which tend to focus on operational matters, while central or divisional mechanisms takes care of strategic and co-ordinating activities. HR must mirror this structure in some way and the Dell solution seems, taken at face value, to be particularly effective.

UNIT 3
EMPLOYMENT RESOURCING: PLANNING AND RECRUITMENT

Introduction

Resourcing is a term applied to the process by which suitable people are identified and allocated to work tasks. It is a function of crucial importance for effective human resource management. Yet the way resourcing is conducted varies considerably from one organisation to another. In fact, there is no right way to set about employment resourcing – it depends on circumstances and the context of the organisation involved (Corbridge and Pilbeam, 1998).

Employees are expensive assets to acquire but many businesses approach resourcing in a relatively unstructured manner. However, as we will discover in this unit (and Unit 4), other employers use sophisticated methods with long-term objectives in mind, often attempting to balance considerations such as:

- satisfying the immediate need to minimise employee costs while maximising worker contribution to the organisation
- fulfilling a longer-term aim of obtaining the optimal mix of skills and commitment in the workforce.

What are the key elements of cost-efficient resourcing? At the heart of the process lies the need to identify work that must be done and the knowledge, skills and abilities required to do it. But it is not sufficient to deal with individual jobs: there are strategic implications to consider. As we noted in earlier units, employers must make choices between hiring permanent employees and using contingent employees or subcontractors. Many businesses outsource non-core activities such as computer support, payroll, catering and cleaning to specialist providers.

Employment resourcing encompasses a range of activities that can include:

- **strategy and planning** – determining future human resource requirements in terms of numbers, skills and location, and deciding whether they should be staffed by permanent employees
- **research** – establishing criteria or competences essential for the performance of particular tasks
- **recruitment** – attracting suitable applicants from within or outside the organisation
- **selection** – choosing the most suitable permanent or contingent workers and subcontractors.

This unit is solely concerned with the first three of these elements. Selection is an extensive topic which justifies consideration in a separate unit.

Objectives

By the end of this unit, you should be able to:

- outline the main purposes and methodologies of soft and hard human resource planning

- explain how human resource planning can be applied to the specific issues of employee turnover and outsourcing

- provide an outline of how information relevant to employment resourcing can be collected, analysed and used to determine staffing needs

- argue for and against alternative strategies to fulfil resourcing requirements.

SECTION 1
Planning and Forecasting

Introduction

How do organisations anticipate their resourcing needs? The first requirement is detailed and accurate knowledge of the current and expected position in terms of:

- what jobs are being done now, and what jobs will be required soon
- by whom
- where
- the skills and knowledge required for these tasks
- the cost implications.

From this knowledge base, businesses can plan and forecast resourcing requirements in the short, medium and long-term. Human resource planning is a process of mapping out the implications of business strategy for the number and type of people required by an organisation. In organisations which take the topic seriously, modern human resource planning is particularly concerned with forecasting skill and competence needs as well as total headcounts. It has consequences for a wide range of human resource activities – such as human resource development, performance management and remuneration – as well as employment resourcing.

We begin this section by examining the purposes of human resource planning. Then we distinguish between hard (or numerical) planning and soft planning which encompasses elements such as skills and attitudes. Finally, we consider how hard and soft planning techniques can be applied to a specific issue – outsourcing.

The aim of this section is to help you to:

- explain the significance of human resource planning
- outline the underlying logic of basic forecasting techniques
- calculate and predict employee turnover
- argue for and against the use of hard and soft forms of human resource planning in specific circumstances such as outsourcing.

1.1   Human resource planning

What is the purpose of human resource planning? How can we use our knowledge of current human resources in an organisation to forecast resourcing requirements next year or, say, in three-to-five years time? Given the rapid rate of change in technology and market needs, is there any value in attempting to undertake this task? Indeed, we might ask whether human resource planning is just a textbook subject? This is a topic of some debate (O'Doherty, 1997).

Personnel textbooks have traditionally promoted techniques known as **manpower planning**. This involves anticipating future demand for staff, allocating different kinds of staff within organisations, and developing systems for calculating human resource requirements based on accurate records and forecasting techniques. Most companies have made simple workforce headcount predictions but only larger organisations, such as the civil service, the armed forces, the Post Office and high-street banks, undertook this type of detailed manpower planning (O'Doherty, 1997). Complex mathematical models were built by specialist planners in these large organisations but, in many ways, this was an unreal process which attracted a great deal of criticism (Corbridge and Pilbeam, 1998). For example, planners were accused of having rigid mindsets with an obsession for numbers which had no prospect of being translated into actual events (Mintzberg, 1994).

Partly as a consequence, modern human resource planners have tended to move away from predicting headcounts towards building 'what if' models or scenarios which allow the implications of different strategies to be debated. However, traditional HR planning techniques have become considerably easier to implement with the spread of human resource information systems which capture key employee information and generate reports and analyses as a matter of course.

FORECASTING FROM THE PRESENT SITUATION

Forecasts of the employee skill mix required can be based on past trends, educated guesswork or more sophisticated models. Some of the most common techniques include:

- extrapolation
- projection
- employee analysis
- scenario building.

Extrapolation

Extrapolation is based on an assumption that the past is a reliable guide to the future. Various techniques are suitable for short and medium-term forecasting, such as time series, trend analysis and measures of cyclical requirements. All rely on present knowledge and do not take the unpredictable into account; these techniques, therefore, are most effective in a stable environment. They tend to do little harm if kept pessimistic. However, enthusiasm and political considerations often encourage undue optimism with expensive consequences.

Projection

This involves basing human resource plans on overall business plans that include sales, production and other workflow estimates produced by operational units. Job analysis and managerial judgement can translate this data into employee requirements.

Employee analysis

Employee analysis profiles the existing workforce to facilitate planning. For example, age distribution has considerable implications for recruitment, promotion and training needs. Obviously, an older workforce is more likely to generate vacancies (as employees retire) than one composed of relatively young people. However, we have to bear in mind that older people are less likely to change jobs than younger members of staff. We examine this topic further later in this unit when we consider how employee turnover can be measured.

The current emphasis on 'knowledge management' (improving workers' skills and knowledge) has produced a need to know the degree to which skills and knowledge are being shared and gained. Pratt and Bennett (1992) argue that 'a basic skills inventory will be invaluable to management, and any personnel records system worth its salt should readily provide details of the skills and attributes of each employee'. We will discover in later units that non-numerical information of this kind is frequently missing even in the most sophisticated human resource databases.

In addition, as we discuss in a later unit, gender, ethnic and disability distributions are essential to monitor progress in achieving an organisation's equality objectives. Such distributions can highlight blockages in the organisation which prevent the achievement of a diverse workforce.

Scenario building

Human resource planners are tending to move away from preparing rigid plans towards providing alternative scenarios. These are speculative assessments of a range of possible future circumstances that aim to clarify direction and identify uncertainty. Organisations have choices available to them, for example hiring temporary staff as opposed to permanent employees to fulfil short-term needs. Different scenarios can be devised which illustrate the consequences of making particular choices.

ACTIVITY 1

From your reading of this section so far, jot down the type of information provided by the different forecasting methods. Then write down the information which you feel may not be revealed by each method. Use the following table to organise your ideas.

Method	Reveals	Does not reveal
Extrapolation		
Projection		
Employee analysis		
Scenario building		

Your answers may have included some of the ideas set out in Table 1.

Method	Reveals	Does not reveal
Extrapolation	Requirements if present conditions continue to apply Definite numbers (headcounts)	Requirements if: ● market conditions change ● technology improves ● competition increases or decreases ● fashion for products and services changes ● legal conditions change
Projection	Requirements if sales and other business forecasts are correct Definite numbers (headcounts)	Requirements if other forecasts are too pessimistic or optimistic
Employee analysis	Depending on the questions asked, can provide detailed profiles of: ● age distribution ● gender distribution ● ethnic distribution ● skills ● knowledge Where blockages are occurring on progress towards skills and diversity targets	Why particular groups are not adequately represented Why skills and knowledge are improving or declining
Scenario building	Range of possible options for the future Assumptions on which options are based	Which specific option to choose Consequences of developments which have not been assumed

Table 1: The characteristics of different human resource forecasting methods

From Table 1, it can be seen that every method has something to offer, but it would appear that each is more appropriate to one set of circumstances than to another. For example, in a fairly stable environment, a small organisation might find that extrapolation was sufficient. But a global company developing a range of fashion products for rapidly changing markets would probably need to use more sophisticated forecasting methods.

PLANNING IN REALITY

What happens in practice? Are these methods really used by many businesses? Research shows that human resource planning is considerably more common in large organisations than small companies (Werther and Davis, 1995).

A survey of 30 large UK organisations in different industrial sectors showed that most had three-to-five year plans (Tyson, 1995). Some retailers kept detailed plans down to just one year but other businesses with major capital investment needs understandably took a much longer view. Most managers surveyed were unhappy with five-year plans seeing them as business constraints.

The study identified three different perspectives on human resource planning amongst the organisations surveyed.

- **Formal, long-range planning**. Adopted by companies which had a planning framework, and constructed in financial terms with written commentaries. All the companies in the study which used this approach consulted widely with stakeholder groups. These organisations had a precise understanding of their staffing situations and a clear programme for the future. This gave human resource specialists a good basis for recruitment programmes. However, detailed planning knowledge was relatively expensive to obtain and could be rendered valueless by unexpected changes in market conditions.

- **Flexible strategies**. Most of the businesses studied used flexible strategies. Plans were amended frequently in response to changing market conditions. Detailed planning was deliberately short-term, often with little in the way of written detail. This allowed speedy reactions to market developments but made life difficult for HR specialists who had little notice of changes in demand for workers.

- **Incremental strategies**. A 'one step at a time' approach with no real commitment to any specific strategy. This approach seemed to have little to commend it since there was no attempt to prepare the organisation for the future.

ACTIVITY 2

The survey of business attitudes and approaches to human resource planning described above involved only a small number of businesses and may not be representative of large organisations in general. However, on the basis of its results, judge whether the following statements are likely to be true or false.

1. Most large organisations have medium-term to long-term plans.

2. There is a significant difference between the planning practices of companies in different industrial sectors.

3. Managers prefer to 'make it up as they go along' rather than have fixed plans, because market conditions are unpredictable.

4. Detailed long-term plans provide a firm basis on which human resource managers can prepare recruitment programmes.

5. Organisations with long-term plans tend to consult widely and spend a great deal of time and effort in their preparation.

6. Most large organisations have fixed plans which do not change over the planned period.

7. Most companies had comparatively broad long-term plans with detail confined to the short-term.

Most large organisations have medium-term to long-term plans. True: the survey did show this finding, but don't forget that it is not necessarily true for all organisations – the survey was based on a small sample.

There is a significant difference between the planning practices of companies in different industrial sectors. Yes. Where there is a big difference in the amount of capital invested by different sectors, there will be a corresponding difference in planning practices. When heavy investment is required to achieve a long-term goal, then more detailed planning and forecasting is practised.

Managers prefer to 'make it up as they go along' rather than have fixed plans, because market conditions are unpredictable. Not true, but they did like flexible plans.

Detailed long-term plans provide a firm basis on which human resource managers can prepare recruitment programmes. True, but the assumptions on which the plans were based could prove unfounded.

Organisations with long-term plans tend to consult widely and spend a great deal of time and effort in their preparation. True: to plan effectively management must gather relevant information about the social, demographic, financial and market environments as well as investigating the internal business environment.

Most large organisations have fixed plans which do not change over the planned period. Not true, most planning is relatively flexible. Some firms revise their five-year plans each year to respond to changes in the business environment.

Most companies had comparatively broad long-term plans with detail confined to the short-term. Yes: as the survey found, the long-range forecast provided a broad framework, but the detailed planning was flexible and short-term.

1.2   Turnover and wastage

We have noted that manpower planners traditionally focused on quantitative measurement. Forecasting (hard planning techniques) has traditionally been preferred to qualitative studies of opinion, attitude, motivation and contribution (soft planning). Human resource planning, as we observed, has become less fixated on numerical measures. (Paradoxically, the increasing use of information technology and management information systems has made numerical data more readily available.) Numbers are associated with objectivity, however, and there will always be some managers who believe that 'facts' – expressed in the form of hard data – justify a distancing from shop floor emotions. It is much easier to sack a number than a real human being.

One of the key concerns of planners – particularly in times of economic growth – has been to ensure that both individual units and the organisation as a whole have the right number of people in place. It would be unfortunate if a high proportion of employees in, say, the finance department retired at the same time without the organisation having made provision for trained replacements to be ready to take over their positions. This process focuses on the concept of employee turnover.

EMPLOYEE TURNOVER

Turnover describes the rate at which people come and go in an organisation. The loss of people is called **wastage**. The two main reasons for being concerned about wastage are:

- the cost of recruiting and training employees can be substantial – high wastage is expensive
- the loss of key personnel can be highly disruptive to an organisation and interfere with the achievement of its plans.

So anticipating wastage is an important element in the planning process, and reducing it is often an important management concern. We now turn to consider methods of measuring wastage. This can be determined by several turnover indices of varying degrees of sophistication.

Central rate of turnover

The central rate of turnover is determined by:

$$\text{Turnover rate (\% staff wastage)} = \frac{\text{Leavers in year}}{\text{Average number of employees that year}} \times 100$$

For example, if 220 people are employed at beginning of year, 260 people are employed at the end of year, and there are 80 leavers during the year, then:

$$\text{Turnover rate} = \frac{80}{(220 + 260)/2} = \frac{80 \times 100}{240} = 33.33\%$$

This indicates that one third of the employees have left during the course of a year. This percentage can be used as a basis of comparison within the organisation (comparing turnover rates between different departments or looking at the trend over a number of years) or with other businesses in the same region or industrial sector. A turnover of 33.3 per cent may seem high at face value, but it may prove to be normal in certain businesses such as fast-food takeaways.

The formula can be applied to smaller groups within the organisation. Indeed, a properly designed computer database or human resource information system can give turnover rates for job types, age ranges, departments, grades and locations at the press of a button. Graphical programmes can highlight trends and areas of concern. Nevertheless, the turnover rate does not tell us why specific individuals are leaving. Try out a calculation for yourself in the following activity.

ACTIVITY 3

Employment figures for different groups of employees at the XYZ Company are shown in the table.

Type of employee	Employees at 31/12/1999	Employees at 31/12/2000	Leavers in year
Manufacturing	315	325	40
Sales	36	32	17
Administration	56	64	12
Others	7	9	1

Using the formula for the central rate of turnover, calculate the percentage wastage for:

- manufacturing staff
- sales staff
- administration staff
- All employees

Discuss your results in the context of the regional wastage figures given in the table below.

Type of employee	Regional wastage
Manufacturing	18.0 %
Sales	27.0 %
Administration	21.0 %
All employees	19.7 %

You should have arrived at the following results.

Type of employee	Regional wastage
Manufacturing	12.5 %
Sales	50.0 %
Administration	20.0 %
All employees	16.7 %

By and large, XYZ Co. is doing well in comparison with other businesses in the region since most of its wastage figures are lower than average. However, there appears to be a high level of turnover in the sales section. Of course this calculation does not give you reasons for this seemingly high rate, but it suggests that turnover in sales is an issue that you might usefully investigate.

Labour stability index

The labour stability index is used to ascertain the percentage of the workforce who have been employed for at least one year. It is determined by the formula:

$$\text{Labour stability index} = \frac{\text{Number of employees with at least one year's service}}{\text{Average number of employees one year ago}} \times 100$$

This index has the advantage of being based on the people that stay as against those that leave, it excludes people who came and went during the year. As we see later in this unit, new recruiters are far more likely to leave than people with a reasonable amount of service. These two types of employee – new recruits and more established staff – need to be distinguished in turnover calculations and forecasts. Many organisations will calculate stability indices for one, three and five years.

ACTIVITY 4

Use the labour stability index to shed further light on the problem of wastage in the sales department at XYZ Co. Use the formula to calculate the labour stability index using the following staff figures:

Sales staff one year ago	Sales staff with one year's service
36	24

Compare the labour stability index with the wastage rate you calculated earlier. Are they significantly different. Why should this be so?

You should have arrived at a labour stability index of 66.7 per cent. This is higher than the wastage index of 50 per cent for sales staff, indicating that there is more of a problem in keeping relatively new staff (those with under one year's service) than those who have been with the company for some time. Nevertheless, a loss of one third of those with a year's service or more still does not compare favourably with the regional wastage average. You may speculate as to why this should be the case but the answer is not provided by the index. Later in this section we discuss ways of finding more information which can help us to understand why there is a retention problem in the sales section.

Cohort analysis

A cohort is a group of employees who were taken on in the same time period. Cohort analysis involves plotting a 'survival curve' to show how many remain and what proportion have left over the intervening period. Again, a computerised human resource information system can generate this analysis from data usually held for normal administrative purposes. Examination of the curve can indicate critical points when, for example, a significant number may have left. Figure 1 indicates a typical pattern.

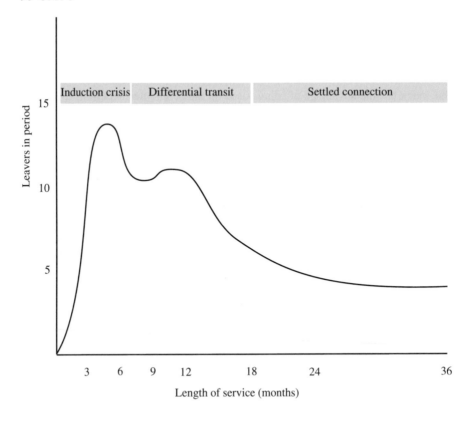

Figure 1: Analysing employee turnover – cohort survival curve

The method pinpoints critical periods and identifies problem areas which should be addressed. Comparing one cohort with another may suggest that the selection procedure used in, for example, 1994 was better than that used in, say, 1998 for recruiting staff with low turnover rates. This method is only suitable for organisations that recruit large numbers of staff at the same time, such as the National Health Service, the armed forces and the police.

CENSUS METHOD

The census method provides a comparative analysis of the length of employee service, numbers in each group, gender, etc. On the basis of historical data, we can calculate how many staff are likely to leave from groups of employees. We might, for example, look at historical wastage rates for newly-recruited males between the ages of 20 and 30, female staff with over five years service aged between 30 and 40, employees over 55 likely to retire in the next five-to-ten years.

Staffing in the National Health Service

In the past, the National Health Service compensated for shortages in the number of trained British doctors by offering posts to overseas medical staff, particularly from south Asia. In 1992, there were 25,333 general practitioners in England and Wales with unrestricted full-time work, and 4,192 had qualifications from south Asia. Some 65 per cent of the doctors with qualifications from south Asia were within 15 years of the average retirement age.

Spread over the whole of the health service, this would pose a problem, but not an insurmountable one. However, most south Asian doctors worked in inner city and other deprived areas, where practices had high caseloads. These practices are likely to prove unattractive to newly qualified staff in the future. So, the turnover analysis has revealed serious problems on the horizon for health authorities, particularly in inner city and deprived areas, and has implications for national policy on doctor recruitment.

Source: Taylor and Esmail (1999)

ACTIVITY 5

Human resource information systems are becoming increasingly common. They offer useful information for a variety of purposes using data entered from recruitment programmes, pay records, annual performance assessments, etc. Write down three important uses of human resource information systems for human resource planning.

Human resource information systems collect detailed information about employees from a variety of sources. This means that data may not have to be collected specially for human resource planning. So, for example, the numbers of recruits, leavers and long-term stayers should be automatically collated, allowing turnover and labour stability indices to be calculated quickly. Similarly, cohort and census analyses may be made using existing information.

EXPLAINING TURNOVER

We have noted that recruits are far more likely to leave a company in the first year rather than when they have completed a reasonable period of service. Why should this be the case? Early work by industrial psychologists identified three critical phases (Hill and Trist, 1953, 1955).

- **Induction crisis** – the relationship between individuals and their organisations is tentative during the first few months. Individuals can feel insecure and may conclude that it is not the right place – or type of employment – for them.

- **Differential transit** – during the first year to eighteen months, employees may put the job 'on trial', evaluating the nature of the work, the discipline required, career opportunities, etc. Absence and accident rates are also higher during this period. At the end of this period, a second induction crisis may lead to further wastage.

- **Settled connection** – after the second induction crisis, employees tend to settle down to the familiar routine or begin to climb the career ladder. The wastage rates for long-term employees are comparatively low.

This pattern of wastage is illustrated in Figure 1. As the length of service increases, the reasons for wastage become complex. Hard planning methods are inadequate to explain the reasons, but statistical analysis of individual employee characteristics may turn up a correlation between turnover and factors such as age, gender, ethnic origin, employees with childcare responsibilities, type or location of job.

ACTIVITY 6

Take a few minutes to think of the reasons why people might leave their employers. Write down as many as possible in the table below, indicating which reasons you think are matters of choice and which are unavoidable. Two examples have been provided.

Leaving by choice	Leaving is unavoidable
Another job	Retirement

Compare your ideas with the examples in Table 2. How many of the reasons suggested could be predicted by the hard planning techniques we have discussed?

It is evident that there is a wide range of possible reasons for employees to leave and many are not predictable even by the most sophisticated statistical analysis. Only the numbers of employees leaving through retirement, dismissal or redundancy can be forecasted accurately within a hard human resource planning exercise. However, organisations with very large workforces and comprehensive human resource information systems may be able to calculate the probability of people leaving due to illness, pregnancy and relocation. Turnover and labour stability indices tend to be similar from one year to the next when large numbers are involved and they provide a useful if blunt predictive instrument.

Leaving by choice	Leaving is unavoidable
Another job	Retirement
Ceasing to work	Death
Illness	Illness
Pregnancy	Pregnancy
Leaving locality	Partner leaving locality
Dissatisfaction with working conditions	Family responsibilities
Dissatisfaction with terms of employment	Dismissal
	Redundancy
Better conditions offered elsewhere	
Returning to full-time education	

Table 2: Reasons for employee turnover

1.3   Integrated planning

A modern human resource planning approach takes a wider perspective than the hard methods described above, attempting to integrate organisational decision-making and resourcing (Reilly, 1998). Hard quantitative techniques associated with manpower planning are combined with soft elements focusing on business developments, organisational culture, attitudes and commitment, and anticipating market conditions and demographic change. An integrated approach to human resource planning is a strategic response based on the interrelationship between productivity, work organisation and technological development. Identifying and planning skills requirements has become a key focus.

An integrated approach to human resource planning may take this pattern.

- **Where are we now?** Survey data (such as a staff audit) is used to produce a qualitative and quantitative picture of the organisation, identifying its strengths and weaknesses.
- **Where do we want to be?** A clear vision is determined with an agreed target date (such as five years) and a set of objectives.
- **What do we need to do?** For example, the organisation may need to introduce new incentive schemes in order to retain skilled staff.
- **Produce an action plan.** Obtain necessary commitment from senior managers. Allocate responsibility for planning and set up a monitoring process.

The current use of human resources is analysed, future surplus or shortage is anticipated, and appropriate changes, probably involving greater flexibility, are considered. For example, an organisation might consider:

- allocating more or different work to existing staff
- combining tasks to reduce the total numbers of employees
- differentiating work to create additional jobs
- putting out work to specialist providers
- replacing workers with machines/computers.

These new ways of operating make challenging demands on management's ability to monitor the performance of individuals or outsourcing services, and to mount development and training programmes.

It is also necessary to assess the availability of potential staff within 'recruiting distance'. The external job market is assessed in respect of factors such as demographic and population trends, environment and transport, the role and impact of other employers, and work-related legislation. Addressing skills shortages through external recruitment may limit career opportunities for existing staff, and cause problems for other employers. This is a particularly important issue for large organisations, such as the National Health Service and the armed forces, and for major employers in small towns.

Human resource planning has been criticised as speculative and over-mathematical (Mintzberg, 1994). Nevertheless, proponents argue that rather than attempting to predict the future, the value lies in challenging assumptions and stimulating thinking (Reilly, 1998). Long-term planning requires a significant degree of organisation, efficient data collection and confidence in the purpose. A shorter time frame may be more compatible with annual procedures such as budget negotiation which incorporates employee costs.

ACTIVITY 7

Review our discussion on soft planning and modern integrated human resource plans. Decide which of the following statements are more true than false, and which are more false than true, briefly giving reasons for your decision.

1. The modern approach does not use any of the hard numerical methods.

2. Integrated human resource planning takes a wide-ranging strategic approach.

3. Identifying skills requirements is a key element of the modern approach.

4. The statistical element of human resource information systems is not of any value for soft planning.

5. The end result of human resource planning is a fixed plan for the next five years.

6. Modern human resource planning is closely linked to performance management and human resource development programmes.

The modern approach does not use any of the hard numerical methods. False: numerical methods are required for initial audits.

Integrated human resource planning takes a wide-ranging strategic approach. True: as we have seen, integrated human resource planning must collect and review a wide range of data about the current and the forecasted business environment.

Identifying skills requirements is a key element of the modern approach. True: at one time, organisations could provide the training needed to do many work activities within a few weeks or months. Today, many jobs require a specialist university-level education which few organisations can provide from their own resources. Consequently, organisations must identify their skills requirements carefully and plan to recruit at the appropriate level.

The statistical element of human resource information systems is not of any value for soft planning. Not entirely true: it is difficult but possible to take measures of skills, attitudes and motivation and record these in a human resource information system.

The end result of human resource planning is a fixed plan for the next five years. False: the intention is usually to provide a flexible plan which can be constantly monitored and updated.

Modern human resource planning is closely linked to performance management and human resource development programmes. True, ideally.

OUTSOURCING

In our debate on flexibility in Unit 2, we discussed how outsourcing is one strategy that can exemplify a hard HR approach. Outsourcing entails a planned decision to give a particular activity (often with the staff who resource it) to a provider outside an organisation. It may be justified on a number of grounds, including:

- lower costs because of the economies of scale available to specialist providers
- greater efficiency due to higher levels of expertise
- lesser management involvement in running an activity which is not fundamental to an organisation's business mission
- greater flexibility, with the ability to change providers if performance is unsatisfactory.

The first justification – of lower costs – is a matter of hard numerical planning and it is typically the major initial reason for outsourcing. In reality, cost reductions are rarely realised (Price, 1997). Continued outsourcing is usually based on gains in quality of service and, in particular, reduction in management involvement. Though reducing management involvement might be welcome, it ignores any consequences for employee enthusiasm, motivation and career interests – all identifiable by soft planning techniques. However, outsourcing decisions are usually taken from the perspective of senior management, often with little thought about the long-term implications of damaged employee morale (Reilly and Tamkin, 1996).

During the 1980s and early-1990s, public sector organisations in the UK such as local authorities were put under pressure to outsource or subcontract a number of functions through competitive tendering. In most cases, the subcontractor with the lowest costs submitted the most competitive tender and won the contract. But lower costs are achieved at a price. Large efficiencies in labour-intensive manual services such as cleaning and refuse collection can not be readily obtained by improved technology, so costs have been cut by reducing quality or by paying lower wages. The firms winning competitive tenders (generally) paid lower wages than local authorities for the same work. It is important to note, however, that judgements in the European Court have ruled against this practice, and thousands of workers have become eligible for compensation. Subcontractors, therefore, now need to find less direct ways of reducing labour costs.

In principle, any business process can be outsourced but the most publicised are computer-based processes such as payroll, accounting and pension administration. Outsourcing information technology requirements is now a major business. It is estimated that 40 per cent of the UK's annual £12 billion IT business will be outsourced in 2000 (Moran, 1998).

Telephone and paper-driven administrative or clerical functions can be given the same treatment. Dedicated call centres using computerised telecommunications systems have taken over much of the work previously handled in local bank and insurance branches. Usually, the business processes and human resources involved are re-evaluated from an IT-perspective, increasing computerisation and reducing the requirement for people.

Outsourcing bank services

Until recently, all major UK banks maintained their own in-house computer systems. Banks have been reluctant to outsource this work fearing security problems and they did not want to upset the banking unions, given the other radical changes taking place in branch networks. Yet, it takes thousands of staff – with skills that are not strictly related to banking – to design, operate and maintain these systems.

In 1998, however, Lloyds TSB announced a departure from this practice and awarded a major contract to EDS, the US computer services company which already handled business worth £1 billion in the UK. Lloyds asked EDS to provide a new personal loans centre, a 'processing platform' for customer loans. No Lloyds TSB staff would be transferred to this centre but paperwork would be taken out of some branches. EDS was to set up and run a call centre for the bank.

At the same time, Bank of Scotland announced that it was forming a joint venture with F1 Group, another computer services company, to provide it with information technology facilities (*The Observer*, 14 June 1998).

Summary

Human resource planning provides a framework for an organisation's people requirements over a defined period. Despite appearing rational and objective, the impossibility of perfect prediction makes planning highly problematic. Plans should be viewed as statements of intent and subjected to continuous review. Human resource planning can take hard and soft forms. A combination of hard and soft approaches is required to meet modern business needs.

SECTION 2
Job Analysis

Introduction

Human resource planning can provide an assessment of future staffing requirements – for example, an organisation might forecast that it needs 100 more employees to handle the development of new products and expansion into new markets. But it is not enough simply to specify the numbers of additional staff that might be needed in the future, the precise jobs that the new staff will undertake must be described and people must be recruited specifically for the particular tasks that need to be done.

Job analysis is the term applied to a group of methods which describe and evaluate the work content and skills required for particular jobs. This section examines different methods of job analysis, ranging from simple, cheap observation to complex and expensive data collection.

If work exists for which people are not immediately available, some basic questions follow:

- what tasks are involved?
- what skills or competences are required?
- are these skills to be found within the organisation?
- should extra people be recruited?
- should the work be offered to contractors or consultants?
- can the work be mechanised or done by computers?

We begin this section by describing some of the ways in which information can be collected for a job analysis. Then we consider various approaches to analysing this information. Finally, we evaluate the use of this analysis to determine vacancies using job descriptions and person specifications.

The aim of this section is to help you to:

- compare and contrast the ways in which job information can be collected
- explain how this information can be analysed
- demonstrate an understanding of the process by which job vacancies are determined from job analysis information.

2.1   Collecting job information

Conventionally, job analysis identifies tasks involved within a specific role using techniques reminiscent of 'scientific management'. Jobs range from 'crystallised' work, such as manufacturing assembly where individual roles are precisely defined, to managerial and professional work which accord considerable freedom and variety (McCormick and Ilgen, 1987). In modern flexible environments, many lower-level jobs are 'broad-banded' or grouped together and allocated a wide range of common tasks.

Job analysis ranges from rudimentary techniques to approaches requiring specialist skills. The simplest methods are 'pen and paper' exercises conducted by observing or interviewing existing staff and supervisors. Another approach is to allow employees to report on the content of their work using an agreed format. Information is also available from records, 'experts', training materials, equipment descriptions, manuals and, possibly, human resource information systems. Smith and Robertson (1993) outline an idealised six-step approach.

1. Collect relevant documents, for example the organisation's training manual covering the post being studied.

2. Ask the responsible manager about the job's purpose and component tasks.

3. Ask the same of post-holders. Request a detailed record of work activities for a week or two.

4. Sit in with post-holders and observe them at work – preferably on more than one day and at different times.

5. Try to do the job yourself.

6. Write the job description.

The data produced by job analysis can be arranged in categories (see table 3).

Attribute	Collect information on
Job identification	Job title, department, grade or level
Relationships	Name/title of immediate boss, number and type(s) of staff post-holder is responsible for, links with other departments
Outputs	The end products or results of the job
Activities	The behaviours or actions of the worker in achieving these outputs
Performance	Required standards, agreed objectives
Individual requirements	Abilities, skills, experience, temperament, training, second language, etc.
Working conditions	The physical and social surroundings of the job such as working space, hours, leave entitlement
Equipment	Computers, machine tools, vehicles, etc. used as an essential part of the job
Other information	Promotion outlets, training available, transfer opportunities

Table 3: A basic job analysis check list
Source: Price (1997)

The next activity asks you to relate this check list to Smith and Robertson's model of job analysis.

ACTIVITY 8

Using the table, rate the likely usefulness of the job-holder, documents or the manager as sources of information about a job. Rank them 1, 2 or 3 for each of the items in the check list – with 1 indicating less useful, 2 useful, 3 very useful. Hint: you might think about a specific job you know well, or focus on a job you have seen performed such as nurse, postal worker or bus driver.

	Job-holder	Documents	Manager
Job Identification			
Relationships			
Outputs			
Activities			
Performance			
Individual requirements			
Working conditions			
Equipment			
Other information			

This is quite a difficult exercise to complete without considerable familiarity with a particular job and its context. You should have also realised that the quality and sources of information will vary from one organisation or department to another. In fact, the process is extremely subjective and depends on factors such as:

- individual personalities and the interest they take in their jobs
- length of experience
- type of job

- quality of management
- manager's experience
- manager's span of control (if managers are responsible for a wide range of different jobs, they are less likely to know the details about specific posts)
- quality of documentation.

Table 4 has been completed with the job of nurse in mind. Your answers may or may not be similar.

	Job-holder	Documents	Manager
Job Identification	3	1	2
Relationships	1	3	2
Outputs	1	3	2
Activities	1	3	2
Performance	3	2	1
Individual requirements	1	3	2
Working conditions	1	3	2
Equipment	1	3	2
Other information	3	2	1

Table 4: Ranking the usefulness of sources of job information for a nurse

Clearly these answers are debatable. Can you see also that reliance on a single worker or manager may result in an extremely distorted view of the job? Obviously, taking information from a large number of people would improve our view of the job. Nevertheless you should have realised that the process of collecting information is not as objective as it may seem at first glance.

In fact, job analysis is by no means a value-free source of information. For example, employees are prone to (Price, 1997):

- **exaggeration** – jobs may be represented as more demanding or complex than they are in reality
- **omission** – routine daily tasks are forgotten in favour of less frequent but more interesting activities.

In contrast, information given by managers may tend towards:

- **understatement** – jobs are described as easier and less complex than in reality
- **misunderstanding** – frequently bosses do not know workers' jobs in any detail.

COMPLEX METHODS

More sophisticated methods can provide extensive data about individual jobs but can be expensive and time-consuming. Generally purchased 'off-the-shelf' from specialist companies, they are now supplied as computer packages.

McCormick's **position analysis questionnaire** (PAQ), including 150 scales with benchmarks covering a variety of jobs, is probably the best-known technique (McCormick and Ilgen, 1987). This system has been criticised for the difficulty it presents for users, requiring a post-college level reading ability to fill in the questionnaires! The US Air Force has funded more accessible methods (see http://www.codap.com). These systems provide a thorough occupational analysis, job description, key function description, performance appraisal form, etc.

From the UK, Saville and Holdsworth's **work profiling system** (WPS) is a computerised, professionally packaged questionnaire system providing a detailed job description and profile of the ideal recruit (see http://www.shlgroup.com). It comprises three overlapping tests, each of 300–400 items. Reports provided by the system include:

- job description
- person specification
- person-job match report
- assessment methods report
- individual development planner
- performance review form
- benchmark report for pay and grades
- competency model.

Professional occupational analysis systems such as WPS are expensive, time-consuming and produce massive quantities of detailed analysis. For many applications this could prove excessive. Simple pen and paper exercises are more economical for one-off jobs, for low numbers of routine functions, and for circumstances requiring very fast decision-making. It takes training and practice to develop confidence in sophisticated systems. For large organisations with complex job patterns and large numbers of employees dealing with similar work, there may be a case for investment in sophisticated systems or the hiring of consultants to conduct the analysis.

2.2   Analysing job information

Having collected detailed job information by one method or another, how do we classify or analyse the data? This depends partly on the nature of the information collected and the analysis technique chosen. The information collected will probably be of four kinds:

- **behaviour description** – overt behaviours taking the form 'uses keyboard' or 'presses switch'

- **behaviour requirements** – general concepts such as 'problem solving' or 'remembering'

- **ability requirements** – more formal psychological expressions such as 'verbal ability' or 'numeracy'

- **task characteristics** – action triggers such as 'nature of instructions' or 'type of display'.

On the whole, it is best to collect as wide a range of data as possible for resourcing, evaluation and training or development purposes.

ACTIVITY 9

Analysis of different jobs requires the collection of different kinds of information (and also different kinds of analysis). For example, an operator's job may be best described in terms of behaviour description and task characteristics, such as 'when the workpiece is in place, operates a lever, checks that work has been completed, replaces workpiece'. A manager's job is more complex and requires information on the behaviour requirements and ability requirements.

State which of the four kinds of information are required for an analysis of these jobs:

- university lecturer
- window cleaner
- astronaut.

The university lecturer's job is marked by a high level of independence and autonomy. There are very few behaviour descriptions relevant to the job – perhaps 'operates a photocopier, and overhead projector as required' might apply. Far more important are behaviour and ability requirements.

The window cleaner's job on the other hand is fairly routine, with behaviour description the most important type of information for job analysis. But a window cleaner who had poor relations with his or her customers would not be employed for long, so it would be important to include an ability requirement, 'forms good relationships with clients'.

The astronaut's job is much more complex. The job includes many highly skilled tasks, as well as requiring a very wide knowledge of several scientific subjects and engineering. Hence a description of the astronaut's job would need to gather all four kinds of information.

From these simple examples you can see that even the task of gathering information for job analysis is not a mechanical routine task to be delegated to clerical staff; you have to carefully work out what information is required, and that might vary for each job you examine.

You also need to appreciate that the job analysis technique may have different emphases. It might be:

- **job-oriented** – a detailed listing of tasks involved in a particular job, such as 'place cream in centre of doughnut' and 'type customer reference number into field a', which produces accurate descriptions of individual tasks that may be difficult to extrapolate to other jobs
- **worker-oriented** – more generalised accounts of behaviour in keeping with flexible work requirements, the newer systems use this approach
- **competence-oriented** – sometimes referred to as attribute or trait-oriented, this produces detailed descriptions of necessary skills, experience and personal qualities.

2.3 Job descriptions and personnel specifications

Traditionally, job analysis was used to generate tight job descriptions, lists of component tasks, and person specifications, the qualities required to do the job. In other words, a job-oriented approach was preferred. Today, there is likely to be a focus on more wide-ranging competences required to perform looser job tasks. Commonly, four main issues are addressed:

- what are the main tasks and activities of the job?
- is it different to that carried out by the previous incumbent?

- which aspects specify the type of candidate required?
- what would the ideal candidate want to know before applying?

JOB DESCRIPTIONS

In the past, job descriptions were regarded as inflexible and definitive lists of tasks. Changes were subject to dispute. Today, employers tend to prefer staff to be ready to take on any required function. Rigid job descriptions would act as a barrier to flexibility and, in any case, technological change would render them out of date almost as soon as they are written.

Conventionally, job descriptions list information such as the job title and the main functions and activities of the job. They have tended to be simplistic and arbitrary, sometimes bearing little relation to everyday reality. Properly compiled, however, they can be valuable statements of the purpose and function of specific jobs. To this end, Torrington and Hall (1995) recommend that job descriptions should be written in a particular style:

- describe tasks in the present tense, starting with an action verb – for example, 'enters customer data on to computer database'
- keep descriptions short, avoiding duplication
- distinguish between tasks carried out personally and those which are supervised, clarifying individual and managerial responsibility
- express performance standards in quantitative terms where possible – for example, 'produce 5 widgets per minute'.

ACTIVITY 10

Using the job description format (see table 5), try to describe a particular job. You may use your own job, or describe any other job you know well.

Identification	Title
	Department
	Grade
	Hierarchical position (and organisation chart)
	To whom responsible
	For whom responsible
	Regular contacts
Job summary	Brief outline of main tasks
	Specific areas of responsibility
	Sensitive lines of communication
Job content	What is done: analysis (advising, tasks)
	How it is done: tools, equipment, treatment, relationships, strengths, mental ability, judgement
	Why it is done: relate job to others – section, department or enterprise
	Standard of performance
Conditions of employment	Pay scale, annual leave, other benefits
	Physical working conditions: hazards, dirt, heat, noise, fumes, weather, uniform, protective clothing, etc.
	Abnormal shift/hours pattern
	Travel away from home
Prerequisites	Skills, knowledge, attitude and behaviour
	Physical requirements: strength, eyesight, hearing, touch, dexterity

Table 5: Format for a job description

You may have found it difficult to follow the format in table 5 exactly. In fact, job descriptions vary from one organisation to another. Table 6 contains another example – note this only covers three categories, identification, job summary and job content.

Job title:	Works Manager
Responsible to:	Production Director
Responsible for:	Production Supervisor, Materials Controller, Quality Controller, Personnel Officer
Main role	To achieve agreed production targets within budget, meeting quality and delivery requirements through the efficient control of manufacturing operations, maintaining good relations and ensuring that staff work together as a team.
Main activities	1. Fulfil manufacturing strategy within budget in line with estimated market demands, ensuring that equipment and staff are available to achieve agreed output and foreseeable additional demands.
Development	2. Continually seek to improve production methods and techniques, making full use of company engineering research and development services.
Operations	3. Maintain close liaison with sales and material supply departments to ensure that capacity is being utilised efficiently and component parts arrive as required.
	4. Ensure that production scheduling fulfils its objectives of meeting programmed delivery dates and optimising wastage, downtime and stock levels.
	5. Ensure that all production operations are progressed and the distribution department is informed of any deviation from programmed delivery dates.
	6. Maintain factory security and all stocks and assets, taking suitable precautions against theft, fire, etc.
	7. Maintain all equipment in good order.
Employees	8. Ensure that factory organisation is the most appropriate for achieving company objectives.
	9. Recruit, train and develop effective employees to meet present and future needs.
	10. Implement company human resource strategies and working agreements.
	11. Maintain good employee relations and morale.
Control	12. Develop an effective reporting system on manufacturing performance and direct a continuous programme of monitoring productivity, quality and costs.
	13. Ensure that corrective action is taken where required to meet budgets and quality standards and report deviations outside agreed control limits to Production Director.

Table 6: Job description for a works manager

PERSON SPECIFICATIONS

Depending on the method used, a job analysis will describe the work to be performed but may not indicate the requisite knowledge, skills and abilities. The conventional Western model of resourcing recommends preparation of a person specification to represent 'the demands of the job translated into human terms' (Arnold et al., 1991).

Person specifications list essential criteria, plus additional desirable qualities which help to filter applicants. Sophisticated forms of competence and worker-oriented job analyses, such as WPS, generate person specifications as part of the package. Moving from job analysis to person specification requires a degree of inference or intuition, and this process is never entirely objective.

Together, job descriptions and person specifications are intended to (Corbridge and Pilbeam, 1998):

- provide an objective focus for matching applicants to job requirements
- communicate a clear idea of the job to applicants – in other words, a realistic job preview
- provide an ongoing basis for performance and training needs assessment.

Rodger (1953) describes a commonly used plan categorising desired qualities under seven headings:

- **physical qualities**, including speech and appearance
- **attainments** – qualifications, membership of professional associations
- **general intelligence**
- **specific aptitudes**, such as numerical ability
- **interests and hobbies**
- **personality**
- **domestic circumstances**.

Since this classification was first devised attitudes and laws have changed. In Unit 6 on equality of opportunity, we will see that legislation on gender, race and disability require scrupulous fairness. Physical qualities and domestic circumstances must be investigated only when they are strictly relevant to the job and unlikely to contravene relevant legislation. To reflect modern concerns, Pilbeam (quoted in Corbridge and Pilbeam, 1998) provides a six-factor categorisation:

- skills, knowledge and competencies
- personality characteristics
- levels of experience
- certificated qualifications
- physical characteristics
- development potential.

Different cultures adopt alternative perspectives. For example, writing before the economic crises of the late 1990s, Whitehill (1990) observed that Japanese companies tended to take a greater interest in personality than technical attributes and looked for a personal philosophy compatible with the corporate climate. They sought employees who desired a stable life. Further, they had to be able to work as part of a group and have no unconventional political or social beliefs. Job-related criteria, such as knowledge of finance and marketing, were regarded as being of little importance, except in industries which demanded highly trained technical specialists.

ACTIVITY 11

Review the material on job descriptions and person specifications. Comment on each of the following statements indicating in what ways they are true or false.

1. Job descriptions should be precise and detailed, listing every activity in minute detail.

2. The process of preparing job descriptions and person specifications is entirely objective.

3. Person specifications should list only qualities that are essential to perform a job.

4. Job descriptions and person specifications are used throughout the world.

5. Job descriptions and person specifications are prepared solely for the employer.

The statements in activity 11 are all partly true, and partly false.

Job descriptions should be precise and detailed, listing every activity in minute detail. Detailed job descriptions are not compatible with flexible working which requires employees to vary their jobs.

The process of preparing job descriptions and person specifications is entirely objective. Job analysis is used in an attempt to make resourcing more objective, but it is inherently flawed since it relies heavily on human judgement.

Person specifications should list only qualities that are essential to perform a job. Person specifications can also include qualities which are desirable but not essential.

Job descriptions and person specifications are used throughout the world. As the discussion on Japanese corporate attitudes shows, job analysis is culturally based.

Job descriptions and person specifications are prepared solely for the employer. They are also used to give job applicants a realistic job preview.

Summary

Job analysis includes a range of techniques; some are relatively simple and easy to use, others are more sophisticated but can be expensive to implement. Job analysis can provide information for a number of human resource activities. Data can be used to prepare job descriptions that detail the tasks an employee is to perform and to write person specifications which outline the characteristics needed for success.

SECTION 3

Recruitment

Introduction

If a decision is made to employ new people – perhaps when human resource planning and job analysis indicate that there are vacancies – the next stage is to attract suitable candidates. This is termed recruitment. This is followed by selection: the process of determining the most suitable applicant among those attracted by a recruitment programme. We discuss selection in some detail in the next unit.

Recruitment is more than a matter of finding as many applicants as possible, it aims to provide a reasonable number of high quality applicants from which the choice can be made. If the recruitment stage is conducted effectively, the selection process becomes much easier. This section begins with an assessment of how appropriate types of recruits can be identified and targeted. We go on to discuss informal and formal methods of recruitment and conclude with an outline of outsourced recruitment through agencies and head-hunters.

The aim of this section is to help you to:

- outline the range of methods available to recruiters
- critically assess the comparative usefulness and limitations of these methods.

3.1   Applicant targeting

Four decades ago, Haire (1959) identified two contradictory approaches to recruitment:

- suitability
- malleability.

Suitability

Find the right person for a job. The individual is the variable in the search – the job is fixed. People are sought with ability and experience to perform determined tasks with minimal training. This has been described as best practice because it is apparently objective. The process follows a logical sequence, asking questions such as:

- what tasks and responsibilities will the job entail?
- what knowledge, skills and abilities will be needed?
- how can these criteria be identified in potential applicants?

This approach assumes that the 'right' or, at least, 'best' applicant for the job can be found. Arguably this approach suffices where the job can be identified very clearly, fits into a 'job box' that separates its functions from any other and demands a particular range of skills. It implies a conservative organisation, interested in matching people to inflexible jobs. It suggests also a preference for the 'kind of people we have always had', shutting the door to non-traditional employees and groups and thereby reducing creativity and experimentation.

Malleability

Find people who fit. Specific job-related criteria do not feature. High-quality people are sought with the right mix of attitudes and personal qualities to fit the prevailing organisational culture. Generally, they are young or relatively inexperienced. Successful individuals can be trained to do specific jobs. This approach focuses on generalists and is typical of Japanese organisations (Whitehill, 1991). It is also conservative in its approach, likely to result in a homogeneous workforce with little diversity of background.

Both approaches are backward looking: the first in terms of an organisation's job structure; the second in relation to its culture. A third strategy – flexibility – meets modern demands (Price, 1997)

Flexibility

Aim for **flexible employees** prepared for future change. Rather than look for people to fill rigid job boxes or have malleable recruits with Plasticine personalities, seek versatile and adaptable individuals. The intention is to recruit employees who can perform in current vacancies, and who also demonstrate a degree of 'trainability' and open-mindedness so that they can be developed to meet changing skill needs.

Approach	Objective	Organisation	HR emphasis
Suitability (Right person for the job)	Get the job done	Traditional Hierarchical Fixed job categories	Job analysis HR Planning Selection
Malleability (Fitting the culture)	Fit in with today's organisation	Small core Strong culture Variable periphery	Appraisal Job training
Flexibility (Employee for tomorrow)	Build a competitive organisation	Flexible Lean	Performance Skills training Development

Table 7: Recruitment strategies
Source: Adapted from Price (1997)

All options, including subcontracting, must be considered carefully before hiring new people. Scenario planning can provide a useful underpinning in forecasting future needs. The flexible approach offers long-term benefits but demands a detailed specification of appropriate competences. It also requires more careful human resource planning, more sophisticated job analysis and high quality recruitment programmes.

ACTIVITY 12

Allocate each of the following sentences or phrases to:

- the right person approach
- the malleability approach
- the flexibility approach.

1. We are looking for a person who can fit into our existing team.

2. This job requires an experienced widget operative able to use the automated sprocket fitter.

3. Our organisation normally recruits school and college leavers who can be trained to fill more senior positions as and when required.

4. You should be able to take on a range of varied activities which may be changed as the company develops to meet new markets.

5. We prefer to look for people who meet the requirements of the job description and person specification as closely as possible.

We are looking for a person who can fit into our existing team. The fitting-in process may require adjustment from the individual (rather than from the team), and the expectation is not so much that the individual currently fits the team but that the recruit will change to fit. This exemplifies the malleability approach.

This job requires an experienced widget operative able to use the automated sprocket fitter. A specific skill for a particular job is required: the right person or suitability approach.

Our organisation normally recruits school and college leavers who can be trained to fill more senior positions as and when required. In other words, 'we take youngsters whom we mould to our culture and requirements' – the malleability approach.

You should be able to take on a range of varied activities which may be changed as the company develops to meet new markets. The indication that the company is growing in a changing environment and wants the applicant to be willing to develop and to grow with it implies that the flexibility approach is adopted

We prefer to look for people who meet the requirements of the job description and person specification as closely as possible. Clearly the recruiters are looking for someone who matches an existing job that is likely to remain the same – the right person approach.

While the activity might suggest that individual organisations adopt a single predominant approach, in reality recruiters may use a combination of these approaches.

3.2 Informal versus formal recruiting

Applicants can be found from within the organisation or from the external job market. Culture and flexibility orientations emphasise using people from the internal employee pool rather than recruiting from the external job market. Internal recruitment, using word of mouth, staff notices, newsletters and vacancy journals, may be on a one-off basis or form part of a planned development programme. In recent years, corporate intranets have been introduced which provide information and data capture facilities on an organisation's system of networked computers.

Intranets are increasingly used to advertise internal job vacancies before details are made available to a wider public.

Recruitment marketing is costly, both in terms of money and time. As an example, PA Consulting reported on a survey of 91 UK graduate recruiters (*Times Higher Educational Supplement*, 21 January 1994). In total, the organisations in the survey reported receiving 318,988 applications for 3,372 vacancies in 1993 – an average of 95 applications for every vacancy; positions with major retail chains and blue-chip corporations attracted 272 applications on average. Businesses recruiting more than 100 graduates spent between £50,000 and £800,000 on their recruitment programmes. Advertising was a small component of total expenditure in comparison with stationery and travel costs. On average, processing applications and compiling a short list took 1,172 hours.

Some firms restrict open recruitment to school-leavers and graduates, with senior jobs filled from within the organisation. This is typical of an approach which emphasises the 'malleable' employee who fits the prevailing culture. This has been the predominant approach in Germany and Japan, whereas American and British organisations have recruited externally at all levels.

External candidates can be attracted through a variety of channels.

Advertising

Recruitment advertising can be placed in local or national newspapers and journals, and, possibly, on radio or television. Specific journals or magazines are favoured for particular occupations such as computing and education. Trade and professional journals are an especially good source of appropriately qualified and experienced candidates.

National newspapers have regular features on specific industry sectors and professions on designated days. Many, for example, have supplements on weekly sections on teaching and information technology. Despite this, they produce large numbers of relatively untargeted applicants at considerable expense.

The local press is unsuitable for professional and other work requiring unusual skills but is a cheap method of attracting applicants who are currently living within easy travelling distance of the organisation.

Professional associations

Professional associations often maintain databases of jobs and CVs (curriculum vitae), and these are increasingly available on the internet.

Government agencies

Jobcentres and the careers service have been the Cinderella of the recruitment market in the recent past, tending to specialise in lower-level jobs and unemployed candidates, but the service is free to employers and employees.

Government training schemes

Government training schemes such as the New Deal offer a low-cost trial system for employers. These are also often linked to vocational qualification programmes.

The milk round

Some recruiters visit schools, colleges and universities, typified by the so-called 'milk round', to promote their career opportunities.

Employment agencies

Many commercial employment agencies have a high street presence and offer a range of fee-based services including (Corbridge and Pilbeam, 1998):

- providing temporary workers
- attracting, preselecting and referring applicants to potential employers
- updating skills to improve applicants' suitability.

Agencies are comparatively expensive, normally charging a percentage of the salary level from the employer for an extended period.

The internet

Corporate websites of major organisations commonly have career pages, often with on-line application forms. Websites are a cheap and easy channel of advertising vacancies for an organisation with its own site.

There are also many on-line newsgroups and other job-based websites. On-line job agencies, for example, are becoming increasingly common with automated CV and job posting. They are relatively cheap as many job-posting websites generate some of their revenue from advertisements.

Head-hunting

Head-hunting is typically a semi-formal search for higher level executive posts. Head-hunting consultants tend to be extremely expensive.

Table 8 shows the relative use of some recruitment methods. Note the table is based on a survey taken prior to the widespread availability of the internet.

Method	Usage
Personal recommendation	35%
Recruitment advertising	27%
Direct approach by employer	13%
Job centre	7%
Recruitment agencies	4%
Unspecified	14%

Table 8: Popularity of different recruitment methods
Source: NOP survey of UK employers, The Independent, *26 October 1995*

ACTIVITY 13

Identify the two methods of recruitment listed in the text that are possibly in breach of equal opportunities legislation.

Personal recommendation and direct approach by the employer are both suspect. On the face of it, they are both subjective and probably biased in favour of people known and acceptable to existing colleagues.

Successful recruitment depends on the choice of method and the budget available. The likelihood of attracting suitable applicants is influenced by the detail and relevance of information given in recruitment advertisements and information packs. High salaries, imposing job titles, promotion opportunities and foreign travel obviously attract more applicants. Considerable effort and money can be invested – or wasted – in recruitment advertising. Too many applications, especially unsuitable ones, create an administrative problem and hinder the selection process. The following example illustrates how companies can deliberately limit the response rate.

> ### *Nissan UK*
> Wickens (1987) describes how Nissan UK deliberately emphasised unattractive aspects of its production-line jobs in order to minimise unwanted applications. Nissan's advertisements stated that:
> - the pace of work would be dictated by a moving production line
> - the work would be very demanding
> - work assignments would be carefully defined and repetitive.

ACTIVITY 14

What channels would you use to advertise vacancies for:

- a computer programmer
- an office cleaner
- a physics teacher.

Write down three appropriate media for each job and provide a brief explanation.

Press advertising should be considered. There are specialist journals and weekly national newspaper features for computing and education – but not cleaning. But national newspaper advertisements may – at some expense – attract large numbers of relatively unsuitable applicants. Local newspapers frequently carry cleaning vacancies but are less likely to attract computer programmers and teachers.

Websites are particularly attractive for computer-minded people. Bodies representing the teaching profession and education authorities may have job sections on their websites. It is unlikely that the internet would be suitable for cleaning vacancies.

Agencies and head-hunters are available for all types of jobs but tend to be expensive. State jobcentres could attract applicants for cleaning jobs. Informal recruiting by word of mouth could apply to both computer programming and cleaning. It is not likely to be appropriate for the teaching profession.

Summary

Recruiting is essentially a process for marketing jobs and attracting good quality applicants. There is a range of channels available by which vacancies can be made known and advertised. They vary in effectiveness and cost, and they must be chosen carefully for each type of job.

Unit review activity

Read the article on *How to determine future workforce needs* (see Resource 3 in the Resources section), and then answer these questions.

1. Is the Tennessee Valley Authority using a 'hard or soft' planning process?

2. What are the main differences between demand and supply data?

3. Who does HR planning at the Tennessee Valley Authority?

4. What information is provided by the human resource information system (HRIS)?

Write about 50 words for each answer. A commentary on this activity is provided at the end of the unit.

Unit summary

In this unit, we addressed the fundamental stages of the resourcing process. Human resource planning emphasises a move away from traditional numbers-driven manpower planning towards a softer approach aimed at fostering debate about an organisation's HR strategies. Job analysis comprises a range of techniques which can be used to develop job descriptions and person specifications. These range from simple pen and paper methods to sophisticated computerised techniques. The recruitment task is to attract appropriate numbers of high quality applicants.

References

Arnold, J, Robertson, I T and Cooper C L (1991) *Work Psychology*, Pitman

Corbridge, M and Pilbeam, S (1998) *Employment Resourcing*, Financial Times Pitman Publishing

Haire, M (1959) 'Psychological problems relevant to business and industry', *Psychological Bulletin* 56:169:94

Hill, J M M and Trist, E L (1953) 'A consideration of industrial accidents as a means of withdrawal from the work situation', *Human Relations*, 6 November

Hill, J M M and Trist, E L (1955) 'Changes in accidents and other absences with length of service', *Human Relations*, 8 May

Mintzberg, H (1994), *The Rise and Fall of Strategic Planning*, Prentice-Hall

McCormick, E J and Ilgen, D (1987) *Industrial and Organizational Psychology*, Unwin Hyman, 8th edn

Moran, N (1998) 'Outsourcing the operation: Where competence is the core issue', *Financial Times*, 7 January 1998

O'Doherty, D (1997) 'Human Resource Planning: Control to Seduction' in Beardwell, I and Holden, L (eds) *Human Resource Management: A Contemporary Perspective*, Pitman Publishing, 2nd edn

Pratt, K J and Bennett, R (1992) *Elements of Personnel Management*, Chapman and Hall, 2nd edn

Price, A J (1997) *Human Resource Management in a Business Context*, International Thomson Business Press

Reilly, P and Tamkin, P (1996) *Outsourcing: a Flexible Option for the Future?*, IES Report 320, Institute of Employment Services

Reilly, P (1998) *Human Resource Planning: An Introduction*, IES Report 312, Institute of Employment Studies

Rodger, A (1953) *The Seven Point Plan*, National Institute of Industrial Psychology

Smith, M and Robertson, I T (1993) *The Theory and Practice of Systematic Personnel Selection*, Macmillan, 2nd edn

Taylor, D H jnr and Esmail, A (1999) 'Retrospective analysis of census data on general practitioners who qualified in South Asia: who will replace them as they retire?' *British Medical Journal*, (318) 306, 30 January 1999

Torrington, D and Hall, L (1995) *Personnel Management: HRM in Action*, Prentice-Hall, 3rd edn

Tyson, S (1995) *Human Resource Strategy*, Pitman

Werther, W B jnr and Davis, K A (contributor) (1995) *Human Resources and Personnel Management*, McGraw Hill College Div., 5th edn

Whitehill, A M (1990) *Japanese Management: Tradition and Transition*, Routledge

Wickens, P (1987) *The Road to Nissan*, Macmillan

Recommended Reading

All major textbooks on human resource management have material on the aspects of resourcing discussed in this chapter. For example, O'Doherty (1997) gives an illuminating critique of the supposed 'scientific' nature of human resource planning. Corbridge and Pilbeam (1998) provide a useful overview of these topics. Links to resourcing-related websites are provided in the 'Resources: plans and strategies' section of the author's *Internet Guide to Human Resource Management* at http://www.hrmguide.com.

Answers to Unit Review Activity

1. The workforce planning process at the Tennessee Valley Authority includes hard and soft elements. Staff numbers are a matter of statistical data collection and projection but 'skills' require some subjective judgement. For instance, benchmarking involves decisions on which criteria staff are to be compared on. Also, the organisation is interested in meeting strategic objectives and reinforcing values which have significant soft components.

2. Demand data are calculated by taking the business objectives and then determining how many people (and with what skills) are required to achieve the objectives. Supply data is based on the existing workforce, without taking any recruits into account. The purpose is to identify the 'demand-supply gap' at various points over the planning period. This gap is met by recruitment – or development. And, of course, there might be a surplus.

3. Planning is seen as a team activity with two types of team: management oversight and actual planning. Management oversight teams are recommended for every business unit, each headed by a senior manager nominated by the chief executive. The belief is that managers are more likely to be committed to the planning process if they take part from the early stages. Planning teams are also recommended for each business unit but they do not have to be composed of managers. Planning teams are directly involved in developing and implementing the plan. The senior human resource person, or someone designated by the senior person, should take charge although this is regarded as a good development opportunity for other managers. Then there are sub-teams for specific aspects which can involve further employees.

4. The human resource information system (HRIS) collects demand (staffing projections) and supply data, and compares the two data sets. It produces reports on the demand-supply gap but, obviously, its reliance on projected data means that these reports must be interpreted with care.

UNIT 4
EMPLOYEE RESOURCING: SELECTION

Introduction

If you don't recruit and select great people, you won't have great employees. And without great employees, you won't have a great company. (Sullivan, 1997)

Unit 3 concluded with an overview of recruitment, the process of attracting suitable applicants. This unit is concerned with the next stage of the employee resourcing process – selecting the most suitable people from these applicants. Selection is a topic of major importance. If people truly are a business' greatest assets, it follows that the selection of new recruits is a matter of crucial importance. World-class companies need world-class employees.

In the past, selection has been about matching people to clearly-defined jobs. In the twenty-first century, the emphasis is likely to be on wider criteria aimed at identifying flexible people able to fulfil multi-skilled roles. Selectors need a broad grasp of human resource strategy to make such choices. They need to understand the direction in which an organisation is intending to go and the kind of people who are needed over the medium to long-term. Human resource specialists have a high profile role in the selection process. Getting it wrong can have damaging consequences on their status and careers and, as we shall see, this has implications for the quality of their decision-making.

Selection procedures are costly, but the consequences of choosing unsuitable recruits can be even more costly. Selection is time-consuming and often involves senior staff. Large organisations increasingly use sophisticated tests and computerised packages which are expensive to buy and require proper training to administer. At face value these procedures may appear to be objective; however, there are underlying issues of validity, reliability, fairness and equality of opportunity which will be discussed in this unit.

Objectives

On completion of this unit you should be able to:

- outline the major concepts of selection
- explain the purpose and basic methodology of the most commonly used techniques for collecting candidate data and making selection decisions
- critically assess a number of selection techniques in terms of validity and reliability.

SECTION 1

Candidate Data and Screening

Introduction

We begin by considering the rationale underlying the selection process. We identify selection as a key lever in the achievement of strategic objectives. We debate whether it is a mechanism for choosing the most competent candidates or, instead, a means of avoiding the risk of taking on unsuitable people. Our discussion moves on to consider the various forms of job application. Finally we focus on methods of pre-screening applicants on the basis of the data they provide and introduce the fundamental concepts of validity and reliability.

The aim of this section is to help you to:

- critically evaluate the underlying logic of the selection process
- understand the essential advantages and disadvantages of basic candidate data collection methods including CVs, application forms, biodata and references
- explain the concepts of validity and reliability.

1.1   Aims of the selection process

What is selection for? A simple explanation is that selection is about finding the best person for the job. In other words, it seeks to match applicants attracted by the recruitment process to the criteria specified by the job description and person specification. However, as we noted in the previous unit, this approach – the best person model – focuses on the short-term need to fill a vacancy.

But this is not the only way to approach selection. In the previous unit we outlined two other models of staffing based, respectively, on the concepts of malleability or 'culture fit' and flexibility. They offer a more strategic approach, placing greater stress on long-term attitudes and behaviour rather than the skills and experience needed for the immediate job. These models are more consistent with the concept of **strategic selection** fostered by increasing links between HRM and corporate strategy (Wright and Storey, 1997).

From this perspective, Sullivan (1997) argues that all selection programmes should aim to identify people who:

- possess competences desired by the organisation
- are capable of self-development without needing company training
- can generate practical ideas
- make few mistakes, do not need disciplining and are rarely absent

- generate higher customer satisfaction, performance assessments, bonus and promotion rates
- do not need close supervision
- stay with the business for a long time
- generate a high return for the money they are paid.

In his analysis, Sullivan embodies the trend towards the use of selection as one of the key levers of human resource strategy. Selection procedures have a crucial role in organisational change by controlling the appointment of staff with desirable attributes or competences to an organisation, and their elevation into significant power positions through promotion. Consequently selection 'supports the achievement of strategic objectives' (Iles and Salaman, 1995). Moreover, selection involves assessment of attitudes and behaviour, a process which is consistent with the emphasis placed on measurement and monitoring within the models of HRM discussed in Unit 1 (Townley, 1989).

ACTIVITY 1

Bonnypark District Council has decided to appoint a development officer. The first task of the successful candidate will be to write a detailed plan for the District's development programme, including a vision for the future, analysis of the current situation and intended projects. The plan is urgently required for a funding submission to the government department responsible for regional development. After this task is completed, the development officer's job will change significantly, probably evolving into a public relations and progress chasing role.

In the first instance, applications are sought from existing employees. Two candidates seem to be worth considering.

Candidate A

Candidate A is a business studies graduate with five years experience in the District Planning Office. She has no experience of marketing or public relations but has been involved in developing the development programme. Her annual performance assessments are given below.

	Overall rating (out of 10)	Comment
Approach to work	7	Conscientious and hard-working but requires guidance on new tasks
Timekeeping and attendance	10	Excellent
Relationship to others	7	Gets on well with everyone but a little reserved
Commitment	7	Has reservations about the council as a long-term employer
Performance on job	9	Meticulous in checking planning applications and following procedures
Knowledge of job	9	Has detailed knowledge of planning regulations
Career and promotion	8	Should do well in a planning environment

Candidate B

Candidate B left school at 18 and worked for six years in the marketing department of a regional newspaper business. Since then, he has had three years experience with the District Parks and Recreation Service. He has no planning experience. His annual performance assessments are given below.

	Overall rating (out of 10)	Comment
Approach to work	9	Enthusiastic and full of good ideas
Timekeeping and attendance	7	Reasonable – occasionally late due to transport difficulties
Relationship to others	9	Presents a friendly and interested personality
Commitment	8	Wants to get on and would prefer to stay with present employer
Performance on job	7	Works unsupervised but does not really identify with the work of the department
Knowledge of job	7	Has adequate but not extensive knowledge of the job
Career and promotion	8	Unlikely to progress in current department but is able to learn quickly and would do well in a people-related function

Based on their experience and current performance, the council's human resources committee feel that candidate A is better suited to the job. However, the committee is concerned that she may not be able to perform quite so well when the initial task of completing the development plan comes to an end.

Using the following table compare the information you have on both candidates with Sullivan's list and ask yourself which candidate appears to be the best strategic selection.

Employee characteristic	Candidate A	Candidate B
Possesses competences desired by the organisation		
Is capable of self-development without needing company training		
Can generate practical ideas		
Makes few mistakes, does not need disciplining and are rarely absent		
Generates higher customer satisfaction, performance assessments, bonus and promotion rates		
Does not need close supervision		
Will stay with the business for a long time		
Generates a high return for their salary		

Obviously you have been given very little information to complete this exercise. Our assessments are in Table 1, and you may have reached similar assessments.

You may have concluded that candidate B is more likely to succeed in the long term as the job becomes largely a PR function. At face value, he seems the better strategic selection. However, candidate A would probably produce a far better development plan. This aspect is crucial since a good plan is necessary in order to obtain funding. The council has an irreconcilable problem. The best solution is to advertise outside the organisation in order to find someone who can perform both the initial task – completing the development plan – and meet the longer-term strategic need.

Employee characteristic	Candidate A	Candidate B
Possesses competences desired by the organisation	Competent to complete the development plan but unlikely to cope well with PR work	No planning experience but likely to be good at public relations
Is capable of self-development without needing company training	Weak	Acceptable
Can generate practical ideas	No evidence from assessment	Good
Makes few mistakes, does not need disciplining and is rarely absent	Very good	Not so good
Generates high customer satisfaction, performance assessments, bonus and promotion rates	On initial task but not in later role	No evidence on initial task but some expectation in later role
Does not need close supervision	Needs supervising for new work	Works unsupervised
Will stay with the business for a long time	Unlikely outside the planning environment	Likely if given a challenging job
Generates a high return for their salary	Initially but, again, not so likely in the long term	Possibly in the long term

Table 1: Assessing the candidates against Sullivan's selection criteria

So far we have discussed recruitment from the perspective of the employer, but now we turn to the role of the applicant and discuss the role of applicants as self-selectors.

CANDIDATES AND CHOICE

Selection is a two-way process: candidates also make choices, they decide which organisations to apply to, and whether to accept a job offer if they are successful in the selection process. Our discussion in the last unit indicated that employee turnover is highest in the period immediately after new recruits are taken on. This happens because some new staff decide that the employing organisation does not fit their working styles or domestic circumstances or meet their career aspirations. It would save considerable trouble and expense if these decisions were made before jobs were offered or accepted.

The costs involved in recruitment and selection can be considerable. In 1997, 16 per cent of full-time employees in the UK changed their jobs for various reasons. In the publishing and leisure industries over a third did so. The UK's Institute of Personnel and Development calculated that it took an average of 10 weeks to recruit a new professional employee, at a cost of £4,861 (Cowe, 1998).

Of course, potential candidates may opt out of the recruitment and selection process at any stage. Advertisements will be read and ignored; application forms will be thrown away; interview opportunities will be declined; job offers may be declined. This 'deselection' is desirable provided that it is the unsuitable rather than the highly competent applicants who remove themselves from the process. To attract and retain highly competent applicants, it is necessary for selectors to be informative and even to sell the organisation to the most suitable people.

CHOOSING THE BEST OR AVOIDING THE WORST?

In the introduction we noted that HR specialists have an important role in selecting new recruits. Their perceptions of the selection process are influenced by three concerns:

- the need to fill vacancies in order to get necessary work done
- the strategic aim of recruiting people with long-term potential for the organisation
- the desire to avoid hiring employees with inadequate skills or experience, and those with undesirable attitudes or behaviour.

Operational managers will emphasise the need to recruit staff as quickly as possible. More senior managers may stress long-term goals. Both operational managers and HR specialists will be wary of taking on unsuitable people. Ironically, selectors may have more to lose from making bad decisions – in terms of status and career prospects, for example – than they have to gain from making good selection choices. Good choices are expected – bad choices are highly visible mistakes. As we can see in Table 2 the consequences of hiring unsuitable candidates can be extensive and expensive. In all cases, selection is a risk-taking procedure.

Management time and effort	Unsuitable recruits require more attention than good people
	Time spent on 'problem' recruits would be better spent on other issues
	Unsuitable recruits interfere with the efficient running of teams and departments, and they require more training effort
Productivity of other staff	Time is lost helping weaker recruits
	Star performers do not like being in the same team as mediocre staff
	A post blocked by a mediocre recruit is not available for a star performer
Creativity	Mediocre staff produce fewer good ideas
	If they are managers, they block ideas that they cannot understand
	Poor quality staff take longer to bring new ideas to market
Company image and public relations	Poor quality recruits give an impression of weakness to competitors and other staff
	Mediocre staffing implies an 'easy touch' to other low quality job applicants
	High staff turnover rates gives a bad impression to high quality applicants
Additional staff cover	Poor quality recruits tend to have greater absence and lateness record
	They need extra training time
	Additional staff required to cover period between dismissal and arrival of replacements
Additional costs	Cost of recruiting replacements
	Mediocre employees lose revenue
	Poor quality staff make more errors and cause complaints
HR time and image	Extra burden of disciplining and firing mediocre employees and recruiting replacements
	Bad selection choices reflect poorly on HR department
	Highly visible example of HR work

Table 2: Consequences of hiring unsuitable applicants
Source: Considerably adapted from Sullivan (1997)

ACTIVITY 2

Reflect on our discussion so far in this section. Then rewrite the following statements to reflect a more balanced and realistic viewpoint.

1. Selectors aim to choose the best person for the job.

2. The purpose of recruitment is to attract the largest possible number of applicants.

3. It is better to hire someone with inadequate competences to do a job rather than leave a vacancy unfilled.

4. You can rely on the HR department to be entirely objective in its selection decision-making.

5. Selectors should never put off a candidate from continuing with his or her application.

6. The concerns that HR specialists have about hiring the 'wrong person' are entirely reasonable.

7. Selectors should be professional and objective – it is not their job to sell the company to an applicant.

8. It is easier to take on people than to dismiss them.

You would have done well to cover the following points in your answers.

Selectors aim to choose the best person for the job. Choosing the best possible candidate is normally the declared objective. However, the desire to avoid making an unsuitable choice may figure more prominently in reality.

The purpose of recruitment is to attract the largest possible number of applicants. The purpose of recruitment is to attract a sufficient, manageable number of suitable applicants – avoiding those who are not suitable – from which selectors can make a choice.

It is better to hire someone with inadequate competences to do a job rather than leave a vacancy unfilled. Sometimes selectors will have no choice but to take on someone who does not possess all the required competences. This may be an acceptable risk, provided that:

- selectors and departmental managers know that this is the case
- the shortfall in competence is not substantial
- managers can redesign the job to fit existing competence levels, or have thought out a programme to develop competence levels to an acceptable level
- the job is not particularly senior
- the individual concerned is hired on a trial basis.

You can rely on the HR department to be entirely objective in its selection decision-making. Selection is not an entirely objective process – it is dependent on human judgement.

Selectors should never put off a candidate from continuing with his or her application. Selectors should gently discourage any applicant from proceeding with an application which will be rejected because of unsuitability.

The concerns that HR specialists have about hiring the 'wrong person' are entirely reasonable. Their concerns are reasonable, but selection is a risk-taking activity and it is essential that selectors are not over-cautious.

Selectors should be professional and objective – it is not their job to sell the company to an applicant. When suitable applicants are difficult to attract, it is essential that selectors promote the organisation to potential employees.

It is easier to take on people than to dismiss them. It is certainly the case that new employees quickly develop psychological bonds and social relationships within the organisation. It may also take some time to discover that an individual does not have the expected abilities. After a point, legal restrictions come into play regarding dismissal, and employees may be entitled to statutory notice periods and redundancy pay.

1.2   Job applications

How do candidates apply if they are interested in a particular job vacancy? In the early part of the twentieth century, people simply turned up at factory gates or offices and inquired about work. Even today, small businesses may continue to offer interviews on the basis of speculative telephone calls. With the exception of specialised and higher-level jobs, however, this approach is unlikely to be successful with larger organisations which tend to formalise the application stage. This formalisation is consistent with the key role of selection as part of a strategic process based on measurement and monitoring (Iles and Salaman, 1995).

Initial telephone calls may be requested, however, as part of **preselection** – a deliberate process of candidate screening. Applicants are invited to telephone a response number which may be partly or entirely automated. Callers are asked to indicate that they possess essential characteristics, such as qualifications or specific experience, before being provided with further information and a (blank) application form. Applicants for call centres and other telephone-handling jobs may find that most of the selection process happens over the telephone. This type of selection process often entails a carefully scripted procedure in which responses are marked on a scoring form.

For all vacancies, the enquiry may be terminated at this point – before it turns into a formal application – if applicant and organisation do not match each other's requirements. However, it is rare for candidates to be rejected over the telephone: this is insensitive and runs the risk of an unpleasant confrontation. More probably, successful callers will be put on the 'fast track' leading to the next part of the process, while unsuccessful applicants are placed on the 'slow track' which goes no further than application form and information pack (Roberts, 1997).

Alternatively, organisations may choose to screen applications by post rather than by telephone. Job advertisements may request interested people to respond by post, either by:

- applying with a letter and curriculum vitae (or résumé)
- requesting an application form and further information.

Large employers typically send out information packs and standardised job application forms. Depending on legal restrictions prevailing in particular countries or states, application forms may ask for:

- personal information – age, gender, health, marital status, address, telephone and other contact numbers
- current employment status – working, unemployed, full-time student
- education and vocational skills – qualifications, certificates, courses taken
- employment record – employers in date order, positions held, responsibilities, reasons for leaving, salary
- additional miscellaneous information – such as memberships, military service, awards, hobbies
- names and addresses of people prepared to act as references.

Application forms should be designed to ensure that all relevant information – regardless of whether or not it is favourable – is supplied by candidates. The forms should be set out so that information of a particular kind appears in the same part of the application so that large numbers of applications can be quickly compared.

ACTIVITY 3

Suppose you are interested in the development officer job at Bonnypark District Council. You phone for, and receive, an application form (see Resource 4 in the Resources section).

You also received a job description and person specification. The person specification for the job is shown in Table 3 – it follows Rodger's seven-point plan, which was described in Unit 3.

The purpose of this activity is to see how effective the application form can be in providing information for the selection process. In this case, we want to find evidence for the essential and desirable features shown in the person specification.

Write down the title(s) of the section(s) – if any – on the application form which provides evidence for each feature in the person specification. (Hint: you might find it helpful to fill in the application form with your own details first.)

Feature sought	Essential	Desirable
Physical makeup	Able to communicate verbally with confidence	None
Attainments	At least two years experience in a business or planning environment	Previous experience of development planning Previous experience of public relations work Knowledge of planning legislation and guidelines
Intelligence	Able to comprehend varied development needs and analyse viability of projects	None
Aptitudes	Able to drive without restriction	Able to: ● complete development plan ● maintain large budget ● analyse financial projections ● organise presentations ● organise conferences ● demonstrate competence with spreadsheet and word processing programs
Interests	None	Development needs of local communities
Disposition	Able to relate well with employees of funding agencies, business organisations, other council employees and community representatives	Contribute to the District Council's good image Cope with unsuccessful projects and day-to-day administration in addition to high profile and successful activities
Circumstances	Able to be away from home overnight to attend conferences and training programmes	None

Table 3: Person specification for development
officer post at Bonnypark District Council

You may have found activity 3 difficult. Hopefully your answers were similar to these:

- physical makeup – could not be obtained directly, but could be inferred from 'employment history', 'positions held outside employment', 'interests and hobbies'
- attainments – might be obtained from 'employment history', although not much detail is requested on the form, and 'the further and higher education' might list relevant vocational qualifications in planning.
- intelligence – as for attainments
- aptitudes – the 'personal history' section asks if the applicant has a driving licence, the form provides no information on the other parts of the specification
- interests – as with attainments, there may also be relevant evidence under 'positions held outside employment' and 'interests and hobbies'
- disposition – could not be obtained directly, but could be inferred from 'employment history' and 'positions held outside employment'
- circumstances – could not be obtained directly, but may be included under 'additional information to support your application'.

Note also that the candidate may also provide information about their attainments and intelligence under 'why do you wish to apply for this job' and 'additional information to support your application'.

You should be able to see from this activity that a standard application form (in this case, one used for every council vacancy) provides a rather hit and miss method of obtaining relevant information for a specific post. A great deal depends on drawing inferences like 'the candidate states that she was planning assistant at XYZ, therefore she can probably complete a development plan'. Of course, the candidate may have worked entirely on checking and approving planning applications for new homes or extensions to domestic dwellings. This would not be of direct relevance to this particular vacancy.

A further issue is that the value of the form depends on the extent to which candidates have tailored their responses to include the features requested in the person specification. Some applicants will read the information provided more carefully than others. Additionally, the headings of the sections included in a standard application form and the space allowed for answers may inhibit candidates from giving full, relevant information. The District Council application form is not helpful in this respect, giving little space for 'positions of responsibility held outside your employment', 'interests and hobbies', 'why do you wish to apply for this job?' and 'any additional information to support your application'. Moreover, the information requested about previous employment is too limited to be of much use to selectors.

Application forms are more useful if they are designed to ask specific questions about individual vacancies, based on job descriptions and person specifications. However, this is expensive and time-consuming. Not surprisingly, most large organisations use standard forms to collect basic candidate information that applies to any job vacancy. But some organisations ask for a great deal of information at this stage. For example, Pizza Hut (quoted by Wright and Storey, 1997) have a nine-page management application form which includes a personality questionnaire.

INTERNATIONAL VARIATIONS

For cultural and legal reasons, there is a significant variation from one country to another in the type of information requested from applicants. For instance, employers in English-speaking countries are generally happy to receive typed two-page curriculum vitae (CVs) or résumés with details of hobbies and interests; French employers prefer short, education and employment-related résumés which are handwritten to allow graphological analysis; Japanese employers may request photographs, copies of official family records and a physical examination report. In some countries requests for photographs can infringe racial discrimination laws.

In the USA, although some professions such as acting and modelling are exempted, it would regarded as discriminatory to request information about:

- ethnicity, national origin or religion
- age or date of birth – instead applicants should be asked if they are above the minimum legal working age
- marital status – because it indicates that applicants are assumed to be heterosexuals and also because some ethnic minority group members are less (and others more) likely to be in a conventional marriage than the general population
- education – this is only acceptable if required by the job
- record of arrests and convictions – because ethnic minority group members are more likely to be arrested than the general population
- credit rating – because ethnic minority group members are more likely to have poorer credit ratings than the general population
- photographs – because they identify gender and ethnic or national origin
- height and weight – because there are significant differences between the sexes and between different racial groups
- specific disability – instead applicants should be asked to confirm that they can do the job.

The approach in the UK is less stringent but considerable care has to be taken to ensure that race or sex discrimination laws are not infringed. We discuss this aspect further in the unit on managing diversity.

SORTING APPLICATIONS

What happens if recruitment advertisements are too successful? Unless organisations apply anti-discriminatory tracking systems with all applications, completed application forms and CVs may disappear into the shredding machine for a variety of reasons. Employers have been known to reject applications on some strange grounds, including because the forms are handwritten (or not), they come from people over 35 and under 27, applicants had 'foreign' names, and worse (see example below).

The 'Boney M' method

A new cable television company in Norwich, England received 5,000 applications in response to its recruitment campaign for production staff (*Independent*, 19 January 1998). Four people were employed to reduce this pile to a more manageable 120 applications. Faced with the absence of unusual characteristics from which to make the choice, they picked out those candidates whose names appeared in songs by the Boney M group.

This example may seem bizarre but it is worth quoting because it vividly demonstrates the lack of care exercised by many recruiters at this stage of the selection process. As we have observed, recruitment and selection can be an expensive exercise involving a great deal of time, effort and thought. Yet candidates may be discarded at an early point with a flippant disregard of their potential.

A possible solution to this problem is to sift applications with computer software. Providers of computerised résumé and application form analysis packages claim their software streamlines the process of short-listing by scanning résumés, identifying suitable candidates, managing documents and producing reports. Integrated computer systems take care of data entry and other administrative burdens, allowing HR staff – as one provider's website claims – to concentrate on 'what's really important: finding and hiring the best people'.

The simplest techniques involve the analysis of a standard CV or résumé which may be filled in over the internet. Alternatively, a paper version is scanned into a computer using optical character reading software. More advanced versions present applicants with on-line questions (see the Macy's example below). The computer is pre-programmed to accept or reject candidates on the basis of criteria decided by HR specialists.

> ### Macy's
> Macy's, the US department store, employs hundreds of additional staff during the peak retail season. Candidates are short-listed for interviewing after going through an on-screen session in which they are given a range of questions. Anticipated answers to these are already graded by HR staff. The computer marks individual responses and decides on those applicants who will be invited for formal interviews – which are conducted by human beings (*Independent on Sunday*, 14 June 1998).

Let's look at one of the computer software packages on the market. Aspen Tree's *ApView* uses mathematical formulas to provide an empirical weighting of the factors which are regarded as leading to successful job performance. In effect, it assigns 'objective values to subjective interview responses' and then ranks these responses by using a sequence of mathematical formulas. The formulas are customised to suit the unique circumstances of individual client organisations.

The company claims that this feature makes their system 'a powerful decision-making tool that, with a keystroke, allows for the systematic and orderly management and evaluation of thousands of applicants'. The system can also deal with multiple-choice answers, open-ended written responses, oral responses given to human interviewers, or any combination of these inputs. Selectors can combine weighted results from different geographic locations, multiple interviews and a variety of dimensions considered important in successful job performance (for example, customer care skills, organising ability or personal warmth).

Yet, both selectors and applicants value human contact, as we see in the next activity.

ACTIVITY 4

Read the article *Fair chance of a job in IT* (see Resource 5 in the Resources section). The article indicates that applicants and employers consider that direct contact at recruitment fairs leads to better job matches. Write down the most important reason for this belief from the employer's perspective.

Probably the most significant argument for direct contact at recruitment fairs is that most applications get no further than the CV and application form stage. This results in an extremely impersonal process, which is often no more than a paper exercise. In particular, there is the problem of 'the one that got away'. It is fairly easy to establish whether or not successful applicants make good employees. But would candidates who are rejected on the basis of the information they supplied on application forms and CVs have been better? It is almost impossible to tell. By opening direct communication before the initial application, there is an opportunity to spot high quality candidates. They can be encouraged to write CVs and fill in application forms in a way which makes the most of their abilities. They can also be motivated to join a company through positive answers to their questions.

1.3   Using candidate data

BIODATA

The council job application form (Resource 4) asked questions about 'positions of responsibility held outside your employment' and 'interests and hobbies'. This is biodata (biographical data), but why do application forms request this kind of information? In most circumstances, it is used for little more than a prompt for interviewers: for example, 'in your application form, you wrote that you were interested in travelling, what kind of travelling have you done so far?'

Biodata is not much used. However, properly formulated biodata questionnaires are known to provide comparatively good predictive information of successful job performance.

Roberts (1997) describes the technique as 'a set of questions framed around coincidences in the lives of people who are good performers'. In other words, people who are good at a particular job are likely to be more similar to each other than a group of individuals taken at random from the general population. These similarities extend beyond education achievement and work-experience, factors which are normally examined in selection procedures. They may tend to share similar views on life, enjoy vigorous sports and visit night-clubs – or, alternatively, prefer spending hours on their home PCs.

Biodata questionnaires can be devised in the following way (Smith et al., 1989).

1. Job or role analysis is used to identify competences or criteria required for desired performance level.

2. A focus group uses brainstorming techniques to generate the biodata items which demonstrate these competences. For example, 'interest in travelling', 'enthusiasm', 'awareness of international events' may be appropriate for a travel agency administrator.

3. Questionnaires are drafted which ask about these items. They are piloted on a large number of existing employees.

4. Replies are then correlated with the performance of those staff. Items which do not correlate highly with good performance or discriminate against particular groups are discarded.

5. The revised questionnaire is given to job applicants.

As Roberts (1997) points out, we do not need to know why these items are significant in order to use them. The method is similar to the scoring systems used by insurance companies. For example, an individual with a profession A might pay a different rate of motor vehicle insurance to another person – with the same model and age of car – working in profession B. The rating is based on the insurance company's record of claims for professions A and B.

ACTIVITY 5

Read the following statements, Which are true and which are false?

1. Biodata stands for biographical data.

2. The biodata technique is not used very much because it is not a good predictor of candidate suitability.

3. The biodata technique requires a large number of people doing similar jobs in order to draft questionnaires.

4. People who have a similar standard of performance on a particular job are likely to be similar in other respects.

5. It is important to understand why a specific item on a biodata questionnaire appears to be related to good performance.

6. Hobbies and leisure interests are examples of biodata items.

The statements 1, 3 and 6 are true. *The biodata technique is not used very much because it is not a good predictor of candidate suitability.* This is false – but, strictly speaking, the method is a predictor of employee turnover rather than suitability. Obviously, however, suitable people are more likely to stay (or be allowed to stay) in a post. The method is not much used because it requires a large number of people doing similar jobs (statement 3), and the fact that it is comparatively expensive and time-consuming to set up. *People who have a similar standard of performance on a particular job are likely to be similar in other respects.* This is also true – but only on average. Some good workers with the same type of job can be completely different in most respects. *It is important to understand why a specific item on a biodata questionnaire appears to be related to good performance.* This is false. It is an actuarial method – we do not need to know why certain items appear to correlate with good performance.

REFERENCES

Virtually every employer asks for references before taking on new people. Yet, although the research evidence on the subject of references is scanty, it shows that that they have little value in making selection decisions (Wright and Storey, 1997; Price, 1997). Applicants invariably nominate referees who are likely to give favourable references. Employers know this, and it is not surprising that they play little part in most selection procedures. Open-ended reference letters are becoming comparatively rare as employers increasingly use standardised proformas asking questions such as:

- how long has this individual been known to you
- how would you rate their general performance – on 1–4 or 1–5 scales, or from very good to unsatisfactory
- how often was this person absent
- would you re-employ this person in the future
- is there any reason why you think we should not employ this person?

The legislation regarding references varies from one country to another. In the UK, referees are legally responsible for providing truthful, accurate and reliable information and they have a duty of care towards the new employer and the former employee. On the other hand, at the time of writing, it does not seem that employers are legally obliged to provide references for former employees. The case of Spring v Guardian Assurance [1994] IRLR 460 brought contradictory and untested assertions from the judges (Barnett, 1999). Lord Slynn concluded that providing references was a *moral* obligation. On the other hand, Lord Woolff considered that references were legally obliged if three conditions were met:

- there was a contract of employment or for services
- the contract relates to an engagement of a class where it is the normal practice to require a reference from a previous employer before employment is offered
- the employee cannot be expected to enter into that class of employment except on the basis that the previous employer will, within a reasonable time, provide a full and frank reference.

On the basis of various authorities, and analogies between the law of negligence and the law of defamation, the Court of Appeal arrived at three statements of general principle (Bartholomew v London Borough of Hackney [1999] IRLR 246):

- employers have a duty to ensure that references are true, accurate and fair in substance
- employers are not obliged to be 'full and comprehensive' since this would impose too high a burden
- employers may not break references down into individual sentences and argue that each specific sentence was factually correct – references must be regarded as a whole.

Finally in this section we briefly consider the issue of reference checking. Most employers in the UK request references but few check that they are valid – with the notable exception of applicants for jobs involving monetary transactions. In the USA, however, candidate screening often leads to extensive checking of applicant credentials and records. US employers often use reference checking agencies. They charge a fee for services which include checks on references from previous employers, credit-worthiness, health records and criminal records.

It should be noted that these activities are potentially discriminatory. Reference checking agencies have also been established in other countries.

ACTIVITY 6

Review our discussion on references. Write about 25 words in each case to amplify the following statements.

1. It is wise to obtain references for all new recruits.

2. Referees selected by candidates will not necessarily provide unbiased references.

3. It is best for former employees to provide references on request.

4. Recruiters should limit reference requests to a short list of factually verifiable items.

It is wise to obtain references for all new recruits. You could consider the different degrees of importance which could be attached to jobs. Is the position being filled junior or senior; does it involve financial responsibility; will it impact on the organisation's image if a bad selection is made; does the position involve influence or staff responsibility? Consider also, the cost of collecting the references, and the cost to the referees of providing them.

Referees selected by candidates will not necessarily provide unbiased references. Candidates are unlikely to suggest people who may give an unfavourable reference, but it is possible to insist on specific individuals such as the applicant's previous immediate manager.

It is best for former employers to provide references on request. The complex legal situation suggests that it is best to provide a clear, short and factual reference based on recorded, non-discriminatory information. References based on unsubstantiated personal opinion would appear to be inappropriate.

Recruiters should limit reference requests to a short list of factually verifiable items. This statement focuses on the essential purpose of obtaining references. They should be used to verify that claims made by candidates regarding positions held, previous responsibility, honesty and attendance – with relevant dates – can be checked. Beyond this we are in the realms of opinion, which may be biased in one respect or another.

1.4 Validity and reliability of selection methods

Before going on to consider interviews and more advanced techniques, we now look at how selection methods can be evaluated. Good selection methods (Smith, 1991) must meet four basic requirements:

- practicality
- sensitivity
- reliability
- validity.

Obviously, selection methods must be **practical**: they must meet the constraints of time and cost. They must be sufficiently **sensitive** to distinguish one candidate from another. It may be, for example, that all candidates who pass through the pre-selection stage have similar educational levels. Ability tests need to discriminate between candidates.

Results must be consistent or **reliable** in three ways:

- test-retest reliability – candidates taking the same procedure a few days apart should score similarly
- inter-rater reliability – different people (interviewers) assessing the same attribute should produce similar scores
- internal consistency – different items or questions meant to measure the same competence should provide similar ratings.

Similarly, there are three measures of **validity**:

- face validity – does it look as if the method is addressing what it is supposed to measure, candidates find 'relevant' questions or tests more acceptable
- construct validity – how well does a method measure a 'construct' such as loyalty or team spirit
- predictive validity – most importantly, how well does the method predict the suitability of applicants for a job?

Validity and reliability can be expressed as coefficients, ranging from 0 to 1.0. A coefficient of 0 indicates that a method is no better than pure chance. A score of 1.0 indicates perfect correlation between the test score and on-the-job performance. Validity scores for selection methods are modest. Based on available research, table 4 provides estimates of validity coefficients for the methods considered in this unit.

Validity range	Selection methods	Rating
0.4 – 0.5 +	Work sample tests Ability tests	Good to excellent
0.3 – 0.39	Biodata Assessment centres Structured interviews	Acceptable
Less than 0.3	Personality tests Typical interviews References Graphology	Poor
0 (i.e. pure chance)	Astrology	

Table 4: Comparative validity of selection techniques
Source: Adapted from Smith (1991)

ACTIVITY 7

Look at the following statements. Three refer to the concept of 'validity' and three to 'reliability' in the context of selection. Identify which relate to validity, and which to reliability.

1. How well does the method predict the suitability of applicants for a job?

2. Different items or questions meant to measure the same competence should provide similar ratings.

3. Candidates taking the same procedure now, and then again in a few days would score similarly on this measure.

4. Does it look as if it is measuring what it is supposed to measure?

5. If different raters used the same selection method on the same candidate they would produce similar scores.

6. How well does a method measure a 'construct' such as loyalty, or team spirit?

Statements 1, 4 and 6 are concerned with validity. Statement 1 refers to predictive validity, statement 4 refers to face validity, and statement 6 is construct validity. Statements 2, 3 and 5 concern reliability. Statement 2 is internal consistency, inter-item or inter-test reliability, statement 3 test-retest reliability, and statement 5 is inter-rater reliability.

Summary

There are significant issues underlying the use of selection methods including objectivity versus subjectivity – some apparently objective methods are more subjective than they seem – the possibilities of distorting or suppressing information by candidates because data-collecting processes are inadequately thought through or analysed, and the fact that no selection method has a particularly high level of validity or reliability.

SECTION 2
Selection Interviews

Introduction

This section examines the role of the formal interview in selection. Interviews have been the subject of a long-standing academic debate that has been largely ignored by selectors. We consider why academic research over several decades seemed to show that interviews had little to commend them in terms of reliability and validity. We also discuss more recent evidence which indicates that interviews *can* be as valid and reliable as any other selection method. Interviews can range from spontaneous and unplanned social conversations to preplanned patterns focused strictly on job-related criteria. Research shows that the latter are far superior at predicting suitable candidates. Interviews can be further improved by using panels and different approaches to questioning.

This section is intended to help you to:

- debate the value of interviews
- outline the methodology of structured interviewing
- critically evaluate some significant interview techniques.

2.1 Interviewing as a selection method

Traditionally, face-to-face interviews are regarded as a crucial part of the selection process. Almost every employer in developed countries uses interviews for jobs other than basic labouring vacancies (Corbridge and Pilbeam, 1998). Applicants would be suspicious of a selection procedure which did not include at least one interview. Interviews provide a social interaction between employer and applicant.

- Interviews meet expectations of common courtesy – it is regarded as a polite way of dealing with people.
- Interviews are good PR, preserving the organisation's good corporate image.
- Interviews constitute a two-way process, providing information to the candidate as well as the organisation. This allows the applicant to find out about the job and its place in the company, career prospects, development and training.
- Interviews allow selectors to sell the organisation when there are few high-calibre applicants available.
- Interviews provide a further screening process, so that statements on application forms and references can be checked for ambiguity and veracity.

Interviews are also thought to be cheap. A common perception is that they can be conducted spontaneously by busy managers – with no preparation required. We discover later in this section that this can lead to inappropriate selection decisions. Ironically, decisions with potentially expensive long-term implications are taken hastily in order to minimise short-term expense and effort.

ACTIVITY 8

Reflect on our discussion so far in this section. In each case write up to 20 words to finish the following statements:

1. Selection interviews enhance the image of an organisation by …
2. Selection interviews are useful for applicants because …
3. Interviews are useful for selectors because …
4. Interviews increase the likelihood of attracting good quality employees because …

Selection interviews enhance the image of an organisation by ... offering a polite reception to applicants, by telling them about the organisation, and by selling the organisation.

Selection interviews are useful for applicants because ... they are provided with information about the company and the job; they give applicants the opportunity to ask questions and to get feedback on their personal history and attributes.

Interviews are useful for selectors because ... they offer an opportunity to check details on application forms and CVs; they give a good image of the company, get extra information and sell the job to high-quality applicants.

Interviews increase the likelihood of attracting good quality employees because ... polite social interaction can provide a favourable view of the company; more information about the job can attract suitable people and good applicants can be sold the job.

The purpose of interviewing can vary since interviews may take place at three stages:

- screening interviews
- formal interviews
- confirmation interviews.

Screening interviews

Screening interviews take place at an early stage of a selection process and may be conducted over the telephone. They are relatively informal information exchanges designed to filter out applicants who do not satisfy basic criteria in the person specification. They also offer an opportunity for job-seekers to drop out of the selection process if the post is not suitable for them.

Formal interviews

Formal interviews are key selection procedures: part of the social ritual which everyone expects when applying for a vacancy. Universities, schools and job clubs advise interviewees to:

- arrive on time, well groomed and dressed appropriately
- project a positive image
- avoid any extravagant gestures or unbusinesslike behaviour
- answer questions fully, no matter how personal or aggressive they may be.

As we shall see shortly, this ritual is understood by interviewers and interviewees alike but its value to the selection process is problematic.

Confirmation interviews

Successful candidates may be invited to 'come and meet the other staff'. These may involve future colleagues, managers or even significant customers. They are relatively informal and may seem relaxing and unimportant to a candidate who has just gone through the ordeal of a formal interview. However, they are a key checking mechanism to confirm the selectors' view on whether this is an acceptable person to work in the organisation.

2.2 Criticisms of interviewing as a method of selection

We noted that the selection interview has long been criticised as an inappropriate procedure for collecting information and deciding on successful candidates. Specifically, they have been faulted on grounds of both validity and reliability. For example, a classic summary of research findings (Webster, 1964) found that:

- interviewers decided (sometimes unconsciously) on candidates, one way or the other, in the first few minutes of an interview
- that interviewees' appearance, voice and mannerisms were the most important factors
- unfavourable evidence countered more strongly than information in a candidate's favour – a single piece of negative evidence was used as justification for rejection in 90 per cent of cases (Bolster and Sprinbett, quoted in Porteous, 1997).
- the process was influenced by feedback provided by the interviewer – in other words, favourable or unfavourable views 'came over' to interviewees which had the effect, for example, of making nervous candidates even more nervous.

Amack (1995) considers that 'interviewing often degenerates into a tacit beauty contest', observing that interviewers favour applicants who are:

- physically attractive
- young and healthy
- quick-witted
- good communicators
- culturally similar to the interviewer
- not particularly nervous
- possessed of the 'normal' range of mannerisms.

These factors are highly significant in an average interviewer's decision-making, outweighing the criteria requested on the person specification.

ACTIVITY 9

Consider the following statements about interviewing. Which are more true than false and which are more false than true?

1. Interviews are face-to-face dialogues between two individuals.

2. It is important to dress and behave appropriately for selection interviews.

3. Applicants can take a casual approach in their initial telephone inquiry about an advertised job.

4. Selection interviews are intended to check that candidates meet the criteria on the person specification.

5. Selectors should not be influenced by the appearance, accent or age of a candidate.

6. It is nice to meet the staff you might be working with if you get the job.

7. Selection interviews are objective.

Interviews are face-to-face dialogues between two individuals. This is true more often than not – but telephone screening interviews are becoming common and, as we see later in this unit, there may be more than one interviewer involved.

It is important to dress and behave appropriately for selection interviews. True. The evidence seems to show that these factors are of major importance despite their (probable) irrelevance to the person specification.

Applicants can take a casual approach in their initial telephone inquiry about an advertised job. False. 'Please telephone for further details and an application form' may actually mean 'contact us for a telephone screening interview'.

Selection interviews are intended to check that candidates meet the criteria on the person specification. True – but other factors seem to outweigh this important function.

Selectors should not be influenced by the appearance, accent or age of a candidate. True – but they are inevitably influenced by these factors.

It is nice to meet staff you might be working with if you get the job. Certainly. But remember that they will form an opinion which may be passed on to the selectors. In effect, this might be a confirmation interview.

Selection interviews are objective. From the evidence presented so far, this statement seems to be false because interviewers are strongly influenced by factors such as appearance. However, we shall soon discover that there are ways of improving the objectivity of interviews.

DISCRIMINATORY EFFECTS

Due to the subjective considerations we have described, it is possible for interviewers to unwittingly discriminate against certain applicants. Amack (1995) argues that traditional face-to-face interviews are potentially discriminatory because they:

- do not significantly enhance predictability of vocational or scholastic performance beyond the evidence available from more objective criteria
- do not measure essential job or educational qualifications
- lack business necessity – candidates with similar backgrounds and interests to the interviewer are favoured, thereby putting members of other social or ethnic groups at a disadvantage
- cause 'discriminatory exclusionary effects' between and among minority groups – for example, highly intelligent candidates with a disability may be offered only menial jobs.

As a result, Amack considers that face-to-face interviews should be used only if they are productivity-related and properly validated.

Available evidence suggests that Amack is correct. For example, Kinicki et al. (1990) found that applicant success could be predicted from three main factors, in the following order of importance:

- attraction – not simply good looks but a wider collection of attributes which an interviewer may find attractive
- gender – whether candidates are the same sex as the interviewer
- interview impression – ability to express ideas, job knowledge, appearance and drive.

Note that the importance of attraction in interview situations can have discriminatory effects. People tend to find members of similar ethnic groups to their own to be more 'attractive' than members of groups which are physically or culturally different.

Applicants are not passive in the interview process. Porteous (1997) describing the interaction of interviewer and interviewee, states that 'the fact that it is a social situation is important ... while they are having what looks like a conversation, it is really more like a duel'. Interviewees intentionally sell themselves in this interaction – sometimes with the acting skills of Oscar-winning performers. They use a process described as **impression management** to create the best possible image of themselves in order to be offered the job (Price, 1997).

It may be, therefore, that interviewing is frequently a case of discrimination rather than selection. However, as we concluded earlier, it is unlikely that the vast majority of selectors or applicants would be happy with selection procedures that did not include interviews (Corbridge and Pilbeam, 1998).

ACTIVITY 10

Read the discussion above carefully then write down how Kinicki's three main factors could be potentially discriminatory. You could use Amack's points – attraction, gender similarity and interview impression – as a check list.

Attraction tells you nothing about vocational or scholarly potential, or job and educational qualifications. In most cases, also, the 'attractiveness' of the applicant is irrelevant to the job. In other words, it is probably not a business necessity – although we should remember that the person specification for customer-facing jobs may require these qualities. Disabilities or ethnic differences might be viewed as unattractive by some interviewers, leading to the exclusionary effects described by Amack. For similar reasons, **gender similarity** is likely to be irrelevant to the person specification and therefore potentially discriminatory.

Candidates who can deliver **impressive** accounts of themselves may facilitate collection of data about vocational or scholarly potential, or job and educational qualifications. However, they may oversell these items. Again, the ability to talk persuasively may not be a business necessity and, since it depends on skills in the dominant language, it may be discriminatory against members of ethnic groups.

2.3   Structured interviewing

There may be good reasons for holding interviews, but it remains the case that while 'cosy chats' can be friendly, unstressful and informative, they do not amount to a valid and reliable method of selection. How can we improve on the situation? Most of the difficulties we have described come from subjective and unstructured approaches. Unstructured interviews are strongly influenced by first impressions, which are often misleading. Since they are often not measuring what they are supposed to be measuring – future performance – their validity can be low. Paradoxically, however, they may produce fairly respectable reliability scores because different interviewers will rate 'impressive' candidates just as highly.

STRUCTURED AND UNSTRUCTURED INTERVIEWS

An interview is an occasion on which two or more people meet and in which one party seeks information and the other provides it.

An **unstructured interview** is one in which the interviewer (or interviewers) asks questions as they occur to them, following no set plan. Unstructured interviews lack validity. Interviewers can be trained to focus on the job rather than the person, but interviewers are people who are always liable to bias and influence by plausible candidates. It is easier to change the process of interviewing so that selectors are made to take a structured, valid and reliable approach (Corbridge and Pilbeam, 1998).

The **structured interview** is one in which the interviewers will have decided in advance what information is required, and usually will have prepared questions beforehand, and planned the order in which the questions are to be put. Structured interviews have been found to give a much better prediction of eventual job suitability than unprepared chats (Corbridge and Pilbeam, 1998, Weisner and Cronshaw, 1988).

A systematic structured interview avoids inquiries into fascinating but irrelevant aspects of a candidate's personal life. Rather it constrains questioning so that the issues discussed are strictly job-related. In small organisations, key work-related questions should be devised and a marking grid prepared to ensure that every applicant is rated on a reasonable sub-set of questions (Roberts, 1997).

Larger organisations may use a process similar to that for biodata questionnaires. Within the constraints of reasonable expense and effort, as many individuals as possible need to be consulted. Information from job analyses can be used and questions related to key competences listed in job descriptions and person specifications. Items can be weighted according to perceived importance and rating forms and a decision grid prepared.

According to Roberts (1997) structured interviews should seem spontaneous. Questioning should flow freely, forming an orderly sequence which takes account of an applicant's individual responses. Interviewers who read out scripted questions in a robotic fashion are not likely to bring out the best in a nervous candidate. Structured interviews are best when selectors can choose from a range of appropriate questions.

ACTIVITY 11

Write down the key differences between structured and unstructured interviews. You can use the table below or write on a separate piece of paper if you prefer.

	Unstructured interviews	Structured interviews
Reliability		
Validity		
Susceptibility to bias		
Fairness		
Relationship to competences or person specification		

You may have come to some of the same conclusions as those shown in the table 5. Of course, both unstructured and structured interviews can vary considerably. It is possible for unstructured interviews in specific circumstances to have high validity, depending on the skill or training of interviewers and their choice of questions. Also, as we pointed out earlier, some customer-facing jobs require competences which amount to impression management. In such cases, an unstructured interview can result in valid measures of these competences.

	Unstructured interviews	Structured interviews
Reliability	Can be relatively good but interviewers are susceptible to impression management.	Should be even better.
Validity	May be low since interviewers are often rating candidates on irrelevant characteristics.	Can be relatively good, depending on the basis on job analysis and competences.
Susceptibility to bias	Very high.	Much reduced.
Fairness	May be discriminatory.	Can be very fair.
Relationship to competences or person specification	Arbitrary.	Can be high.

Table 5: Key differences between structured and unstructured interviews

MULTIPLE AND TRAINED INTERVIEWERS

One of the main concerns with conventional interviewing is the reliance on a single interviewer. Rejected applicants may (sometimes correctly) feel that they are turned down because of bias. There is something inherently unfair in having one's career decided by what may seem to be the whim of a single individual. From an equal opportunities perspective, there is a worrying lack of independent evidence should rejection lead to accusations of discrimination.

The panel or board method has been used to overcome these difficulties. Panels normally consist of two or more interviewers. Classically, the panel consists of:

- a chairperson
- an operational assessor, from the line department which holds the vacancy
- a personnel assessor.

Operational and personnel assessors ask questions related to their expertise. The operational assessor focuses on job knowledge and technical expertise. The personnel assessor examines motivation, career commitment and people-related competences. The chairperson may do little more than 'top and tail' the process or pick up on any topic which seems to merit more attention.

In practice, organisations may vary this procedure considerably. Boards of as many as nine assessors have been known. One organisation when interviewing for its graduate entry scheme seats three assessors in front of a candidate – and one behind (as described to the author by a student).

The panel format is seen as fair but intimidating. An alternative approach compromises between the single interviewer and panel methods. Individual selectors interview candidates on a one-to-one basis and then meet to discuss their findings. This is commonly seen as being less stressful.

The value of structured interviewing is enhanced if assessors are given training on questioning technique.

- Ask open rather than closed questions. Open questions, commencing with 'why', 'what', 'when' and 'how' can not be answered with short 'yes' and 'no' answers. Candidates are made to think and to develop on their answers.

- Use funnelled questions, in which a broad general question, such as, 'you say you have travelled widely, where have you been?', is followed by more incisive and probing questions, such as 'what have you learned about different cultures on your travels?', 'you say you dislike some aspects of male office culture – which aspects in particular?', 'can you think of any reason why this should be so?', 'in what ways does it affect your relationship with male workers?' (The first question is called a funnel, the subsidiary questions are called probes.)

- Use both factual and hypothetical questions. Candidates can be asked to deal with a realistic problem to gauge speed of thought, imagination and practicality.

- Use supportive body language and mannerisms to put candidates (relatively) at ease.

ACTIVITY 12

This is a list of statements about interviewing. Which of these statements are true and which are false.

1. In the context of panel interviewing, questions about the applicant's knowledge of the job for which they have applied will be asked by the personnel interviewer.

2. Funnelling is a method which allows interviewers to obtain deeper, more job-relevant and significant answers to a question.

3. Chairpersons take an active role in questioning a candidate.

4. A closed question is one which can be answered briefly – typically with 'yes', 'no' or a stated fact such as the name of the previous employer.

5. Operational assessors are interested in job expertise or specific competences required for a vacancy.

6. Interviewers can ask questions which have nothing to do with the job.

In the context of panel interviewing, questions about the applicant's knowledge of the job for which they have applied will be asked by the personnel interviewer. False. Personnel assessors normally focus on motivation, career commitment and people-related competences

Funnelling is a method which allows interviewers to obtain deeper, more job-relevant and significant answers to a question. True. Remember that it should not be over-done or it may seem like interrogation!

Chairpersons take an active role in questioning a candidate. There are no hard and fast rules, but generally the main questioning is done by operational and personnel assessors. The chairperson would not normally engage in lengthy questioning.

A closed question is one which can be answered briefly – typically with 'yes', 'no' or a stated fact such as the name of the previous employer. True. As this information should be obtainable from application forms and CVs, it is best to use open questions in interviews.

Operational assessors are interested in job expertise or specific competences required for a vacancy. True.

Interviewers can ask questions which have nothing to do with the job. True – provided that they are testing for a desired competence such as problem-solving or imagination.

Summary

Research shows that many interviewers make decisions about candidate suitability on the basis of spurious and superficial characteristics. However, the much-maligned interview can, depending on the method used, be a better predictor of suitability for the job than commonly believed. Structured and multiple interviews are more likely to produce valid conclusions, especially if they are based on a job analysis. Good questioning styles can be learned, including methods designed to elicit more revealing answers such as funneling and open question techniques.

SECTION 3

Advanced Selection Methods

Introduction

This section evaluates a number of relatively sophisticated selection methods including psychometric tests, work samples and assessment centres. Psychometric tests are psychologically based methods of rating candidates on a variety of dimensions or scales. Work samples are used to give a sense of realism to the selection process, testing applicant performance on elements of the job. Assessment centre is a term given to a set of procedures that include a range of selection methods and multiple assessors. The section concludes with a discussion of validity and reliability in selection.

The aim of this section is to help you to:

- outline the advantages and disadvantages of psychometric tests
- explain the usefulness of work samples and assessment centres.

3.1   Psychometric tests

Psychometric tests are used extensively by larger organisations. In principle, tests can measure any psychological characteristics such as personality traits, intellectual abilities, competences, career interests. 'Pen and paper' versions date from the early twentieth century and computerised versions are becoming common. Among the best known tests are:

- 16PF – a sophisticated statistical technique designed to measure 16 personality traits identified by the occupational psychologist Robert Cattell on the basis of factor analysis

- MBTI – the Myers Briggs type indicator, which determines the personality type an individual best matches, has its origins in Jungian psychoanalytic theory

- OPQ – the occupational personality questionnaire, developed by Saville and Holdsworth, scores candidates on 30 dimensions (or scales) and compares the results against an ideal profile for a particular job.

There are innumerable other psychometric tests, many being sold by 'consultants' with no psychological training or real understanding of the value of such tests. Intriguingly, there is no evidence that results from these type of personality tests have any value in predicting work performance (Martin, 1998; Roberts, 1997). Some tests also suffer from a lack of face validity. In other words, the questions they include do not seem to have any relationship to the job being applied for.

In comparison with interviews, tests give the impression of being objective. A test must surely be scientific if there is a 'right' or 'wrong' answer. Applicants may tell tales at interviews, beam friendly smiles at interviewers and otherwise sell themselves as the best candidate. But tests have to be answered truthfully. Or do they?

Sample test questions

Number ability tests set various problems. One type is the progression.

Write down the next two numbers in this series:

5   10   8   16   14   28   26   ?   ?

Personality tests are intended to investigate characteristics such as introversion or extraversion. In other words, are you shy or outgoing? You might be asked a question such as:

On a scale of 1 (I agree strongly) to 5 (I disagree strongly), indicate your response to these statements:

1. I like to sit in my room reading novels   1   2   3   4   5

2. I get nervous when I meet new people   1   2   3   4   5

3. I love parties   1   2   3   4   5

4. I feel enthusiastic about giving a speech 1   2   3   4   5

5. I prefer working quietly on my own   1   2   3   4   5

Career interest tests check out aspirations and other factors which suit a candidate for a particular range of jobs. Questions may follow a pattern of this kind.

Which of the following tasks would you prefer?

Working with children

Using computers

Dealing with adult customers

Do you have a preference for?

Spreadsheets

Word processing

Picture scanning

ACTIVITY 13

Look at the personality and career interest test questions in the panel above. Suppose you were applying for a job as a journalist, how would you answer the questions?

You may have decided to answer these questions in the following way. On the personality tests, many real journalists might say:

I like to sit in my room reading novels	Perhaps 4 or 5
I get nervous when I meet new people	Probably 5
I love parties	Towards 1
I feel enthusiastic about giving a speech	Perhaps 1 or 2
I prefer working quietly on my own	Perhaps 3 or 4

On the career interest tests, aspiring journalists may express a preference for 'dealing with adult customers' (although journalism involves computers these days) and for 'word processing'.

Now complete the next activity before we continue with the commentary.

ACTIVITY 14

Unfortunately you failed to get the journalism job because more experienced candidates had applied. You desperately need some work to pay your mortgage. Now you find yourself at a selection procedure for a position as a payroll administrator. How would you answer the same personality and career interest test questions?

This time your answers to the personality test might be:

I like to sit in my room reading novels	Possibly 1 or 2
I get nervous when I meet new people	Maybe 2, 3 or 4
I love parties	Perhaps 4 or 5
I feel enthusiastic about giving a speech	Again 4 or 5
I prefer working quietly on my own	Ideally 1

On the career interest tests, you might express a preference for 'using computers' (although payroll administrators do deal with other staff) and for 'spreadsheets' (figures, figures and more figures).

Of course, if you are a truthful person you will have given the same responses both times. However, many people will give different responses depending on the answer they think is expected. It is fairly obvious that selectors expect journalists to be outgoing, communicative – good with people and words. Payroll administrators, on the other hand, may be expected to work on their own for lengthy periods and prefer numerical work. Candidates and selectors know what is expected in both circumstances. In practice, therefore, many tests are no more 'objective' than interviews.

In fact, we can distinguish between two categories of psychometric test.

- **Suitability tests** – these include personality profiling and career interest tests, and are comparatively easy to answer untruthfully. Test-constructors have a number of means to reduce the effects of lying and distortion. For example, questions can be planted for which answers would have to be detrimental to the candidate if answered truthfully. Questions can also be presented two or three times using different phraseology to check that answers are consistent.

- **Ability tests** – this kind of test, such as the number progression example given earlier, is almost impossible to distort. A candidate either does, or does not, know the right answer. It is possible to guess with multiple-choice questions, but scores based purely on chance are predictable and comparatively low.

Research shows that suitability tests are poor predictors of performance, whereas ability tests are good predictors – if they are appropriate (Pickard, 1996). Number, geometric or other ability tests should only be used where these abilities are critical to job performance.

As with any selection procedure, tests can be discriminatory. In Canada, for example, if a test which has not been validated rejects a disproportionate number of people from a particular ethnic group or of one race, sex, religion or national origin, it violates the Canadian Human Rights Act.

In the United Kingdom, there have been several instances where tests have been found to discriminate against individuals whose first language is not English. For example, eight guards of Asian origin took the UK train operator British Rail to an industrial tribunal on the grounds that the tests it used to assess applicants for promotion to driver were discriminatory. Verbal reasoning tests were used which were not directly related to the job and were especially difficult for people whose second (or third) language was English. British Rail admitted that the tests were unfair and revised its selection techniques on the advice of the Commission for Racial Equality.

COMPUTERISED TESTING

Kleeman (1998) argues that computers are excellent for assessment and testing purposes. Assessment is repetitive, and every candidate should be tested in exactly the same manner. Human assessors will vary in their approach from one applicant to the next, so computer assessment increases the reliability of a test. Other advantages of using computers include:

- the assessment procedure is precisely controlled – computers will follow specific instructions exactly
- the assessment benefits from speed – applicants appreciate rapid feedback
- people are not good assessors – humans make mistakes, are liable to personal bias and get bored marking test papers.

There are several difficulties in using computers for testing. Traditional test formats may not be suitable for present-day computer software packages. The rigidity which is useful for standardising the delivery of tests can cause insurmountable problems. Multiple choice or simple factual formats can be readily computerised but the computer must be told the 'right' answers to mark them correctly. Any input which is allowed to deviate by as much as a comma from these answers will be marked as incorrect. An open-ended or essay type response cannot be reliably assessed by a computer.

ACTIVITY 15

Reflect on our discussion about tests. Write down some comments on whether these statements are more true than false, or more false than true.

1. Computers are better than humans at marking test papers.

2. Applicants can angle their responses to ability tests to match the answers they think the selectors want to receive.

3. Human assessors vary the way they make judgements on different candidates.

4. Lying in suitability tests – such as those devised to assess career interests – can be controlled by repeating questions with slightly different words.

5. Essay type answers must be marked by human assessors.

6. Ability tests are the best and most easily assessed predictors of performance.

Computers are better than humans at marking test papers. They are useful for cut-and-dried answers where there is no room for variation. Answers to open questions have to be marked by human assessors.

Applicants can angle their responses to ability tests to match the answers they think the selectors want to receive. They can in some cases, but most ability tests have 'right and wrong' answers and applicants would do better to get the highest possible score of right answers.

Human assessors vary the way they make judgements on different candidates. True. Even the best-trained assessor shows occasional bias or fatigue.

Lying in suitability tests – such as those devised to assess career interests – can be controlled by repeating questions with slightly different words. True to some extent but this is only partially effective as a method. In most cases, it is likely to be time-consuming and impractical.

Essay type answers must be marked by human assessors. Largely true, although computer packages are improving.

Ability tests are the best and most easily assessed predictors of performance. True, but only where the abilities which are tested for are relevant to the job.

3.2   Work samples and assessment centres

Interviews and tests produce hypothetical responses to questions of the 'what would you do if...?' variety. Applicants can often guess the response sought by the assessor. Candidates use impression management to give the best possible images of themselves and there is no certainty that they would perform in such an appropriate fashion in real life. Work samples provide the opportunity to test applicants on real aspects of a job.

Work samples are tasks or 'mini-jobs' designed to evaluate key competences required by a particular job. Carefully designed tests offer a relatively high degree of validity. They should include some elements of the context in which the job takes place. Simple forms include:

- laying some courses of bricks – appropriate for bricklayers
- typing tests – for keyboard operators
- dealing with a series of scripted telephone calls – for call centre operators.

'In-basket' or 'in-tray' exercises are often used for administrative and managerial jobs. Candidates are given a selection of letters to respond to; reports to analyse, spreadsheets to complete, meetings to prioritise, presentations to prepare, etc.

Work samples are time-limited and marked according to a scoring system determined in advance by 'experts' in the relevant jobs. They often feature as part of an assessment centre.

Assessment centres are procedures and not necessarily places. They are expensive to set up, requiring considerable time and effort. Not surprisingly, they have been described as the Rolls-Royce of selection methodology. They were first used during the Second World War to evaluate officer candidates and have since spread to industry. They are regarded as being particularly good predictors of performance since they can serve to improve reliability and validity by integrating multiple selection techniques (Corbridge and Pilbeam, 1998). In fact, the methodology addresses many of the weaknesses in job selection discussed in this unit. There are three key elements of an assessment centre:

- evaluation of applicant competences, personality, motivation and behaviour on a number of dimensions
- assessment of a group of candidates at the same time to provide comparison
- use of several trained members of the organisation as assessors, facilitators and observers.

How is an assessment centre conducted? They can vary considerably, often being designed specifically to meet the needs of individual organisations. They can also be used for promotion and assessing the development needs of existing staff. Typically, six or more participants are assessed as a group, but not in competition with each other.

The procedure may last from one to three days. Candidates are presented with a number of selection procedures, including at least one work simulation. This may consist of practical work samples, role plays, group exercises or in-baskets, designed to demonstrate key competences for the job in question. Other items normally include interviews and tests. Three or more trained assessors observe the simulations and conduct interviews. They take notes and rate candidates on predetermined criteria. They take it in turns to observe different applicants.

When the procedures are completed, assessors take one or more days to share observations and reach agreement on their evaluations (Byham, 1984). The final assessment for each candidate is typically presented in a summary report. This gives details of the candidate's strengths and development needs and an overall rating of his or her suitability for the job.

Roberts (1997) lists a range of advantages and disadvantages to using assessment centres. Advantages include:

- the focus on key elements of the job directly addresses the suitability of candidates for the position
- the variety of techniques and assessors gives a full and balanced picture

- they are interesting for candidates, allowing them to meet several people from the organisation
- they give candidates a flavour of the work involved, providing a realistic job preview
- there is some evidence that assessment centres are better at predicting successful candidates than other methods.

On the other hand, there are several disadvantages:

- the exercises involved can seem demeaning to some applicants, particularly at senior level
- exercises may seem too obvious, so that candidates can 'act' for the short period of time required – this might not be sustainable in a real job
- this is an expensive technique which is also very demanding on management time.

There are also issues of stereotyping and discrimination which need to be carefully watched. The selection of exercises involves a degree of prejudgement about the kind of candidate expected. Physical exercises can be overtly discriminatory against some applicants.

ACTIVITY 16

Read these list of statements. There is at least one word or phrase missing in each statement. Write in the missing word(s).

1. .... are tasks or 'mini-jobs' designed to evaluate key competences required by a particular job.
2. The variety of techniques and assessors used in an .... gives a full and balanced picture of candidate suitability.
3. .... or .... exercises, including letters to answer and reports to analyse, are often used for administrative and managerial jobs.
4. The .... is an expensive technique which is also very demanding on management time.
5. Assessment centres allow an evaluation of applicant ...., ..., ... and .... on a number of dimensions.
6. Assessment centres may include ...., ..., ... or ...., designed to demonstrate key .... for the job in question.

Here are the complete statements. *Work samples* are tasks or 'mini-jobs' designed to evaluate key competences required by a particular job. The variety of techniques and assessors used in an *assessment centre* gives a full and balanced picture of candidate suitability. *In-basket* or *in-tray* exercises, including letters to answer and reports to analyse, are often used for administrative and managerial jobs. The *assessment centre* is an expensive technique which is also very demanding on management time. Assessment centres allow an evaluation of applicant *competences*, *personality*, *motivation* and *behaviour* on a number of dimensions. Assessment centres may include *work samples*, *role plays*, *group exercises* or *in-baskets*, designed to demonstrate key *competences* for the job in question. (You could also have included *tests* and *interviews* in your answer for the last statement.)

3.3 Use of different selection methods

We have considered a range of selection methods but to what extent are they used in practice? Large organisations typically use lengthy selection processes. A survey by Capita Ras showed that 60 per cent of applicants short-listed for posts offering salaries of more than £40,000 said they had been involved in extensive selection procedures (*PM Online*, accessed March 1998). Most respondents believed the procedures made selection fairer and were keen to receive feedback. A relatively small proportion of organisations use work samples and assessment centres in their selection procedures. Table 6 compares the use of different selection methods in the top companies of the UK and France.

Method	UK companies	French companies
Application forms	93%	98%
Interviews	93%	94%
More than one interview	60%	92%
References	74%	11%
Cognitive tests	70%	50%
Handwriting	3%	77%
Biodata	19%	4%
Assessment centre	59%	19%

*Table 6: Comparison of the relative use of different
selection methods in UK and French companies
Source: Based on Shackleton and Newell (1991)*

It is interesting to note that handwriting analysis is extensively used in France, whereas it is thought to have little predictive value in the UK. However, some British employers have used graphologists.

The drug addict?
A candidate applying for a junior position in Warburg's computer department sent in an excellent CV and had two excellent interviews, seeming both able and confident. However, Warburg used handwriting analysis as part of its selection process. His handwriting sample was unusually cramped and badly squashed, with crooked lines, spidery letters. It looked like the writing of a badly educated child. The graphologist concluded on this evidence that he may have been a drug addict. He was turned down for the job (*Independent on Sunday*, 20 October 1991).

Summary

This section examined problematic issues associated with relatively advanced methods of selection. It demonstrated that the apparent objectivity of many psychometric tests is fictitious. Assessment centres and work sample simulations are expensive but comparably good predictors of job performance.

Unit summary

Selection is a topic at the heart of human resource management. No other HR activity offers the same high-profile exposure to individual error on the part of generalist or specialist people managers. Selection depends on less than satisfactory methodologies, and touches on a number of sensitive and contentious areas of human resource management, including equal opportunities, performance assessment and human resource development.

References

Amack, L O (1995) 'Discriminatory Effects of the Face-to-Face Selection Interview', *LawInfo Forum*

Barnett, D (1999) from www.barnett.co.uk website, accessed 10 August 1999

Byham, W (1984) 'Assessing employees without resorting to a "centre"', *Personnel Management*, 55 (October)

Corbridge, M and Pilbeam, S (1998) *Employment Resourcing*, Financial Times Pitman Publishing

Iles, P and Salaman, G (1995) 'Recruitment and selection' in Storey, J (ed.) *Human Resource Management: A Critical Text*, Routledge

Kinicki, A J, Lockwood, C A, Horn, P W and Griffith, R W (1990) 'Interviewer predictions of applicant qualifications and interviewer validity: aggregate and individual analyses', *Journal of Applied Psychology*, 75

Kleeman, J (1998) 'Now is the time to computerize pen and paper tests!', Question Mark Computing Ltd, 1998

Martin, J (1998) *Organisational Behaviour*, International Thomson Business Press

Pickard, J (1996) 'The wrong turns to avoid with tests', *People Management*, August

Porteous, M (1997) *Occupational Psychology*, Prentice Hall

Price, A J (1997) *Human Resource Management in a Business Context*, International Thomson Business Press

Roberts, G (1997) *Recruitment and Selection: A Competency Approach*, Institute of Personnel and Development

Smith, M (1991) 'Selection in organizations', in M Smith (ed.) *Analysing Organizational Behaviour*, Macmillan

Smith, M, Gregg, M and Andrews, R (1989) *Selection & Assessment: A New Appraisal*, Pitman

Sullivan, J (1997) *Why Employment Is a Strategic Function: the Business Impacts of a Bad Hiring Decision*, International Personnel Management Association Assessment Council

Shackleton, V and Newell, S (1991) 'Management selection: a comparative survey of methods used in top British and French companies', *Journal of Occupational Psychology*, 64 (March)

Townley, B (1989) 'Selection and appraisal: reconstituting social relations' in Storey, J (ed.) *New Perspectives on Human Resource Management*, Routledge

Webster, E C (1964) *Decision Making in the Employment Interview*, Eagle (Montreal)

Weisner, W H and Cronshaw, S F (1988) 'A meta-analytic investigation of the impact of interview format and degree of structure on the validity of the employment interview', *Journal of Occupational Psychology*, 61

Wright, M and Storey, J (1997) 'Recruitment and Selection' in Beardwell, I and Holden, L (eds) *Human Resource Management: A Contemporary Perspective*, Pitman Publishing

Recommended Reading

Most major textbooks on human resource management contain useful material on selection. Two recent texts offer more detailed reading: the book by Gareth Roberts (1997) is well-written and up-to-date but does not match references to the text; the book by Marjorie Corbridge and Stephen Pilbeam (1998) is more academic in its approach. *The Internet Guide to Human Resource Management* provides extensive links and notes in its recruitment and selection section at www.hrmguide.com.

UNIT 5
PERFORMANCE MANAGEMENT

Introduction

The term performance management dates from the same time as the Harvard model of human resource management and originates from a related source (Beer and Ruh, 1976). However, its meaning has often been unclear; the term has been used to describe performance appraisal – the top-down rating of employees by their line managers – but also to denote a more comprehensive and wide-ranging linking of individual performance to that of the whole organisation. In line with the latter approach, Armstrong and Baron (1998) define performance management as: 'a strategic and integrated approach to increasing the effectiveness of organisations by improving the performance of the people who work in them and by developing the capabilities of teams and individual contributors.'

Performance management is a key human resource management process that provides data for a range of other human resource activities. In particular, it supplies essential information for rewarding and developing employees.

Objectives

On completion of this unit you should be able to:

- explain the relationship between performance management and other people management systems
- outline the main reasons why measuring performance is not straightforward
- evaluate criticisms of performance management based on empirical research
- argue the case for making performance management a discrete area of HRM

SECTION 1
Managing Performance

Introduction

Why is performance management important? There are obvious benefits to any business if individual and team performance can be managed to achieve organisational objectives. But performance management is concerned not only with *what* is achieved but also with *how* it is achieved. Performance management plays a pivotal role in an organisation's human resource framework. Improving performance requires the effective management of continuous development, addressing 'the core competences of the organisation and the capabilities of individuals and teams' (Armstrong and Baron, 1998). Performance management has a key function in the integration of HR processes and initiatives since it provides the raw information on how well individuals and work teams are performing and developing. It follows, therefore, that performance assessment is also a measure of the effectiveness of an organisation's human resource activities.

We begin this section by discussing the reasons for assessing and managing performance. Then we consider how comprehensive performance management systems can be organised. Finally we evaluate the underlying concepts involved in performance measurement.

This section is intended to help you to:

- explain why performance is assessed and managed
- justify the creation of performance management systems
- outline the underlying concepts of performance measurement.

1.1   Performance management systems

What is the purpose of performance management? Based on a major survey of performance management practice undertaken by the Institute of Personnel and Development in the late 1990s, Armstrong and Baron (1998) argue that there are two central propositions used to justify performance management.

- First, people (as individuals or teams) will try their hardest to perform well if they 'know and understand what is expected of them' and have also been involved in specifying those expectations.
- Second, people's ability to meet performance expectations is based on their levels of capability, the level of support provided by management, and the organisation's processes and systems and the resources available to them.

In practical terms, Armstrong and Baron contend that performance management aims to:

- assist in the achievement of sustainable improvements in an organisation's overall performance
- serve as a lever for change in the development of a more performance-oriented culture
- increase employee motivation and commitment
- give individuals the means to develop competences, improve job satisfaction and reach their full potential to the benefit of individuals and organisation
- improve team spirit and performance
- offer a mechanism for regular dialogue and improved communication between individuals and their managers
- provide an outlet for individuals to express their aspirations and concerns.

It is clear from the survey that there is a considerable variation in the use and expectations of performance management between different organisations. Hendry et al. (1997) state that 'many people now believe that performance management covers a raft of cultural, communications and development issues, which may or may not lend themselves to measurement. It can mean different things to different organisations, or even to different groups within the same enterprise.'

Gallup workplace audit statements

Gallup Selection has developed a package designed to monitor employee satisfaction and provide the basis for a performance management system. Employees are asked to rate on a scale of 1–5 the extent to which their experience is reflected in these 12 statements.

1. I know what is expected of me at work.
2. I have the materials and equipment I need to do my work right.
3. At work I have the opportunity to do what I do best every day.
4. In the last seven days I have received recognition or praise for good work.
5. My supervisor or someone at work seems to care about me as a person.
6. There is someone at work who encourages my development.
7. In the last six months, someone at work has talked to me about my progress.
8. At work, my opinions seem to count.
9. The mission/purpose of my company makes me feel my job is important.
10. My associates (fellow employees) are committed to doing quality work.
11. I have a best friend at work.
12. This last year, I have had opportunities at work to learn and grow.

Positive responses were found to correlate with employee loyalty and commitment. For example, a chain of electrical superstores found that responses from staff at the 25 best-performing branches were significantly more favourable than elsewhere in the organisation.

In addition, organisations with high employee ratings were said to significantly outperform rivals on customer satisfaction (by 38 per cent), profitability (27 per cent), employee retention (22 per cent) and 'hard' productivity measures (22 per cent). Perhaps the positive employee ratings cause the better business performance. On the other hand, it may be that employees in the better performing units are generally more satisfied with their work, and this is reflected in their responses to the questionnaire. Further research is needed to address this question and to assess long-term impact on profitability.

Gallup has developed a training system to enable effective middle managers to respond appropriately to the results of surveys among their staff. It is hoped that this will improve both employee performance and also develop the managers' own potential.

Source: Adapted from Caulkin (1998)

ACTIVITY 1

Reread the preceding section and reflect on Armstrong and Baron's views on the purpose of performance management. To what extent does each statement in Gallup's workplace audit reflect Armstrong and Baron's two central propositions? Make comments about the relevance of each of the 12 Gallup statements to Armstrong and Baron's propositions.

Table 1 sets out our assessment of the relevance of the Gallup statements to Armstrong and Baron's propositions. You may have come to similar conclusions. In general, it seems that the audit statements are a better measure of the second than the first proposition.

Statement	Proposition 1	Proposition 2
1. I know what is expected of me at work	Matches closely	Not directly relevant
2. I have the materials and equipment I need to do my work right	Not directly relevant	Matches closely – resources
3. At work I have the opportunity to do what I do best every day	Relevant to the proposition	Not directly relevant
4. In the last seven days I have received recognition or praise for good work	Not directly relevant	Matches closely – support
5. My supervisor or someone at work seems to care about me as a person	Relevant to the proposition	Matches closely – support
6. There is someone at work who encourages my development	Relevant to the proposition	Matches closely – support
7. In the last six months, someone at work has talked to me about my progress	Matches closely	Matches closely – support
8. At work, my opinions seem to count	Matches closely	Not directly relevant
9. The mission /purpose of my company makes me feel my job is important	Not directly relevant	Relevant to the proposition
10. My associates (fellow employees) are committed to doing quality work	Not directly relevant	Relevant to the proposition
11. I have a best friend at work	Not directly relevant	Relevant to the proposition
12. This last year, I have had opportunities at work to learn and grow	Relevant to the proposition	Possibly relevant

Table 1: Relevance of Gallup audit statements to Armstrong and Baron's propositions used to justify performance management

PERFORMANCE MANAGEMENT AS A PROCESS

From the process perspective, modern performance management is a strategic process incorporating performance assessment (or appraisal). Such a process could include the following stages (Corbridge and Pilbeam, 1998):

- define organisational goals
- set individual or team objectives
- agree training and development plans
- conduct performance appraisal
- provide regular feedback
- allocate rewards
- develop individual career plans.

But, in every case, effective performance management requires an organisation to do three things well (Cascio, 1996):

- define the characteristics of good – as opposed to average or bad – performance
- facilitate (help) employees to perform well by removing obstacles
- encourage performance through reward, praise or promotion.

Performance management can be critically important to organisational effectiveness, but it is also of major significance to employees if there is a direct link between their performance and their pay or career progression. Of late there has been a move to distance pay from performance management but where performance-related pay exists, a valid connection between employee performance and employee pay must be established (Armstrong and Baron, 1998). Consequently, the definition and measurement of good performance can be controversial topics.

Business strategists have been slow to develop an interest in the motivation and performance of employees despite the often-quoted mantra that 'people are our greatest assets'. However, integrated performance systems have appeared in some organisations. Bevan and Thompson (1991) describe a model performance management system as follows:

- the organisation has a shared vision of its objectives or a mission statement that is communicated to its employees
- there are individual and departmental performance management targets, related to unit and wider organisational objectives
- there is a regular formal review of progress towards achieving the targets
- there is a review process that identifies training, development and reward outcomes
- the whole system is itself evaluated – feeding back changes and improvements.

Such a system embodies three central features:

- an objective-setting process which defines performance goals in the form of measurable outputs, accountabilities and training/learning targets
- a formal assessment system which communicates regularly set performance requirements
- links between performance requirements and pay – particularly for senior managers.

The intention is that the performance management system should be owned and implemented by line managers. Human resource specialists provide an internal consultancy, helping and advising line managers to develop the system.

British research has indicated that most large organisations have some form of performance management process but comparatively few have an integrated and formal system of this kind (IRS, 1998). There remains an inconsistency in approach towards performance management and different interpretations of the concept. Bevan and Thompson (1991) found two contradictory themes.

- **Reward-driven integration**. Emphasising performance-related pay (PRP) with a consequent undervaluing of any other human resource activities, especially human resource development.
- **Development-driven integration**. Human resource development activities directed at long-term objectives.

It seems that reward-driven integration was dominant in the UK, reinforcing the prevalent cash flow driven, short-term orientation of British organisations. However, during the 1990s there was a shift in the direction of development-driven integration (IDS, 1997; Armstrong and Baron, 1998).

Bevan and Thompson are not the only authors to outline a model performance management system, Another approach is described by English (1991). He suggests that a rational performance management system should have the following characteristics:

- a clear statement of what is to be achieved by the organisation
- individual and group responsibilities which support the organisation's goals
- all performance to be measured and assessed in terms of these responsibilities and goals
- all rewards based on employee performance
- organisational structure, processes, resources and authority systems designed to optimise the performance of all employees
- an ongoing effort to create and guide appropriate organisational goals and to seek newer, more appropriate goals.

To achieve such a system, English (1991) advocated a need for agreement among all critical parties on what is to be performed. Cascaded objectives from the top should be plotted on a control system so that all staff are working in the same direction and nothing is overlooked. There also needs to be an effective way to measure desired performance – 360-degree feedback (which is discussed later in this unit) may be the most appropriate solution.

Other conditions needed to achieve English's rational system include:

- a reward system tied directly to performance
- an environment conducive to successful performance
- a communication programme to gain understanding, acceptance and commitment to the system
- creation of a performance-based organisational culture.

ACTIVITY 2

Compare and contrast the account of the approach taken by English with the model outlined by Bevan and Thompson in this section. In what ways do they differ? Try to pick out three main differences.

There is a considerable overlap between the two approaches but they differ in terms of emphasis and precision. You may have concluded that the approach taken by English is more prescriptive (do it like this ...) than that taken by Bevan and Thompson. There is a also a much stronger emphasis on rating, measurement and integrated objectives within English's model. A further difference is that Bevan and Thompson distinguish two distinct emphases within different performance management systems: one focused on performance-related pay, the other on development. English does not draw a distinction between these two orientations.

1.2   Foundations of performance assessment

Townley (1994) argues that performance assessment is one of several HR techniques which 'classify and order individuals hierarchically'. In other words, it is intended to rate employees on supposedly objective criteria or standards that determine good performance. Behind this statement we find problems in defining 'good' performance and making distinctions between the effective and the ineffective. For example, Bates and Holton (1995) contend that performance is 'a multi-dimensional construct, the measurement of which varies, depending on a variety of factors'. So the measurement of performance can vary according to (Armstrong and Baron, 1998):

- personal factors – the skills, competence, motivation and commitment shown by an individual
- leadership factors – the support, guidance and encouragement given by managers, supervisors and team leaders
- systems factors – the information technology, administrative and communication systems, and other facilities provided by the work organisation
- situational factors – pressures and changes within the organisation's internal and external environment including market and economic developments, career opportunities.

Later in this section, we see that traditional appraisals rated individuals on psychological features or 'traits' which embraced work-related attitudes and personality characteristics (Chell, 1992). They tended to ignore situational and systems factors. Modern performance management is more likely to relate these to competences (which also are seen to be conceptually problematic under close examination) and the circumstances in which individuals must work.

Traditionally, performance assessments of employees and managers have been treated differently. Employee assessments have emphasised a variety of psychological characteristics considered to be essential for good performance; management ratings, on the other hand, have focused on results. Murphy and Cleveland (1995) see this dichotomy as reflecting the two main groups into which performance data can be categorised:

- judgmental or subjective measures
- non-judgmental or objective measures.

The distinction between the two types of measure has become increasingly blurred as new forms of assessment have been introduced, such as those based on competences, objectives and 360-degree feedback (which is discussed later in this unit).

Performance assessment has probably existed in one form or another since people were first organised into working groups. But a significant tradition derives from the scientific management approach of FW Taylor and his followers, which dates from the beginning of the twentieth century. Formal rating scales first appeared in the American military and then found their way into industry, particularly from the 1950s onwards (Armstrong and Baron, 1998). Variously described as merit-rating or performance appraisal, these systems depended on subjective judgements of various factors. For example, managers could be asked to judge their staff on questions such as:

Rate 'attitude to work' on a 1–5 scale, with a paragraph of comments.

In essence, such measures were based on an evaluation of psychological traits: supposedly consistent features or patterns of behaviour demonstrated by an individual over time. As a result, trait-based assessments or appraisals often took the form of barely disguised personality tests.

Does effective work performance depend on personality characteristics alone? If you recall the wide range of factors affecting performance described by Armstrong and Baron, it is apparent that the answer is no. Certainly, some aspects of individual personality may be highly relevant to the performance of a specific job – for example, sales people must demonstrate a friendly disposition towards clients. But other factors can be equally important. Sales people, regardless of basic personality, are more likely to be friendly if they are happy in their work and motivated to do well.

But, assuming that personality characteristics are at least partly significant, is it possible to rate them accurately or objectively? On the basis of a review of research findings, Murphy and Cleveland (1995) drew four conclusions.

- Appraisers make 'global evaluative judgements' in almost every context and that attempts to prevent this are likely to be fruitless. In other words, appraisers tend to make sweeping judgements about appraisees based on very limited evidence.

- Appraisers are prone to a wide variety of biases – mostly unconscious.

- More people are given above average than below average ratings. In statistical terms, this means that assessments are skewed towards the positive. Murphy and Cleveland attribute this **rater inflation** to the close working relationships which often develop between managers and their staff. This bonding leads to bias in the way that employees are assessed – favoured employees will be assessed generously. Rater inflation is most common when managers assess staff that they have personally selected or promoted.

- Appraisers rate appraisees partly on their own implicit theories about people. In other words, they have notions about what makes people tick that over-ride their observations of the way that people have actually behaved.

Another reason that managers tend to make higher ratings is their awareness of organisation politics. Price (1997) suggests three 'political' factors which encourage high ratings.

- **Preserving morale**. People like being praised. Positive performance assessment is normally taken as a compliment – whether or not the employee deserves it. It gives managers the chance to develop a comfortable working atmosphere and boost morale.

- **Avoiding confrontation**. Negative assessments have the opposite effect. Managers may choose not to risk upsetting employees.

- **Management image**. Managers with poorly-rated staff may be suspected of being in charge of a badly-run department. They run the risk of receiving equally poor personal performance assessments from their own superiors. Conversely, the presence of highly-rated staff members gives the impression of an efficient department.

Attempts have been made to prevent rater bias by using assessment criteria that are more directly work-based. This introduces its own range of problems. For example, should we include factors such as 'knowledge, potential and overall worth' and, if so, what weighting should be attached to any of these attributes (Townley, 1994).

Not all managers tend towards above average ratings. Perhaps paradoxically, people who rise through the ranks are likely to demand unrealistically high levels of performance from their staff. Murphy and Cleveland (1995) argue that this is due to a distorted view of their own past performance – they remember the successes and forget any poor quality work.

Organisational success also influences the conduct of performance management. Assessors (and those being appraised) may vary their standards depending on their perception of the organisation's overall performance, their career prospects and, consequently, their feelings of security and optimism. The emotional background to assessment can be directly affected by the prevailing culture of the organisation. Arguably, attempts to develop a strong, cohesive culture encourage a closer agreement between raters on the standards they expect.

Delayering and downsizing have had the effect of increasing the ratio of staff to managers throughout the Western business world. As a consequence, managers have a greater number of assessments to conduct on people they know less about. Widespread structural changes in large organisations also bring new combinations of people together with little knowledge of each other – but, perhaps, fewer long-standing prejudices.

ACTIVITY 3

Based on the evidence we have presented on performance assessment, which of these statements are more likely to be true than false and which more false than true?

1. Traits are relatively permanent features of an individual's personality.

2. Supervisors appraise their staff purely on their performance during the appraisal period.

3. Rater bias is due to the personal likes and dislikes of appraisers.

4. Rater inflation is a tendency to increase the rating of preferred individuals.

5. It is best for appraisers to avoid negative assessments.

6. Managers who work their way up the promotion ladder tend to be kinder appraisers than those recruited from outside an organisation because they understand the specific problems of the business.

7. Performance assessments are a relatively new feature of working life.

Traits are relatively permanent features of an individual's personality. True – this is a definition of traits. However there is some disagreement between psychologists on the degree of permanence (or even existence) of traits.

Supervisors appraise their staff purely on their performance during the appraisal period. False – the intention is that they should confine themselves to actual behaviour and effort in the appraisal period but frequently their judgements go beyond these constraints. In practice, raters tend to widen the grounds for their judgements to include an appraisee's earlier or later behaviour and incorporate their own psychological interpretations which may well be completely irrelevant.

Rater bias is due to the personal likes and dislikes of appraisers. Partly true, but many other factors are also involved including the personality of the rater and office politics.

Rater inflation is a tendency to increase the rating of preferred individuals. Arguably true, but in fact Murphy and Cleveland found that there is a tendency for appraisals as a whole to be skewed towards the positive. One reason may be that raters are reluctant to criticise. Another is the desire to avoid the impression of running a poor team or department.

It is best for appraisers to avoid negative assessments. False – but there are often compelling reasons why raters tend to avoid negative assessments in line with the comment on rater inflation.

Managers who work their way up the promotion ladder tend to be kinder appraisers than those recruited from outside an organisation because they understand the specific problems of the business. False – it appears from Murphy and Cleveland's review that insiders tend to be tougher on their staff.

Performance assessments are a relatively new feature of working life. False – they have been in place for decades.

1.3   Performance objectives

An alternative approach is to focus on the goals which an individual needs to achieve rather than the employee's psychological characteristics. Here, in contrast to the trait-perspective, the emphasis is on the results attained by the employee rather than the manner of working. The long-standing approach of management by objectives (MBO) is one such technique aimed at tying performance ratings to unambiguous, measurable and relevant personal objectives (Drucker, 1954). In fact, as Murphy and Cleveland (1995) point out, MBO systems are not based solely on objective measures because setting goals, targets and objectives is a subjective process, often renegotiated during the assessment period. In this section we first look at how management by objectives should operate in theory. We then present the views of critics who argue that the system does not work so well in practice.

Theoretically, the process starts at the top of the organisation with senior managers agreeing their own set of individual objectives based on the strategic goals of the business. Each manager has objectives that are relevant to their area of responsibility and cascades them in the same way to subordinates. Employees at each level take on personal targets and goals over which they have direct control but all objectives are interlocked and contribute to overall business strategy.

Management by objectives has four essential stages:

- goal setting
- action planning
- self control
- periodic review.

Goal setting

Goal setting is central to the process of managing by objectives. Goals must be specific, targeted, verifiable and required, and they must be attained in an agreed period of time. Their achievement should indicate real progress. Goals must be:

- **challenging**, stretching beyond comfortable performance
- **attainable**, being feasible, realistic, and cost-effective
- **measurable**, specific, quantifiable and verifiable – they are best expressed in a form which includes numerical targets such as 'reduce complaints by 5 per cent'
- **relevant**, directly related both to the employee's work and to business goals.

Action planning

Individuals need to work out how they will achieve their objectives, asking questions such as what, who, when, where, and how a goal can be attained.

Self control

Employees are given an active role in setting their own objectives and action plans. Management by objectives can be an empowering process that encourages commitment to the business. But continuous feedback is required so that staff can control progress towards achieving objectives.

Periodic review

Progress towards goals needs to be reviewed regularly so that individuals and their managers are certain that they are on, rather than off, target. This requires a coaching approach from managers who should help to remove obstacles in the way of achieving the goals.

The thinking behind management by objectives has been absorbed into modern performance management, with a greater emphasis on team, as opposed to individual, goals. Cascio (1996) argues that setting specific, challenging goals tells everyone what is expected from them and inevitably leads to higher levels of performance. In fact, Cascio contends that goal-setting of itself leads to an average productivity improvement of 10 per cent. According to Cascio, this is achieved by:

- directing attention to the specific performance required to achieve, say, an additional 5 per cent measured customer satisfaction
- mobilising necessary effort to achieve higher performance standards
- fostering a persistent attitude about higher performance standards.

However, as we will discover in the next section, goal attainment must be measured accurately and consistently to achieve these benefits.

ACTIVITY 4

The direct labour operation servicing Bonnypark District Council has appointed a new supervisor within its Parks and Roads department. Five key objectives have been agreed for this year. Your task is to choose the most appropriate measure from the three alternatives provided for each objective.

Objective 1: Expenses for contracted services will be held to previous levels.

Suggested measure:

(a) 100% of budget for road maintenance to be spent
(b) expenditure kept to minimum
(c) increase expenditure by no more than 0% on the previous year

Objective 2: To provide the lighting in parks necessary for security and safety.

Suggested measure:

(a) Bright light in 80% of park areas
(b) 20 lights to be installed or maintained for every 10 acres of park
(c) No more than 10 upheld complaints from residents about park lighting during period

Objective 3: To meet the council five-year plan for road maintenance.

Suggested measure:

(a) 10 miles of streets in urban area to be resurfaced
(b) 100% of budget for road maintenance to be spent
(c) No more than 10 upheld complaints from residents about road maintenance during period

Objective 4: Provide an improved level of satisfaction amongst residents regarding pavements.

Suggested measure:

(a) 2.3 miles of pavements in urban area to be checked and replaced where necessary
(b) 100% of budget for pavement maintenance to be spent
(c) No more than 10 upheld complaints from residents about pavement condition during the period

Objective 5: Keep senior management informed promptly of developments.

Suggested measure:

(a) Arrange regular meetings with senior managers
(b) Complete monthly reports as soon as possible after the end of each month
(c) Monthly reports to be completed and submitted by twelfth of following month

---

The most appropriate measure for objective 1 is choice (c). This measure is precise – and it is taxing because, taking inflation into account, it involves a small reduction in real terms on the previous year. Alternative (a) is not taxing the individual and alternative (b) is vague.

For objective 2, we suggest choice (b). Alternative (a) may seem precise but, in fact, it is subjective – what is 'bright' light? Alternative (c) is not relevant because residents may not be aware of security and safety problems.

The most appropriate measure for objective 3 is choice (a). Again, this is a precise measure. Spending the budget – alternative (b) – does not specify an outcome; alternative (c) is irrelevant to the wording of the objective.

Choice (c) is appropriate for objective 4. The objective is all about residents' satisfaction. The other two alternatives do not measure this directly.

For objective 5, use measure (c). Both the other alternatives are imprecise.

This activity should have given you a clear idea of the nature of objectives within management by objectives. They need to be precise (preferably with a number, percentage or date included), measurable and reasonably stretching.

At this point we will move on to a discussion on the difficulties experienced with the MBO approach.

CRITICISMS OF MANAGEMENT BY OBJECTIVES

Armstrong and Baron (1998) describe management by objectives as being 'now discredited'. Why should this be the case? Perhaps the most common criticisms of management by objectives have been those directed at the paperwork involved and the administrative burden that the process places on small organisations. Fowler (1990) also specifically attacked the artificial and managerially obsessed nature of MBO, which seemed to most employees to be an imposition from on high bearing little relevance to their work. More systematically, the concept was criticised at an early stage by Levinson (1970) on grounds that remain valid today.

- Most people work within a social system. Even the best performer may fail to achieve objectives because of the (in)action of colleagues, subordinates or managers.

- Formal MBO systems emphasised measurement and quantification. But most jobs have subtle, informal aspects that could be neglected in the pursuit of measured objectives. For example, good customer service may involve spending time with customers that will not necessarily result in an immediate sale. This could be regarded as 'wasted' in terms of achieving objectives. An overly quantitative MBO system might allocate strict time limits for individual transactions. This would be counter-productive for the organisation, however, since it is likely that future sales would diminish as a consequence.

- The MBO system defines objectives as organisational, but most people work to further their own personal objectives. If there is no clear link between the two, the MBO process is unlikely to be a motivator for effective performance.

ACTIVITY 5

What do you consider to be the three greatest strengths and, conversely, the three greatest weaknesses of management by objectives as a method for assessing performance. Jot down your reasons for each choice. Write about 10–20 words in each case.

Management by objectives is comparatively objective in that – unlike trait-based systems – it depends on precisely defined targets which can be measured unambiguously. Another strength is that objectives must be work-related and important to the conduct of the job; it is not based on possibly irrelevant aspects of personality or behaviour. Additionally, the cascading nature of objectives means that they are tied to strategic business goals from the top down.

In terms of weaknesses, you could have made the observation that management by objectives has often proved to be a top-down or, at least, managerially inspired process which imposes a simplistic set of objectives on people at the bottom of the hierarchy. A further weakness is that this can result in objectives which 'miss the point' of the job – in other words, they do not reflect the complexities or subtleties which are particularly relevant in customer-facing jobs. Also, objectives derived from organisational goals may not connect well with individual aspirations and hence do not motivate good performance.

Summary

The assessment and management of performance is a key function of human resource management. Several theorists have advocated a systematic approach which links performance management to other elements of HRM. A variety of approaches can be taken towards performance assessment, based on either psychological or organisational criteria. Traditional trait-based methods are liable to bias and inflated ratings from supervisors. A longstanding alternative is the use of management by objectives. But this method also has deficiencies, which we shall consider next, particularly in respect of the organisational context of performance.

SECTION 2
Measuring Performance

Introduction

Performance assessment is the nearest we have to a scientific system of measurement in human resource management, since it is aimed at evaluating individual effectiveness and commitment and linking employee performance to business objectives. In the resourcing process we try to predict the performance of new recruits: performance management tells us if we were right or wrong. As another illustration, change initiatives may attempt to develop a creative corporate culture, increase commitment or increase the efficiency of work systems: performance management confirms the success or failure of these initiatives.

However, devising and implementing a meaningful system of measurement may be problematic. According to Armstrong and Baron (1998) 'what gets measured is often what is easy to measure. And, in some jobs, what is meaningful is not measurable, and what is measurable is not meaningful.'

Performance management is concerned with measurement at different levels. It encompasses:

- organisational measures, which can be internal or benchmarked against the performance of industry competitors

- team performance measures, for example quality standards, team output and productivity

- individual measures including both traditional appraisals, where employees' immediate line managers complete appraisal forms, and self-assessment, where individuals assess themselves against rating criteria or agreed personal objectives

- peer assessment, in which team members and colleagues provide assessments

- upward appraisal, where managers are appraised by their staff

- 360-degree feedback, in which the appraisal process includes anyone with direct knowledge of an individual's work such as peers, direct reports, managers and internal customers.

We begin this section with a discussion on organisational and team measurement. Then we consider the respective merits and drawbacks of methods used for individual assessment. In particular, we identify the practicalities and difficulties of each form in relation to the overall purpose of performance management.

This section is intended to help you to:

- outline the range of assessment methods available to modern organisations

- evaluate the advantages and disadvantages of a number of significant methodologies

- explain the terminology of performance assessment.

2.1   Traditional appraisals

'Appraisal is seen as essentially an exercise in personal power. It elevates the role of the supervisor by emphasising individualism and obscuring the social nature of work.'

Storey (1989)

In many organisations, performance management is equated with a rating system known traditionally as appraisal. Despite a revised perspective which treats performance management as a wide-ranging process, many line managers still equate performance management with annual appraisals and their negative aspects (Hendry et al., 1997). Appraisals, often disliked by both employees and managers, generally involve a formal annual exercise based on form-filling and counselling interviews (Armstrong and Baron, 1998). The HR function is charged with organising the paper distribution and then policing the process, coercing often unwilling participants into completing the forms and conducting one-to-one confrontations with appraisees about their judgements.

In most cases, the person conducting the appraisal is the immediate supervisor or line manager. This assessment is countersigned by his or her manager, perhaps with further comments. This is a paternalistic method sometimes known as the 'father and grandfather' system. Despite the range of alternative methods now available, 90 per cent of organisations continue to use the traditional top-down method although there is less emphasis on rating and formality than was the case a decade ago (IDS, 1997).

Few managers who complete appraisal forms are trained psychologists, but they are expected to make fine judgements on personality traits and personal qualities. There are innumerable variations in methodology but, in the traditional model, many appraisal forms asked for a numerical rating on a scale of 1 (excellent) to 5 or 7 (appalling). Instead, or in addition, a supplementary written comment might be requested. This takes the form of a carefully – or indifferently – crafted paragraph of criticism or praise. The rating element is particularly disliked and some organisations have eliminated formal rating from their appraisals (Armstrong and Baron, 1998).

Finally, in the traditional model, there is an obligatory overall judgement on the individual's suitability for promotion and a summary of any development or training needs. This may be followed by the appraisee's own comments and further remarks by the appraising supervisor's own manager. Completed forms are duly signed by all contributors and become part of the organisation's human resource records. They may reappear as evidence at promotion boards, training courses and management development programmes.

Today, most appraisal forms are shown to employees, who often have the option of adding their own remarks if they disagree with any aspect of the manager's assessment. As we see later in this unit, modern performance management systems emphasise dialogue rather than assessment. However, the traditional form was arguably designed to achieve behavioural consistency (Townley, 1994) – that is to say, conformity with the standards, norms or image required by the person completing the assessment. Although to a degree this might coincide with the organisation's overall aims, this approach is inconsistent with a more modern emphasis on individuality, flexibility and creativity.

The traditional process is reinforced at the appraisal or counselling interview. Cascio (1996) observes that employees often react to appraisal interviews in negative ways:

- often employees are less certain about their standing in the organisation after the appraisal interview than they were before it

- employees tend to regard their line managers less favourably after the interview than before it

- staff members make few constructive changes in their working behaviour after appraisal interviews.

Cascio concludes that the paternalistic 'tell and sell' approach which characterises so many appraisal interviews is incompatible with the concept of employee empowerment. (We discuss alternative ways of delivering performance feedback later in this unit.)

Fairness, judgement and interpretation of results and behaviour are key issues of performance management. Serious efforts have been made to deal with its deficiencies including:

- detailed measurement of behaviour

- results-based systems

- process assessment.

One popular approach to the detailed measurement of behaviour is **behaviourally anchored rating scales** (BARS). Comparatively inexpensive to maintain, this approach requires job 'experts' to develop rating scales based on real-life behaviour analysed by the critical incidents methodology. The rating scales force appraising managers to make relatively objective judgements, placing individual behaviour in the context of the business as a whole, rather than on personality traits. This approach is unsuitable for situations where new technology or procedural changes require frequent updating of scales.

Another popular technique is **behavioural observation scales** (BOS). Similar in construction to BARS, in this approach assessors list the frequency of occurrence of specific behaviours within a defined period rather than making comparative judgements of better or worse performance.

The **results-based** methods are an extension of goal-based systems such as management by objectives from top management to lower level employees. In such systems, staff are assessed on their personal or team achievements, expressed as clear performance targets. For example, a production team may be given the objective of reducing defects by 20 per cent in a year. How they do this is not the subject of assessment. Of course, objectives are more difficult to define for some jobs, especially those which are people-related.

Process assessment is a different approach which emphasises how goals are achieved. This approach often focuses on compliance with quality procedures or levels of service. It is more in tune with the views of advocates of integrated performance management systems such as Armstrong and Baron.

ACTIVITY 6

A vacancy has occurred in head office for a high-flyer. The marketing, research, accounts and production departments each have people well qualified for the job and, it appears, these candidates are of nearly equal merit. As a step in the selection process, managers of these different departments have been asked to carry out appraisals on the candidates. Head office will use these appraisals to draw up its short list.

Explain any doubts you have about the validity and fairness of this approach.

The motives of the appraisers are important. There might be a benefit to a manager having an ex-subordinate in head office, where he or she might act as a contact, source of information, or influence. So there might be a bias to score departmental members favourably. (You may also think of reasons for an unfavourable bias.)

Even if the different managers conducting the appraisals are scrupulously honest, they might unconsciously be using different scales. For example, Mrs Affable of marketing rates most people as 8, reserving 5 for weak employees. Whereas, Mr Stringent from accounts is stingy with each grade, and marks the average as 5. With few candidates there is no statistical process so that can even out this potential bias in the grading process.

If the appraisals require assessment of such factors as communication, leadership, sense of humour, strategic orientation (as many do), it is common for different raters to interpret these words in different ways; so they are actually rating the candidates on different traits and therefore not providing fair comparisons.

Candidates who don't succeed may feel that their managers did not do their best for them, and this might create resentment that lasts long after the appointment. The process also reinforces the hierarchical nature of the organisation. A candidate's immediate boss intervenes in the selection process, in a way he or she would not do with an application for an outside job.

The skills required at head office are unlikely to be precisely those required by employees in either marketing, accounts, production or research. So it is possible that even if the appraisal process is unbiased, candidates' current jobs might not provide sufficient evidence to score key competences needed for the new job.

It is quite likely that you have additional doubts; but these should be enough to cause you to question the process. What better way could be devised? Perhaps a more precise focus on the competences – the skills and qualities – required by head office would be an improvement. We turn now to consider this approach to appraisal.

2.2   Competence approaches

Recently there has been a marked trend towards performance management systems that assess performance in terms of competences. **Competences** are behavioural constructs or dimensions of desirable abilities.

Job analyses or job descriptions generally produce large numbers of tasks as components of individual jobs. It is difficult to measure performance and train people for large numbers of tasks, but comparatively simple to do so for a relatively small number of competences. On analysis, we may find that many of the tasks within a specific job are inter-related, requiring common skills or behaviours. As a result it is possible to put tasks into groups requiring one or a few core skills. These are competences. A particular job may involve 50 to 100 tasks, but the position can be described more simply if the necessary skill, knowledge and behaviours can be expressed in terms of 5 to 20 core skills or competences.

A university lecturer, for example, needs to be able to explain complex concepts in tutorials, deliver lectures, and justify research funding at academic meetings. These are different tasks but they all require skill in verbal communication. This is a competence required for the job of lecturer. Similarly, an electrician must be able to strip off the correct amount of cable, cut the exposed wire to the correct length, inset socket boxes into the wall at the correct depth, place switches at the same heights, support wires at correct intervals and so on. Each of these activities requires the competence of 'uses a (tape) measure accurately'.

Competence is a critical variable for the achievement of both individual and organisational success. It implies either an immediate or potential capability to reach a high standard of performance. As human resource strategy becomes more influential, performance management is more closely integrated with overall business performance. Strategists emphasise the core competences of organisations which are made up of the individual competences of its staff. As with management by objectives, competence requirements and goals can be cascaded from the top so that all employees are performing in an integrated fashion. (You may find in your reading that some writers use the term 'competency' instead of 'competence' as a label applied to the desired organisational attributes.)

Boyatzis (1982) elaborates the concept of competence as 'an underlying characteristic of a person which results in effective and/or superior performance in a job'. He considers that a competence may be a:

- **trait** – a characteristic or personal quality of the individual, such as self-confidence

- **motive** – a drive or need related to a particular goal which causes the individual to strive for improvement, such as a higher salary

- **skill** – such as the ability to influence others

- **self-image** – the perception of oneself and where one stands in relation to others, such as a belief in one's creativity

- **social role** – the perception of norms and social behaviour which are expected or admissible
- **body of knowledge**.

This framework covers a wide range of possibilities, some of which are relatively fixed (traits) and others which may be developed (knowledge and skill). Boyatzis further divides competences into types and levels. In his framework, types are geared to behaviour requirements so that 'leadership', for example, is associated with conceptualisation, self-confidence and oral presentation. In practice, most organisations have attempted to define competences in more tangible terms.

The methodology does not take account of the origins of a particular 'behaviour'. Competence-based performance measurement focuses on having and attaining high levels of appropriate competences for specific roles. Although psychological in nature, competences are more closely job-related than traditional trait-based criteria. As such, they may not be quite as prone to subjective assessment and personal bias. However, competence is a construct which many psychologists find difficult to accept since individual competences can consist of a mixture of learned and inherited qualities. Some organisations, such as ICL and HSBC have adopted capability as a more meaningful term. Many other organisations seem to be defining competences which are little different to old-fashioned psychological traits (Armstrong and Baron, 1998). To this extent, they suffer the same conceptual and measurement problems as those discussed earlier in this unit.

The ambiguity and complexity of the concept has led Collin to raise some controversial questions (cited in Armstrong and Baron, 1998).

- How can discrete competences be identified? Can they be distinguished from their contexts and inter-relationships and the tacit knowledge they hold?
- Are there generic competences which are common to a range of jobs?
- If competences are identified, are they the most important features of a job?
- Can competences be measured? If so, against which criteria?

In practice, a variety of approaches have been taken to deal with the difficulties exposed by such questions. For example, Armstrong and Baron (1998) contend that competences can be analysed by addressing these points.

- First, what are the elements of the job – the main tasks or key result areas?
- Second, what is an acceptable standard of performance for each element?
- Third, which skills and what knowledge does a job-holder need to possess to be fully capable in each job element – and at what level?

- Fourth, how will they or their managers know that they have achieved the required levels of competence?

Determining a set of competences appropriate to a particular job requires knowledge not only of essential skills and abilities but also of an organisation's strategic objectives and the culture within which they can be achieved. Typically, this information is gathered through interviews and questionnaires conducted with people performing or managing similar jobs, often in workshops dedicated to the purpose. The group can focus on three main topics (Armstrong and Baron, 1998).

- What are the most important things that you have to be capable of doing in the job?
- In each part of the job, what do you need to do to perform well?
- How do you know that you are doing the job well?

Data from the job analysis or collection exercise is first analysed and grouped as clusters of behaviours. Each cluster represents a competence and is given a title. The title is not important but it is essential that there is a logical relationship between the behaviours which form a competence. For example, two analysts may respectively use the terms 'problem-solving' and 'decision-making' for the same set of behaviours.

Human resource specialists

Zeneca identified these competences as being necessary for human resource specialists in its International Personnel and Training Group.

Conceptual thinking	Concern for standards
Strategic thinking	Concern for impact
Adaptability (cultural)	Strategic influencing
Flexibility	Results orientation
	Development orientation

Consultants in the field use a range of methods to prepare competence lists, some of which are used on an off-the-shelf basis for common types of jobs. The concept of competence will be further discussed in respect of vocational qualifications in the unit on human resource development.

ACTIVITY 7

Use Boyatzis' classic typology to indicate the nature of each of the key competences identified by Zeneca as being necessary for its human resource specialists. In other words, which of the following terms best describes each competence: trait, motive, skill, self-image, social role, body of knowledge. Use the table below to jot down your choice, or use a separate piece of paper.

Competence	Type
Conceptual thinking	
Strategic thinking	
Adaptability (cultural)	
Flexibility	
Concern for standards	
Concern for impact	
Strategic influencing	
Results orientation	
Development orientation	

There are different ways of interpreting these competences. You may agree with our classification on most of them:

- conceptual thinking – skill
- strategic thinking – skill
- adaptability (cultural) – trait, also self-image and social role
- flexibility – trait
- concern for standards – motive
- concern for impact – motive, social role, self-image
- strategic influencing – skill, social role and self-image
- results orientation – trait, motive
- development orientation – trait, motive, social role.

As you can see, some competences are (or can be regarded as) a mixture of two or more categories. Also, it is not necessary for all of Boyatzis' types to be represented in the competences for a particular job.

2.3 Assessing organisations and teams

Despite the great emphasis on teams in modern management thinking, few organisations seem to have developed methods for assessing team performance (Armstrong and Baron, 1998). Armstrong and Baron identify several factors that can affect team performance:

- clarity of team goals expressed as expectations and priorities
- the way in which work is allocated to a team
- dynamics of team processes – cohesion, ability to deal with internal pressure and conflict, and relationships with other teams
- a team's ability to manage itself in terms of setting targets and priorities and monitoring its own performance
- quality of leadership to set direction of the team
- skills of individual team members, including multi-skilling
- systems and resources provided to support a team.

It may be that the great value attached to teamwork does not suffer close examination. Purcell et al. (IPD, 1998) found that productivity is improved by teamwork, but participation and the quality of working life may actually be reduced. They attributed the latter finding partly to the increased pressure in teams to achieve stringent performance targets and also to oppressively close monitoring of individuals and groups. This has been described by Garrahan and Stewart (1992) as management by stress, further intensified by individual workers watching and criticising each other.

Belbin (1993) considers that the effectiveness of a team depends on a balanced mix of competences and temperaments. Optimum performance is only achieved by selecting individuals who are capable of performing a full set of team roles.

ACTIVITY 8

Read the article *Out of the tick box* (see Resource 6 in the Resources section). This gives more details about a programme of research by the Institute of Personnel and Development which found considerable changes in the practice of performance management over the previous decade. Write down the three most significant changes you can identify in this article. Justify the reasons for your choices in about 100–150 words.

You may have observed that the survey indicated a trend towards less simplistic measures of performance, moving away from ticking rating boxes on standardised forms towards dialogue focused on development. This is in line with a trend away from the practice of using appraisal as a top-down imposition by the organisation upon individual employees. Equally, there seems to be a reduction in the formal, bureaucratic aspect of the process. Instead, performance management is becoming more of a participatory process in which individuals take an active part in their own assessments. You could also have identified a tendency to distance performance-related pay (PRP) from ratings. Inevitably, there is often (perhaps usually) a link between performance assessments and performance-related pay but ratings appear to be the most unpopular part of the performance management process. Accordingly, some organisations have tried to engage in assessments which do not have formal ratings.

360-DEGREE PROFILES

Multi-source or 360-degree performance assessment is a rating system using multiple raters, a variety of perspectives and peer-to-peer feedback. It evaluates an employee's performance with information collected from:

- an employee's work colleagues
- managers
- any staff reporting to the employee
- internal and (exceptionally) external customers.

Large US corporations have used the method extensively in some form for over a decade. It is becoming common in other countries, such as Australia and the UK. Its supporters argue that it is more effective in improving performance than other kinds of assessment. In particular, it is regarded as being fairer than methods which depend on the views of an immediate superior.

Kettley (1996) argues that the increasing prevalence of flatter organisational structures has encouraged the trend to use 360-degree performance assessment. These organisations have multiple reporting lines and managers have greater spans of command, making performance assessments by single line managers inappropriate.

Kettley also points to the role of 360-degree feedback schemes in reinforcing 'desired management behaviours'. As the feedback comes from sources closest to individual employees, it can play a significant part in developing the kind of culture the organisation wants.

A 360-degree profile firstly involves devising a skill model or competence framework listing essential job skills and behaviours. A performance measurement survey is defined on the basis of this skill model. Each employee is then asked to recommend between 8 and 12 raters for his or her personal review. These may include any individual who has direct knowledge of the employee's working performance, including peers, bosses, staff and internal customers – or even external customers. The employee's immediate supervisor selects 6 to 10 of these raters to complete performance surveys, rating the individual on each skill area. Ratings are commonly given on a scale of 1–10. The supervisor should try to widen the circle of raters beyond the employee's friends. Reports are gathered together and the appraisee receives a summary giving the raters' assessments of the employee's performance. Strengths and development needs are highlighted.

The perceived benefits of 360-degree performance assessment include:

- employees get a better appreciation of how they are viewed from other people's perspectives allowing them to see their own strengths and weaknesses more clearly
- a broader range of rater information is available
- because survey responses are anonymous, the aggregated feedback is likely to be more honest
- the requirements for successful performance and career advancement are made clear to employees
- there is a clear focus for discussion between supervisors and employees
- human resource development programmes can be focused more effectively
- it is easier to identify team strengths and development needs
- teams are directly involved in debating their own performance.

ACTIVITY 9

Your manager (or tutor) has asked you to nominate 12 people, who know your work well, to rate your performance. Who would you choose, and why? Jot this down on paper. Then look through your list again. If your manager (or tutor) asked you to narrow your list down to six people, who would you leave out? Explain why.

Your natural inclination might be to make up the list from friends or even relatives and to exclude anyone who could give an unfavourable view of your work. However, it is better to make sure that the list includes as wide and diverse a range of people as possible – and include even those who could be critical. It is sometimes difficult to think of enough people who do know your work but remember that this method allows you to nominate people who are a level above or below you, as well as colleagues working alongside you. In addition, you can nominate customers, people you deal with in the course of work or study, suppliers, and so on. Similarly, when you reduce the list to six, you will need to consider which people represent the most balanced range to reflect the full nature of your work or study.

Managers can start the process by asking their own staff to rate them. This demonstrates commitment to the method and encourages acceptance from employees. It also gives an early indication of individual rating styles. As with any rating system, the 360-degree system suffers from both over-generous and under-generous assessors. These need to be identified and given further training before rating anyone else. Every participant in the assessment must be briefed about the purpose of the exercise and coached in how to rate the desired qualities.

In a study of large British employers, the Institute of Employment Studies found that the majority used organisational values or core competences as a basis for feedback criteria (Kettley, 1996). Their feedback schemes were mostly limited to managers and focused on how they led, coached, managed and developed staff. The dimensions they measured were clustered around managing relationships, managing self or personal style, leadership, decision-making and developing others.

Feedback results could be unstructured or statistical. Unstructured feedback allowed managers to summarise comments as they saw fit, using the information for a personal development plan (PDP). Statistics from questionnaires were most useful when they highlighted variances between the managers' rating of themselves and those provided by others.

Most of the firms studied by the Institute of Employment Studies used a questionnaire to collect information for a predetermined framework. The organisations felt that the advantages were that:

- the nature of the questions familiarised participants with the organisation's values
- scored items were easier to analyse than unstructured comments.

Kettley observes, however, that a highly structured questionnaire can make the feedback 'flat and inexpressive' and makes the whole procedure less interesting for participants.

DIFFICULTIES WITH 360-DEGREE FEEDBACK

It requires a considerable culture change for many businesses to provide 360-degree feedback. It is not advisable to introduce the method in organisations which are involved in major reorganisation or downsizing. In these cases, it is likely to add to mistrust and heighten employees' fears of losing their jobs.

As with any initiative, 360-degree feedback requires the enthusiastic backing of senior managers to succeed. One common reason for scepticism is the massive bureaucracy involved. Traditional appraisals have been unpopular partly because of the work involved in rating single individuals. As 360-degree feedback requires a minimum of six raters per assessment, each with an average of 20–30 rating categories, it is clear that the form-filling and paperwork can mushroom. Not surprisingly, data-scanning, on-line forms and report producing software have become popular solutions for the problem. Nevertheless, conducting a 360-degree feedback in a large organisation can be a disruptive process.

The anonymity of 360-degree feedback has disadvantages as well as advantages. Some raters choose to write intemperate comments that are picked up when feedback analysis reports are used for development purposes. Raters can bear unexpected grudges, or have a strange sense of humour. Malicious or jocular remarks inevitably register with readers, whether or not they are based on fact.

ACTIVITY 10

Read the article *Companies evaluate employees from all perspectives* (Resource 7 in the Resources section).

What do you consider to be the three greatest strengths and, conversely, the three greatest weaknesses of 360-degree profiling as a method for assessing performance. Jot down your reasons for each choice. Write about 10–20 words in each case.

You might have listed some of these strengths: the diverse range of opinions and evidence brought to the process of assessment; the considerable range of perspectives – above, below, sideways, internal, external; honesty from anonymity of assessments; the benefits for team-based management; and the fact that valuable feedback from so many perspectives offers great learning opportunities.

In terms of weaknesses, you could have noted that 360-degree profiling can be very bureaucratic, generating large numbers of forms which require analysis. Collectively, it can be extremely time-consuming for participants who might be involved in assessing numerous people, and the anonymity can allow unchallenged malice to be introduced into the process.

Summary

This section investigated different approaches to performance measurement. Traditional downward appraisals have been much criticised and we looked at newer techniques for improving on these approaches. Competences (or capabilities) have become a fashionable addition to performance management methodology but there are difficulties at both theoretical and practical levels in identifying competences which have real worth. Upward feedback and multi-source or 360-degree feedback can reinforce the sense of reality by obtaining information on performance from a greater range of sources.

SECTION 3

The Consequences of Performance Management

Introduction

Recent research for the Institute of Personnel and Development indicates that the way people are managed has more impact on measurable business outcomes such as profit than investment in technology or in research and development (Caulkin, 1998). As we observed earlier, this has led some companies to develop comprehensive, integrated performance management systems. In this section we discuss the consequences of performance feedback with respect to individuals and work teams. Finally, the impact of performance management on redundancy and downsizing is evaluated.

The purpose of this section is to help you to:

- critically evaluate the consequences of performance feedback on individual and group working behaviour
- explain the relationship between performance management and pay
- outline the implications of performance assessment for redundancy, deselection and downsizing.

3.1   Performance feedback

Feedback is the term sometimes given to the report the appraisee receives towards the end of the performance assessment process. The nature of feedback varies according to the method and strategic purpose of performance assessment. In traditional appraisal systems, feedback consists of being allowed to read the assessment form, followed by a counselling interview. In an extensive review of research evidence on performance feedback, Murphy and Cleveland (1995) identify the following inherent conflicts:

- appraisees 'desperately want feedback, but they also want to hear only positive feedback and tend to dismiss negative feedback'
- appraisees want feedback to include information which is not readily available to them
- appraisees do not want to be lectured, typically they need to talk for approximately the same amount of time as they listen
- performance feedback can be an extremely uncomfortable process for the appraiser, combining the roles of judge and counsellor

- despite all the conflicts involved, feedback is regarded by most participants as being of considerable benefit to individuals and organisations.

Appraisals require line managers to be amateur psychologists in the rating exercise and pseudo-counsellors in the feedback process. A face-to-face discussion between line manager and appraisee can be difficult if the assessment is critical. Not surprisingly, both participants may demonstrate some avoidance behaviour. Managers have been known to inflate ratings in order to avoid confrontation. Critical assessments do not go down well and should be counselled with sensitivity.

There is no doubt that feedback is more readily accepted if (Kettley, 1996):

- feedback is focused on development
- broad-based competences are rated, rather than narrow job-related abilities.

A poor assessment of an individual's personality traits is perceived as an attack on that person's very being. No matter how it may be couched, it is interpreted as 'you do not like me'. Competence-based measures are not so threatening and are seen as being more objective. Feedback is most effective if it forms part of a HRD assessment centre or management development programme. The 360-degree systems have a further advantage of team feedback. Individual team members receive feedback but the team as a whole can also be given aggregate results.

From the organisational perspective, it is surely inadequate to try to improve employee performance just once a year. Sports coaches constantly monitor and encourage athletes to achieve peak performance. Businesses need to do the same with their employees to maintain the continuous improvement that gives a competitive edge.

Armstrong and Baron (1998) set out a number of points to be covered by a performance review:

- achievement of objectives, analysing why they have or have not been achieved
- levels of competency attained under each competency heading
- contribution by individuals or teams to upholding core values
- achievement of elements of their personal or team development plans
- items for future consideration such as aspects of performance to be improved, strengths to develop, and training needs
- feelings about work – its nature and scope, demands on the individual or team, chance to use or develop skills and abilities
- views of the individual or team about the support given by team leader or manager.

Armstrong and Baron see the process as being partly a stock-taking exercise, but also, and more importantly, a chance to look forward to development opportunities, challenges and improvements.

Fowler (1996) recommends several key points for effective feedback. In the feedback interview supervisors should:

- be specific, avoiding generalities and linking particular events or behaviours to performance ratings or comments
- justify requests for changed behaviour
- be constructive – focus on learning opportunities based on ratings or comments
- avoid argument, aim for a practical discussion that incorporates the appraisee's point of view
- avoid commenting on relatively permanent aspects of personality or attitudes which are unlikely to be changed, instead concentrate on behaviour and its effect on performance.

Give regular feedback – not just once a year – and do so as close to 'learning events' as possible.

The appraisee's role in the process should not be neglected. Encourage self-reflection so that appraisees have the opportunity to realise the consequence of behaviour for themselves. Encourage the appraisee to develop an action plan.

Finally, as a supervisor, consider your part in the process. Take feedback yourself – discussion should be two-way and include some upward feedback. This is a topic which we address more fully in the next section. Be open and helpful so that employees are encouraged to come for regular feedback.

ACTIVITY 11

Reflect on the views of Murphy and Cleveland, Armstrong and Baron, and Fowler regarding the best ways to provide performance feedback, and then comment on this case study.

Stella was contacted by Eric, her recently promoted head of department, during a coffee break in the crowded staff room, for what (to her astonishment) was to be her first and only appraisal. Eric was busy and as they sat down a colleague asked Eric to sign his travel expenses form. The conversation began with Eric telling Stella that, while her performance was good, Eric did not want just 100 per cent but 106 per cent. In particular, he made the point that when inviting visitors to the firm a map should be provided – it wasn't good enough just to give directions. Eric believed that this was a good company with fine people in it and that he hoped that Stella would be successful in her future career. As the coffee break had ended, Eric stood up and went out with a colleague who had been hovering nearby wanting to speak to him.

Consider in particular the feedback interview, the frequency of feedback, Stella's role and Eric's part in the process.

You will probably have organised your response differently, but I hope you will have covered most of these points.

In the feedback interview, there were no performance ratings or comments to be discussed. The only specific point was that a map, not directions, should be provided for visitors. To suggest that a map be sent rather than simple directions may seem to make good sense, but it does appear to be a rather small matter compared to other aspects of any job. The request for 106 per cent performance was a nonsensical generality.

Rather than focus on learning opportunities, the specific point about the map is trivial and does not focus on significant issues. The interview seems to have picked up one point rather than to have been based on carefully collected data. Indeed, we might add this advice to that from the quoted authors: focus attention on the key aspects of the job, and base the interview on data, not impressions.

The recommended approach to appraisal and feedback is to encourage appraisees to recognise their own behaviour and its consequences, and to develop their own action plan. In contrast, Eric acted as if the interview was a chance to reinforce his authority in a top-down confrontation rather than to help Stella to develop her own abilities. There was no discussion; Stella's point of view was not sought. The interview was one way, authoritarian, far from open, and unhelpful. It is improbable that Stella would willingly seek feedback from Eric.

To sum up. As he was 'recently promoted' it is possible that this was the first appraisal interview Eric had ever conducted. This case illustrates some of the many ways in which appraisals can be badly handled, and leads us to a final recommendation: ensure that appraisers are trained.

UPWARD FEEDBACK

Historically, performance management has emphasised assessments which are top-down and imply a degree of power play on the part of more senior staff. As we have noted, however, there has been a trend towards constructive, developmental approaches with a move away from ratings. Equally, it has become acceptable to take views of individual performance from a wide range of perspectives, as in 360-degree profiling. In line with these developments, some organisations have adopted upward feedback, a process in which managers receive comments and criticisms from their subordinates. In some cases, this involves an intermediate or facilitator who organises the process and maintains a positive and non-acrimonious climate.

Upward feedback has many benefit for managers – it is not appraisal, it is not linked to standardised competences, and it does not affect remuneration. Instead (Forbes, 1996):

- it delivers candid, accurate feedback from the team to their manager
- it is based on how a team perceives the actions of their manager
- it is not a system of judgement 'but only asks him or her for more, less, or the same of a broad series of behaviours'
- equal weight is given to leadership, management, task and people factors
- the facilitator provides confidential feedback, first to the manager, then between the team and their manager
- team members and the manager can compare their understanding of what is required, bringing areas of misunderstanding or disagreement out into the open.

Because upward feedback is not formal appraisal, managers lose the fear of being judged. Generally, upward feedback begins with the most senior executive and cascades downwards with each level in turn taking turn to receive feedback from their direct reports.

Upward feedback allows individual and team action plans to be produced, which can improve co-operation between team and manager (Forbes, 1996). Managers are encouraged to vary their style and emphasis. Ideas, problems, and suggestions can be collected from a range of teams. These can be used to set up new cross-functional teams or aid business process re-engineering.

The process allows training requirements to be clearly defined and linked to specific outcomes for the team. Indeed it can be used as a benchmarking exercise, allowing organisations to map how employees, managers and senior executives perceive development requirements in different behavioural areas.

Upward feedback also helps smooth the path to empowerment and self-management. Moreover, it creates a more open culture where different forms of performance assessment can be introduced.

Of course, there can also be disadvantages with upward feedback. Managers with assertive and ambitious staff may find themselves at the receiving end of destructive comments designed to undermine their confidence and authority – and nobody likes hearing unfavourable assessments of their performance. Knowledge that they will receive the views of their staff may influence some managers to be less firm or directive in their behaviour, even when circumstances would suggest that this would be appropriate. Managers are also less likely to be critical or demanding of their subordinates in order to reduce the likelihood of unfavourable feedback in return.

ACTIVITY 12

Which of these statements are true and which are false?

1. Upward feedback is a form of performance assessment in which subordinates appraise their line managers.

2. There is an important role for a facilitator in this process, to ensure that a positive exchange of views takes place.

3. The process can be part of a detailed benchmarking procedure in which managers and their teams can be rated on a large number of criteria.

4. Feedback is only provided to the individual managers concerned.

5. Upward feedback is useful for deciding changes in organisational structure.

6. Upward feedback encourages better and more open communication between managers and staff.

Upward feedback is a form of performance assessment in which subordinates appraise their line managers. False – this is a feedback rather than an appraisal process.

There is an important role for a facilitator in this process, to ensure that a positive exchange of views takes place. True – there is a risk of conflict in situations where facilitators are not used.

The process can be part of a detailed benchmarking procedure in which managers and their teams can be rated on a large number of criteria. True.

Feedback is only provided to the individual managers concerned. False – upward feedback procedures vary considerably between the relatively few organisations which use the method. But usually there is feedback back to the manager's team and feedback may be collated for other uses in some organisations.

Upward feedback is useful for deciding changes in organisational structure. True – it may indicate the need for collaboration between teams or new cross-team groupings.

Upward feedback encourages better and more open communication between managers and staff. Possibly true, although there is a risk of managers changing their behaviour to avoid adverse criticism from subordinates.

3.2 Performance management and pay

Performance management is a controversial subject but the greatest controversy has been caused by the relationship between performance and pay. Pay or reward management is a complex topic – a sensitive and controversial area that has been extensively debated at both practical and theoretical levels (Armstrong, 1996). The rewards (or compensation) people receive for their contribution to an organisation includes monetary and non-monetary components. But reward management is not just a matter of compensating employees for their efforts: it is also about the incentives necessary to attract, motivate and retain talented people. Some incentives, such as public recognition – for example through 'employee of the month' schemes – may have no monetary value at all.

Reward or compensation management links pay and other benefits to the achievement of an organisation's objectives. According to Torrington and Hall (1995) employers have a mix of objectives for reward management, including the:

- prestige to be gained from being a 'good payer'
- need to be competitive to ensure a sufficient supply of employees
- need for control over workers
- need to motivate and improve the performance of workers
- need to control costs.

Employees also have needs and objectives in respect of pay. Torrington and Hall (1995) suggest that these include:

- the purchasing power to maintain their standard of living
- the feeling that they are being paid a 'fair rate'
- the rights to a fair share in profits or the country's wealth
- the need to maintain relativities in comparison with other workers
- the need to be recognised.

Pay is not simply a matter of rewarding employees for the work they have done. Pay policies and rates must fit the recruitment and retention needs of an organisation. The job market is increasingly competitive, particularly for skilled staff, and recruiting and keeping high quality people is crucial for business survival. Many organisations provide attractive pay packages for new recruits but fail to give due consideration to the importance of reward systems aimed at keeping and motivating the talented people they already have (Price, 1997).

In terms of motivational psychology, organisations should aim to create a working environment that provides both intrinsic reinforcement from inherently satisfying aspects of a job and external rewards and recognition through, for example, pay, incentives and promotion. These 'motivations' should be directed to working behaviour which contributes to organisational objectives (Porteous, 1997).

To fit this motivational relationship, rewards need to serve three key purposes in a real working situation (Wilson, 1995):

- they must have a positive impact on employee behaviour
- pay mechanisms should focus effort on serving an organisation's customers
- remuneration needs to enhance workplace collaboration.

Wilson defines the purpose of pay in the context of performance management as 'a method for reinforcing the value-added contributions of each individual through the application of their talents, the growth of their capabilities, and the performance of their actions consistent with the key success factors of the organisation'.

Achieving this can enhanced by using these five guidelines. Reward systems should be:

- **specific** – focus pay on desirable behaviour with a clear connection (for the employee) between action and business result
- **personalised** – both employee and employer should consider the level of pay to be 'worth the effort'
- **immediate** – rewards are given 'as timely as necessary to reinforce the desired behaviours that achieve desired results'
- **contingent** – results are seen to be achievable but not easy
- **sincere** – rewards are contingent on taking particular actions or achieving results.

It is clear that, to meet such guidelines, information is required on how employees are behaving and reacting to any incentives or rewards that they may be offered. Performance management offers a way of collecting this information. But how close a relationship should there be between performance management and pay?

PERFORMANCE-RELATED PAY

Armstrong and Baron (1998) observe that whereas 85 per cent of organisations with performance management surveyed by the Institute of Personnel Management in 1992 had performance-related pay (PRP), only 43 per cent of those in the equivalent 1997 Institute of Personnel and Development survey had PRP. None the less the 1997 survey showed that pay differentials remained an important motivating element in many performance management schemes. In general, performance-related pay has been presented as an extra reward, taking pay scales above former maximum points for staff performing exceptionally. More recently the survey showed that there has been a trend towards discretionary pay based on attainment of competences. In other words, the link seems to be moving from directly-linked performance and pay towards a relationship between performance and pay mediated by human resource development.

In principle, it seems fair that employees should receive rewards in proportion to their contribution to a business. Theoretically, discretionary pay schemes benefit both employers and staff by emphasising efficiency and effective job performance which leads to higher productivity. If higher pay is targeted at the most competent performers, they are encouraged to stay with the organisation and continue to perform at a high standard.

According to this view, properly directed pay can reinforce appropriate behaviour.

Well-designed discretionary pay schemes can focus effort on organisational targets and encourage a results-based culture. However, these links must be justified and real if they are not to demoralise other members of the workforce.

A 1998 Institute of Personnel and Development survey covering 1,158 respondents found that 40 per cent were using PRP (Armstrong and Baron, 1998). It seems that most companies convince themselves of the merits of PRP – 59 per cent of those surveyed had introduced PRP in the previous five years. But then many discontinue its use for various reasons – 23 per cent of those currently without PRP had tried and abandoned the system between 1990 and 1998. Those in favour of PRP emphasised its impact on the behaviour of the highest performers. Not surprisingly, it seems that people who benefit personally from PRP like it!

How do PRP systems function? Performance-related pay can be related to the performance assessment of the individual, group (team), department, or company. There are several systems in common use, though they can be classified into two broad types – assessment-related pay schemes and collective performance schemes (Price, 1997).

Assessment-related pay schemes

Merit pay is paid as a component of an annual increase, usually on the basis of an overall performance assessment. This is a long-standing method, commonly regarded as an effective motivator. Budgetary considerations frequently undermine its motivational value when the level is set too low.

Individual incentives may also be given as unconsolidated (one-off) payments or gifts such as holidays, golf sets or vouchers.

Collective performance schemes

These include **bonuses** which are paid to all staff in a business unit, department or team. As with all collective performance rewards, bonuses are intended to reinforce corporate identity and performance.

Another collective scheme is **profit-related pay**. Employees are allocated a sum equivalent to an agreed proportion of business profits.

In the USA, executive **share option schemes** have become common and these initiatives are spreading to other countries. Senior staff benefit from the continued success of the business by being allowed to purchase shares at some point in the future at a fixed price. If the company is successful and the share value increases, the executive gets a greater reward. Share options are viewed as important incentives to motivate key people.

There is clearly a body of opinion that performance-related pay must be a good thing – but the evidence for its effectiveness is not overwhelming. Famously, the search for a positive relationship between PRP and good performance was described by Fletcher and Williams (1992) as being like 'looking for the Holy Grail'.

We noted that people being rewarded by PRP showed a good response. What effect does performance-related pay have on average and poor performers? It seems that they are often unhappy with the system. As an example, a survey of Inland Revenue employees in the UK found considerable dissatisfaction and concluded that the process was demotivating most staff. Reasons included (Price, 1997):

- upward movement of targets: employees found themselves on a treadmill which was continually being speeded up – the goalposts were being moved
- employees were being assessed by managers who did not know them
- performance pay for junior employees was restricted by budgetary constraints but this limitation did not seem to apply to senior officials
- objectives were often imposed rather than negotiated
- subjective criteria led to disagreements on the quality of performance, leading to a perception of unfairness
- individual targets were not compatible with team performance.

Low inflation has further reduced the value of performance-related incentives. Merit payments of a mere 2–3 per cent are not perceived as much reward for exceptional performance. They may even be regarded as insulting.

The Organisation for Economic Co-operation and Development (OECD) conducted a study in 1994–5 on performance pay in the public sector. The survey included 965 middle and senior managers in Australia, Denmark, Ireland, the UK and the USA (quoted in Price, 1997). It found that:

- performance pay schemes were not easy to understand
- the schemes were not generally accepted by managers
- there was no clear link between actual performance and performance pay awards
- awards were too small to motivate the managers

- they were not distributed fairly and equitably
- subjective performance appraisal ratings had a negative effect on managers' own motivation and their perception of the assessment systems

In fact, performance pay was valued less than challenging work opportunities, a sense of accomplishment, recognition, achievement, and respect and fair treatment from colleagues. Why then does PRP remain popular? This may be for one of two reasons.

First, the concept of relating pay to effort or results is simple – and simplistic. Performance-related pay sounds good in tough statements about employee performance in the public sector. It fits nicely into soundbites on television and headlines in tabloid newspapers.

Second, it seems like common-sense. The notion of performance-related pay appeals to people who do not think deeply about the issue and are unaware of the conflicting evidence.

ACTIVITY 13

Read the article *In the classroom, pride and passion mean more than performance pay* (see Resource 8 in the Resources section). Write an evaluation of the likely success of the government's policy of introducing performance-related pay in order to improve the quality of teaching. How many points raised in our discussion are reflected in this article? Try to establish the main points in favour of PRP and the main points against. Write about 80–100 words.

This article covers a large number of the issues we have already discussed. You may feel it shows that the government is convinced of the merits of PRP and is seemingly unaware of the arguments against the system. There are several strands to the argument for and against the use of PRP. You might have noted, for example, that like nursing the teaching profession attracts people who are not necessarily motivated by money. In which case, the use of a pay-based motivational system seems destined not to have an impact on many people in the profession. You might also have highlighted some illustrations of the main complaints of PRP such as underfunding. If rewards cover only a small percentage of good performers, or offer limited extra pay, the system may be very limited in its impact.

3.3   Feedback and human resource development

In the UK, the Investors in People initiative has given performance management a distinctive part to play in the strategic development of human resources. In particular, it defines the responsibilities of line and senior managers in reviewing employee performance. Investors in People's guidelines state that managers are responsible for meeting staff regularly to discuss training and other development with a view to continuously improving performance. This could involve internal or external training, including national vocational qualifications such as NVQs or SVQs.

Robinson and Robinson (1998) argue that people involved in human resource development (HRD) should take on the role of performance consultants: 'partnering with clients for purposes of enhancing human performance in support of business needs and goals. The outputs from this role are strong relationships with clients, identification of potential opportunities for working together, and achievement of human performance improvement.' They view trainers as troubleshooters, moving around a business and dealing with performance problems when and where they occur. The main focus, according to Robinson and Robinson, should be on the identification of underlying causes for inadequate performance. These causes could be:

- organisational, for example inadequate preparatory training
- procedural, such as ineffective systems
- personal, including inadequate competences.

Trainers take on a much wider role than that of classroom delivery within a performance management process of this kind.

Andersen Consulting has designed a model for performance consultants which links the individual and organisational factors that underlie effective performance (Ives and Torrey, 1998). The model lists organisational performance factors such as:

- processes – what are they supposed to do?
- culture – what social and political factors affect performance?
- physical environment – where are people asked to work?

It also covers individual performance factors including:

- direction – what direction do people receive?
- measurement – how are they measured?
- means – do they have the tools to enable good performance?
- ability – do they have the skills and knowledge to perform well?
- motivation – will they perform well?

The importance of performance management in the integration of assessment and development is further discussed in the unit on human resource development.

REDUNDANCY, DOWNSIZING AND DESELECTION

'It is the quality of the staff ... not the quantity, which is the essential factor in downsizing. As we all know from experience, where there are programmes of voluntary redundancy, it is often the most skilled employees who go first because they are more marketable outside.'

Thomson and Mabey (1994)

It is ironic that managers in charge of redundancy programmes tend to focus purely on target numbers, with little or no thought about the quality of the staff leaving the business. Retention strategies for key staff are even more important during periods of redundancy. Performance management provides an ideal mechanism for the best staff to be identified and nurtured at this point.

Job security is considered to be a prerequisite for an effective human resource strategy. Yet a recent UK survey (*Labour Force Survey*, Autumn 1998) indicates that a general sense of *insecurity* is expressed by more than 50 per cent of the workforce, compared with two-thirds when recession was at its worst in the 1980s. However, this is countered by data indicating that most people do not face a significantly higher risk of having to leave employment. The typical length of time in a job declined by four months from 1985 levels to five years and two months in 1995. Men over the age of fifty have suffered the biggest reduction in job tenure, often as a consequence of redundancy. Women under fifty, especially those with children, have seen an increase in tenure over the same period. The ageing of the population has also contributed to increased job tenure.

Nevertheless realistic planning must consider possible redundancies resulting from company failure, rationalisation or reduction in demand for products and people. Companies using portfolio planning are likely to take financial decisions without regard to the welfare of employees. Human resource management in such organisations will be tough-minded, favouring employees in some business units over others. Those in less successful areas stand the risk of being disposed of more readily.

As we shall see in the unit on employee relations, during the 1960s and 1970s this aspect of employment was conducted on an adversarial basis, often involving trades union disputes. 'Last in, first out' was the rule. More recently organisations have tended to select staff they wish to release on the basis of behavioural, financial or other criteria. This deselection implies some form of systematic procedure to decide who will lose their job.

Performance management has its darker side in such a situation. Inadequate performers may be targeted and dismissed perfectly legally if adequate evidence is collated and warnings given of the need for improvement in feedback sessions.

ACTIVITY 14

Write down three of the most important consequences of performance management for the development and retention of employees. Justify your reasons in a total of about 100 words.

You may have observed that there is a close link between performance management and the development of employees through national vocational qualification schemes. This is especially true of competence-based performance management. You could also have identified a change in the function of in-house trainers to act as troubleshooters, using performance assessments as diagnostic procedures to determine areas in which people need training and development. This places an emphasis on understanding the causes of inadequate performance. Finally, performance management is of considerable importance in employee retention or deselection particularly when organisations are making reductions in their overall staffing.

Summary

This section examined the consequences of performance management on individuals and workforce as a whole. There are contradictions between theory and reality in the way performance management systems are organised. In particular, feedback has a variety of implications because of individual differences in motivation and expectations. A key issue is the relationship between performance assessment and reward management. The relationship between performance management and choice of individuals for redundancy is a further topic of importance.

Unit review activity

Read the article *Missed a motivator* (see Resource 9 in the Resources section). In the article Redhouse says: 'In the past, we have put in so-called incentive and recognition plans, and they have not fulfilled the expectations because we have failed to engage at the heart of the business debate.'

How far do you agree that the failure of incentive schemes and other attempts at performance management follows from a failure to engage in debate? Or, would you attribute this failure to other factors?

Study the article carefully and identify other explanations for the failure of these plans.

Unit summary

This unit examined the subject of performance management and varying approaches to methodology and assessment. Performance assessment has moved away from traditional trait appraisal towards the more complex concept of competences. Feedback is increasingly important, developing from authoritarian downward 'counselling' to upward and 360-degree feedback systems. There remains a link between performance management and reward but the relationship has become more complex in recent years.

References

Armstrong, M (1996) *The Handbook of Personnel Management Practice*, Kogan Page

Armstrong, M and Baron, A (1998) *Performance Management: The New Realities*

Armstrong, M and Murlis, H (1998) *Reward Management: A handbook of Renumeration Strategy and Practice*, Kogan Page

Bates, RA and Holton, E F (1995) 'Computerised performance monitoring: a review of human resource issues', *Human Resource Management Review*, Winter

Beer, M and Ruh, R A (1976), 'Employee growth through performance management', *Harvard Business Review*, July–August

Belbin, M (1993) *Team Roles at Work*, Butterworth-Heinemann

Bevan, S and Thompson, M (1991) *Merit Pay, Performance Appraisals and Attitudes to Women's Work*, IMS Publications

Boyatzis, R (1982) *The Competent Manager*, Wiley

Cascio, W (1996) 'Managing for Maximum Performance', *HR Monthly*, September, Australian Human Resources Institute

Caulkin, S (1998) 'How that pat on the head can mean money in the bank' *The Observer*, 19 April

Chell, E (1992) *The Psychology of Behaviour in Organisations*, Macmillan

Corbridge, M and Pilbeam, S (1998) *Employment Resourcing*, Financial Times Pitman Publishing

Drucker, P (1954) *The Practice of Management*, Harper

English, G (1991) 'Tuning up for performance management', *Training & Development Journal*, April

Fletcher, C and Williams, R (1992) 'The route to performance management', *Personnel Management*, October

Forbes, R (1996), 'Performance Management', *HR Monthly*, November, Australian Human Resources Institute

Fowler, A (1990) 'Performance Management: the MBO of the '90s?' *Personnel Management*, July

Garrahan, P and Stewart, P (1992) *The Nissan Enigma: Flexibility at Work in the Local Economy*, Mansell

Hendry, C, Bradley, P, and Perkins, S (1997) 'Missed a motivator?, *People Management*, 15 May

IDS (1997) *Performance management*, Study No. 626, Incomes Data Services

IPD (1998) *Getting Fit, Staying Fit: Developing lean and responsive organisations*, IPD Research, Institute of Personnel and Development

IRS (1998), 'Using human resources to achieve strategic objectives', *IRS Management Review*, Vol. 1:2, July

Ives, W and Torrey, B (1998) 'Supporting Knowledge Sharing', *Knowledge Management*, April/May

Kettley, P (1996), *Personal Feedback: Cases in Point*, IES Report 326, Institute of Employment Studies

Levinson, H (1970) 'Management by whose objectives?' *Harvard Business Review*, July–August

Murphy, K R and Cleveland, J N (1995) *Understanding Performance Appraisal: Social, Organizational and Goal-based Perspectives*, Sage

Porteous, M (1997) *Occupational Psychology*, Prentice Hall

Price, A J (1997) *Human Resource Management in a Business Context*, International Thomson Business Press

Robinson, D G and Robinson, J C (1998) *Moving from Training to Performance – A Practical Guidebook*, Berrett-Koehler

Storey, J (ed.) (1989) *New Perspectives on Human Resource Management*, Routledge

Torrington, D and Hall, L (1995) *Personnel Management: HRM in Action*, Prentice-Hall, 3rd edn

Townley, B (1994) *Reframing Human Resource Management*, Sage

Thomson, R and Mabey, C (1994) *Developing Human Resources*, Butterworth-Heinemann

Wilson, F M (1995) *Organizational Behaviour and Gender*, McGraw-Hill

Recommended Reading

Performance Management: The New Realities by Michael Armstrong and Angela Baron (1998) is a wide-ranging text which conveys the full flavour of the subject. Kevin Murphy and Jeanette Cleveland's *Understanding Performance Appraisal: Social, Organizational and Goal-Based Perspectives* (1995) provides a detailed analysis of research on the performance assessment process over three decades. *Reward Management: A Handbook of Remuneration Strategy and Practice* (1998) by Michael Armstrong and Helen Murlis is the fourth edition of the most comprehensive text available on the relationship between performance and pay. Links to articles and updates are given in the performance management section of the *Internet Guide to Human Resource Management* at http://www.hrmguide.com.

Answers to Unit Review Activity

One of the main explanations offered in the article for the failure of performance management systems, repeated at several points, is that in most organisations there has been a lack of a clear connection between individual behaviour and business objectives. This seems to be a major issue in the context of performance-related pay, where financial reward is often disconnected from achievement of strategic objectives. Individuals might be motivated and individual goals might be assigned, but unless these individual goals contribute to organisational goals, the system will not deliver the results intended.

Another issue is the lack of understanding about what actually motivates employees. Some managers believe that money is the main motivator, whereas others believe that only intrinsic factors (for example, a sense of pride in one's work, achievement, and responsibility) motivate them. If the reward system does not offer rewards people want, then it is unlikely that employees will be motivated to obtain them.

A further difficulty is rewarding people appropriately as they work through a long project. It is difficult to tie reward to success of the project, since that might not be achieved for some years. A distant reward is much less of a motivator than one near at hand. It is important for people to see the results of their efforts and the rewards they produce. Rewarding performance speedily is much more easily applied to activities such as producing or selling.

Finally a substantial problem lies in the way that performance management systems are created. 'HR, finance and strategic planning ... do not collaborate at all in the development of their various processes.' This results in a misalignment. A further misalignment occurs within HR. There is a need to get all HR processes to work together, instead of each one – development, selection, reward, and so on – operating as a stand-alone process.

The line manager is a weak link in many systems. Line managers need to view performance management as a developmental and motivational process rather than an exercise in control.

I think that you will agree that correcting these defects in a management performance system will be more effective than simply debating the issues. The authors appear to identify the need for alignment as the key issue.

UNIT 6
EQUALITY OF OPPORTUNITY

Introduction

In this unit we explore the nature of unfair discrimination in the workplace and consider a range of factors that limit equality of opportunity, noting a number of levels at which access to opportunities can be denied or enhanced. We examine discrimination on grounds of age, disability, gender, race and background. Finally we study the impact of positive action and positive discrimination, and the role of legislation in addressing underlying attitudes and behaviour.

Equality of opportunity is both an issue of social justice and sound economic sense. Discrimination on the basis of race, class, or gender is demonstrably illogical and unfair. Discrimination is also a waste of scarce skill and creativity.

Success is said to depend on the conjunction of preparation and opportunity. The first element is largely within individual control. However, access to opportunity involves additional external factors such as economic conditions and the attitude of others. Promoting equality of opportunity is not an act of benign altruism designed to facilitate individual achievement. Neither should it be viewed as simply being 'politically correct'. As well as being morally unethical, denial of opportunity damages organisational effectiveness by reducing the diversity of ideas, abilities and experiences essential for competitive performance.

Objectives

On completion of this unit you should be able to:

- explain the argument that equality of opportunity is both a matter of social justice and economic sense
- critically assess the limitations of legislation and other initiatives against discrimination
- outline the subtle, far-reaching, informal barriers that limit equality of opportunity.

SECTION 1

Equal Opportunities in Context

Introduction

Society, in diverse ways, determines who is given opportunity and who is denied opportunity. Inevitably, some people are offered greater opportunity than others. This imbalance has a number of negative effects on individuals, organisations and the communities in which they live, work and operate. The imbalance may operate in subtle ways or appear in the form of overt discrimination.

Discrimination has been defined as prejudice plus power, where prejudice is commonly viewed as the opposite of tolerance leaving underlying power relations unaddressed (Husband, 1991). It operates when people who have the power to recruit, promote or reward choose to exercise that power in ways which intentionally or unconsciously demonstrate a preference for one group against another. We will see in this unit that excluding or disadvantaging people on the basis of 'otherness' is both irrational and counterproductive for individuals and organisations alike.

The UK, like many other countries, has established a number of legal constraints and voluntary guidelines covering a variety of forms of discrimination, including that based on gender, race, disability and age. The underlying intention has been to tackle overt discrimination. There have been measurable effects in some areas, specifically gender and race, but less impact in others. Subtler forms of discrimination are more difficult to tackle as evidenced by public concern in the late 1990s about institutional racism in organisations such as the Metropolitan Police.

We begin this section by examining evidence of discrimination in the workplace that prevents equality of opportunity. Then we consider the various philosophies of equal opportunity including affirmative action. Finally we consider some organisational frameworks which can assist members of disadvantaged groups.

The aim of this section is to help you to:

- explain the wide range of barriers to equality in business organisations
- outline the benefits of a diverse workforce
- define specific approaches to equality of opportunity, such as affirmative action and positive discrimination.

1.1   Discrimination and inequality

Discrimination in employment takes a number of overt and subtle forms. Discrimination may be on the basis of:

- **age** – exclusion of younger or older workers by use of arbitrary age boundaries at recruitment, promotion and retirement
- **disability** – preventing people with special needs taking on jobs that they are capable of performing
- **gender** – restricting certain types of jobs to male or female applicants without valid reason
- **race** – favouring members of one community, ethnic group, religion, nationality or colour over others.

In addition, there is discrimination on the basis of **background**. People may be excluded from jobs or particular positions on the basis of social factors such as class, religious denomination, education, home address; those in power reserving the best opportunities for applicants from similar backgrounds to their own. In addition, those deemed socially undesirable, such as ex-offenders, are actively discriminated against.

Three main elements of discrimination are apparent (Corbridge and Pilbeam, 1998):

- direct discrimination
- indirect discrimination
- victimisation.

Direct discrimination

Direct discrimination occurs when an individual has less favourable treatment than another on grounds of disability, race, sex or marital status. Direct discrimination is comparatively easy to identify because of its explicit nature. An example would be the use of different criteria in promoting male employees than in promoting female employees.

Indirect discrimination

Indirect discrimination is a more subtle and less obvious to detect. Here certain conditions or requirements are applied which are more easily satisfied by one group than another. For example, a minimum height requirement would allow more male than female candidates to be considered; a requirement for an unnecessarily high standard of written or spoken English will favour well-established, educated groups over recent immigrants from non-English speaking countries. Employers can objectively justify certain indirectly discriminatory conditions within current legislation – as we discuss later in this unit – but if the case is brought to a tribunal it would have to be shown that there is a genuine and substantial reason for the requirement.

Some issues of indirect discrimination come from stereotyping particular jobs into male or female work. Paradoxically, this has affected men in particular; as the availability of traditional full-time manual jobs has declined, men have been applying for part-time service jobs which have been historically taken by women.

Victimisation

Victimisation is less favourable treatment by an employer because of actions taken by an employee to assert a right, make an allegation or 'whistleblow', concerning a matter of alleged discrimination.

ACTIVITY 1

Read the previous section carefully. Then consider the hypothetical cases given below. Classify each case as either:

- direct discrimination
- indirect discrimination
- victimisation.

1. Candidate X is female. She has been told that she is ineligible for the post of shop assistant because she is over 55.

2. Candidate Y is female. She has been told that she is ineligible for the post of shelf-stacker because she is under 1.68 metres (5O 6OO).

3. Candidate A is a recent refugee from the Balkans. His first language is Serbo-Croat. He applied for a shelf-stacking job in a supermarket but was told that his spoken English was not good enough.

4. Candidate F is of African-Caribbean origin. He has taken a complaint to an industrial tribunal because of his failure to pass a promotion board. He alleges racial discrimination. His manager has refused to let him take annual leave (holiday entitlement) in order to prepare his case for the tribunal.

5. Candidate M is male and has been told that the job of receptionist is only open to women – so he need not bother to apply.

6. Candidate N has been concerned at the way her boss promotes staff. She believes that he has been only promoting white men and has told various senior members of staff. Her manager has given her twice the normal workload and is threatening to discipline her for failing to cope.

Note that not all these forms of discrimination are unlawful – you are not expected to know the detailed legislation involved at this stage.

Hopefully you will have appreciated that none of these hypothetical cases is entirely clear cut. Each involves interpretation of the contrasting views held by employer and candidate.

Candidate X's case is an example of direct discrimination on age grounds, but note that this is not unlawful in the UK at the time of writing

Candidate Y's case could be interpreted as indirect discrimination under the Sex Discrimination Act as men are more likely to satisfy the requirement than women. The employer may argue that high shelves are more easily stacked by relatively tall people. However, the employer could provide aids such as step-ladders. (Besides, how are short customers to reach such high shelves?)

Candidate A's case could be regarded as indirect discrimination under the Race Relations Act, as it is unlikely that a high standard of spoken English is required for the job. However, the issue of communication is problematic.

At face value, candidate F's case appears to be victimisation although most companies restrict the right to unplanned annual leave which might damage productivity. Candidate's M case is direct discrimination, if the statement could be proven. And, finally, candidate N's case is likely to be victimisation.

THE BENEFITS OF EQUAL OPPORTUNITY

What are the benefits of equal opportunity to employing organisations? Ross and Schneider (1992) argue that there are clear and beneficial consequences from the promotion of equal opportunities.

They argue that a diverse workforce provides a richer perspective than that obtained from a narrow range of backgrounds. The greater variety of experience and points of view can lead to more creative ideas for product and service development and better appreciation of market needs. Other benefits include:

- a wider range of creative suggestions for dealing with issues and problems
- enhanced performance through recruitment and promotion of the best people, rather than clones of the existing workforce
- an environment in which high-performing people are more likely to stay, because the organisation values everyone and encourages all staff to develop and realise their talents
- enhances productivity through improved motivation and commitment
- greater profitability through reduced wastage and recruitment costs.

Attitudes towards equality of opportunity have a complex basis in real organisations. Goss (1994) links reasons for promoting diversity to different models of human resource management. The human capital perspective (compatible with hard HRM) holds that impeding the progress of any group is irrational because it prevents optimal use of an organisation's human resources. Goss suggests that this represents a shallow commitment 'capable of being adopted or abandoned, in line with legal or economic expediency'. The problems are exemplified by **tokenism**, the expectation that isolated individuals can represent a disadvantaged group. For example, if one woman is appointed to an otherwise all-male board of directors, this might be deemed to be a demonstration of commitment to equal opportunities for women. Tokenism does not produce the benefits outlined by Ross and Schneider.

The other main perspective is that of social justice: fairness and equity. Goss contends that the social justice perspective (compatible with soft HRM) is more likely to produce organisational and social benefits – despite its emphasis on overriding ethical dimensions rather than economic benefits. This is because the social justice approach is usually more thorough in intent and practice, avoiding the tokenistic pitfalls of the human capital perspective.

ACTIVITY 2

Read the five statements below. Which are consistent with the views presented by Goss and/or Ross and Schneider, and which are not consistent? Write one or two sentences for each statement to explain your conclusions.

1. Placing a member of a disadvantaged group on a company board of directors is an excellent way of furthering the cause of equal opportunity.

2. The human capital approach to human resource management is often used to hide a lukewarm attitude towards equal opportunities.

3. It is best to have employees with similar backgrounds and interests because they are more likely to get on well and form harmonious working teams.

4. It is all very well to be concerned with fairness but business depends on taking hard decisions to gain the greatest competitive advantages.

5. Encouraging everyone to aim for promotion, regardless of their gender, ableness, age or ethnic origins is foolish because it is misleading and will only lead to disappointment for the majority.

There is an element of truth in all of these statements. Yet, you may have concluded that, apart from the second statement, each is inconsistent to some degree with the views of the authors we have considered.

Placing a member of a disadvantaged group on a company board of directors is an excellent way of furthering the cause of equal opportunity. Of course, it is better to have one person from a specific disadvantaged group than none but Goss argues strongly that this is tokenism. He considers that it is an ineffective way of furthering equal opportunities if senior managers think that one representative of a particular group is sufficient. Also, members of any group are individuals in their own right: a quota of one individual does not further the other group members' personal rights to equal opportunity.

The human capital approach to human resource management is often used to hide a lukewarm attitude towards equal opportunities. Developing human capital is a fundamental element of HRM. As such, improving the range and depth of skills and experience is advantageous to any organisation. However, Goss contends that it is often a mask for compliance with legislation or industry guidelines which is swiftly dropped when economic circumstances are difficult, or legislation is relaxed.

It is best to have employees with similar backgrounds and interests because they are more likely to get on well and form harmonious working teams. Obviously it is important to encourage co-operation and teamwork and people naturally gel more easily if they have a great deal in common. However, as Ross and Schneider point out, a restricted range of backgrounds produces a narrow breadth of experience and limits the range of creative and unusual ideas.

It is all very well to be concerned with fairness but business depends on taking hard decisions to gain the greatest competitive advantages. Goss holds that the social justice approach leads to a deeper commitment to equal opportunities than that gained from a hard-nosed economic viewpoint. Ross and Schneider argue that the business case for equal opportunities is irrefutable. In the long run it makes more sense than decisions based on short-term economic considerations.

Encouraging everyone to aim for promotion, regardless of their gender, ableness, age or ethnic origins is foolish because it is misleading and will only lead to disappointment for the majority. Clearly, it is inappropriate to make promises about promotion and career development that can not be realised. However, Ross and Schneider make the point that when people realise that there are no unnecessary barriers in their way and that the organisation will support and assist individual development, numerous benefits unfold.

1.2   Ethical and social dimensions

Discriminatory practice has become institutionalised in many societies. Most countries demonstrate over-representation of one particular social group at the top of their institutions. Members of different, and less-advantaged, groups accumulate further down in the scale of power, status and income. Consequently, skills and abilities are not used to the full and alternative perspectives are wasted. A variety of approaches can be taken towards this problem. We now examine a highly influential model which addresses different levels of equal opportunity.

LEVELS OF EQUAL OPPORTUNITY
Straw (1989) argues that equal opportunity can be addressed at three significant levels.

- **Equal chance** – everyone has the same right to apply for vacancies or be considered for a position. However, in the absence of effective legislation and monitoring, some people will encounter formal or informal barriers. For example, employers may choose to ignore applications from people living in areas considered undesirable.

- **Equal access** – there are no barriers to entry into organisations. However, members of disadvantaged groups may be restricted to lower levels of work. Discrimination results from institutional barriers: appraisal methods may favour certain groups; promotion requirements, for example mobility, may deter those with childcare responsibilities. Conventional norms and procedures, not *formulated* to diminish opportunities, may nevertheless have this effect on all disadvantaged groups (Braham et al., 1992).

- **Equal share** – Straw describes this as the ideal situation, with free access and representation achieved at all levels. The only barriers are justifiable and legal.

This model provides a useful progression for any organisation or society wishing to eliminate discrimination.

POSITIVE AND AFFIRMATIVE ACTION

Positive affirmative action refers to actions taken to enhance the chances of individuals from disadvantaged groups. The selection processes for employment, training and promotion are particular areas of concern. In this section we review the problems, and different solutions, within the selection process.

Selectors tend to consciously or unconsciously pick people with similar characteristics to themselves, or to seek people who bear the closest possible resemblance to the previous post-holder. This leads to the phenomenon of **cloning** – more formally termed elective homogeneity – when organisations employ an undiverse workforce (Smith and Robertson, 1993).

Recommendations for the selection of particular individuals that come from friends, from a consultant's executive search (or headhunt), or from the same narrow range of school or university recruitment are inevitably discriminatory in their effect (Corbridge and Pilbeam, 1998). These restrictive practices are unimaginative at best. They threaten the organisation's effectiveness by stagnating in the past and ignoring the potential to be gained through diversification.

A strategy of **positive action** has been adopted by some governments and major employers. Recruitment for employment and training is achieved by open competition, but under-represented groups are assisted and encouraged to apply for jobs and training, and to join support groups and mentoring schemes. This positive action encourages individuals, and gives them greater confidence to apply for jobs and go through selection procedures.

Positive discrimination is a more controversial approach that requires a predetermined proportion of posts to be filled by members of under-represented groups. Several countries, including the USA, Australia and South Africa, have enacted legislation for positive discrimination under the label of affirmative action. In South Africa, affirmative action led to a substantial increase in the proportion of senior positions held by black managers in just one year – from 2.5 per cent in 1994 to 9.5 per cent in 1995 (South African *Sunday Times*, 21 January 1996). However, as we can see from the following example, affirmative action can have difficult consequences.

Affirmative action versus civil rights

A school in New Jersey, USA decided to make one of two teachers redundant. They had identical skills but one was black, the other white. They fired the white teacher, citing New Jersey's affirmative-action policy. The white teacher sued the school board under the Civil Rights Act 1964, which makes it illegal for employers to discriminate on the basis of race. Eventually the school board reached an out of court settlement, agreeing to pay $433,500 including salary arrears to the white teacher.

Source: *PM Online*, 15 May 1998

Positive action is lawful in the United Kingdom. The Sex Discrimination Act 1975 and the Race Relations Act 1976 allow employers to encourage applications from a gender or racial group which has been under-represented in a specific type of work over the previous 12 months. However, both Acts make it unlawful to exercise positive discrimination in the actual selection process unless ethnicity or gender is a defined 'genuine occupational qualification'. Genuine occupational qualifications cover modelling and acting jobs and a limited range of other occupations.

ACTIVITY 3

Allocate each of these terms to one of the definitions which follow:

- positive action
- equal share
- cloning
- equal access
- positive discrimination
- equal chance.

1. A quota system giving a predetermined proportion or number of jobs to a particular group or groups

2. A situation with no barriers where all groups are represented more or less in proportion to their numbers.

3. Everyone being allowed to apply but no legislation or other mechanism to prevent them being turned down because of factors such as their gender, origin or disability.

4. Members of disadvantaged groups are encouraged, mentored and developed to increase their chances of success in a selection or promotion procedure.

5. Members of disadvantaged groups are allowed into an organisation at basic levels of employment, but hidden barriers prevent them from reaching the most senior positions.

6. Selection of people similar to those who have already done well in an organisation.

Definition 1 is positive discrimination, definition 2 is equal share, definition 3 is equal chance, definition 4 is positive action, definition 5 is equal access, and definition 6 is cloning.

EQUAL OPPORTUNITY POLICIES

We have discussed discrimination in selection, and different approaches an organisation might adopt to reduce it. We now consider company-wide policies that might affect discrimination in every area of activity. Many organisations have adopted an equal opportunities policy – in a publicised and accountable manner – committing them to non-discriminatory human resource management. Both the Equal Opportunities Commission and the Commission for Racial Equality have issued codes of practice which encourage the adoption of such policies.

Molander and Winterton (1994) assert that an effective equal opportunities policy should:

- allocate overall responsibility for policy to a specified senior executive
- be agreed with employee representatives
- be effectively communicated to all employees
- be based on an accurate survey of existing employees
- audit human resource practices for equal opportunities implications
- set equal opportunities objectives within human resource strategy
- allocate training and development resources to fulfil objectives.

One measure of the effectiveness, or otherwise, of equal opportunities policies is the proportion of people from disadvantaged groups achieving positions of influence and power. This can be ascertained from an equal opportunity audit.

Coussey and Jackson (cited in Corbridge and Pilbeam, 1998) contend that the need for an equal opportunities audit should be triggered if:

- managers complain of lowered standards
- managers complain that their ability to take decisions has been taken away
- employees allege positive discrimination and resent the equal opportunities policy
- women and ethnic groups do not believe the equal opportunities policy
- women and ethnic group members do not apply for new jobs or promotion
- there are tensions between groups, complaints of unfairness or cases taken to employment tribunals
- the equal opportunities policy attracts derision
- results are not achieved.

ACTIVITY 4

Bonnypark District Council has published an equal opportunities policy and code of practice. Extracts are shown in the case study below. To what extent does it meet the criteria laid down by Molander and Winterton?

Bonnypark District Council – Equal Opportunities Policy

Statement

Bonnypark District Council is committed to equal opportunities in all its activities. This commitment will be demonstrated through active promotion of the council's code of practice. It is the intention of the council that no job applicant or employee will receive less favourable treatment on the grounds of marital status, gender, sexual orientation, disability, race, nationality, ethnic origin, political belief, religion or social class. Selection and promotion criteria will be continuously reviewed to ensure that all applicants are treated solely on the basis of job requirements and relevant personal merits, and are not disadvantaged by any conditions or requirements which cannot be shown to be fully justifiable.

Code of practice (abridged)

The council will maintain a programme of action to promote its policy of equal opportunities. The Chief Operating Officer will have overall responsibility for implementation of the policy. The head of each department will have responsibility within that department. The Head of Human Resources will be responsible for ensuring that all central human resource activities relating to recruitment, promotion, training and career development meet the code of practice.

A working group will meet quarterly to develop and oversee the effective operation of the policy on equal opportunities. The group shall consist of three council representatives and three representatives of recognised trade unions.

Copies of the policy statement and code of practice will be distributed to all existing staff and to new employees of the council.

Procedures for recruitment, promotion and career development

- All job descriptions and personnel specifications will be reviewed to ensure they reflect the needs of the post.

- All publicity and information material concerned with recruitment will state that Bonnypark District Council is an equal opportunities employer.

- Content and placement of recruitment material and advertisements will be reviewed to ensure that applications are encouraged from all suitable candidates.

- All requirements, such as qualifications or language ability, which are irrelevant to the needs of the post will be removed from selection criteria.

- Requests from candidates for flexible forms of employment such as job sharing or part-time arrangements will be considered sympathetically.

Language

The council will endeavour to use non-discriminatory language in all written and spoken communication.

Training for interviewers, assessors, managers and team leaders

Guidelines on the code of practice will be issued to all those involved in making decisions such as selection, performance assessment and development. All training programmes, particularly those concerned with management and team leading, will include an equal opportunities component.

Monitoring

The working group will advise on monitoring applicants and employees and will determine the procedures to be followed in all cases of complaint or grievance. Monitoring forms will be determined in consultation with the Joint Union Consultative Committee. Submission of information specifically for monitoring purposes will be voluntary for all employees. Such information will be treated confidentially and within the terms of the Data Protection Act.

At Bonnypark District Council, overall responsibility is allocated at a high level but distributed, or cascaded, to heads of individual departments. This is probably realistic in a large, distributed organisation but could lead to some differences in approach in different departments. Trade union representatives are involved in the working group which has a significant input into the process of implementing and monitoring the policy. It is arguable whether the policy is effectively communicated to all employees: everyone gets a copy – but will they read it?

The case study does not state whether an audit of existing employees and practices has taken place. Completion of monitoring forms is voluntary, so it is difficult to see how an accurate picture of equal opportunities can be drawn. Similarly, we don't know whether there has been an audit of human resource practices. However, the initial statement makes it clear that equal opportunities are to be embedded in the most fundamental activities of the human resources department. Training and development resources are allocated to support the policy, through it is not clear whether these are sufficient to achieve the objectives.

From our look at the Bonnypark policy it is clear that management have attempted to go a long way towards establishing a non-discriminatory organisation. Even so, there are areas in which some improvements might be possible. Bonnypark is seeking to eliminate the human and economic costs of discrimination, but the policy fails to attempt to capitalise on the potential benefits of individual differences. We turn next to consider how organisations might make greater use of the talents within their organisations by the effective management of diversity.

1.3   Management of diversity

The concept of management of diversity is a comparatively new term in human resource management. Managing diversity extends beyond the notion of equal opportunity. The key difference is the focus on individuals and their potential, rather than on traditionally disadvantaged groups. The fundamental justification is that valuing people for their different and various experiences enriches the organisation. It is consistent with the HRM approach discussed in Unit 1 since it requires integration and co-ordination of a wide range of HR activities.

Royal Dutch-Shell

Royal Dutch-Shell is one of the world's largest multinational oil companies. Some 80 per-cent of its employees are neither British or Dutch, but the company has traditionally had a British and Dutch male-dominated corporate culture. However, Royal Dutch-Shell is now encouraging the appointment of women and people from a broader range of nationalities to top management. It intends to increase the proportion of women in the top 400 posts from 4 per cent to 20 per cent over a five-year period.

This transformation is driven by Shell's failure to respond to rapid change in its business environment. Critics argue that a more diverse management group would have made a better job of responding to sensitive issues such as human rights abuses in Nigeria and the scrapping of the Brent Spar North Sea oil rig.

Shell has conducted a study into management diversity as part of its long-term strategy to transform the heavily bureaucratic organisation into a nimbler competitor. The study revealed that without some form of positive action, the make-up of its senior managers in 10 years – in terms of nationalities and gender – would be almost the same as those of its present top managers.

Source: *Financial Times*, 13 January 1998

Ross and Schneider (1992) hold that managing diversity has five key dimensions that distinguish it from equal opportunities. They contend that managing diversity:

- is internally driven, rather than externally imposed
- is focused on individuals not groups
- is concerned with diversity not equality
- addresses the total organisational culture – not just systems
- is everyone's responsibility, not just the personnel/HR function

The basis of their argument is that the values of managing diversity should be internalised by individuals and therefore becomes part of the organisation's culture.

ACTIVITY 5

Read the 10 statements below. Indicate which five apply to the equal opportunities approach, and which five apply to the managing diversity perspective.

1. A focus on inclusiveness and the needs of all employees.

2. A focus on needs of specific groups such as women, the disabled, etc.

3. All members of a specific group treated as if they had the same needs and experiences.

4. Leadership from personnel/human resources.

5. A recognition that each individual has a unique combination of needs and experiences.

6. Does not involve positive action.

7. Makes use of positive action and other mechanisms to draw attention to the needs of particular groups.

8. Business-focused.

9. An emphasis on moral, ethical and social matters.

10. Likely to be more acceptable to line managers.

The management diversity perspective is reflected in statements 1, 5, 6, 8 and 10. The other statements illustrate an equal opportunities approach.

Managing diversity involves specific actions by the organisation to assist individuals in achieving their potential despite any barriers or disadvantage. Setting up a mentoring system is an important example of how organisations can assist this process.

MENTORING

In Greek mythology, Mentor was the guide of Odysseus and Telemachus (Antal, 1993). In contemporary society, mentoring is the use of personal experience to provide confidential, structured support and feedback. Mentoring can be used to support people in a range of circumstances from young unemployed to higher management. Megginson and Clutterbuck (1995) define mentoring as 'off-line help by one person to another in making significant transitions in knowledge, work or thinking'. (Note, 'line' in this definition refers to the line management relationship.)

The British government's New Deal for the unemployed, announced in 1997, initially targeted 18–24 year olds who had been out of work for more than six months. The scheme has since been extended to older age groups. The initiative places heavy emphasis on the role of trained volunteer mentors to encourage self-confidence among those involved in the scheme.

Within organisations, mentoring typically is offered to junior members of staff following a similar career path, or with comparable circumstances outside work, to that of their mentor. Mentors are normally more senior but have no line responsibility for the learner. Mentoring skills are useful to most managers, but it is best to keep line management issues separate. Mentors should be interested in developing themselves and others, and they must inspire trust and respect in the people they mentor. Mentoring has been found to be particularly effective in preparing people for high-profile or challenging positions, and in offering psycho-social support within the work context (Megginson and Clutterbuck, 1995).

Mentors perform four main roles:

- **coaching** – for example, showing how a task is performed or a problem solved
- **facilitating** – for instance, through creating opportunities for junior staff to use new skills
- **counselling** – such as talking through the consequences of a particular course of action

- **networking** – taking a junior to another 'expert' for advice on specific issues.

Mentors are of considerable value when supporting individuals from an under-represented group as we can see from the following example.

Aer Rianta

Aer Rianta – the organisation responsible for managing Dublin, Cork and Shannon airports in the Republic of Ireland – initiated a mentoring scheme in 1993. At the time all senior posts in the company were held by men. It was decided to break the glass ceiling (invisible barrier) to women's progress by equipping female staff with skills and confidence.

The mentoring scheme began with 18 women managers who volunteered to be mentored by senior male managers within Aer Rianta. Originally the women were paired with senior male colleagues as understudies but this was developed into a more conventional mentoring arrangement.

The success of mentoring relationships varied considerable. The most successful were those which had these '**relationship components**':

- commitment
- openness
- encouragement
- investing time (in preparation and follow-up as well as meetings)
- demonstrating interest
- trust and confidentiality
- clear objectives
- developing a career path
- feedback
- sharing experience
- questioning
- being a critical friend.

The mentoring arrangement allowed women to realise that they could do the senior jobs and that there was no mystique about senior management posts.

Source: Clutterbuck (1995)

ACTIVITY 6

Study the report on the mentoring scheme at Aer Rianta. For each of the four mentoring roles – coaching, facilitating, counselling and networking – write down the five most significant relationship components relevant to each role.

You may have concluded that all of the relationship components have value in each of the four roles. The following table gives our choice, yours may be different.

Role	Relationship component
Coaching	Encouragement Clear objectives Feedback Sharing experience Being a critical friend
Facilitating	Commitment Clear objectives Developing a career path Feedback Questioning
Counselling	Openness Encouragement Trust and confidentiality Sharing experience Being a critical friend
Networking	Commitment Openness Investing time Trust and confidentiality Developing a career path

Table 1: The relationship components important in each mentoring role

Summary

Equality of opportunity is both an issue of social justice, and for business organisations, an issue of economic and operational effectiveness. Discrimination is a waste of scarce skill and creativity. Discrimination can be addressed at three levels: equal chance (giving everyone the right to apply for positions), equal access (giving everyone an equal opportunity of access to organisations) and equal share (with free access and representation at all levels).

Some organisations pursue affirmative action and positive discrimination policies to correct under-representation in the workforce. However, these approaches can be controversial and, in many countries, positive discrimination is illegal under anti-discrimination legislation.

Managing diversity focuses on realising the potential of all individuals, in contrast to the more traditional equal opportunities focus on disadvantaged groups. Mentoring is one practical approach to fostering equal opportunity and of managing diversity.

SECTION 2

Race, Ethnicity and Gender

Introduction

This section evaluates equality of opportunity based on factors which all people have at birth: their 'race' or ethnic origin and gender. Multicultural societies in the twenty-first century have major problems in ensuring fairness between people of different racial origins. Some countries have introduced legislation to make discrimination illegal. Attitudes have changed considerably in a generation: in many societies, for example, women expect and demand full equality in the workplace. Discrimination based on ethnicity and gender is often institutionalised in society and organisations. The issue of childcare and family-friendly work practices is central to achieving equal opportunities between female and male staff.

This section is intended to help you to:

- outline the degree of inequality remaining in the workplace between people of different race and gender
- explain the concept of institutional discrimination
- evaluate the effectiveness of government legislation and HR policies on the achievement of equal opportunities
- assess the impact of measures to provide childcare facilities on gender discrimination.

2.1 Race and ethnicity

Race is a commonly used term, though it has little biological foundation. It refers to the supposed physical characteristics of a group of people; ethnicity refers to cultural differences. Within any country, you may find populations with diverse 'racial' and ethnic origins. Typically, diversity is readily apparent in language or skin colour. However, less obvious factors, such as family customs or religious difference may be highly relevant. Few countries have true equality between these groups.

In the UK, around 2 million people (6 per cent) come from non-white racial and ethnic groups, of whom just over a million are in paid employment and a further quarter of a million are seeking work (CRE, 1997). Some 97 per cent of the UK's ethnic minority population live in England – with 47 per cent residing in London. Most of the remainder are concentrated in major population centres such as Birmingham.

Racism is a very common but complex phenomenon, and it is by no means always expressed in overt hostility and prejudice. Media attention on the more extreme demonstrations of racism, such as neo-fascist violence, tends to obscure and excuse subtler and more insidious forms. This is exacerbated by the inability of many people to perceive and acknowledge the structural advantages that contribute to the success of dominant groups. Ben-Tovim et al. (1992) criticise the ideology of 'colour blindness' which:

- fails to appreciate the pervasiveness of racism
- confuses racism with urban deprivation and class inequality
- is conveniently compatible with a range of political opinions
- classifies racism purely as overt and deliberate discrimination.

Colour blindness, they argue, also accommodates the 'universalistic ideologies and practices of public administration' – in other words, applies identical rules, approaches and expectations to everyone, regardless of any racial or other differences.

Rationalisations for ignoring other forms of racism include contentions that raising the question of racism is divisive, and that the problems of ethnic minorities are the same as those experienced by the general population, the working class, people living in inner cities or other less specific categories. Considering racism purely in terms of disadvantage or prejudice (that is, opinions and attitudes) rather than actual behaviour, leaves underlying power relations unaddressed (Husband, 1991).

Widening the definition of discrimination to include indirect or institutional racism improves our understanding of the barriers against ethnic minorities and represents an important shift of emphasis from intent to outcomes (Husband, 1991). Dominelli (1992) highlights a general failure to make connections between 'the personal, institutional and cultural levels of racism'. Virtually unrecognised in business, the concept of institutional racism is a contentious issue in the public sector – see, for example, the Metropolitan Police's responses to the murder of Stephen Lawrence (*The Guardian*, 30 January 1999).

The Stephen Lawrence affair

Stephen Lawrence was an 18-year old black man murdered on the streets of South London in April 1993. None of five white racist suspects has been convicted. An internal Metropolitan Police inquiry initially concluded that 'the investigation progressed satisfactorily and all lines of inquiry had been correctly pursued'. Mounting evidence of police incompetence and racist treatment of the victim's family eventually led to a public inquiry,

The public inquiry published its report in February, 1999. It recommends radical changes to the policing of racial crime, concluding that institutional racism played a part in the collective organisational failure demonstrated in the investigation of Stephen's Lawrence's death and its aftermath.

ACTIVITY 7

Reflect on the distinctions drawn between 'racial prejudice' and 'institutional racism' in our discussion above. Which of these statements are more true than false and which are more false than true.

1. Institutional racism is found in public sector organisations but not in private sector companies.

2. Racism always takes the form of overt prejudice against people from minority groups.

3. People should be treated in the same way regardless of their colour, ethnic origin or culture.

4. Ethnic minority groups have the same work problems as any other disadvantaged part of the population, such as poorer people in the inner cities.

5. Talking about different forms of racism only makes the problem worse.

6. Institutional racism is a unique form of discrimination which does not apply to any other disadvantaged group.

Institutional racism is found in public sector organisations but not in private sector companies. The authors we have cited in this section would argue that institutional racism may be largely unrecognised in the private sector but it certainly exists.

Racism always takes the form of overt prejudice against people from minority groups. Few people show overt prejudice – or even believe that they are racist. Nevertheless the nature of institutional racism is that it operates on the assumptions and expectations of the majority population. Inevitably, people whose experiences and beliefs do not coincide with these assumptions and expectations will be disadvantaged. Also, institutional racism involves stereotypical beliefs held by members of the majority population which are detrimental to members of minority groups. Why do police officers stop far more youths of African-Caribbean than European origins?

People should be treated in the same way regardless of their colour, ethnic origin or culture. This sounds eminently fair but Ben-Tovim and others would argue that this approach denies the right of minority groups to be different.

Ethnic minority groups have the same work problems as any other disadvantaged part of the population such as poorer people in the inner cities. There is a considerable element of truth in this statement but Husband and others would say that the problems of ethnic minority groups are exacerbated by different forms of discrimination.

Talking about different forms of racism only makes the problem worse. Ben-Tovim regards this as colour-blindness – a form of denial which does not help to bring racism to the surface in order to counter it.

Institutional racism is a unique form of discrimination which does not apply to any other disadvantaged group. Other groups also experience institutional discrimination: women, disabled people, older people, people with criminal records, people who have had a lengthy period of unemployment. In some societies, religion and caste are also used as grounds for exclusion from job opportunities.

LEGISLATION

In the UK, the Race Relations Act 1976 defined **direct** racial discrimination as treating one person less favourably than another because of his or her colour, race, nationality (including citizenship), or ethnic or national origins. In line with our earlier discussion, **indirect** discrimination is held to have occurred when a requirement or condition which applies equally to everyone has unequal and detrimental impact on a particular racial group, and cannot be justified. An example would be the requirement for a higher standard of English than that strictly necessary to perform a job. This would be indirectly discriminatory against recent immigrants whose first language was not English.

Within the UK, the Commission for Racial Equality (CRE) is empowered to advise both victims of discrimination and employers about their rights and responsibilities, to negotiate between parties, and to provide legal representation. The Commission can also take action against discriminatory advertisements and in cases where people have been told to discriminate on racial grounds. Failure to follow the CRE's employment code of practice may be used as evidence at an industrial tribunal but is not illegal in itself. Where an organisation is found to have discriminated on grounds of race, a binding non-discrimination notice is issued.

Northern Ireland has separate legislation against discrimination on grounds of religious affiliation. Legislation against discrimination on grounds of race remains comparatively rare outside the UK. In a European context, the CRE notes that:

> 'Neither the Treaty of Rome nor the European Convention on Human Rights provides explicit protection from racial discrimination. Furthermore, the protection afforded by the domestic legislation of other European countries is very limited. This means that, while people coming to Britain have the protection of the Race Relations Act, those going to other European countries from Britain will find far fewer legal safeguards. The CRE's concern is that there should be a rapid improvement in protection from racial discrimination across Europe, and that the Race Relations Act should not suffer dilution in any future attempts to harmonise laws across the Community.'

(CRE, 1998)

2.2 Gender

All human societies divide members into categories named 'female' and 'male'. These two groupings are defined on the basis of diverse cultural assumptions about appropriate characteristics, attitudes and behaviours which are attributed, sometimes arbitrarily, to males or females. Gender depends on a complex interaction of genetics, psychological and social factors, all susceptible to ambiguity. Perceptions of gender difference have traditionally been used to justify male domination of societies in which women have been restricted to subordinate and undervalued roles in their working lives.

GENDER STEREOTYPES AND REALITIES

Bevan and Thompson (1992) found that men and women placed different values on behaviour in the working environment:

- men preferred and aspired towards qualities that were essentially **individualistic** and **competitive**, such as intelligence, dynamism, energy, and assertiveness

- women tended to favour qualities of a more **co-operative** and **consensual** nature, such as thoughtfulness, flexibility, perceptiveness, and honesty.

They concluded that women are disadvantaged by the over-representation of male managers who evaluate female staff against their own (male) norms of behaviour. Men are more likely to be offered training or promotion even when women have comparable appraisal ratings and job descriptions. In addition, women tend to underestimate their own skill levels and may show a lack of assertiveness that further inhibits their progress.

The participation of women in the employment market has increased rapidly, but their share of senior jobs remains disproportionately low. In the 1990s, men occupied between 95 and 97 per cent of senior management posts in the USA's biggest corporations. In the UK, women still occupy just 33 per cent of managerial and administrative positions, 6 per cent of police sergeant posts and 15 per cent of legal partner positions. In general, women earn only 80 per cent of men's average hourly wage – an improvement of a mere 7 per cent in 20 years (Equal Opportunities Commission website, accessed 3 September 1999).

In an attempt to explain this situation, Strebler et al. (1997) argued that the progression of women employees may be limited by:

- the assessment of their training needs by line managers
- relatively greater importance given to technical than personal competences – giving women less challenging objectives
- their own perceptions of their training needs.

In general, they found that women felt their managers to be less able to identify their strengths and weaknesses than male employees did.

Strebler et al. (1997) argue that competency headings (and their associated behavioural indicators) should be checked carefully to make sure that they apply equally to both male and female employees. They propose this check list:

- review whether self assessment and peer assessment could not be used in addition to line manager assessment of competences, and consider monitoring ratings of individual competences for possible discrepancies
- ensure wherever possible that the skill and competency frameworks developed or purchased are based on a representative sample of both men and women
- develop guidelines to control gender bias and stereotypes in the assessment process, and monitor ratings of competency performance for men and women

- investigate whether the different competency profiles drawn by line managers, and the choice of competency level for individual jobs, are free of bias and relate to individual performance
- train line managers and staff to interpret competency headings and be aware of the potential biases in interpretation, particularly if leadership is one of the competences assessed.

Women may respond to these inequalities by adopting strategies traditionally associated with male workers. Alternatively, women managers are more likely to regard themselves as enablers of other people. Strebler et al. (1997) found that women stressed competence in managing and developing people. In contrast, men paid more attention to visibility and knowledge of internal politics. Women considered it important to open up opportunities and provide information, building the confidence of their staff and encouraging them to develop and use their skills. But, in support of Bevan and Thompson's earlier work, Strebler et al. concluded that men seem to be more likely than women to be given training for career advancement and this made a greater impact on their promotion prospects.

ACTIVITY 8

On the basis of the surveys conducted by Bevan and Thompson and by Strebler, which of these qualities are more likely to be preferred by women and which by men? Remember that these are generalisations – every individual is different.

Technical competences	Intelligence	Personal competences	Developing other people
Individualism	Enabling other people	Energy	Co-operation
Dynamism	Flexibility	Perceptiveness	Assertiveness
Thoughtfulness	Competitiveness	Honesty	Consensus

Qualities likely to be preferred by men are technical competences, intelligence, individualism, energy, dynamism, assertiveness and competitiveness.

Qualities likely to be preferred by women are personal competences, developing other people, enabling other people, co-operation, flexibility, perceptiveness, thoughtfulness, honesty and consensus.

LEGISLATION

Many countries have adopted legislative mechanisms designed to reduce entrenched inequalities. However, they vary considerably in strength and focus. One of the more common approaches, followed by states in the European Union among others, makes it illegal to pay different wages for comparable work or to discriminate on grounds of sex. In the UK, relevant legislation – the Equal Pay Act 1970 and the Sex Discrimination Act 1975 – has been in place for nearly thirty years. The Equal Opportunities Commission was formed under a provision of the Sex Discrimination Act to monitor implementation of both Acts.

However, such strategies make slow progress against subtle psychological and practical organisational barriers that continue to place hurdles in the way of women at work. In Australia, the Affirmative Action (Equal Opportunity for Women) Act 1986 requires all private sector organisations with 100 or more employees to develop policies designed to remove barriers in the path of female staff. However, the Australian Council for Equal Opportunity in Employment did not collect any data on compliance with this Act until 1997 and its effect remains unknown. Worryingly, a survey in 1997 found that 70 per cent of men and 44 per cent of women in the Australian finance industry considered that 'managers should be able to employ who they want without having to worry about EEO (equal employment opportunity)' (*HR Monthly*, June 1997).

Read the article on *The low down: work and family* (see Resource 10 in the Resources section). What does this tell you about the effect of legislation on equal opportunities for women? The issue of childcare is becoming increasingly important as we shall see in the next section.

2.3   Gender roles and responsibilities

Prejudices of individual employers continue to reinforce some of the barriers facing women in paid employment. These include fundamentally confused attitudes about the complex position of women in contemporary society. Negative attitudes abound: women really should be homemakers and primary child-carers; they are unreliable because of domestic crises; they are not truly dependent on their income; the are tied and inflexible; they are not suitable for positions of responsibility in the workplace.

In Britain, male (old boys') networks are a principal factor in the perpetuation of discrimination against women (Wilson, 1995). These pervasive informal cliques operate in many sectors of the employment market. They may be based on family or professional ties, and tend to attribute undue precedence to past attendance at particular schools or universities. Networks are reinforced by ostensibly social contact, such as playing golf, which has an additional self-justifying role in securing privilege. Men devote 500 per cent more time than women to such networking activities, as a result men are seven times more likely than women to get unadvertised jobs through personal contacts (Wilson, 1995).

Networks also have a positive function by facilitating communication and support for those in similar and often isolated positions. When women attempt to join a male network on an equal basis, they may be viewed as aggressive or sexually provocative. An alternative approach, sometimes to be preferred, is to develop women-only networks. For example, in the UK groups such as Women in Shell, Women in Banking, the City Women's Network foster the careers of their members through job referral, advice, contacts and support. Senior women managers in education formed a Through the Glass Ceiling group in 1990.

The United Nations asserts that 'in no society do women enjoy the same opportunities as men' (*The Financial Times*, 11 December 1995). As we noted in the last section, the concept of a glass ceiling describes the invisible barrier which has to be breached if women are to achieve higher promotion. This barrier becomes increasingly apparent as it is reached and is reinforced by the attitudes of those already in power (usually men), manifested in their preferential treatment of people like themselves, and compounded by structural inequalities. As we shall see in the next section, there is pressure to equalise parental rights in respect of paid and unpaid leave, especially in the early years of a child's life, in line with the European Union's Parental Leave Directive. However, childcare provision, equal and minimum pay, pensions and part-time workers' rights are all issues which arguably affect women more than men.

ACTIVITY 9

Read the article entitled *Flexibility comes out of flux* (see Resource 11 in the Resources section). This article gives some case studies on the use of flexible working practices to improve the position of women at work. Write brief notes on each flexible working practice. Explain its key features and why you think it is significant.

Reviewing these initiatives, draw up three generalisations relating to improving the opportunities for women.

We have not attempted to summarise each example of flexible working. However, in reviewing the scheme at the Bank of Montreal, for example, you might have noted how employee-generated ideas on part-time working allowed three-day shift patterns to be organised. This initiative was effectively organised and communicated to employees. At Price Waterhouse, modern technology released female workers from having to come to their regular workplace. They no longer had to access files manually, for example.

The article contains many other examples of flexible working practices and these are some of the generalisations which can be drawn from them:

- there is a wide variety of strategies and tactics for improving the position of women at work by increasing the flexibility of conditions of employment
- it is best for as many suggestions as possible to come from the employees involved
- employees should be involved in any decisions
- these flexible options should be catered for within personal development plans and overall business strategies.

There are other generalisations which you might have spotted.

CHILDCARE RESPONSIBILITIES

In the UK, equal opportunities strategies focused on women tend to have particular emphasis on the need to respond to childcare responsibilities. The Fairness at Work Bill – before parliament at the time of writing – will extend paid maternity leave to 18 weeks, thereby implementing the European Union's Parental Leave Directive. This places the UK behind other European countries such as Denmark, the Czech Republic and France but well ahead of USA, Australia and New Zealand where parental leave is left to the discretion of employers. Only 62 countries provide the minimum of 14 weeks recommended by the International Labour Organisation. However, Denmark's initial commitment to 13 weeks' paid leave for both parents placed a strain on industry (*The Guardian*, 3 February 1999).

Identifying reliable and flexible care providers is a stressful and expensive process. Only one child in nine under the age of eight years is able to secure a place in registered care facilities. As a consequence, nearly 50 per cent of working parents rely on unregistered carers (Daycare Trust, 1997). A full-time child minder in Britain costs up to £100 a week, a private nursery up to £180 (figures from Joseph Rowntree Foundation, 1998).

The European Commission has actively encouraged provision of childcare facilities although generally there is insufficient available provision (see table 2). In France, Belgium and Greece, registered child-minding services are free for children under three years of age. In Japan, a public day nursery place costs the equivalent of just £90 a month. Cost of childcare receives tax credits in the USA. Elsewhere, costs vary considerably but facilities in the UK are amongst the most expensive, with participation correspondingly lower. In an attempt to encourage the return of skilled women to work, tax concessions for workplace childcare were introduced in the UK in 1990.

The Daycare Trust (1997) estimates that overall only 10 per cent of UK employers contribute towards childcare costs. Table 3 details the contributions from some of Britain's major employers. Even ignoring the implications for equal opportunities, this lack of investment is surprising. Avoiding the considerable costs incurred in recruiting and training replacement staff is one example of the significant advantages of retaining experienced employees.

Country	Monthly cost (£)	Normal arrangement	% involved under 3 years age	% involved 3 years to school age
Austria	121	Public day-care centre	3	69
Belgium	Free	Public nursery school	18	95
Denmark	97	Crèche, authorised home daycare	60	79
Finland	72	Public daycare centre	25	50
France	Free	Public nursery school	33	99
Germany	42	Public nursery school	4	68
Greece	Free	Relative or public daycare centre	5	>50
Irish Republic	184	Private child minder or crèche	3	82
Italy	73	Public daycare crèche	6	95
Luxembourg	102	Private daycare or crèche	10	55
Netherlands	164	Daycare centre	<10	93
Portugal	65	Private social solidarity institute	15	53
Sweden	64	Public daycare	32	63
UK	347	Registered child minder	7	66

Table 2: Childcare provision in Europe
Source: *Adapted from Bradshaw, S, Kennedy, S, et al. (1996)* The Employment of Lone Parents, *Family Policy Institute*

Note: Figures for Germany relate to West Germany

Company	Employees ('000s)	Childcare subsidy	Workplace nursery	Extra maternity benefits
Barclays	97	No	No	No
Bass	76	No	No	18 weeks full pay
BAT Industries	84	No	No	18 weeks full pay, career breaks
BG	70	Yes	No	7 weeks full pay, loyalty incentives
Boots	80	No	No	No, but career advice and support
BP	67	No	Yes	Pay according to length of service
BT	149	No	No	Assessed individually
HSBC Holdings	107	Yes	Yes	46 weeks unpaid leave
ICI	68	Yes	Yes	Top-up pay, unpaid year off
Lloyds	62	Yes	Yes	63 weeks unpaid
NatWest	98	No	No	No
Post Office	193	No	No	18 weeks full pay
Safeway	67	No	No	18 weeks full pay plus bonus
Sainsbury	82	Yes	No	No, but career breaks
Tesco	71	No	No	No

Table 3: Workplace childcare arrangements in largest UK employers
Source: Adapted from 'Industry's crèche economy'
The Guardian, *12 November 1997*

ACTIVITY 10

The European Commission has actively encouraged the provision of childcare facilities; but how well is it succeeding? Consider tables 2 and 3 and judge to what extent the Commission is successful in encouraging uniform public provision and in-work childcare provision.

How far do governments and companies feel that they should provide for child care? These questions might help your analysis.

- From a parent's perspective, which European countries offer the cheapest childcare opportunities?
- Conversely which are the most expensive?
- In which European countries are parents most likely to be offered childcare for children under 3 years of age?
- And in which countries are they least likely to be offered childcare for children under 3 years of age?
- Which countries offer the greatest likelihood of childcare facilities for children between 3 years of age and formal school age?
- Which countries offer the least possibility of childcare for children between 3 years of age and formal school age?
- Overall, which company surveyed offers women parents the best terms?
- Which company surveyed appears to be the least generous?

It is impossible to say to what extent any of the provision has been due to the encouragement of the European Commission, but it is clear from the very uneven provision that this encouragement has not been uniformly effective.

In terms of the detail about the provision in different countries, Belgium and Greece provide free care, while provision is most expensive in the United Kingdom, followed at some distance by the Irish Republic.

Parents in Denmark are most likely to be offered childcare for children under 3 years of age. Provision is poorest in Austria and the Irish Republic – but notice that provision in Greece is also poor which means that the 'free' provision is not very helpful. Provision of childcare facilities for children between 3 years of age and formal school age is almost universal in France, closely followed by Italy and the Netherlands. Provision is poorest in Finland, Portugal and, probably, Greece.

The fact that there is a wide difference in the level of public and in-work provision, suggests that while some employers can see the value of childcare, in the UK the government does not.

It is interesting that some companies such as HSBC do provide for childcare, but other banks like Barclays do not. This suggests that the arguments for making provision are not wholly convincing to all business people, or possibly that the culture of some organisations resists this provision. It would be interesting to find out the banks' arguments for these different policies.

HSBC and Lloyds offered extensive periods of unpaid leave and both also gave childcare subsidies and provided workplace nurseries. However, some women might prefer companies such as ICI or BP that provided some additional financial benefit. Barclays, Tesco and NatWest seemed to be the least generous.

Summary

This section examined inequality of opportunity in regard to race, ethnic origin and gender. Most major countries have multicultural populations and a balanced society requires fair treatment for all, regardless of race and ethnic origin. Institutional mechanisms and glass ceilings prevent full equality in employment. Women continue to be poorly represented in higher positions. Childcare provision is an important mechanism for increasing women's opportunities in the workplace. However, the provision of publicly funded childcare in Europe is very uneven and workplace childcare support is very patchy.

SECTION 3

Other Forms of Discrimination

Introduction

Regardless of race or gender, everyone may be subjected to other forms of discrimination because of life events and personal circumstances. People with disabilities form a large proportion of the population but seem to be invisible to many employers. Older employees are a valuable resource in countries where the availability of skilled young people is reducing because of demographic trends. Ex-offenders also represent a considerable resource despite employer resistance,

This section is intended to help you to:

- outline the difficulties people with disabilities face in obtaining employment and the continued ineffectiveness of government measures to remedy the situation
- explain the merits of employing older workers
- evaluate the effectiveness of programmes to increase the employability of ex-offenders.

3.1 Disability

We now consider discrimination against people with physical and mental disabilities. You might like to consider your attitudes and views on these statements, and review your ideas when you have studied this section:

- disabled people form a fairly homogenous group for the purposes of employment

- disabled people experience prejudice directed against them

- mentally ill people are more likely to be unemployed than people with other disabilities

- the disabled make up a very small proportion of the population

- organisations which already employ disabled people are more likely to employ additional people with disabilities than other organisations

- interviewers should not focus on disability

- employers who do not employ disabled people usually have good reasons for not employing them

- partly because of their disability, most disabled working people are unhappy at work.

In Great Britain, disabled people make up nearly a fifth of the population of working age (men aged 16–64, women aged 16–59) . However, they comprise only 11 per cent of people in employment (*Labour Force Survey*, Autumn 1998). Of the 8.7 million disabled people in the UK, 6.2 million people have a long-term disability or health problem which either has substantial adverse impact on day-to-day activities (as covered by the definitions of the Disability Discrimination Act 1995) or limits the range of work they can do.

The Labour Force Survey shows that there are 2.8 million disabled people in employment. But levels of employment vary considerably according to the type of disability. For example, people with hearing impairment, diabetes and skin conditions have much higher rates of employment than those with learning disabilities or mental illness. On average, disabled employees earn around 10 per cent less per hour than the non-disabled. In addition, this differential in wage rates is compounded by the shorter working hours of many disabled employees.

MENTAL DISABILITY

The mental health charity Mind found that in 1996, 31 per cent of disabled adults generally were in employment, but the figure for those with mental health problems was only 13 per cent. Productivity lost through mental health problems cost the British economy approximately £14 billion in 1996. American research suggests that about 70 per cent of people with a serious mental illness identify work as a principal priority. Some 38 per cent of British psychiatric service users reported experiencing intimidation and bullying at work because of their condition (*The Scotsman*, 28 November 1997).

EMPLOYMENT QUOTAS

In the UK, voluntary schemes for employment of disabled people on a quota basis proved largely ineffective because of inadequate enforcement and monitoring. A study by the Institute of Employment Studies (Honey et al., 1993) indicated that few of the organisations surveyed in the early 1990s had 3 per cent of their workforce registered disabled (the legal requirement for employers with 20 or more employees).

REASONS GIVEN FOR NOT EMPLOYING DISABLED PEOPLE

In a survey, 75 per cent of companies who did not employ people with disabilities claimed the main reason was that they had no applications from people with a disability (Honey et al., 1993). Just 20 out of the 482 organisations surveyed stated that they had rejected a disabled applicant because their disability was seen as barrier for employment in a particular job. However, most organisations perceived certain jobs as being unsuitable for people with disabilities. Manual jobs were frequently cited as inappropriate because they were physically demanding, or there were associated health and safety issues. The researchers concluded that such opinions were based on stereotyping, with employers making a common association between 'wheelchair' and disability.

In another study, Dench et al. (1996) found that employers regarded people with difficulties in seeing or having mental handicaps and learning difficulties as the most difficult to employ. People with mobility problems (in contrast to findings in earlier studies) were perceived as being less difficult. Less problematic were conditions such as hearing difficulties, allergies and skin conditions, heart and circulation problems, epilepsy, and diabetes. The least discrimination occurred where disabilities were least noticeable.

EMPLOYMENT POLICIES FOR PEOPLE WITH DISABILITIES

Less than half of surveyed organisations had explicit policies on the employment of people with disabilities – and just one quarter had clear written policies (Honey et al., 1993). Large companies were most likely to have policies, particularly those already employing disabled people. A mere one in five organisations said they were actively trying to recruit people with disabilities. Again, larger organisations were most positive. A third of companies with disabled employees said they were actively seeking to recruit more. Honey concluded that there was a general antipathy towards disability issues – able-bodied recruiters were not affected and seemed to pursue an 'out-of-sight, out-of-mind' policy. On the other hand, organisations with disabled employees were impressed by their generally high levels of commitment and motivation.

COMPARATIVE DISADVANTAGE OF DISABLED PEOPLE

The queasy attitude of many able-bodied and mentally-resilient people helps to perpetuate the fact that people with disabilities continue to be amongst the most disadvantaged in the workplace. A further issue is that, unlike discrimination on grounds of race, colour or sex, the disabled are not seen as a specific group. Anyone can be disabled. Paul Miller (Equal Employment Opportunities Commission in the USA) stated that:

> 'The nature of disability discrimination is more intensely personal as opposed to group-directed. People with disabilities are generally not perceived as being members of a group that a particular employer dislikes or discriminates against. While there may be some employers who have a specific animus towards disabled people, such malevolence is more visible against people of colour in the form of racism or against women in the form of sexism. Malevolence is not often the prime motivation for excluding people with disabilities from the workplace. Rather, pity towards, discomfort with, and fear of people with disabilities are more likely to shape the stereotypes.'

DISCRIMINATION EXPERIENCED

Not surprisingly, Meager et al. (1998), in a survey of over 2,000 disabled people of working age, found that 16 per cent of those who were or had been economically active experienced discrimination or unfair treatment in a work-related context. Of that group, most said had been discriminated against by an employer (41 per cent) and/or potential employer (42 per cent). Most commonly, discrimination took the form of:

- assumptions by interviewers that disabled job applicants would not be able to perform as well as non-disabled persons
- job interviews focused on the applicant's disability, rather than his or her ability to do the job
- instances of disabled people being dismissed because of their disability.

However, Meager et al. found that most of those disabled people who were, or had been, in work reported broad contentment with current or recent jobs, and their treatment by employers.

Why not now go back and check your responses to the statements we asked you to consider at the beginning of the section. To reinforce the material, here are the statements with the true position.

Disabled people form a fairly homogenous group for the purposes of employment. On the contrary, people with disabilities form a very diverse section of the population and, in general, employers seemingly do not perceive the disabled as a single group.

Disabled people experience prejudice directed against them. By and large, the forms of discrimination experienced by the disabled are qualitatively different from the prejudice experienced by some other minority groups. Also, the disabled group is more heterogeneous than other disadvantaged groups, and individuals suffering different degrees of disability experience different degrees of discrimination.

Mentally ill people are more likely to be unemployed than people with other disabilities. There appears to be more fear among employers towards individuals with mental disabilities. This runs somewhat counter to the observation that people with noticeable disabilities experience more discriminated than people with less visible disabilities.

The disabled make up a very small proportion of the population. In fact, almost 20 per cent of the working age population are disabled in some way, but they represent only 11 per cent of the employed population.

Organisations which already employ disabled people are more likely to employ additional people with disabilities than other organisations. This phenomenon may arise because employers who have employed some disabled people already are more open-minded in the first place. Alternatively, disabled employees make employers realise that many perceived problems associated with the disabled are imaginary.

Interviewers should not focus on disability. One of the main reasons why disabled people experience discrimination is that many interviewers ask questions about the disability and how the candidate copes, rather than focusing on his or her ability to do the job.

Employers who do not employ disabled people have good reasons for not employing them. The reasons given by employers are mainly based on prejudice or stereotypical beliefs. It appears that the reasons given for rejection are often unfounded, and are based on false assumptions for example, that a high standard of English is required for a backroom warehousing job.

Partly because of their disability most disabled working people are unhappy at work. On the contrary, most disabled people are happy with their jobs. It is conceivable that this is partly because they have overcome discrimination to get a job, but also because they can cope with the work and overcome any extra difficulties their handicap presents.

LEGISLATION

We consider the legislation that has been introduced to offer some degree of protection for people with disabilities; as you study this section, compare it with what you know about sex discrimination legislation.

Recent legislation currently seems destined for the same fate as the older quota system. A prime example of a missed opportunity is offered by the Disability Discrimination Act 1995. This made discrimination against disabled employees or customers illegal in the UK but crucially excluded those with impairments vaguely defined as 'substantial'.

The UK Disability Discrimination Act 1995 defines disability as 'a physical or mental impairment which has a substantial and long-term adverse effect on a person's ability to carry out normal day-to-day activities'. Impairment covers any physical impairments which affect the senses (such as sight and hearing), and mental impairments including learning disabilities and mental illness. To be substantial, an impairment must be more than minor. With the exception of spectacles and contact lenses, artificial aids or medication are not taken into account in considering whether an impairment is substantial. Long-term effects are those which have lasted, or are likely to last, for at least 12 months, or for the rest of the life of the person affected.

Disability organisations have argued for a broader definition of disability similar to that contained in the Americans with Disability Act, a piece of US legislation which covered those people perceived to be disabled. This definition would allow the focus to be on the misconceptions and stereotypes shown by people who discriminate rather than intrinsic characteristics of individuals who experience discrimination. Such a definition moves away from the medical model of disability towards the social exclusion model preferred by many disability activists. In other words, the activities of disabled people are restricted by consequences of social organisation (such as transport and access) as much as by impairment.

The Disability Discrimination Act makes it unlawful for organisations with 20 or more staff to discriminate against current or prospective employees with disabilities because of a reason relating to their disability. The Act covers recruitment and retention of employees, training and development, promotion, transfers, and the process of dismissal. Employers are also expected to make reasonable changes to any employment arrangements or premises which substantially disadvantage a disabled employee or applicant – taking cost and other effects into account.

The Act states that discrimination occurs if a disabled person is treated less favourably than someone else because of their disability and if such treatment cannot be justified. Employers may justify less favourable treatment if they believe that there is a relevant or substantial reason. However, they must consider whether the reason could be overcome by making changes to working premises or employment arrangements.

Employers with fewer than 20 staff are excluded from the employment provisions of the Act. It is legal for them to discriminate against disabled persons and they are not obliged to justify their actions, however they are encouraged to follow good practice guidelines. The Act also specifically excludes operational staff employed in the armed forces, police, prison services, fire service or anyone employed on board ships, aircraft or hovercraft.

The Disability Discrimination Act led to the creation of the National Disability Council (NDC), which advises the government on discrimination against disabled people. A separate body – the Northern Ireland Disability Council (NIDC) – covers Northern Ireland. Unlike the Commission for Racial Equality or the Equal Opportunities Commission, the NDC and NIDC have no enforcement powers and were not given a remit to investigate individual complaints. These bodies have also been criticised for their undemocratic constitutions and for the fact that they are underfunded – the National Disability Council receives £250,000 a year, compared with £7 million for the Equal Opportunities Commission. Partly in response to these criticisms, a more powerful organisation, the Disability Rights Commission is replacing the NDC in April 2000.

ACTIVITY 11

Compare the information you have been given on the Sex Discrimination Act 1975 and the Disability Discrimination Act 1995. Do the provisions listed in the table below cover one or both Acts?

Provision	Sex Discrimination Act	Disability Discrimination Act
A statutory monitoring body which can oversee the implementation of the Act		
Monitoring body able to pursue individual cases of grievance		
Monitoring body adequately funded		
Allows justifiable discrimination in certain cases		
Provides exemption for certain occupational categories		
Applies to all employing organisations regardless of size		

See table 4 for a comparison between the provisions of sex and disability discrimination legislation. It summarises the situation at the time of writing (September 1999).

Provision	Sex Discrimination Act	Disability Discrimination Act
A statutory monitoring body which can oversee the implementation of the Act	Yes	Yes, but relatively toothless
Monitoring body able to pursue individual cases of grievance	Yes	No
Monitoring body adequately funded	Comparatively	No
Allows justifiable discrimination in certain cases	No	Yes
Provides exemption for certain occupational categories	Yes	Yes
Applies to all employing organisations regardless of size	No	Does not apply to companies that have fewer than 20 employees

Table 4: Comparing the provisions of the Sex Discrimination Act and the Disability Discrimination Act

3.2 Age discrimination

The prevalence of discrimination on grounds of age often goes unrecognised. In the absence of legislation, job vacancies commonly target applicants from a narrow age range, recruitment to the European Commission being a significant example (Price, 1997). In the early 1990s, about 30 per cent of employment advertisements in the UK carried discriminatory references to older workers (Heasman, 1993). Half of these indicated a maximum age limit of 35 years. While overt restrictions may be less common now, use of terms like 'youthful' and 'dynamic' carry the implicit message that older workers need not apply. Ironically this restriction often is associated with a degree of required experience that is much more compatible with a mature applicant.

Although discrimination is found across the age range, a survey by the Employers' Forum on Age (EFA, 1997) found that 80 per cent of workers over fifty believed they had been turned down for a job because they were too old. This may be attributed to direct discrimination, or to cost, skill or institutional factors.

The entrenched assumption that people over 45 years old are not worth recruiting, promoting, training or retaining goes against the increasing demographic trend, especially in developed countries, where people over this age already represent one-third of the workforce. Common stereotypes about older workers suggest that they are slow to learn, are less willing to accept and adapt to new technology, and lack enthusiasm for training. Research, however, shows that older workers are more reliable and conscientious, more loyal and committed to the organisation, have better interpersonal skills, work harder and to greater effect, and are just as productive as younger staff (Bevan and Thompson, 1992).

According to this survey, while older workers may be less suitable for work involving heavy physical activity or the continuous rapid processing of information, they perform better than younger colleagues in jobs requiring accuracy, reliability and use of experience. In the UK, the B&Q chain of Do-it-Yourself home improvement superstores is a rare example of an organisation adopting a strong anti-ageist policy. It is so rare, that the chain is able to promote its highly successful use of mature staff at all levels in marketing and PR campaigns. However, B&Q's policy tends to be viewed by other organisations as a curiosity rather than as effective resourcing.

More commonly, older workers are perceived as not portraying the right kind of image. A youthful workforce is preferred, especially when they have direct contact with customers, in the belief that this will make the organisation appear efficient and modern. Extensive downsizing in organisations throughout the Western world has been achieved in large measure through early retirements. The result is that many companies – with the exception of their senior managers – are entirely staffed by people under fifty. Canada, France, New Zealand and the USA are rare examples of countries where ageism in employment is illegal.

A case of age discrimination

Television news broadcasting in the USA is inundated with cloned pairs of regular presenters: a man of any age and a younger, glamorous woman. This pattern is repeated in 90 per cent of local stations. In January 1999 a Connecticut court awarded the equivalent of £5.2 million in compensation to Janet Peckinpaugh, age 48, who sued the WFSB network on grounds of gender and age discrimination. She had lost her job after ten years as a prime-time news presenter following the appointment of a new male presenter (age unknown) from a rival station.

Ms Peckinpaugh indicated that she had forgone other employment opportunities on the understanding that she would be allowed to 'grow grey' in her present role. In awarding twice the sum claimed, the jury technically found WFSB-TV liable on grounds of gender discrimination, but the issue of age was inextricably linked. The case is subject to appeal at the time of writing.

Sources: Adapted from *Independent on Sunday* (31 January 1999) and *The Independent* (30 January 1999)

The absence of legislation in the UK to address discrimination on grounds of age can be attributed to lack of commitment on the part of both employers' organisations and government. Having failed to support a Private Members Bill through Parliament, the UK government put forward a voluntary code of practice for employers in June 1999 which includes the provisions on a number of employment issues.

Recruitment

- Avoid using age limits or age ranges in job advertisements.
- Think carefully about the language used in the advertisements.
- Think strategically about where job advertisements are placed.

Selection

- Where possible, use a mixed age interviewing panel.
- Avoid making age an integral part of the application process.
- Select purely on merit.

Promotion

- Advertise promotion opportunities through open competition.
- Ensure that interviewers ask job-related questions.

Training and development

- Make sure that age is not a barrier to training.
- Ensure that all employees are aware of training and development opportunities and encourage staff to make use of them.

Redundancy

- Candidates for redundancy should be considered on objective, job related criteria.

Retirement

- Retirement policy should be based on business needs, giving individual employees as much choice as possible.
- Flexible retirement schemes should be used wherever possible.
- Pre-retirement support should be made available for employees.

A report by the Employers Forum on Age (BBC News, 7 September 1999) indicated that the code of practice was having 'little or no impact'. A third of the 430 employers surveyed said they were 'completely unaware' of the code. Two-thirds said the code had made no difference to the way they ran their businesses. At that point, the government had spent just £70,000 in promoting the code of practice to 34,000 organisations.

ACTIVITY 12

Jot down three of the most significant reasons why age discrimination against older workers should be countered. For each reason you select, write down how the UK government's voluntary code of practice might help.

You may have suggested some of these reasons why age discrimination is an important issue.

- The age balance of the population is changing. With an increasing proportion over 45, it makes sense for companies to look for scarce employees among older workers.
- Older workers are more reliable and conscientious, more loyal and committed to the organisation, have better interpersonal skills, work harder and to greater effect, and are just as productive as younger staff.
- They perform better than younger colleagues in jobs requiring accuracy, reliability and use of experience.

The voluntary code of practice should encourage the removal of overt age barriers, open up jobs to all ages; advocate selection on purely job-related criteria by open-minded people, and allow for flexible retirement ages. There are numerous other good points in the code but it may well fail because of its voluntary nature.

3.3   Ex-offenders

It could be argued that discrimination against applicants with a recent or serious criminal record is the most understandable manifestation of prejudice. The question posed by the most sympathetic manager is likely to be 'when does an ex-offender really become "ex"?' In the UK, the Rehabilitation of Offenders Act 1974 allows some convictions to be regarded as 'spent' after prescribed periods. With the exception of jobs requiring exceptional levels of trust – such as medicine, accounting, care and control of young people – job applicants do not have to declare their convictions after the rehabilitation period. In practice, however, the Act is virtually irrelevant because the rehabilitation periods are so long: seven years, for example, for an individual over 17 years old imprisoned for up to and including six months.

The position of ex-offenders articulates the importance attributed to reliability and loyalty in employment. It helps to highlight the nature of risk taken by all employers.

In addition to the nature of their offending, people with criminal records may have inadequate job-seeking skills for a variety of reasons, including those that may have led to their offending, such as:

- lack of social stability and work experience
- unrealistic expectations leading to underachievement or overoptimistic salary targets
- poor motivation, reflecting past failures or a belief that success will be short-lived
- gaps in education or training
- ignorance about negotiating the job market.

Two-thirds of offenders in contact with the Probation Service may be unsuitable for the vast majority of job opportunities because of numeracy or literacy problems (source: personal communication with a regional Probation Service).

A proactive approach to employment of ex-offenders

A resettlement prison in the suburbs of west London caters for long-term prisoners eligible for parole and with a release address within the M25 motorway system orbiting the city. Careful appraisal and extensive risk assessment by multi-disciplinary professionals draws on a variety of sources:

- written reports dating from before the sentence
- direct observation of the individual in various group settings
- performance in respect of agreed work, training and behaviour targets
- merit awards during the sentence
- feedback from voluntary external community work placements.

Towards the end of their sentence, inmates are assisted to apply for full-time employment that can be undertaken initially from the prison and continued after release on parole licence.

Employers develop confidence in the fact that such people are preselected on considerably more rigorous grounds and come with more detailed objective references than normally is the case. Problems such as unsubstantiated absenteeism are non-existent and employees demonstrably have a great deal to lose. In addition, those prisoners without previous experience of consistent employment gain in self-esteem and are committed to the opportunity to restructure their lives.

ACTIVITY 13

We noted in an earlier unit that employee selection is a risk-taking activity: there is always a chance of taking on an unsuitable recruit. Write 50–70 words on how the risks of recruiting an unsuitable employee are reduced by taking on someone from the resettlement prison described above.

You might have concluded that the resettlement prison provides many of the conditions and measures associated with assessment centres described in an earlier unit. In other words, prisoners are assessed in a number of ways by different people. In fact, the amount of information collected is extensive and detailed – much more so than that provided even by an assessment centre. Also, the resettlement period involves external voluntary or paid work so that realistic measures can be made of an individual's performance in a working context. All in all, a recruiter has far more reliable information available than would be expected for a conventional recruit. However, it must also be acknowledged that the resettlement centre is biased towards getting its clients into work, and there is a risk of a favourable bias affecting even 'objective' assessments.

Summary

This section discussed the difficulties experienced by disabled people, older workers and ex-offenders in obtaining work and fulfilling careers. The reasons behind this are complex and, in many ways, less likely to be ameliorated by government legislation and public concern. These groups incorporate a wide spectrum of individuals who can not be treated as uniform groups with the same needs and difficulties. Employer resistance to equal treatment is often due to ignorance and lack of awareness rather than prejudice.

Unit review activities

1. Read the article *Looking for a colour blind employer* (see Resource 12 in the Resources section). Identify and outline the main reason why employees from disadvantaged groups, such as women and ethnic minorities, fail to reach higher positions in significant numbers. Write about 70–100 words to explain your conclusion.

2. Answer the following questions.

   a) What proportion of the population of working age are disabled?

      5%   10%   15%   20%?

   b) What percentage of the employed population are disabled?

      5%   10%   15%   20%?

   c) People with different disabilities suffer different amounts of discrimination at work. Which groups suffer most, people with mentally disability, or those with physical disability?

d) In what ways is disability discrimination demonstrated:

>   lower earnings

>   lower wages

>   fewer jobs

>   all of the above

e) Mental health problems cost the UK economy about

>   £1 million or less

>   £10 million

>   £100 million

>   £10 billion or more

f) How well did the voluntary quota system work, in which employers with 20 employees were asked to ensure that at least 3 per cent of their workforce were disabled people?

>   very well

>   moderately well

>   poorly

g) State two reasons employers give for not employing people with disabilities. What other reasons might there be?

h) How common is it for firms to have written policy statements regarding the employment of people with disabilities (regardless of whether these policies are followed)?

i) Approximately what proportion of employed people with disabilities experience discrimination in a work-related context?

>   1%   5%   10%   15%   20%   25%

Unit summary

In this unit, we examined hurdles to achieving equality of opportunity and the nature of discrimination that disadvantages certain groups. Differing approaches have been taken throughout the world in terms of legislation, positive action and positive discrimination. Theoretical understanding has been enhanced by analysing discrimination at various levels of opportunity. Disadvantage is not uniform and specific forms of discrimination can be identified such as those on grounds of age, disability, gender, ethnic origin and background.

References

Antal, A B (1993) 'Odysseus' Legacy to Management Development: Mentoring', *European Management Journal*, Vol 11, No 4, December

Ben-Tovim, G, Gabriel, J, Law, I and Stredder, K (1992) 'A political analysis of local struggles for racial equality' in Braham et al. (1992) *Racism and Anti-Racism: Inequalities, Opportunties and Policies,* Sage/OUP

Bevan, S and Thompson, M (1992) *Merit Pay, Performance Appraisals and Attitudes to Women's Work*, IMS Publications

Braham, P, Rattansi, A and Skellington, R (eds) (1992) *Racism and Anti-Racism: Inequalities, Opportunities and Policies*, Sage/OUP

Clutterbuck, D (1995) 'Breaking the Glass Ceiling at Aer Rianta, Dublin' in Megginson, D and Clutterbuck, D *Mentoring in Action*, Kogan Page

CRE (1997) *Employment and Unemployment Fact Sheet*, Commission for Racial Equality

CRE (1998) *European Union and Racial Discrimination*, Commission for Racial Equality

Corbridge, M and Pilbeam, S (1998) *Employment Resourcing*, Financial Times Pitman Publishing

Daycare Trust (1997) Information pack on day care

Dench, N, Meager, S and Morris, S (1996) *The Recruitment and Retention of People with Disabilities*, IES Report 301, Institute of Employment Studies

Dominelli, L (1992) 'An uncaring profession: an examination of racism in social work' in Braham et al. ibid.

EFA (1997) *Managing the size and balance of your workforce*, Employers' Federation on Age

Goss, D (1994) *Principles of Human Resource Management*, Routledge

Heasman, K (1993) 'The case against ageism', *NATFHE Journal*, Autumn

Honey, S, Meager, N and Williams, M (1993) *Employers' Attitudes towards People with Disabilities*, IES Report 245, Institute of Employment Studies

Husband, C (1991) 'Race, conflictual politics and anti-racist social work: lessons from the past for action in the '90s' in *Setting the Context for Change: Anti-Racist Social Work Education*, CCETSW

Meager, N, Bates, P, Dench, S, Honey, S and Williams, M (1998) *Employment of Disabled People: Assessing the Extent of Participation*, Institute for Employment Studies

Megginson, D and Clutterbuck, D (1995) *Mentoring in Action*, Kogan Page

Molander, C and Winterton, J (1994) *Managing Human Resources*, Routledge

Price, A J (1997) *Human Resource Management in a Business Context*, International Thomson Business Press

Ross, R and Schneider, R (1992) *From Equality to Diversity: A Business Case for Equal Opportunities*, Pitman

Smith, M and Robertson, I T (1993) *The Theory and Practice of Systematic Staff Selection*, Macmillan

Straw, J M (1989) *Equal Opportunities: The Way Ahead*, Institute for Personnel Management

Strebler, M, Heron, P and Thompson, M (1997) *Skills, Competencies and Gender: issues for pay and training*, IES Report 333, Institute of Employment Studies

Wilson, F M (1995) *Organisational Behaviour and Gender*, McGraw-Hill

Recommended Reading

The most influential book on the subject is *Diversity in Action: Managing the Mosaic* by Rajvinder Kandola and Johanna Fullerton (IPD, 1998). In general, the subject is treated somewhat scantily in most general human resource text books. Perhaps the best treatment is seen in 'Discrimination' by Sally Howe in *Employee Relations* by Hollinshead et al. (Financial Times Pitman Publishing, 1999).

The UK's Commission for Racial Equality (http://www.cre.gov.uk) and the Equal Opportunities Commission (http://www.eoc.org.uk) have extensive websites. Links to similar bodies in other countries, articles and other websites can be found at http://www.hrmguide.com, particularly within the managing diversity section.

Answers to Unit Review Activities

Unit review activity 1

The answers to this activity could be quite involved because we are dealing with a complex issue which is not fully understood. The article pinpoints institutionalised discrimination as the most significant mechanism that limits the success of under-represented groups. This is a (sometimes subtle) set of barriers and prejudices which block and undermine the progress of people from disadvantaged groups into the higher levels of an organisation. You might have considered the difficulty in monitoring the effectiveness of any attempts to overcome institutionalised discrimination – as much as anything because of the years, or even decades, involved. You could also have mentioned that there is still a reluctance to introduce any form of positive discrimination in the UK, unlike some other countries.

Unit review activity 2

a) 20%

b) 10%

c) Some 31 per cent of all disabled people find employment but only 13 per cent of people with a mental disability.

d) All of the above.

e) One estimate quoted is £14 billion.

f) Few companies employed 3 per cent so the quota system did not work well.

g) No applications from people with disabilities. Some say that mobility is a problem, others that the disability prevents applicants from doing the job. However, it appears (to some researchers) that these are not genuine reasons, and that prejudice and stereotyping is a more plausible explanation.

h) Between 25% and 50% have such policies.

i) About 15% have experienced such discrimination.

UNIT 7
EMPLOYEE
RELATIONS

Introduction

On 6 October 1999, about 800 workers walked out of Ford's Dagenham (UK) plant – not in protest over wages and working conditions, but over the way in which they were being treated. They complained that management was guilty of condoning racial discrimination, bullying, physical violence and disrespect and that although Ford had adopted equal opportunities and anti-racist policies, these policies were not being carried out.

The Dagenham incident demonstrates that the topic of employee relations covers more than the economic link between management and workers. It also encompasses social relationships in which justice, fair play, and the exercise of power and authority play a part. These social and control relationships, which are often not directly addressed, underlie many of the problems of dealing with employee relations.

Partly because of political and legislative changes, we will see that the subject of modern employee relations carries wider connotations than the industrial relations of the past. In many of today's organisations, staff may communicate directly with management or indirectly through representatives. The scope of employee relations therefore encompasses one-to-one negotiation between employer and employee, as well as larger-scale dealings that involve trade unions and staff associations. In this unit, we examine both the informal processes and formal mechanisms involved in all relations between organisations and their employees, though we give more attention to the economic relationship.

For companies in member states of the European Union (EU), the European Commission has had an increasing influence on this aspect of human resource management. It advocates co-operative and flexible arrangements between individual employees and their employing organisations. This attitude accords with the social partnership perspective of many European countries and contrasts strikingly with the confrontational style of the 1970s and 1980s. Consequently, an important part of our discussion covers the role of EU (as well as national) legislation, including the function of works councils and supervisory boards.

Objectives

By the end of this unit you should be able to:

- outline the varied mechanisms for conducting employee relations
- explain the role of arbitration and industrial tribunal systems in resolving conflict
- understand the role of negotiations and bargaining as approaches to conflict resolution within employee relations.

SECTION 1

The Industrial Relations Tradition

Introduction

At first sight, it may seem that the obvious focus of employee relations should be on monetary or other rewards, involving some balance between acceptable pay (to the employee) and reasonable cost (to the employer). But the topic of employee relations goes beyond the issue of money to include a number of other concerns, both collective and individual, including:

- working hours and conditions
- length of paid leave and other social benefits
- freedom (or not) for workers to deal with tasks in their own way
- involvement in decision-making.

Pay and other benefits may still be negotiated, but modern employee relations addresses the more fundamental question of how the power relationship between employee and employer is played out in the workplace.

Today, employee relations is based on a rather different set of assumptions to the older industrial relations approach. To fully appreciate the scope of modern employee relations, we need to start by understanding the earlier industrial relations. Employee relations involves an assumption that employees and management share common interests in making the organisation profitable. By contrast, industrial relations placed a greater emphasis on the different interests of employees and management.

The aim of this section is to help you to:

- outline the origins and key developmental phases of the industrial relations tradition
- explain changes in attitudes towards employee relations in recent decades.

1.1   Industrial relations and collectivism

The employment relationship between workers and employers is a problematic concept. Despite increases in the number of self-employed in recent years, most people of working age continue to offer their time and effort to an employer in exchange for pay. The employment relationship is based, therefore, on an economic exchange between employer and employee. However, it is not an economic exchange like any other, since it is also a power relationship where:

- employers have formal authority, directing human resources towards specific objectives in order to maximise profit (reward) for the organisation
- employees have the (usually informal) ability to frustrate the achievements of this goal in order to achieve their own individual or collective objectives.

According to Hyman (1989), this power element always provides scope for conflict within the employment relationship as employers try to generate profit from their workers' efforts and employees try to equalise the balance of reward. Hyman argued that industrial relations – as the subject area was then known – should focus on the 'study of processes of control over work relations'. In other words, it should concentrate on the mechanisms by which control was exercised or resisted at work. Much of this debate revolves around the rights or presumptions of managers to manage, and the concepts of unitarism and pluralism that will be considered later in this unit.

ACTIVITY 1

Let us take this matter of the employment relationship a little further. It has been argued that the employment relationship is:

- an economic bargain between employer and employee
- a power relationship, in which the employee surrenders his or her right to autonomy to the employer

From your experience of work, either in casual, temporary or full employment, which statement do you think is the best description of the employment relationship.

Not only is the employment relationship an economic bargain but it is also a power relationship in which the employee surrenders autonomy. Both statements, therefore, describe elements of the employment relationship. But is this the same for professional working relationships? For instance, how would you describe the relationship between doctor and patient, or solicitor and client? In these relationships, professionals usually hold on to their status and authority, even though the clients make the payments.

Now think about skilled self-employed people working in trades such as plumbing, or domestic appliance repairs. Like the doctor, they have wide knowledge, skills, and qualifications; they have to keep up to date by regularly attending courses.

What are their expectations about the way they should be treated? As professionals? Or as employees? How do you regard them?

How should employees of a factory, who might also be skilled plumbers or electronics technicians, be treated at work? As professionals or as people to be supervised, controlled, ordered, and managed?

The point of this discussion is to indicate that the employment relationship is not just about money; it is partly about the way in which people treat each other – and specifically about how managers treat employees. The employment relationship also involves the submission and obedience of the employee, and the exercise of authority and control by management. While every human might be different, there are many people who do not take readily to subservience and the arbitrary use of power, perhaps resenting the subordination that they are made to feel by some managers.

These feelings of resentment can sometimes boil over into strikes and walk-outs, if employees feel that management is using its power inappropriately – or failing to use it as we saw in the Ford example at the beginning of the unit.

The view that industrial relations is concerned about power and control is rooted in the phenomenon of collectivisation, a feature of nineteenth century and early twentieth century industrial relations. The period was characterised by employee militancy and rapidly increasing trade union membership in response to considerable technological change and growth of employment in large factories located within urban centres (Hollinshead et al., 1999).

Organisations which represent people at work are often categorised as **trade unions**, a term which derives from the collectivisation (union) of workers within their respective trades, such as engineering, coal mining or garment sewing. One view is that trade unions were initially established as friendly societies to help promote the welfare of individual workers in difficult times, when there were no state security benefits or pensions (Cox and Parkinson, 1999). Sinclair (1999), on the other hand, contends that they originated as craft-based bodies designed to protect skilled workers from competition through control of apprenticeships and local pay rates. That is, a union was designed to protect one group of workers against others.

Described as a mixture of movement and organisation (Flanders, 1965), trade unions combine practical representation at an organisational level with a quasi-political role so that they may:

- aim to protect and improve their members' pay and conditions of employment
- campaign for government legislation and policies that benefit people at work.

We consider trade union organisation in more detail later in this unit.

As individuals, most nineteenth century employees had too little power to influence employers and protect, let alone improve, their conditions. Collectively, however, it was possible to withstand employer power to some degree. Hence workers increasingly banded together in their own locality, and then within industry-wide or national trade unions, to protect mutual interests and seek improved pay and conditions. Even so, at the end of the nineteenth century a mere 12.5 per cent of workers in Britain were members of trade unions. By 1970, however, membership throughout the UK had increased to 56 per cent for all male employees and 30 per cent among women workers (Hughes and Pollins, 1973). But from the late 1980s, there has been a steady decline from this peak level of representation.

ACTIVITY 2

If it was true that employees resented the exercise of power by harsh employers, can you suggest some reasons why trade union membership was so low during the nineteenth century?

It should be remembered that membership of trade unions was a courageous and sometimes foolhardy activity in the late nineteenth and early twentieth century. Whole workforces could be penalised for union activity. It is also worth noting that the same could be said of union membership during the Thatcher period from the late 1970s to the early 1990s. In both periods, the attitudes of government and the legislation in force were not supportive of collective bargaining.

At first, collectivisation was essentially defensive. Victorian employers were frequently aggressive in their tactics: some cut wages when labour was plentiful, demanded extra work without increasing pay, and imposed dangerous or unhealthy work conditions. But, as trade unions began to exercise some power, they pressed for collective bargaining procedures in which they would be given the right to represent their members in pay and other negotiations. Sidney and Beatrice Webb first publicised the term collective bargaining in the early 1900s, arguing that it was simply the collective equivalent of individual bargaining, aimed at achieving economic advantage for union members (Webb and Webb, 1902).

From our earlier discussion on the role of power and control in the employment relationship you might disagree with the Webbs. (As we shall see later in this section, the Webbs' classical definition has been challenged.)

Since 1902, the function of unions has broadened out from concern solely with the employment relationship. Sometimes they took on overtly political aims with some unions, for example, promoting the election of a Labour government. In other cases, unions have been concerned with social justice issues which went beyond the confines of their members' places of work, for example, offering support for the anti-apartheid movement during the 1970s. The rail unions have taken on the matter of rail safety which, of course, is in the interests of passengers as well as their members.

STATE INTERVENTION

The Conciliation Act 1896 marked a turning point. It was the first attempt by the state to achieve reasoned bargaining procedures as an alternative to strikes, lockouts, dismissals and intimidation. This Act set the scene for UK industrial relations throughout most of the twentieth century, together with the introduction of limited government support for joint consultation, especially in nationalised industries.

Joint consultation included collective bargaining, where employers recognised trade unions and their officials as legitimate bargaining agents acting on behalf of employees (members) in matters such as pay, working conditions, other employment benefits and work allocation.

What did this mean in practice? The Donovan Commission (1968) stated that the basis of collective bargaining was that 'employees do not negotiate individually, and on their own behalf, but do so collectively through representatives'. As a trade-off for collective bargaining and representation, individual employees were often asked to subordinate their own personal career and reward aspirations to the greater good of a union's wider membership (Cox and Parkinson, 1999).

ACTIVITY 3

Employees who continue to work during a strike are often reviled and abused. But the non-strikers might be seen to be exercising their own individual rights to choose a course of action they judge to be correct.

Provide an explanation for the strikers hostility towards the non-strikers.

Trade unions have power only if members act together. By joining a union, employees surrender their rights to negotiate individually in return for the union negotiating on their behalf. If some union members fail to support the union, they weaken the ability of that union to support all employees. The power of other individual employees – as expressed through the union – is weakened.

By way of summary, try this next activity.

ACTIVITY 4

The nineteenth century probably seems remote and, perhaps, irrelevant to you but key elements of modern employee relations can only be explained if we understand concepts which date from that time. Try this quiz to see if you have absorbed the main points of this section.

Choose the most appropriate ending for each of these statements from the options supplied.

1. The employment relationship is:
a) the personal relationship between a worker and his or her line manager or boss.
b) a label for the complex economic and power relationships between employees and employers.
c) an economic exchange of work for pay.

2. The first trade unions were:
a) national organisations designed to bring workers' rights and conditions to the attention of governments and politicians.
b) groupings of workers coming together to protect themselves from aggressive and unfair employers.
c) small 'friendly societies' or craft-based bodies in which workers came together to provide each other with welfare benefits in times of hardship and maintain the value of their skills.

3. Collectivisation is:
a) a process in which people work together to share pay and benefits from their employment.
b) a way of increasing the industrial power of ordinary workers by acting together to preserve or improve pay and conditions.
c) a concentration of people in one place to increase efficiency and cut costs.

4. Trade unions evolved into:
a) entities which were a mixture of movement and practical organisation with wide-ranging objectives.
b) political organisations.
c) bodies which represented every worker in the country.

5. Collective bargaining is:
a) a process in which all workers meet together to discuss pay and conditions with their employers.
b) a process in which national trade union representatives meet employer representatives to set basic rates of pay and conditions within a particular industry.
c) a process in which trade union representatives are recognised by an employer as having the right to negotiate pay and conditions on behalf of their members.

The most appropriate conclusion to statement 1 is ending b. For statement 2, option c is most nearly correct. But remember that historians disagree on this matter. One view is that unions were initially established as friendly societies to help promote the wellbeing of individual workers before the Welfare State was established (Cox and Parkinson, 1999). Sinclair (1999), on the other hand, contends that they originated as craft-based bodies designed to protect skilled workers from competition through control of apprenticeships and local pay rates. The most appropriate endings for the remaining three statements are endings b, a and c, respectively.

TRADE UNION STRUCTURE AND MEMBERSHIP

Trade unions played a major role in traditional industrial relations. Today, they remain an important element of the industrial scene with 238 registered trade unions and a total membership of over eight million (Sinclair, 1999). The Trade Union and Labour Relations (Consolidation) Act 1992 defines trade unions as permanent or temporary organisations consisting wholly or mainly of workers of one or more description whose principal purposes include regulation of relations between workers of that description, and employers or employers associations.

Within the system of collective bargaining trade unions may take a variety of forms. However, a common structure includes these elements:

- **the membership** – individuals who pay an annual subscription to belong to the union

- **local trade union representatives** – often called shop stewards, elected by the membership to act as intermediaries or negotiators with management

- **local branches** – giving support to union members within a locality, with a branch secretary usually elected by the local membership

- **district and regional offices** – often these employ full-time union officials to provide advice and support to union members and representatives within local branches

- **union headquarters** – providing a further layer of support to the membership and typically administering benefits, arranging legal support and campaigning for improvements to legislation and working conditions.

- **general secretary** and a **national executive committee** – elected by the membership, providing overall co-ordination and representation at the highest level.

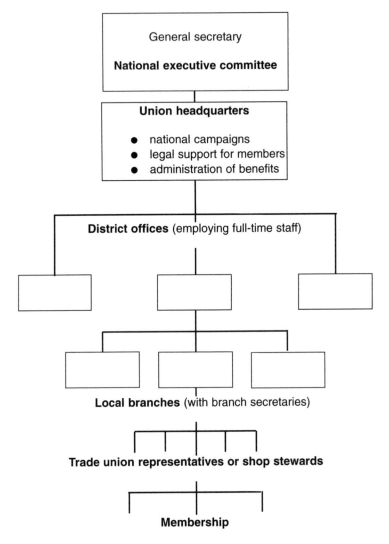

Figure 1: The structure of a typical UK trade union, 1990s

Figure 1 might suggest that the individual member is very remote from the general secretary, but this need not be the case. The individual member usually has the right to attend branch meetings, and may express opinions and put forward suggestions for discussion. If these ideas are adopted as branch resolutions of the branch, they might go the whole way to the top, and might eventually be adopted by the union. On the other hand, in recent years there has been talk about a gulf between the shop floor (ordinary members) and branches. This gulf may have led some members to become disenchanted with union membership. It is quite easy in any democratic organisation for those members who wish to be actively involved (activists) to become much more influential than ordinary members, and even to formulate and progress policies that would not be endorsed by the wider membership.

In serious disputes, the general secretary may get involved. In the Dagenham walk-out, for example, Bill Morris then general secretary of the Transport and General Workers Union (TGWU), contacted the Ford's president in Detroit, to review the management processes at Dagenham that had failed to prevent this particular dispute flaring up.

UK TRADE UNIONS

Some unions continue to cover specific jobs, such as the National Union of Journalists (NUJ) or the Association of University Teachers (AUT). Others embrace related industries such as the Banking, Insurance and Finance Union (BIFU), whose members have a range of jobs in the financial sector. The largest unions in the UK, such as UNISON and the Transport and General Workers Union (TGWU), are the product of mergers of individual unions and cover a very diverse membership from unrelated sectors of industry.

At a national level, trade unions in the UK are loosely affiliated within the Trades Union Congress (TUC). The TUC represents over 80 per cent of all trade union members (McIlroy, 1995). The General Council of the TUC organises annual conferences and conducts policy between conferences. A variety of regional (for example, separate Scottish and Welsh TUCs) and special interest groupings (such as the Black Workers' Conference) reflect the diversity and range of membership.

The TUC has four key functions (Sinclair, 1999).

Regulating conflicts

The TUC regulates conflicts between trade unions, for instance in recognition disputes over new industries. When a new industry becomes established, such as the call centre industry or electronic printing, different trade unions might wish to represent the workers in these industries – partly as a way of gaining more members – and would each seek recognition from employers. But an employer might accept only one union. The conflict between the unions can be negotiated under the auspices of the TUC.

Providing services

The TUC provides educational, research, financial and legal services for its affiliates. The cost of running a college to teach shop stewards and members topics of importance such as negotiating skills and employment law would be too great for a single union to shoulder. But by combining, unions together can support prestigious colleges such as Ruskin.

A political voice

The TUC is the political voice for the trade union movement, especially in relation to government. Once again, the voice of a single union might pass unheard, or differences between individual unions might weaken their case. But by presenting a united front, and expressing a common view, unions can together make a contribution to the political and social life of the country.

An international role

The TUC represents the UK trade union movement internationally, for example within the European Union. At an international conference it is the concerns that are common to UK unions, rather than the individual concerns of separate unions, that need to be heard. Also, it would not be practical for each union to represent its members internationally. For these two reasons some kind of joint representation is needed.

TRADE UNION MEMBERSHIP

We have discussed the historical reasons for the rise of trade unions but, you might wonder, why should employees join them today? In a British Social Attitude Survey, Sinclair (1999) found that reasons were given for joining a union included:

- to protect existing jobs
- to improve working conditions
- to improve pay
- to have more say over management's long-term plans
- to reduce pay differences at work
- to work for equal opportunities for women.

We mentioned earlier that membership of unions fluctuated. Before reading on, you might like to think of some of the factors that may influence people to join or not. Research suggests that the following are the main factors associated with union membership:

- state and employer attitudes – if government or employing organisations are negative towards trade unions, employees are discouraged from joining
- company size – in general, collective representation is more common in larger organisations and almost unheard of in very small firms
- type of occupation – manual and blue-collar workers have tended to favour trade unions more than 'white-collar' employees
- type of industry – there has been a concentration of union members in large manufacturing and privatised state industries.

Note that this analysis helps to explain some of the decline in union membership. Blue-collar workers have suffered more redundancies in recent years, similarly large manufacturing companies and privatised state industries have taken the brunt of closures in periods of economic downturn. In other words, today's labour force has fewer jobs which have traditionally been unionised. We will examine reasons for decline in trade union membership and influence in more detail later in this section.

ACTIVITY 5

Read the section on trade unions carefully and jot down your thoughts on these questions. Write about 30–50 words for each question.

Trade unions vary considerably in the types of work they cover. Can you give example of one type of trade union that is likely to have lost membership heavily in the last 10–15 years? Explain why this might be the case.

Can you suggest a type of union that might have done better in retaining and perhaps increasing its membership in recent years?

Unions that represent single industries (or are focused on a range of related occupations which have comparatively large numbers of unskilled manual or blue-collar jobs), especially those where technology has led to large reductions in employment levels, have suffered declining memberships. Shipbuilding and coal mining are obvious examples of industries in which job losses have caused falls in union membership.

In considering which unions have retained or increased membership, perhaps you might have thought of 'umbrella' unions that embrace diverse trades, some of them in high-growth areas of the economy such as information technology. The advantage to a union of not having all its eggs in one basket is that loss of membership in one area can be compensated for in another. This is exactly the strategy that some unions have embraced. The advantage to employees of joining an 'umbrella' union is that the costs of union activity is spread over a greater membership than would be the case in a specialist union.

1.2   The evolution of industrial relations

Before moving on to more recent events and the development of modern employee relations, we will discuss the implications of industrial relations as it was practised prior to the Thatcher revolution of the late 1970s to the early 1990s.

INDUSTRIAL RELATIONS RULES

You may have come across reference to rules in your reading about industrial relations in the twentieth century. In this next section, we talk about the rules, consider the form they took, what behaviour they governed, where they came from, and assess their advantages and disadvantages.

Within the typical industrial relations climate prevailing in large state and manufacturing organisations throughout much of the twentieth century, workplace relations were governed by a system of rules (Flanders, 1965). These may have been unrecognised and sometimes informal. According to Flanders, industrial relations rules appeared through a number of guises in:

- legislation and statutory orders
- trade union regulations
- collective agreements and arbitration awards
- social conventions
- managerial decisions
- accepted 'custom and practice'.

Flanders distinguished between procedural and substantive rules. In essence, **procedural rules** determined who could do what and how they could do it on both sides of the employment relationship. This included the ways in which collective bargaining took place, the stages involved and how agreements were arrived at and formulated. Procedural rules determined the behaviour of trade union representatives and their counterparts on the employer side. **Substantive rules**, on the other hand, governed the outcomes of those procedures. They laid down the ways in which employees and employers operated the individual contracts of employment between them, the rights and obligations of specific job roles and their respective status.

These rules arose through a mixture of historical factors, including:

- traditions and customs within a particular industry or geographical region
- ideas and practices circulating among employers, managers and supervisors at an organisational, industrial or national level
- beliefs and habitual practices of individual trade unions and their representatives
- state legislation, courts and tribunals
- the negotiating history of individual organisations.

Rules were sometimes written down in company handbooks. More often they circulated as an informal set of agreed procedures described as 'custom and practice'. The outcome was a complex web of rules which entangled all the participants in prescribed sets of behaviour. The existence of such rules reinforced the traditional industrial relations preference for a formal structure of negotiation and bargaining.

Flanders also emphasised the disproportionate power relationship between individual employees and their employers that could only be partly redressed by collective bargaining. In his analysis of collective bargaining as a system of rules, he moved away from the Webb's simple definition of collective bargaining described earlier.

ACTIVITY 6

Jack has turned to Eve Winters the shop steward to help him in his difficulty. He had been promised overtime and on that basis had bought furniture on hire purchase. There is a written note from Jack's supervisor (amounting to a contract) confirming that Jack would be given the overtime. Now, owing to an unexpected downturn in orders, his employers have cut all overtime.

Eve knows that, although there is a formal company rule to eliminate overtime, it would be possible to find Jack the money in two or three other ways if she could chat to his manager.

However the rules state that Eve can not deal with a matter about earnings – it has to go to the local branch secretary. The supervisor and manager would also know that they could not talk about the 'contract' since all legal matters have to go through the company secretary.

Argue the case for and against regulating people's conduct by such formal rules. State what you think might happen in practice in this case.

In order to maintain consistency across an organisation, rules have to be made and followed. If different managers made up their own solutions to problems, workers would find they were being treated differently from co-workers. Because of the different treatment they would feel unduly privileged or disadvantaged, and, in the latter case, they would complain – further conflict could be created by attempts to resolve this disadvantage. A second justification for some rules is to ensure that matters are dealt with by experts in the relevant fields – legal matters are dealt with by solicitors, for example. On the other hand, in many situations people of good will can find an acceptable compromise that suits them all, without having to go through formal procedures.

There are several disadvantages to guiding human behaviour and interactions by rules. The formal procedures that are intended partly to ensure consistency may take so long to complete that injustice is done by the delay. The rules may restrict the range of solutions so that no suitable solution is found in a particular case. The application of rules to situations may be inappropriate, since situations can arise that were not foreseen by the rule-makers. Rules tend to be rigid and inflexible and do not allow for changes in social attitudes, or changes in other circumstances.

In the particular case outlined in the activity, what happens in practice would depend on the climate of the organisation. If the union wants a battle, it may have a good legal case to bring against the company. On the other hand, if there is an atmosphere of co-operation and trust, then (in spite of any rules) an informal contact could be made between Eve and Jack's manager. Jack could find himself being offered, say, an additional job as a part-time security officer.

So, though collective bargaining is surrounded by rules as part of the protection of both sides, the rules themselves do have both advantages and disadvantages

COLLECTIVE BARGAINING

We mentioned earlier that there has been some debate about the nature and purpose of collective bargaining. According to Flanders (1965) it is not simply the collective equivalent of individual bargaining as advocated earlier by the Webbs, since:

- individual bargaining is essentially an economic exchange resulting in an agreement
- collective bargaining is a process that establishes rules for exchange.

Fox (1975) disagreed with Flanders' assumptions, arguing that neither individual nor collective bargaining necessarily resulted in agreement. Also, Flanders contended that collective bargaining was a political process (using the term political in its widest sense). Union and employer representatives negotiated levels of pay, working conditions, grade demarcations, holiday entitlement and so on as if they were politicians debating in Parliament. Fox, on the other hand, held that the passion and commitment shown by many union representatives indicated greater sincerity and conviction than was shown by most politicians.

It seemed natural to some organisations to use the same collective bargaining (or similar) process for matters of discipline or employee grievance. Within such systems, staff had no responsibility for determining their own required performance levels, times of attendance or (in some large organisations) work procedures. It could be argued that employees were – in effect – controlled as much by their trade unions as by their employers.

ACTIVITY 7

Based on Flanders' views and the comments by Fox, which of these statements are true and which are false?

1. Flanders considered that industrial rules were formal, written statements that laid down how management and trade union representatives should behave in the process of collective bargaining.

2. Procedural rules define how management and trade union representatives should behave in the process of collective bargaining.

3. Substantive rules set the ways in which the outcomes of collective bargaining, such as the rights and obligations of jobs, should be conducted.

4. Rules are determined by government legislation at a national level.

5. Custom and practice refers to the rules laid down in company handbooks.

Flanders considered that industrial rules were formal, written statements that laid down how management and trade union representatives should behave in the process of collective bargaining. False – many 'rules' are informal and unwritten.

Procedural rules define how management and trade union representatives should behave in the process of collective bargaining. True – this is Flanders' interpretation.

Substantive rules set the ways in which the outcomes of collective bargaining, such as the rights and obligations of jobs, should be conducted. True.

Rules are determined by government legislation at a national level. This is partly true because governments do legislate on employee relations issues but many other 'rules' derive from different sources such as company history, local agreements and others.

Custom and practice refers to the rules laid down in company handbooks. False. This term generally refers to historical 'rules' which have evolved over time. Of course, some of these can find their way into company handbooks.

PLURALISM AND UNITARISM

Changes in twentieth century industrial relations can be interpreted as a shift from the dominance of unitarism at the beginning of the century, to an essentially pluralist perspective for most of the middle period, and then a re-emergence of the unitarist view in the final decades (Cox and Parkinson, 1999). Pluralism involves a recognition that participants (stakeholders) in an organisation may have different goals and interests and that a key function of industrial relations is the recognition of these differences and the conflict they may engender. This is significantly different to the unitarist – essentially managerialist – approach held by nineteenth century employers who demanded that employees follow their instructions without thought in a 'master and servant' relationship (encapsulated in an Act of Parliament of the time) or face legal consequences. As we shall see, this unitarist approach came back into fashion with Thatcherism and the advent of human resource management.

Whether you adopt the 'management has the right to manage' (unitarist) philosophy or not, you should recognise that adopting it is a value judgement. Alternatively, you might take the view that every person engaged in an enterprise has the right as a person to express their views, to retain responsibility for their own actions and moral choices, and accordingly management's rights are limited. This again, is based on a set of value judgements.

Nicholls (1999) identifies a number of shortcomings in unitary theory.

- Unitarism fails to recognise that management and employees have different interests. It assumes that managers know best and the 'better' managers will look after the interests of all employees.

- Unitarists explain countervailing forces, such as opposition from trade unions or interest groups, as a response to their failure to understand management motives. Better communication is frequently proclaimed as the solution to problems. In fact, better communication might simply heighten the conflict, when it becomes even clearer that there is a difference of interest; for example, when management wants to hold down wages and unions want to raise them.

- Conflicting views are regarded as deviant, requiring aggressive responses that might include legal action or dismissal.

- Modern managerialists often attribute conflict to the failure to create a cohesive corporate culture. This belief is very narrow, overlooking the many different possible sources of conflict.

Managers might define unitarism as team spirit characterised by a common purpose. Today, it reflects the central concern of HRM that employees, whether managers or lower-level workers, should share the same objectives and work together to achieve them. From a unitarist perspective, conflict is viewed as negative and damaging to an organisation's effectiveness. Pluralists, on the other hand, hold that conflict is natural and may be healthy if channelled through a constructive process of negotiation and collective bargaining.

But the pluralist perspective also has shortcomings (Nicholls, 1999).

- Pluralism implies a belief that democratic institutions will resolve differences between management and workers. It is arguable that within the capitalist system there are in-built inequalities that cannot be resolved democratically.

- It presupposes the existence of a common set of rules and procedures to guide behaviour in the workplace, ignoring different values, objectives and individual circumstances.

- It is based on the (usually false) assumption that there is a roughly equal distribution of power between participants. Unless each side holds roughly the same power, the bargaining process is skewed in the direction of the more powerful party. Power rather than justice wins the argument.

- There is reliance on the power of negotiation and bargaining to achieve a compromise between employees and employers. This can be a rather crude instrument, time consuming and expensive, and it sometimes creates problems for the future, particularly when the power of one side is greater than that of the other.

- There is an acceptance of modern capitalist structures without questioning their inherent biases and inequalities. For example, it could be argued that there seems to be an in-built bias in favour of the owners and managers, thus giving them an unfair advantage in negotiation.

Prior to the Thatcher administration, a succession of British governments tried to reform and stabilise industrial relations. They took a pluralist perspective, emphasising a need for industrial democracy. As we see in the next section, although the process failed, it served to highlight the deficiencies of traditional industrial relations.

ACTIVITY 8

Ignoring the truth or falsity of these statements or phrases, decide which of them apply to unitarist and which to pluralist perspectives.

1. Everyone in an organisation should be committed to the same set of objectives.

2. Conflict is an inevitable and healthy demonstration of different points of view.

3. A strong corporate culture will eliminate conflict.

4. Democratic institutions will protect the interests of workers.

5. Conflict is dangerous and divisive.

6. Conflict can be resolved by achieving compromise through negotiation and bargaining.

7. A managerialist outlook.

8. Good communication is a solution to many organisational problems.

Statements 1, 3, 5 and 7 exemplify a unitarist perspective. Indeed, statement 3 defines modern unitarism as found in some accounts of HRM. Statement 8 is also essentially unitarist in the context of our discussion although communication can always be improved. Statements 2, 4 and 6 illustrate pluralist perspectives.

1.3   Individualism and Thatcherism

Industrial chaos in the 1960s and 1970s involving large-scale strikes (walkouts or withdrawal of labour) was instrumental in the downfall of governments in the UK. Not surprisingly, industrial relations became a major issue in politics and contributed to the rise of Thatcherism (which included a right-wing, anti-union agenda espoused by Prime Minister Margaret Thatcher and her followers).

Industrial chaos, low productivity and hostility to change were blamed on trade unions by much of the press (Price, 1997). Margaret Thatcher considered herself mandated to restrict industrial action and confine the power of trade unions.

Cox and Parkinson (1999) argue that, as a consequence, the nature of industrial relations changed dramatically from the late 1970s. Specifically, they attribute this to an ideological shift towards the free market in which a 'rugged entrepreneurial individualism reflected the values of individual innovation and creativity and the potential high reward associated with it'. Individualism has the following values (Legge, 1995):

- the value of the individual (as against the collective)
- the right of the individual to advance and be fulfilled at work
- individual initiative, energy and drive
- self-reliance
- personal acceptance of responsibility
- willingness to take risks
- expectation of benefits from work and innovation.

Conservative governments under Margaret Thatcher and John Major regarded trade unions as an impediment to the spread of these values (Cox and Parkinson, 1999). They introduced a succession of legislation that reduced the power of unions (see table 1).

Act of Parliament	Main measures
Employment Act 1980	Picketing: change in definition of lawful picketing – restricted to employees' own place of work; no more than six people; secondary action restricted.
	Closed shops: 80 per cent support required in ballot required to legalise closed shop agreements.
	Statutory recognition procedure repealed.
	Unfair dismissal and maternity rights restricted.
Employment Act 1982	Change of definition of trade dispute – further restriction.
	Employers awarded right to obtain injunctions and sue for damages.
	Right of compensation if dismissed due to closed shop agreement.
	Clauses requiring only union labour removed from commercial contracts.
Trade Union Act 1984	Requirement for executive elections every five years by means of secret ballot.
	Ballots required for political fund every ten years.
	Secret ballots must take place before any industrial action.
Public Order Act 1986	Trade union members able to obtain injunction if no secret ballot before strikes.
	Compensation for members disciplined for not following majority decisions.
	Inspection of union finances.
	Unions no longer allowed to pay fines on behalf of officials or members.
	Action taken to preserve post entry closed shop made illegal.
	Additional restrictions on election ballots and industrial action.
	Control on union election addresses.
	Commissioner appointed to provide independent scrutiny of unions.

Employment Act 1989	Restrictions on the work of young people and women lifted.
	Small employers exempted from providing detailed information of disciplinary procedures.
	Paid time off work for union duties restricted.
	Abolition of redundancy rebates.
	Written reasons for dismissal only required after two years employment.
Employment Act 1990	All secondary action made unlawful.
	Liability for unions for any wildcat action taken by an official unless written repudiation sent to all members using prescribed set of words.
	Workers taking unofficial action may be selectively dismissed.
	No longer lawful to refuse employment to non-union members.
Trade Union and Labour Relations (Consolidation) Act 1992	Consolidation of all collective employment rights, including trade union finances, elections, time off and dismissal.
Trade Union Reform and Employment Rights Act 1993	Individuals able to seek injunctions against unlawful action.
	Requirement for seven days notice of ballots and industrial action.
	Abolition of wages councils.
	Union financial records to be available for scrutiny.
	Increased penalties against unions failing to keep adequate accounts.
	All strike ballots must be postal; independent scrutiny imposed.

Table 1: Summary of UK employee legislation introduced by Conservative administrations
Source: Price (1997)

Partly as a consequence of this legislation, Legge (1995) identifies six key changes in this period.

Decline in trade union membership

There was a decline in trade union membership and density. The reasons for this are complex but include changes in workforce composition and the effects of unemployment and recession during much of the period. Legge dismisses many simplistic arguments about changes in trade union membership which are valid for formerly large-scale manual industries (such as coal mining and steel production) but do not apply elsewhere. She argues that a shift towards smaller-scale industries and management hostility towards collective bargaining (underpinned by legislative change) are also important factors. A further explanation is that unions were poor at promoting themselves and recruiting members in new industries.

Abolition of the closed shop

Closed shop is a term used to describe a situation where all employees within a particular work unit, or all those performing a specific range of tasks (trade), are obliged to become members of a recognised trade union – whether they wish to or not. The Employment Act 1980 made it difficult to create or maintain closed shops; the Employment Act 1982 further restricted the possibility of closed shops by requiring regular secret ballots and banning the use of contracts that specified union-only workers. Eventually the Employment Act 1990 removed any possibility of a closed shop by making it unlawful to refuse employment to non-union members.

Decline in trade union recognition

Widespread privatisation removed the obligation on formerly state-owned corporations such as BT to recognise trade unions. This may not have had much direct effect but privatisation was often followed by considerable job reductions and contracting out of activities such as catering and security to companies which did not recognise trade unions. Similar contracting-out arrangements affected trade unions in organisations remaining in the public sector such as the National Health Service.

Decline in collective bargaining

There was a decline in the coverage and scope of collective bargaining, especially in the private sector. Employers in the private sector, particularly those in secondary or service organisations offering comparatively low-skill jobs, generally did not give workers the opportunity to organise collectively – in line with the spirit of government legislation. This was compounded by the increasing importance of this sector of the economy as larger organisations outsourced or contracted out work which they had previously performed in-house.

Introduction of single-employer bargaining

There was a move away from multi-employer to single-employer bargaining, paralleled by a move away from multi-establishment to single-establishment bargaining. This trend was encouraged by government on the grounds that costs and conditions varied around the country. Accordingly Conservative governments emphasised a matching model approach to human resource management (discussed in Unit 1) with pay and other conditions being negotiated locally. In general, this weakened union power which had stressed, and often made a principle of, equality in pay and conditions throughout the country. The changing attitude struck at the heart of the collectivist tradition by playing one union, or union branch, off against another.

Reduction in industrial action

There was a reduction in the number of strikes, number of workers involved in strike action and the number of working days lost. Strikes and other trade union actions were once common themes in British newspapers and television news. We have already noted that the disruption and political instability they caused were important in laying the grounds for a long period of Conservative government. A conjunction of tightening legislation, fear of unemployment and reduced trade union authority led to a relatively steady decline in the number of strikes.

ACTIVITY 9

Our discussion of Karen Legge's views indicated that legislation enacted under Conservative administrations contributed to the six key changes she identified. Look through the Acts of Parliament listed in Table 1 and identify the Acts that could have contributed specifically to each of the changes.

You should have realised that the legislation had a profound effect on the power and influence of trade unions. In various ways, it had a direct impact on issues such as trade union membership, closed shop agreements, trade union recognition and reduction in industrial action.

Other issues were not directly addressed by legislation but the restrictions on trade union activity, organisation and unrest affected the broad climate of employee relations. This in turn led many employers to distance themselves from any interaction with unions or to engagement in formal collective bargaining as it had been understood in previous decades.

Key changes	Acts of Parliament contributing to change
Decline in trade union membership	Indirectly, all the Acts listed in Table 1
Abolition of the closed shop	Employment Act 1980 Employment Act 1982 Public Order Act 1986
Decline in trade union recognition	Employment Act 1980 Trade Union Act 1984
Decline in collective bargaining	Indirectly, all the listed Acts
Single-employer bargaining	Indirectly because of the change in style of employee relations
Reduction in industrial action	Employment Act 1980, in relation to picketing Employment Act 1982 Trade Union Act 1984 Public Order Act 1986

*Table 2: Impact of employee relations legislation
enacted by Conservative administrations*

Summary

This section reviewed the origins of collective bargaining and trade unionism. Early industrial relations were characterised by collectivisation to defend workers against exploitative employers and the development of formal bargaining arrangements. In the second half of the twentieth century, industrial relations can be seen as a shift from a pluralist perspective – a recognition that participants in an organisation may have different goals and interests, and implicitly recognising a role for unions in managing the conflict these differences might engender – to a unitarist view, which assumes that a strong corporate culture will eliminate conflict. Legislation enacted by the Conservative administrations in the 1980s and 1990s, other changes inspired by a climate of individualism exemplified by Margaret Thatcher, and market competition have shifted the power balance between unions and employers.

SECTION 2

Human Resource Management and Employee Relations

Introduction

In this section, we move on to consider the role of HRM and other management developments in the new employee relations which enveloped traditional industrial relations within a wider agenda. We discuss the relationship between 'HRM (as a managerialist perspective) with employee relations, now including individual as well as collective bargaining. European influences are steadily influencing employee relations practices in the UK and we give particular attention to the notion of social participation and to the roles of works councils and supervisory boards. Finally we conclude with an evaluation of employee involvement in Europe.

The aim of this section is to help you to:

- outline the relationship between HRM and employee relations
- explain and evaluate the concept of social partnership
- outline the functions of works councils and supervisory boards
- critically assess the implications of employee involvement in business decision-making.

2.1   Strategies for employee relations

What is the relationship between the new employee relations and human resource management? HRM has been accused of being instrumental in changing the nature of employee relations. It has been described as an anti-union philosophy involving strategies such as (Guest, 1989):

- withdrawal of recognition from existing unions
- awarding more generous awards to non-union members than those who remain unionised
- neutralising union power by means of no-strike agreements, single union deals and pendulum arbitration.

Hendry (1995) identified a number of pressures which pushed personnel managers away from their traditional roles as intermediaries between employees and management. There was a trend towards adopting a more managerialist stance in the HRM vein, whether or not they titled themselves human resource managers. In the 1980s, according to Hendry, personnel managers had become 'firefighters', attempting to deal with local (and, sometimes, national) disputes in an ad hoc manner without effective and co-ordinated strategies.

Part of the problem, as identified by Hendry, was the prevalence of informal, behind-the-scenes dialogue between personnel managers and trade union representatives which frequently ended in fudged compromises which did nothing to rectify major competitiveness problems in much of British industry. Through the Thatcher period, however, significant changes in the legislative background and a renewed confidence in managers' right to manage swung the balance of power towards management and began to emphasise individual as opposed to collective employee relations.

As we observed earlier, Conservative administrations considerably changed the power balance between unions and employers in the UK during the 1970s and 1980s. The turn-of-the-millennium Labour government has done little to redress that balance. In recent years, unions have played a subdued and apparently ineffective part in workplace relations. In the manufacturing sector, for example, major closures and massive redundancies have taken place which unions have been powerless to prevent.

The Labour government only partly redressed the situation with its Employment Relations Act 1999, loosely modelled on the US system. Adoption of European directives has also allowed unions to regain representation in large organisations in the form of company-wide works councils. (Works councils are discussed in a later section.)

Nevertheless many employees continue to be members of trade unions or staff associations. Pay rates, working hours and conditions continue to be negotiated and discussed. However, there has been a movement away from formal structures. For example, negotiation has taken on a greater individual rather than collective emphasis. This is exemplified by greater use of:

- **personal contracts**, where pay and conditions vary from one individual to another, without collective bargaining
- **team briefings** to cascade management communication about change downwards throughout the organisation, with no initial union negotiation
- **quality circles**, discussing improved working practices directly between staff and line managers, bypassing the unions traditional 'middle-men' role.

Unions frequently tried to resist these changes since they removed a key element of their power: the ability to filter information to staff and thus control the rate of change. In many organisations, collective bargaining has become confined to the essential topics of basic pay, holiday entitlements and representing staff in disciplinary hearings (Cox and Parkinson, 1999).

Read the article entitled *Phone workers' brain strain* (see Resource 13 in the Resources section). Consider how the call centres described in this article are an illustration of modern HRM-based employee relations.

TYPES OF EMPLOYEE RELATIONS

The influential models of HRM we have considered in this module advocate comprehensive people management, based on strategy and interconnecting aspects as diverse as recruitment and reward structures. The role of unions can be undermined by the channels of communication and influence opened up by HR initiatives. Emphasis on team-working and socialisation also works towards creating a belief that unions are not as necessary as they once were. In general, the interaction between human resource management and employee relations is complex. Guest (1995) describes four types of employee relations as they relate to a HRM framework:

- new realism

- traditional collectivism

- individualised HRM

- the black hole.

New realism

There is a high emphasis on industrial relations and human resource management. Management and unions approach employee relations as a joint activity, emphasising their mutual interest in the process. Formal union representation and direct management-employee communication exist alongside each other. But Guest expresses doubts as to whether hard HRM and strong trade unionism can coexist in the same organisation.

Traditional collectivism

There is industrial relations without human resource management. The old pre-Thatcher ways continue in many organisations but this form of arrangement is declining.

Individualised HRM

There is human resource management without industrial relations. Management negotiates directly with employees without union representation (and, probably, without union recognition). There may be comparatively high levels of pay in, for example, new technology and financial sectors but low pay in low-skill sectors such as cleaning. However, with the exception of US-owned businesses in the UK, this approach seems to have been largely adopted in a piecemeal rather than strategic fashion (Hollinshead, 1999).

The black hole

There is no human resource management or industrial relations. An increase in non-union environments and slow adoption of HRM as a methodology of people management probably means that this form is becoming prevalent. Ironically, growth in small firms, especially in secondary and service sectors, exposes an increasing number of workers to traditional (that is to say amateur and unsophisticated) management practices uninfluenced by any form of HRM, whether soft or hard.

ACTIVITY 10

Using Guest's model, which type of industrial relations best fits these situations?

1. A small software enterprise run by a recent graduate. Currently there are six staff and all receive high rates of pay in comparison to industry norms. Pay rates are determined between the owner and individual members of staff. They are expected to work long hours to develop leading-edge software.

2. A large retail operation with a nationally recognised brand name on its several hundred stores. Staff receive good rates of pay. They have the right to belong to a staff association but there is no recognised union.

3. A clothing company employing about thirty people sewing garments, mostly in their own homes. Most are women, many with children or other dependants, living in area which still has unemployment problems. Pay is low and staff who complain quickly find themselves out of a job. The garments are produced for an upmarket design label and sell in smart shops at premium prices.

4. A large automotive components company, which manufactures, packages and distributes replacement parts for a number of well-known cars. The union is well-organised and 85 per cent of staff are members. It is recognised by the company. Employer and trade union representatives negotiate pay and conditions each year.

5. This cleaning company competes for contracts in hospitals and offices. Staff are paid at the national minimum rate but they are given good training and supervisors are effective. The company does not recognise any trade union and does not negotiate on pay.

You will probably have realised that the types provided by Guest do not necessarily match these examples exactly (nor any others in the real world). However, it is a useful typology when trying to understand how and why organisations conduct employee relations in the way that they do.

The small software enterprise is probably best viewed as individualised HRM although it may have elements of the black hole stereotype. The large retail operation is also individualised HRM but the company has gone some way towards new realism in that it recognises a staff association. The clothing company exemplifies the black hole type in its exploitative arrangement. The large automotive components company uses traditional collectivism. The cleaning company is individualised HRM.

SINGLE UNION AGREEMENTS

One significant feature – multi-union representation within individual organisations – distinguishes British employee relations from those of many competitor countries. Single-union representation has been portrayed as a strength of German employee relations in comparison with the situation in British companies where several unions may be involved in a single workplace. Large organisations that have made inward investments in the UK over the last 20 years, especially those from the Asia-Pacific region, have encouraged single-union deals in their British subsidiaries. (This contrasts with many US corporations that have newly invested in the UK, which have tended to avoid any form of union presence.)

A single-union agreement gives one union sole and exclusive recognition for most or all of an organisation's employees. In practice there have not been many single-union agreements (Salaman, 1998). As a rule most agreements have had extra elements extending beyond sole recognition rights including, for example:

- a mechanism for employee involvement such as an employee council which actually conducted negotiations with management
- harmonised terms and conditions of employment within the organisation
- a no-strike clause linked within an arbitration mechanism for disputes.

Companies such as Nissan have attracted bids from British trade unions that have competed with each other to provide the most management-friendly terms. These so-called 'beauty contests' ensure that the winning union is likely to be fairly compliant and supportive of management aims (Salaman, 1998). There has been much discussion of the value of unionisation dictated on management terms and the level of membership in single-union businesses tends to be relatively low. Nevertheless, some unions have actively promoted themselves as being more than willing to enter into single-union agreements.

EMPLOYEE RELATIONS IN NON-UNION ORGANISATIONS

One of the critical differences that is supposed to distinguish employee relations from industrial relations is that the former encompasses non-union organisations whereas the latter is primarily concerned with trade union-led collective bargaining. This may be an artificial distinction since union membership reached only 45 per cent of the UK workforce at its peak in 1979 (Hollinshead, 1999). In practice, therefore, there must have been some form of negotiation about employment matters taking place at that time between management and non-union members, albeit of a limited, unitarist character. However, the issue has come to prominence because of the decline in membership and weakening of union power in recent decades.

Successive Conservative governments marginalised trade unions in the 1980s and early 1990s, providing a favourable climate for non-union organisations. The entrepreneurial spirit they engendered, together with growth in small service sector companies and large-scale US investment, further encouraged the trend. Hollinshead (1999) attributes considerable importance to US-owned multinationals which brought an anti-union influence to bear on management thinking, supported by an array of communication and reward techniques which were directed at individuals with no requirement for intermediaries such as trade unions.

Non-unionism is not necessarily total in such enterprises. Internal groupings of employees may be allowed to form staff associations or consultative committees. In fact, these may be encouraged as instruments of commitment. On the other hand, external interference in the form of national institutions and outside trade union officials are not welcomed.

Guest and Hoque (1995) attempted to explain why organisations with totally different characteristics and philosophies took a non-union route. They characterise employers as good, bad, ugly and lucky. Good employers are characterised as large companies which are dominant in their sector. They have clear HR strategies, reward packages paying above market rates policies which encourage compliance of employee behaviour and attitudes with the organisation's declared norms and values, high levels of job security and satisfaction and excellent communication systems. However, this enlightened soft HRM regime is dependent upon success. Once such organisations lose product leadership or face economic difficulties they are likely to abandon the good approach and switch to hard HRM with job cuts and closures.

Bad employers, in contrast, have no choice but to offer poor terms of employment and low job security because they operate in secondary sectors supplying a small number of customers and subject to intense price competition. Clothing manufacture is a good example of a sector dominated by 'bad' employers. Ugly employers make a deliberate choice to give employees minimal rights. In both cases, trade union recognition is seen as an interference and a barrier to keeping employee costs to the bare minimum.

The final type of employer is what Guest and Hoque term lucky. This type is likely to be small and owner-managed or family-managed. Management is unprofessional, opportunistic and pragmatic. Trade unions are not opposed but ignored. Pay is usually low and dependent on the prevailing business conditions.

ACTIVITY 11

Try matching the five companies profiled in Activity 10 to the stereotypes provided by Guest and Hoque. Try to characterise each employer as either good, bad, ugly or lucky.

Again, you may have found that it is not necessarily easy to bracket the examples with the types provided by Guest and Hoque. This is the case with all simplified typologies. However, we can make the attempt. The small software enterprise appears to be best described as a lucky employer but with some good features. The large retail operation is a good employer – but watch out if the competition gets tough. The clothing company is definitely an ugly employer. The large automotive components company is probably a good employer. The cleaning company is a bad employer in this typology, but due to market conditions they appear to have no choice.

2.2 Impact of the European Union: social partnership and employee involvement

So far, we have examined the topic of industrial relations in its free market context, exemplified by the UK and USA in the 1990s. In contrast, continental European countries tend to favour a social market approach, tempering capitalist free market economics with measures designed to mitigate its more socially-damaging effects. The social market approach features (Price, 1997):

- government encouragement of investment in production and product development – and, therefore, in job creation
- regulation of workers' rights and employers' obligations, ensuring consultation on major changes and restrictions on staff dismissal
- provision of extensive social benefits, adding considerable social costs to the payroll of commercial organisations.

The prevailing attitude in the European Union is steadily impacting on British companies. This is reflected in the adoption of EU directives in recent UK legislation designed to encourage a social partnership between employers and the employed. As we will see, a recent example is the requirement that all large companies operating in two or more member states of the EU must have Europe-wide works councils. The effect is to underpin the function of collective representation and, in particular, the role of trade unions.

SOCIAL PARTNERSHIP

The way in which an employer deals with staff depends upon a number of factors. These include the prevailing national culture and its assumptions about the respective roles, duties and privileges of employers, managers and workers. Such assumptions can vary considerably from one country to another. They are also embedded in national legislation governing the conduct of employee relations.

We have noted that legislation and managerial attitudes in the UK during the Thatcher period strongly emphasised management power. The situation was not replicated in Germany where companies operated within a social market and a legislative system that advocated a balance of power between employee and employer. This was reinforced by a rule-based system of employee relations relying on:

- detailed 'codetermination' laws, requiring worker participation in determining basic employment conditions
- formalised consultation procedures about major company changes such as plant closures
- protected employee rights.

Industrial organisation in Germany involves parallel business and union structures based on the regional states. German unions mirror employer organisations (trade associations): individual trade unions cover single industries or groups of related industries, and 90 per cent of employers belong to trade associations which are organised hierarchically at regional and national level. This is quite different from the situation in many other countries where unions may focus on particular crafts and professions or might be general and unfocused. The single industry unions form part of a national umbrella organisation – the DGB, the Confederation of German Trade Unions. This is a similar entity to the TUC in the UK, ACTU in Australia and AFL/CIO in the United States.

The effect of having single industry unions is to minimise disputes between different types of employees within a single organisation. The UK, in particular, has a tradition of multi-union representation in which different groups of workers within the same organisation belong to separate unions. Not only is there room for conflict between management and unions, but also between unions representing different groups of workers. Demarcation disputes and squabbles between different unions over issues such as 'who uses new equipment' have been unpleasant features of British industrial relations but virtually absent in Germany.

The German system, initiated by the wartime Western allies – France, UK and USA – embodies principles of social harmony and industrial democracy which, paradoxically, are conspicuously absent from the US and British industrial relations traditions. The system is based on codetermination laws featuring supervisory boards and works councils. The German tradition of employee relations consolidates a considerable degree of employee involvement and consultation within formal social partnerships between businesses and their workers. This approach to employee relations has been strongly resisted by free market businesses in the predominantly Anglo-Celtic countries.

Does participation work, or are US and UK companies right to resist it? A report for the Involvement and Participation Association by Guest and Pecci (*PM Online*, March 1998) argues that businesses which resist any form of employee participation are losing competitive advantage. In the survey, 65 per cent of companies which reported allowing staff comprehensive involvement in major business decisions, such as long-range planning and product development, feel that they benefit against their competitors. The report (*Benchmarking the Partnership Company*) incorporated information from major British companies including Scottish Power, the John Lewis Partnership, Rover, Remploy and HP Bulmer. However, a high degree of participation is not widespread in the UK. It seems that many British managers are unable to contemplate placing a high degree of trust in their staff.

Participation does not necessarily either involve or exclude unions, though 70 per cent of the companies in the Guest and Pecci survey had some union involvement (Scottish Power had three). Partnership takes place through formal bargaining mechanisms with union (or employee) representatives and different forms of individual involvement, including self-managed teams. Partnership requires a high degree of trust on both sides, with commercially sensitive information being made available to employees and everything being open to debate. Rover continued its partnership culture despite having new owners and some drastic changes to face in the near future.

The study concludes that the best partnership programmes take place when 'a set of mutual commitments and obligations' exists between a business and its workforce. The set includes commitment to business objectives, job security and direct employee involvement in job design, human resource development and training. According to Guest: 'The most striking thing is that partnership pays off. Organisations have a better psychological contract, there is greater trust between employees and employers and performance is higher.' Employee and management responses demonstrated similar beliefs in the effectiveness of partnership programmes.

ACTIVITY 12

Summarise the similarities and differences as you see them between:

- traditional British industrial relations
- the German approach
- new partnership ideas in the UK.

Write about 80–100 words. You might like to compare and contrast two of these approaches at a time.

You may have concluded that traditional British industrial relations is quite different from the other two approaches, whereas there are some similarities between the German system and new partnership ideas in the UK. Trust is a key element, with low trust between employers and employees in the traditional British system and much higher levels of mutual trust in the other two approaches. Alternatively, you could have focused on the 'us against them' or adversarial attitude implicit in traditional British industrial relations compared with the partnership of shared interests found in the other systems.

2.3   Types of employee involvement

The European Union (*European Works Council Directive 94/45/EC*) has directed that a business must set up an EU-wide works councils if the company has:

- headquarters in a member state
- a minimum of 1,000 employees
- at least 150 employees in each of two or more EU member countries.

The directive is aimed at transnational companies of any nationality, and includes companies based outside the European Union. So, for example, a US company with operations in Europe which met the EU's criteria would also have to set up a works council.

The directive requires that each business must inform its works council of the general progress of the company. Also, they must consult the works council about any significant change to working methods or company organisation including planned closure of factories or restructuring. The directive is not specific on the way works councils should function, or the method of consultation, but does have an annexe giving a model format which organisations are recommended to adopt. German and French-based companies based their EU-wide works councils on their existing national formats whereas British and Irish companies, with no previous tradition, have taken diverse routes.

National laws in most EU countries require all companies to establish their own works councils – the UK and Ireland being two notable exceptions. In Germany, for example, works councils have the following rights (Lawrence, 1993):

- **codetermination right** – the ability to give or refuse consent on issues such as appointment of an employee to a new position, transfers within an organisation, transfers between wage groups, start and finish times for a working day, and introducing shift work or overtime
- **consultation right** – the right to be consulted over planning matters including plant closure, new factory development, investment decisions and business policy
- **information right** – the right to be kept informed about company performance and prospects.

These rights provide German workers with a much higher level of access to company information and involvement in decision-making than their equivalents in the UK. The system also means that many of the consultative functions (handled by trade unions in the UK) are embedded within the works council system. German research indicated that the existence of works councils does no harm to the economic prosperity of organisations, in comparison with businesses in countries such as the UK where works councils remain rare (Salaman, 1998).

All businesses in Germany with 2,000 or more employees must also have a supervisory board, half of whose constituent members are elected by the workforce including managers with the other half representing shareholders. Board members are elected every four years. The purpose of supervisory boards is to monitor and evaluate business performance and organisational change. They are separate from the main or management boards – which are effectively composed of shareholder representatives – that have ultimate authority in large German firms. Conflict between supervisory and management boards has been infrequent, largely because differences tend to be resolved informally. However, if the supervisory board cannot agree with major decisions taken by management, the chair of the supervisory board has the casting vote. The chair is a shareholder representative. This structure has smoothed German employee relations, by and large, but decision-making can be slowed by its complexity.

A recent survey on employee consultation (*HR Network Online*, 1998) investigated over a hundred European multinationals. Despite the relative lack of legislation on employee involvement in the UK, British employers were found to inform their employees on developments and consult the workforce about major issues more than their counterparts in several other EU countries.

The survey made the following key findings.

- The level of employee involvement is no lower in the United Kingdom than in EU member states which have legally prescribed employee involvement procedures.
- The method of involvement by which information and consultation take place is dependent on the legislation of individual countries. In some countries it is, for example, direct to employees, in others through trade unions or representative committees.
- UK employers are more likely to consult workers on productivity and competitiveness than their French equivalents.
- There is a lower likelihood of joint decision-making about redundancies in the UK than in Germany.
- Because of the absence of legal prescriptions, methods of employee involvement are more diverse in the UK than in most other EU countries.
- There was no evidence that multinationals are 'playing one country off against another' across Europe.

It is clear from this survey that the different business cultures in Europe have different expectations of employee involvement. Standardised corporate policies on consultation and information do not seem appropriate as yet. At the time of writing, Ireland and the UK are alone in the European Union in being without national legislation on establishing works councils. The European Commission's harmonisation instincts may lead to pressure for conformity from Brussels and it is likely to press for legislation on the establishment of local works councils throughout the EU.

ACTIVITY 13

Check out your understanding of the works council and supervisory board systems with this short quiz.

1. Which of these organisations is required to have a European Union-wide works council?
   a) A French company with headquarters and 3,756 employees in France. It also has 96 sales staff located in Belgium, Italy, Ireland, Germany and the UK.
   b) A US corporation with its European headquarters in Dublin. It has manufacturing plants in Ireland, Scotland and the Netherlands, each with over 600 staff.
   c) A British distributor with a total of 845 staff, including 175 in France and 157 in the Netherlands.

2. What information must businesses legally supply to their EU-wide works councils?
   a) Information about profitability and expansion plans.
   b) Information about a television advertising campaign.
   c) Information about the planned closure of a factory.

3. What is a consultation right as it applies in Germany?
   a) A right to be kept informed about planned changes.
   b) A right to accept or refuse planned changes.
   c) A right to be consulted about planned changes.

4. In the German system, what is a supervisory board?
   a) The main board of directors.
   b) A board made up of workers' representatives and managers.
   c) A board made up in equal measure of workers' representatives and shareholder representatives.

5. On the basis of the survey discussed in this section, which of these statements are true?
   a) Methods of employee involvement are more varied in the UK than elsewhere in the European Union.
   b) There is a higher probability of consultation about redundancies in the UK than in Germany.
   c) Multinationals play one country off against another in the EU.
   d) UK employers consult employees more often on productivity and competitiveness than French employers.

In question 1, the US corporation is required to have a works council; it meets the criteria because it has over 1,000 employees in the European Union and more than 150 in each of two or more countries. The French company has more than 1,000 staff but it does not have 150 staff in each of two or more EU countries. The British distributor has fewer than 1000 staff.

In question 2, businesses must supply information to EU-wide works councils about profitability and expansion plans and planned factory closure. They do not need to provide information about television advertising campaigns.

In question 3, the consultation right, as it applies in German law, gives employees the right to be consulted over planning matters including plant closure, new factory development, investment decisions and business policy. Therefore, answer c is correct.

In question 4, in the German system, a supervisory board is made up of equal numbers of workers' representatives and shareholder representatives (answer c).

In question 5, statements a and d are true, statements b and c are false.

Summary

This section developed the account of how industrial relations based on collective bargaining evolved into a wider-ranging form of employee relations which encompassed non-union organisations. HRM and related managerialist concepts have had an important influence on the development of employee relations with an emphasis on the individual rather than the collective. European legislation also has increasing influence on the conduct of employee relations in the UK, introducing the concepts of social partnership, works councils and supervisory boards. These and other forms of employee involvement are becoming issues of importance in modern employee relations.

SECTION 3
Conflict, Bargaining and Discipline

Introduction

This section is about conflict between employees and the organisation and the ways in which it can be resolved. Conflict can take place at an organisational level, involving collective bargaining or negotiation. It can also occur between an individual and the organisation's management or another employee, sometimes leading to issues of discipline or grievance. The twin processes of discipline and grievance are amongst the most difficult and legislated areas of human resource management. Conflict can be healthy but generally tends to be disruptive and damaging to all involved. At its worst it can develop into legal or quasi-legal problems which HR managers are often asked to resolve.

The aim of this section is to help you to:

- outline key elements of the processes of negotiation and bargaining
- explain the key ACAS recommendations for dealing with conflict
- evaluate the role of industrial tribunals and arbitrators in dealing with disputes between employers and employees
- outline the effect of legislation in the processes of discipline and arbitration.

3.1   Conflict

Conflict occurs when the wishes of one person or group may be thwarted by those of another. It may be hidden, seething below the surface. Or it may be expressed verbally, physically or indirectly (as in industrial sabotage), and commonly can be manifested by a drop in co-operation between parties or by outright hostility

Conflict can occur over several kinds types of issue:

- **conflicts of interest** – where one group gains at another's expense
- **conflicts of values** – where parties disagree about the morality of a course of action
- **systemic conflicts** – where the operation of one system impinges on another so, for example, recruitment might alter the gender balance which is being protected by the equal opportunities system.

There are several ways of handling conflict. These include to:

- ignore it, hoping it will blow over
- accept the conflict but minimise its consequences
- separate the contending parties – where possible
- clarify the issues over which conflict is taking place in the hope that clarity will lead to an understanding of the parties' different perspectives, and that will provide a resolution
- try to reach a workable compromise between the parties through negotiation.

We do not have the space to examine the different kinds of conflict and different strategies for resolving it, so in this section we focus on the principal approach to conflict resolution adopted within employee relations – negotiation and bargaining.

NEGOTIATION AND BARGAINING

Negotiation has become something of a science in employee relations. The days of amateur negotiators concluding deals in smoky rooms are certainly numbered, if not over. Today, management and union representatives are likely to have been trained in bargaining techniques, entering negotiations with clear objectives and preplanned strategies.

Nevertheless there remains an ideological gap between many of the protagonists on the employer and employee sides of any dispute. Union representatives are likely to favour industrial democracy and hold beliefs in fairness and increasing levels of pay. Management negotiators may see union resistance to changes in working practice or job losses as a barrier to efficiency and demands for extra pay as unjustifiable increases in cost. Put simply, both sides may have valid arguments based on completely different perspectives. Bad negotiators will fail to recognise the opposition's point of view.

Walton and McKersie (cited in Fox, 1975) outlined two main approaches to collective bargaining – distributive bargaining and integrative bargaining.

Distributive bargaining

Here, one of the parties tries to achieve gains at the expense of the other – each side tries to maximise their own share of a limited resource. Negotiating a pay increase can be regarded as distributive bargaining, since one side gains at the other's expense. The most important feature of distributive bargaining is the power one side has to inflict damage on the other (through strikes or lock-outs, for example) if there is no move towards an acceptable agreement. This is also described as competitive or 'I win, you lose' bargaining.

Integrative bargaining

Here there is a more trusting attitude to bargaining as both sides work through issues in a problem-solving approach which could result in mutual benefits. This is sometimes described as co-operative or 'you win, I win' bargaining.

Clearly, these two approaches reflect different degrees of mutual trust and willingness to share information. Hence communication is critical since negotiators can make disputes worse when:

- one or other of the sides (perhaps both) do not have clear goals
- the negotiators do not understand the details of the dispute sufficiently well
- the two sides are in dispute over issues which mask the underlying problem.

Naïve management and union negotiators tend to use competitive language such as 'winning the battle' and 'fighting the enemy'. Yet, in most cases, winning a battle does not guarantee winning the war. In the context of employee relations, creating sore losers in one dispute simply encourages a return fight and greater intransigence over relatively minor changes in the future.

More sophisticated negotiators aim for an integrative or co-operative 'I win, you win' settlement where both sides feel that they have gained something from the bargaining exercise. Lyons (1988) has put forward this four-stage model of the bargaining process.

- **Initial positioning** – the two sides put forward their demands firmly, showing no sign of any possible agreement. At this point it seems often that there is no hope of resolving the dispute. Typically, if a large organisation is involved, the media present the situation as a bitter and uncompromising battle made all the more newsworthy if the participants hurl abuse at each other.
- **Testing** – the protagonists begin to tire of the argument. Slowly, the two sides begin to probe one another's points of view, testing which points are totally immovable, and which could be the basis of a compromise.
- **Concession** – proposals are put forward more formally and mutual concessions are made.
- **Settlement** – the two sides reach agreement and a package is determined which may bear little resemblance to either side's initial demands.

The basis of successful negotiation lies in a 'tit for tat' exchange of concessions in the third stage of Lyons' model. For this to happen, it is necessary for there to be a balance of power (real or illusory) between both sides. If, for example, management have real power, perhaps threatening closure of a factory in an area of high unemployment, the balance is absent. In this case, the union negotiators will find it difficult to wring any meaningful concessions from the employers.

Negotiation demands these personal qualities and skills which may not be entirely realised through training.

- **Ability to analyse**. This requires a long-term perspective, seeing the dispute as part of an ongoing process in which employees and employer will have to continue to deal with each other. It also demands the ability to understand the strengths and weaknesses of the other side's arguments.

- **Ability to argue effectively**. Negotiation involves reasoning: participants have to be able to put forward convincing arguments forcefully but not aggressively.

- **Ability to give and sense signals of co-operation**. Negotiators need to be able to 'read' small cues of compromise and concession.

- **Attention to detail**. A deal may be concluded but it will fall apart quickly if all the details are not taken care of in the formal agreement.

ACTIVITY 14

Read the article entitled *Unattractive contracts* (see Resource 14 in the Resources section). Evaluate the approach of the university vice-chancellor in the light of the discussion on negotiation and bargaining. Why have negotiations failed at the university?

Note that no account of a negotiation provides all the information you might want. But make the best judgements you can with the information provided. Write about 80–100 words.

You might consider:

- whether this a case of distributive or integrated bargaining?
- did the negotiation follow the stages in Lyons' model?
- to what extent did the vice-chancellor demonstrate good negotiating skills?

You may have found that the account of this industrial dispute was difficult to analyse fully because (as is often the case) it does not provide a full account of the issue. However, you would probably define the case as an example of distributive bargaining gone wrong. It is hard to tell quite how well the process matched Lyons' model but bargaining clearly failed before the 'tit for tat' stage was reached. You might have concluded that the vice-chancellor did not have (or, perhaps, deliberately refrained from using) the negotiating and bargaining skills we have described in this section.

3.2   Discipline

Individual countries vary considerably in both the amount and the nature of legislation regarding employee discipline. Legislation aside, most large organisations have their own well-defined set of internal procedures for disciplinary cases. Typically presented in the form of a company handbook, usually forming part of a formal employment contract, businesses have rules on:

- **absence** – including rules on reporting absence due to sickness and other causes, mechanisms for authorising annual leave, requirements for medical certificates
- **health and safety** – covering, for example, the need for protective clothing, rules on smoking, dealing with hazards
- **timekeeping** – hours of attendance, mechanisms for flexitime and clocking-on, rules on lateness
- **using company facilities for personal reasons** – this may cover vehicles, telephones, photocopiers, internet access, stationery, etc.
- **discrimination** in the workplace against customers or fellow workers on the basis of disability, race, gender, and so on
- **gross misconduct** – the most contentious area, covering offences which could justifiably lead to instant dismissal.

The Arbitration, Conciliation and Advisory Service (ACAS) classification of offences which can be included within the term gross misconduct lists:

- serious negligence involving unacceptable loss, damage or injury
- deliberate damage to company property
- fighting with or assaulting another person
- serious incapability due to the effects of substance misuse such as alcohol and illegal drugs
- fraud, theft and deliberate falsifying of records
- unauthorised access to computer data
- serious acts of insubordination.

ACTIVITY 15

Which categories of disciplinary offences do the following cases fit?

1. Repeatedly turning up 15–20 minutes late for work.

2. Using company stationery for personal use.

3. Taking a sum of money from the department's petty cash without intending to return it.

4. Taking a day off because of a hangover.

5. Hitting a colleague.

6. Reading a file containing a colleague's pay records without authority.

You will probably have observed that these cases are all subject to interpretation. Often you would prefer to have more information about what happened, why it occurred and to what extent before making up your mind.

Let's look at these cases in turn. Persistent lateness is a timekeeping issue and it would not be regarded as gross misconduct. Using company stationery for personal use is not normally regarded as gross misconduct. However, taking petty cash (without intending to return it) is gross misconduct. Taking a day off because of a hangover should be covered by absence procedures. Hitting a colleague and reading a file containing a colleague's pay records without authority are both instances of gross misconduct.

DISCIPLINARY PROCEDURES

The Arbitration, Conciliation and Advisory Service (ACAS) advocate a procedure for dealing with disciplinary offences which is cautious, carefully staged and meticulously recorded. The process is intended to be fair to the employee and prevent the employer from any subsequent liability to action in the courts or industrial tribunals. The procedure is based on these principles:

- no disciplinary action is to be taken against an employee until the case has been fully investigated
- employees should be advised of the nature of the complaint against them and given the opportunity to state their case before any decision is made
- every employee may be accompanied by an employee representative or work colleague during a disciplinary interview
- employees should not be dismissed for a first breach of discipline except in cases of gross misconduct
- employee should have the right to appeal against any disciplinary penalty imposed.

In minor cases, the problem is best dealt with on an informal basis. For more serious cases the standard ACAS model for disciplinary procedures follows this (simplified) sequence.

1. When conduct or work performance is not acceptable, employees should first be given a formal oral warning

2. In the case of a serious offence, or if unsatisfactory conduct continues, the employee should be given a written warning. This should give details of the complaint, the improvement required and the timescale.

3. When there is no improvement, or there has been some action which is serious enough to justify a single written warning but not dismissal, a final written warning is given to the employee. This should detail the complaint, warn of dismissal if there is no acceptable change of behaviour, and advise of the right of appeal.

4. If the employee does not heed the warning, the result is normally dismissal. This should be actioned by the appropriate senior manager. The employee should receive a document providing written reasons for dismissal, the date of termination of employment, and a statement of the right of appeal.

In other words, ACAS suggest that **verbal warnings** are used for less serious cases which cannot be resolved through an informal discussion; **written warnings** are used for serious cases or cases where there has been no improvement after an oral warning – further written warnings will follow if there is still no improvement; **written statements detailing the nature of the offence** should accompany written warnings and further stages in the disciplinary process; **formal appeals** should be allowed after formal written warnings or notice of termination; **dismissal** only occurs for gross misconduct or repeated offences which have been dealt with through the disciplinary process.

3.3 Arbitration mechanisms

On occasions, conflict between an employer and a member of staff may require external intervention, possibly by arbitration or a legal tribunal. Many countries have taken the view that an impartial, legally constituted body has a part to play in some circumstances. In the UK, ACAS provides a range of services including arbitration and facilitating employment tribunals. It is a widely respected and influential body which has had a changing role under different governments.

It is a state-funded but independent body with 600 staff located in nine offices around the country. ACAS provides telephone assistance from its public enquiry points, handling 442,000 calls during one year (*ACAS 1997 Annual Report*). Just over half of the enquiries (53 per cent) came from individual employees, the rest being mostly from employers and trade unions. In order of frequency, callers asked about:

- wages and holiday pay (35 per cent)
- discipline and dismissal (20 per cent)
- redundancy and transfer of undertakings (16 per cent)
- maternity rights (8 per cent).

Disability issues and the effect of European law on employment rights were also major topics.

In the UK, ACAS has been given a stronger role in arbitration by the Labour government. ACAS was already required to try and promote an agreed settlement in most statutory employment rights disputes, but now it has authority to conciliate in cases of redundancy payment claims. Under the Employment Rights (Disputes Resolution) Act 1998, ACAS has a duty to conciliate if an application is passed to an employment tribunal regarding redundancy pay entitlement for dismissals occurring after 1 October 1998. ACAS conciliators make contact with all the parties involved to determine whether the claim can be resolved without needing a tribunal hearing. Some 4,770 such cases were registered by the Employment Tribunal Service in 1997–98, representing about six per cent of the caseload for the period.

EMPLOYMENT TRIBUNALS

Employment tribunals may take a variety of forms. German labour courts can make legally binding judgements whereas British tribunal decisions do not set a precedent in law and cannot establish criminal behaviour. However, they create a set of values which can influence industry as a whole.

Employment tribunals are not courts, but are designed to give speedy, expert, cheap and informal resolution to a whole range of employment disputes. Appeals from employment tribunals are heard by the employment (appeals) tribunal, and the High Court. The tribunal chair will be legally qualified and will be supported by two lay assessors, one drawn from each side of industry.

The *ACAS 1997 Annual Report* reported that, for the tenth year in succession, claims to industrial tribunals reached a record high. In 1997, ACAS received nearly 107,000 claims on issues connected to individual employment rights. This was a 6.5 per cent increase on 1996, (in the preceding two years the rises had been about 10 and 15 per cent). The number of claims has more than doubled between 1990 and 1997. However, there has only been a 2 per cent rise in the number of individual cases. The explanation lies in a growing tendency for cases to include two or more areas of complaint (for example, unfair dismissal and breach of contract).

The largest number of claims – two out of every five – concern alleged unfair dismissal. An equivalent proportion of cases was accounted for by claims regarding protection of wages and breach of contract. Cases of discrimination remained at a comparatively low level: in 1997 there were 6,600 cases of sex discrimination, 2,900 of race discrimination and, in the first full year of the new legislation, 1,400 for disability discrimination.

ACAS claimed considerable success in its attempts at individual conciliation, with just 30 per cent of claims proceeding to a tribunal hearing. The achievement was particularly good with cases under the new Disability Discrimination Act – only 18 per cent of 568 completed cases going as far as a tribunal (*ACAS 1997 Annual Report*).

ACTIVITY 16

A large UK company operating on fairly hard HRM principles wishes to set up an internal arbitration service. As a first step you have been asked to recommend, in outline, how the arbitration service should be organised. Write a brief paper for the HRM Director outlining your thoughts for the service.

In your paper you should cover:

- the aims of the service and benefits to the company
- who should staff it
- who will pay for it
- what are the expected types of complaint
- at what stage, if at all, would individual employees be allowed to access the service
- how would access be provided?

An arbitration service must be seen to be independent by both sides to a dispute. This means that the service must not be in the control or pay of either side. However, given limited funds some compromise may have to be made on this issue, and how you make this compromise is a matter for your judgement.

The suggested aims of the service are to provide a means of settling disputes between management and employees in a way that is acceptable to both sides.

The benefits to the company are expected to be:

- avoidance of adverse publicity when disputes go public or to tribunal
- maintenance of effective working relationships between management and workers
- reduction in the severity of conflict by limiting escalation.

In the interests of economy and independence it is suggested that the administrative element of the service would be run by the union and paid for by the company. Adjudicators would be independent, and appointed from a panel created jointly by unions and management. It is recommended that services of the arbitrators would be paid for by the company.

If complaints follow the national pattern, then the company can expect these types of case (in order or frequency):

- wages and holiday pay
- discipline and dismissal

- redundancy and transfer of undertakings
- maternity rights
- disability issues
- employment rights under European Law.

However, the distribution of cases might be different, reflecting particular issues that might arise within the company and the style of company management.

Employees would be expected to exhaust the existing disciplinary and grievance procedures before making formal reference to the arbitration service. However, facilities should be in place to enable employees to obtain information at any time informally by telephone or letter.

ACTIVITY 17

Which of these statements are true and which are false?

1. ACAS does not have the right to conciliate on redundancy payment claims.

2. The most common claim to ACAS is for unfair dismissal.

3. The largest number of telephone calls received by ACAS were concerned with unfair dismissal.

4. The majority of grievance claims go to an employment tribunal.

5. British employment tribunals can make judgements which set a precedent in law.

Statement 2 is true, the other statements are false. Note that the largest number of telephone calls received by ACAS concern with wages and holiday pay, and that most grievance claims do not reach an employment tribunal, they are resolved informally.

Summary

In this section we considered the negotiation and bargaining process which depends more upon analysis and participant training than is apparent in the media. The internal and external mechanisms for handling discipline and arbitration in organisations are also amenable to analytical thinking. It is advisable to follow ACAS recommended procedures for dealing with disciplinary cases, following a careful and fair sequence of verbal and written warnings.

Unit review activity

This activity invites you to move beyond the nuts and bolts of employee relationship and union organisation and to think about the wider roles of trade unions.

Read the case study below on 'getting off the fence in Ulster'. Then:

- identify the issues that underlie trade union activity in Northern Ireland
- discuss whether it is appropriate for trade unions to involve themselves in issues that go beyond the workplace.

Getting off the fence in Ulster

In Northern Ireland there is a close correlation between religious affiliation and political belief. Most Catholics support the republican movement, and most Protestants support allegiance to the United Kingdom. For many years the minority Catholic community has been disadvantaged in comparison to the Protestant majority with regard to finding jobs, getting promotion, political influence and housing.

As they should represent both Protestant and Catholic workers, trade unions in Northern Ireland have avoided taking one side or the other in the political struggle between the two communities. But when the simultaneous referendums held in Northern Ireland and the Republic of Ireland came out in favour of the Good Friday Agreement, the Irish Congress of Trade Unions lent its weight in support. "That was a difficult decision," said Mrs Inez McCormack, the elected president. Not all unions would endorse the Congress position, since they would be unable to secure the agreement of their Loyalist members.

Some politicians from the UK mainland had hoped that working class solidarity could overcome the sectarianism in the province, but as Mrs McCormack points out, this was very unrealistic. "It would be like in the southern states of the USA in the 1960s, if you had tried to fight the issues of equality without accepting the issues of black and white."

One of the consequences of the Good Friday Agreement is that working class Protestants were more willing to address issues of equality and human rights. Previously any such discussion would have been seen as having a hidden agenda – to admit Catholics into political equality with Protestants – and so would be fiercely resisted.

The change in attitude and the new mechanisms introduced by the Agreement have assisted those Unionists concerned with equal opportunities in respect, for example, of fair treatment for minority groups, women and the long-term unemployed.

Unit summary

This unit has introduced you to the topic of employee relations. We identified a reorientation of the subject from the confrontational industrial relations of the past to more conciliatory interpretations. The effects of European Union directives have been particularly important in the context of works councils and supervisory boards. Grievance, discipline and negotiation are important topics which need to be handled sensitively and with due regard for the possible legal consequences.

References

Cox, P and Parkinson A (1999) 'Values and their impact on the changing employment relationship' in Hollinshead, G, Nicholls, P and Tailby, S (eds) (1999) *Employee Relations*, Financial Times Pitman Publishing

Donovan Commission (1968) *Royal Commission on Trade Unions and Employers' Associations*, HMSO

Flanders, A (1965) *Industrial Relations – What is Wrong with the System?*, Faber and Faber

Fox, A (1975) *Beyond Contract: Work, Power and Trust Relations*, Faber and Faber

Guest, D (1989) 'Personnel and HRM: can you tell the difference? *Personnel Management*, January

Guest, D and Hoque, K (1995) 'The good, the bad and the ugly – employment relations in non-union workplaces', *Human Resource Management Journal*, 5 (1)

Hendry, C (1975) *Human Resource Management: A Strategic Approach to Employment*, Butterworth-Heinemann

Hollinshead, G (1999) 'Management' in Hollinshead, G, Nicholls, P and Tailby, S (eds) (1999) *Employee Relations*, Financial Times Pitman Publishing

Hollinshead, G, Nicholls, P and Tailby, S (eds) (1999), *Employee Relations*, Financial Times Pitman Publishing

Hughes, J and Pollins, H (1973) *Trade Unions in Great Britain*, David and Charles

Hyman, R (1989) *The Political Economy of Industrial Relations*, Macmillan

Lawrence, P (1993) 'Human Resource Management in Germany', in Tyson, S, Lawrence, P, Poirson, P, Manzolini, L and Vincente, C F (eds) (1993) *Human Resource Management in Europe: Perspectives for the 1990s*, Routledge

Legge, K (1995) *Human Resource Management, Rhetoric and Realities*, Macmillan

Lyons, P (1998) 'Social Interaction' in Cowling, A G, Stanworth, M J K, Bennett, R D, Curran, J and Lyons, P (1998) *Behavioural Sciences for Managers*, Edward Arnold, 2nd edn

McIlroy, J (1995) *Trade Unions in Britain Today*, Manchester University Press

Nicholls, P (1999) 'Context and Theory in Employee Relations' in Hollinshead, G, Nicholls, P and Tailby, S (eds) (1999), *Employee Relations*, Financial Times Pitman Publishing

Price, A J (1997) *Human Resource Management in a Business Context*, International Thomson Business Press

Salaman, C (1998) in Salaman, C, Mabey, G and Storey, J (eds) (1998) *Strategic Human Resource Management*, Sage Publications

Sinclair, J (1999) 'Trade Unions' in Hollinshead, G, Nicholls, P and Tailby, S (eds) (1999), *Employee Relations*, Financial Times Pitman Publishing

Webb, S and Webb, B (1902) *Industrial Democracy*, Longman

Recommended Reading

Employee Relations (1999) edited by Graham Hollinshead, Peter Nicholls and Stephanie Tailby provides a comprehensive overview of the subject in a readable and accessible manner. Links to articles and useful websites are provided in the employee relations section at http://www.hrmguide.com.

Answers to Unit Review Activity

Some of the issues underlying working life in Northern Ireland include:

- **the political future of Northern Ireland** – that is, whether to agree to power sharing between Catholics and Protestants, or to continue to support the previous political arrangement

- **sectarianism** – the relative dominance by Protestants in employment as well as housing and politics in Northern Ireland has generated long-term grievances from Catholics in the workplace, so trade union activity has been affected by this issue which, of course, comes from outside the work environment

- **working class solidarity** – a reference is made to the sense of solidarity between all members of the working class, not just between workers in the same trade or organisation, and arguably this sense of solidarity is something that has helped to maintain the class system within the UK, and explains the willingness of one union to support another (although much restricted during the Thatcher era)

- **equal opportunities** – in England, Scotland or Wales this means giving women the same opportunities as men or treating different ethnic groupings in the same way, but equal opportunities has different implications in Northern Ireland; giving Catholics and Protestants equal opportunities would help to reduce the sectarian and political division between the communities.

While the immediate concern of union members might be with pay and conditions within the workplace, these matters are shaped by outside forces at many different levels. For example, unions are concerned at work with safe working conditions, so they would be keen to support the introduction of health and safety legislation that would force unwilling employers to provide satisfactory working conditions – they would have to be involved in politics. A second example: the unequal distribution of wealth in the UK, affects the relative position of union members. This difference reinforces power and privilege for the rich at the expense of the less well off (including most union members). Measures to reduce inequity would reduce the imbalance of power, which is why many unions once argued for 'the [state] ownership of the means of production'.

A person's life is predominantly affected by work. The same work could be good for employees at work, but bad for their domestic lives and their families. For example, an oil exploration company wants to fly its geologists to any point in the world at short notice. This might lead to an exciting and welcome experience for the employee, but leave his or her partner and family in difficult circumstances. So justification for a union's existence is not merely that it makes working conditions for employees better but that it works towards making their members' whole lives better. If that is accepted, then the unions might be properly interested in all factors that affect their members' lives. There is no reason to stop working for the improvement of people when they leave the factory gate. Unions could be quite properly interested in world peace, a better environment, road safety, and any other aspect of life that affects their members.

UNIT 8
HUMAN RESOURCE
DEVELOPMENT

Introduction

Human resource development (HRD) is a strategic approach to investment in the skill, expertise and capabilities of an organisation's employees: its human capital (Nadler 1970). It provides a framework for self-development, training programmes and career progression to meet an organisation's future skill requirements. HRD draws on other human resource processes, including resourcing and performance assessment to identify actual and potential talent. Effective development begins with induction and the identification of potential talent but development is not just the responsibility of the organisation – individuals must develop themselves.

In the first section we consider macro-level issues of human resource development such as the role of the state in developing a national framework for HRD. In the second section we concentrate on human resource development at the organisational level, discuss attitudes towards training and evaluate the concept of the learning organisation. Finally, we outline the arguments for specific development programmes geared towards particular types of employee.

Objectives

By the end of this unit, you should be able to:

- evaluate the roles of the state, organisations and individual employees in the human resource development process
- assess the suitability of different forms of human resource development such as vocational education and informal learning
- explain the concept of the learning organisation
- relate your own career plans to HRD theory and practice.

SECTION 1

Human Resource Development at National Level

Introduction

Human resource development is an area of human resource management significantly influenced by the commitment of the state towards developing the country's human capital. In this section we discuss the ways in which national initiatives have been organised and implemented in the UK in recent years. We begin with a discussion of human capital and attitudes towards training, especially in small companies.

The aim of this section is to help you to:

- evaluate the role of the state in providing a national framework for human resource development

- critically analyse the suitability of national schemes such as Investors in People as templates for effective vocational education and training.

1.1   Human capital

The rise of a nation's living standards, the level of employment and the availability of a skilled workforce are closely interrelated. The realisation that human capital is a key to a country's economic success has led to action by a succession of governments to increase the quality and quantity of training activities in the UK. Jobs are generated by economic growth but they can only be filled if suitably skilled people are available.

A shortage of skilled people is a limiting factor on the economy. This limitation acts in a number of ways. For example, small information technology businesses may be unable to expand as quickly as they would like because of the difficulty in finding people with the right skills. A Computer Economics survey estimated that more than 90 per cent of IT firms recruited in 1997 and 83 per cent of these experienced some difficulties in obtaining the right staff (Beard and Breen, 1998). The following example illustrates the issue.

Oracle

Oracle, a leading-edge IT software company, requires a steady supply of university graduates to expand its workforce. Having invested a considerable amount of money training them, it tries to keep these recruits. Vance Kearney, vice-president in charge of UK human resources, stated: "We recruit 150 graduates a year and we make sure we keep them with good benefits. Our people are permanently being headhunted. Most of the time we hang on to them because of the benefits. Also, they can work with the latest technologies and their skills are staying in the mainstream." 主流)

Source: Adapted from *Financial Times*, 7 January 1998.

Oracle is a large company and you may like to think about the implications of its strategy for smaller companies. Can small businesses afford the time and money to chase high-quality recruits and reward them highly enough to ensure they stay for a reasonable period of time? We consider the problem later on in this section.

A further issue is that UK companies may have to pay premium rates for scarce skills in comparison to their competitors in some other countries where the skill base may be higher. This gives overseas competitors a significant cost advantage. Levels of training and education vary significantly between different countries and the record in the UK seems particularly bad. For example, a skills audit commissioned for a 1996 British government White Paper, *Creating the Enterprise Centre of Europe*, found that:

- 30 per cent of young people in the 16–17 age group were judged to be inadequate in numeracy
- 21 per cent were inadequate in oral communication
- 32 per cent were judged to have a poor business ethic.

Another factor is that higher education in the UK has been focused on academic disciplines rather than the acquisition of technical skills. Sapsford and Tzannatos (1993) conclude that the British education system – particularly at the higher levels – is not adding much to the country's human capital. Instead, education acts to provide a cheap and easy selection filter for recruiters who consider that job-seekers with paper qualifications are better than those without. Given these comments, you might like to consider why you are studying this subject!

Government action can influence uptake and participation in training by businesses. But Ashton and Felstead (1995) argue that the training infrastructure in Britain has a tradition of minimalism – in other words, it has always been poor. They contend that the tradition dates from the nineteenth century when the pioneers of industrialisation could compete successfully in both national and international markets with a comparatively low-skill workforce.

Employers who needed skilled employees did not turn to the educational system but, instead, resorted to on-the-job training. In some industries employers could draw on what remained of the medieval apprentice system to provide skilled craft workers such as printers and furniture makers. Traditionally, apprentices were young people who agreed to work for a skilled craft worker over a fixed number of years in order to learn trade skills.

Ashton and Felstead go on to argue that the spread of US management methods throughout most of the twentieth century further allowed employers to squeeze out the skill requirements of production. Mass production depended on simple, repetitive machine operation with little need for craft expertise. Together with an overall decline in the importance of manufacturing to the British economy, this led to the virtual elimination of the apprenticeship system. In contrast, 50 per cent of German school-leavers are involved in apprenticeship schemes covering over 300 occupations. In the 1980s, over 90 per cent of German employees had completed at least three years of craft training, compared with just 10 per cent in the UK (Price, 1997).

At the beginning of the 1990s Stevens and Walsh (1991) pointed to the fact that a significant proportion of the British workforce was in 'danger of becoming trapped in a low-skills, low-quality equilibrium with low initial education and poor skills leading to low productivity and a predominantly low-quality market orientation'. In the next part of our discussion we consider how successive governments attempted to improve on this situation.

ACTIVITY 1

Jot down the main factors that you feel have led to the UK's inadequate training infrastructure. Imagine you had been given responsibility for improving the country's skills base. What solutions would you propose?

You may have come to the conclusion that you were being asked to deal with a very serious problem – a problem deeply rooted in the UK's industrial culture for over a century. A solution is not likely to be easily found to change attitudes and patterns of behaviour which are so well-entrenched. You might also have thought that there is an element of 'buck-passing' in that different governments assumed that industry would deal with the problem, and vice versa.

What solutions would you propose to deal with the problem? You may have decided to continue with the voluntary approach to training or chosen to introduce an obligatory system that forced organisations to provide a certain degree of training. Perhaps you thought of creating a system of skills training involving formal courses, provision by colleges and universities, and recognition of awards or qualifications. You might have suggested that governments provide cash benefits or tax allowances to organisations and individuals that actively pursue training and development.

You may have thought of several other good ideas. Compare your thoughts with the actual decisions taken by governments discussed in the next part of this unit.

1.2   National initiatives

The poor state of training in the UK has caused concern for decades. The Industrial Training Act 1964 led to the creation of a number of Industrial Training Boards (ITBs) that operated in a variety of forms for around 20 years. They imposed a levy on employers, monitored training on an industry-wide basis and tried to improve quality. The industry-by-industry approach was unpopular with some employers and also did not reflect the underlying structural changes in British industry we described earlier, such as the decline in manufacturing (Ashton and Felstead, 1995).

In the 1970s a more directive approach was taken with the creation of a centralised Manpower Services Commission (MSC) which began the process of developing a national vocational education and training system. The MSC was eventually abolished in favour of a market solution for training in which employers determined their own training levels. Ashton and Felstead (1995) argue that the MSC had failed because the Thatcher government diverted efforts towards ineffectual training programmes focused on the unemployed. We shall discuss an evaluation of one such scheme that appears to show that this view is not correct. Under the Labour administration elected in 1997, the 'New Deal' for the unemployed increased the intensity and coverage of these type of training programmes in an attempt to eradicate long-term unemployment by tying participation to financial support.

TRAINING FOR WORK

Training for Work (TfW) was the main training programme for the adult unemployed administered by the Department for Education and Employment until 1998. It was replaced by work-based training for adults. Unemployed school-leavers were dealt with by a parallel Youth Training scheme. TfW provided skills training – often recognised in the form of national vocational qualifications (NVQs) – job search training and work experience for unemployed people who had been out of work for six months or longer. Unemployed people with special needs, including disabled people, ex-service men and women, victims of large scale redundancies, job market returners, individuals with literacy or numeracy needs, and former detainees were exempted from the six month requirement.

Participation in the scheme was voluntary, and not all eligible unemployed people who were offered a place chose to accept it. TfW places were limited, however, so the scheme was also oversubscribed and many people who wanted a place were not offered one.

Payne et al. (1999) found clear patterns of characteristics that distinguished participants in the scheme from non-participants. In general, participants were younger, had academic qualifications, had worked before and had less experience of unemployment than non-participants. Payne et al. conclude that while being disadvantaged, TfW participants tended not to be the most disadvantaged among the unemployed.

Payne et al. also found that people from these groupings were more likely to participate than others:

- women with dependent children of school age
- people without a driving licence but having regular access to a vehicle
- people who had last worked in clerical or secretarial occupations

- people who had previously been on government programmes for the unemployed.

People less likely to be participants included:

- women with children under school age
- people who had long-term health problems or disabilities
- tenants in both social and private housing
- people who had no GCSE or GCE O-level passes at high grades
- people with vocational qualifications equivalent to NVQ level 2 or higher
- people of Indian subcontinent origin
- people who had both a driving licence and had regular access to a vehicle
- people who had never held a job.

As we have already observed, such schemes are commonly regarded as being ineffectual. However, Payne et al. found evidence to the contrary. Their research showed that TfW gave its greatest boost to job entry chances immediately after participants finished the programme but it also boosted long-term job chances of people who did not start work immediately on leaving TfW. In the first 17 months after leaving the scheme, participants spent 50 per cent more time working than non-participants. After 36 months, 49 per cent of participants had a job compared with 37 per cent of non-participants. That is to say, of a group of 25 participants, 12 had a job after three years, compared with only 9 people from a similar group who did not have training.

Of course, the people who participated in TfW may simply have had characteristics (which had nothing to do with the scheme) that were more highly valued by prospective employers than those possessed by non-participants. However, Payne et al. used matched comparison groups to provide similar participants and non-participants for their study and claim that this was not an issue.

ACTIVITY 2

Review the preceding discussion. To what extent does the evidence presented by Payne et al. disprove the contention by Ashton and Felstead that government programmes to help the unemployed were ineffectual. Jot down 30–40 words to support each side of the argument.

Taken at face value, the study by Payne et al. appears to show that the TfW did make a contribution towards helping participants obtain and remain in jobs. The difference was larger than could be explained by chance, but the difference of 12 per cent (in job holding after three years) was not enormous.

In support of Ashton and Felstead you could have noted that TfW was oversubscribed and selective in its offers and did not encompass all the unemployed people who could have benefited from the scheme. You might argue also that participants in the scheme were unrepresentative of the general population, that they were a self-selecting group of people who were likely to have fared reasonably well without the programme. But then you may have defended Payne's conclusions by noting the attempts to match the characteristics of those participants and non-participants included in the study in order to control for this variable.

TARGETS AND FRAMEWORKS

We now turn to current national training structures in the UK. By the time you read this section everything may have changed again, so we will be considering not merely current details, but we will try to indicate the trends in government thinking, and the principles, if any, on which it works.

The last Conservative government established national targets for education and training to be achieved by the year 2000. The aim was to 'improve the UK's international competitiveness by raising standards and attainment levels in education and training to world-class levels by ensuring that:

- all employers invest in employee development to achieve business success
- all individuals have access to education and training opportunities which meet their needs and aspirations
- all education and training develops self-reliance, flexibility and breadth in particular through fostering competence in skills.'

In England and Wales, the National Advisory Council for Education and Training Targets (NACETT), founded in 1993, was give responsibility for specifying training targets in more detail. Targets were prepared in 1995 in respect of foundation learning and lifetime learning to be achieved by the year 2000 (NACETT, 1996).

In **foundation learning**, the year 2000 targets were:

- by age 19, 85 per cent of young people to achieve five GCSEs at grade C or above, an Intermediate GNVQ or an NVQ level 2
- 75 per cent of young people to achieve level 2 competence in communication, numeracy and IT by age 19 and 35 per cent to achieve level 3 competence in these core skills by age 21
- by age 21, 60 per cent of young people to achieve two GCE A-levels, an Advanced GNVQ or an NVQ level 3.

In **lifetime learning**, the year 2000 targets were:

- 60 per cent of the workforce to be qualified to NVQ level 3, Advanced GNVQ or two GCE A-level standard
- 30 per cent of the workforce to have a vocational, professional, management or academic qualification at NVQ level 4 or above
- 70 per cent of all organisations employing 200 or more employees, and 35 per cent of those employing 50 or more, to be recognised as Investors in People.

These may have been laudable targets but there is little evidence of their achievement. As we have noted, direct government intervention and funding has been aimed at unemployed school-leavers and adults with little expenditure on skills training for people in employment. The government's Training Agency functioned through market mechanisms, exhorting employers to provide their own skills training on a voluntary basis. However, new framework initiatives were introduced.

- **Scottish vocational qualifications** (SVQs) and **national vocational qualifications** (NVQs) – covering England, Northern Ireland and Wales – provide recognition of competence levels in non-academic areas directly related to work. Other initiatives such as **Skills Seekers** and **Modern Apprenticeships** served to provide funding and facilities for young people to achieve these qualifications.
- **Training and enterprise councils** (TECs) in England and Wales and **local enterprise companies** (LECs) in Scotland were charged with organising and encouraging training and development within companies in their locality.
- **Investors in People** (IiP) is a scheme designed to provide a template for planned training aimed at closing the skills gap in order to achieve business objectives.
- **Lifelong learning** is an umbrella term which encompasses a variety of learning initiatives generally aimed at ensuring that skills are constantly updated throughout life.

Collin and Holden (1997) argue that 'what is emerging in the UK is a systematic, self-reinforcing framework for VET (vocational education and training) rather than, as hitherto, a patchwork of piecemeal initiatives'. They point to training targets as having a role in directing, motivating and reinforcing the other initiatives such as vocational qualifications and IiP. A key element of this emerging framework is the emphasis on having observable and definable outcomes that can often be measured. The new Labour government is in the process of restructuring the organisations responsible for these initiatives at the time of writing.

NATIONAL VOCATIONAL QUALIFICATIONS

National vocational qualifications (NVQs) and Scottish vocational qualifications (SVQs) were first introduced in 1986 to provide such a framework (Walton, 1999). They are intended to cover a wide range of occupations and qualifications in the UK. They were designed to unify and replace a diverse collection of different vocational education and training (VET) awards. NVQs and SVQs are supposed to be more relevant and useful qualifications with five levels of competence from basic skills at level 1 through to professional and management skills at level 5.

The national framework also provides links to academic qualifications. General national vocational qualifications (GNVQs) provide an alternative to A-level and Scottish Higher qualifications. GNVQs allow students to:

- acquire basic skills
- develop a body of knowledge which underpins their vocation
- achieve a range of core skills.

A combination of vocational and core skills provides a platform for students to move into further or higher education, or continue in their vocation.

Each NVQ or SVQ is based upon an industry's own standards with a clear statement of the performance that an individual must show to indicate competence in particular occupations. NVQs and SVQs are divided into levels and units that are then subdivided into measurable competences. They are presented as having the following advantages:

- they are objective performance benchmarks
- assessment takes place in the workplace
- the logical structure provides clear progression paths for learning
- there is an in-built system of quality assurance
- they offer national recognition of an individual's competences.

A promotional document produced for a training and enterprise council lists further benefits offered to employees and employers. It suggests benefits of NVQs and SVQs to employers are:

- they improve employee performance
- they enhance an individual employee's ability to do a particular job
- they help motivate staff
- they increase productivity
- they make it more likely that good employees are retained
- quality of products and services is improved
- staff are prepared for future demands of the organisation

- they provide a framework for cost-effective, relevant training
- flexibility in working practice is encouraged
- competent staff give a competitive advantage
- there is an in-built measurement of performance
- skill gaps can be recognised and filled
- NVQ/SVQs can be integrated with internal (or external) quality systems.

For individuals, NVQs and SVQs:

- offer nationally recognised certification
- permit clear routes to progress in their careers
- provide recognition of their work competences and levels of responsibility
- allow unit certification, allowing progress to a full NVQ/SVQ
- are part of their career development
- offer recognition of any relevant prior experience and achievement
- are open equally to anyone, regardless of gender, ethnic origin or age.

NVQs and SVQs relate to specific jobs and careers. Standards are reviewed regularly because of changes in a particular sector or type of job, ensuring their continued occupational relevance. Their flexibility allows entry to the framework at levels suitable for people with different kinds of experience. Prior qualifications are not required and trainees obtain certificates for specific units or full NVQs and SVQs. They are not time-limited, so people can work at their own speed. They do not involve formal examinations and written tests are uncommon. The emphasis is on allowing individuals to demonstrate the competences they have gained in a practical fashion.

Despite the claimed benefits, the system has attracted a great deal of criticism including (Corbridge and Pilbeam, 1999):

- a belief that too many people see it as a simple solution to a complex problem
- generic qualifications do not take account of the considerable variations between work roles in different organisations – for example, HR managers in different organisations may do very diverse jobs
- there is an assumption that the essence or essential characteristics of a job such as HR manager are known
- they provide a template against which competences can be measured but if a trainee already has those competences, they do not develop the individual any further
- if someone is judged sufficiently competent, employers may be reluctant to offer further training

- by definition, they are job-related so that learning is narrowly focused
- they serve to maintain the status quo (reach and maintain standards needed now) rather than serve as instruments of HRD (developing for the future).

Perhaps the most common complaint is directed at the bureaucratic and mechanistic nature of the system, involving masses of paperwork.

The following example gives an illustration of an externally provided course leading to an NVQ or SVQ.

Hairdressing NVQ/SVQ level 2

Entry requirements

No qualifications are necessary. Hairdressers must be physically fit, neat, clean and well groomed. They must be artistically inclined, have good colour sense and have manual dexterity. It is not a suitable career for people with allergies or breathing difficulties as some hairdressing preparations are known to aggravate these conditions.

Attendance and length of course

Full-time for five terms. As well as their college-based work, students spend one day a week at a commercial hairdressing salon.

Course content

Practical hairdressing

Theoretical knowledge

Instruction in using and handling hairdressing preparations and equipment

Manicure

Stock control

Art and photography

Health and safety

Physics

Progress

This qualification leads on to:

- NVQ/SVQ level 3 Hairdressing
- Supervisory NVQ/SVQ level 3 Hairdressing
- NVQ/SVQ level 4 Management

Career

Career openings exist in salon work in the United Kingdom and abroad including work in theatre and television, health and leisure clubs, passenger liners, reception work, mobile hairdressing, and technical and sales representation.

It seems that academic opinion may not support the claims made by people involved in promoting NVQs and SVQs. To help you understand the different arguments try this exercise.

ACTIVITY 3

We listed a number of alleged benefits for employers of NVQs and SVQs. In the light of the criticisms outlined above, how far do you think they are plausible?

Use the table to structure your comments or write them on a separate piece of paper if you prefer. To get you started, we have provided an (incomplete) example.

Claimed benefit	Comments
They improve employee performance	Many factors affect employee performance: improving competence may not alter performance.
They enhance an employee's ability to do a particular job	
They help motivate staff	
They increase productivity	
They make it more likely that good employees are retained	
Quality of products and services is improved	
Staff are prepared for future demands of the organisation	
They provide a framework for cost-effective, relevant training	
Flexibility in working practice is encouraged	

Competent staff give a competitive advantage	
There is an in-built measurement of performance	
Skill gaps can be recognised and filled	
They can be integrated with internal (or external) quality systems	

SVQs and NVQs improve employee performance. This is a rather sweeping claim. An employee's performance may be held back by poor motivation, poor supervision or other factors, other than a lack of competence. S/NVQ training brings people up to a standard of competence but does not enhance or develop them beyond this point unless an employer is committed to doing so. Similar criticisms apply to the claim that *they enhance an individual employee's ability to do a particular job.*

They help motivate staff. This is true to an extent but if development is limited to the requirements of their current jobs the system could act as a demotivator.

They increase productivity. This is true only to the extent of reducing defects and lost time. They do not encourage the leaps in imagination which lead to major improvements in productivity. Their emphasis on predetermined specific objectives, might even institutionalise rigidity and a lack of flexibility and innovation.

They make it more likely that good employees are retained. No evidence has been presented for this. Is it not just as likely that employees will find it easier to find other (better paid) jobs?

The quality of products and services is improved. Since the system is focused on conformity this is probably the case.

Staff are prepared for future demands of the organisation. It seems that they are more likely to be prepared for past and present demands.

They provide a framework for cost-effective, relevant training. To an extent this is valid, but the bureaucratic nature of the system imposes costs in terms of filling in paperwork and making detailed assessments.

Flexibility in working practice is encouraged. Theoretically true, but the rigid template surely encourages conformity to old ways rather than flexible and novel ways of doing the job.

Competent staff give a competitive advantage. Not when staff only gain competences found elsewhere the same industry. More a matter of keeping up with the best than gaining an advantage.

There is an in-built measurement of performance. This is a template which measures generic competence for the type of job but jobs differ from one organisation to another. Peculiarities in one organisation may go unmeasured.

Skill gaps can be recognised and filled. Yes, but what about requirements in the future?

NVQ/SVQs can be integrated with internal (or external) quality systems. True theoretically.

ACTIVITY 4

Now evaluate the supposed benefits for employees, again taking account of the criticisms we have mentioned. Again you can use the table to structure your comments if you wish.

Claimed benefit	Comment
Offer nationally recognised certification	
Permit clear routes to progress in their careers	
Provide recognition of their work competences and levels of responsibility	
Allow unit certification, allowing progress to a full NVQ/SVQ	
Are part of their career development	
Offer recognition of any relevant prior experience and achievement	
Are open equally to anyone, regardless of gender, ethnic origin or age	

NVQs/SVQs offer nationally recognised certification. Yes, but how many employers take much notice? A national qualification is of value if the employee is to move around the country in search of jobs. But of less value to individuals who are not geographically mobile.

They permit clear routes to progress in their careers. Employers may choose not to allow their employees further training.

They provide recognition of their work competences and levels of responsibility. Yes, this is certainly true.

They allow unit certification, allowing progress to a full NVQ/SVQ. In theory true, but again employers may choose not to develop their staff further.

They are part of their career development. They can be if they are allowed to develop further.

They offer recognition of any relevant prior experience and achievement. Yes, but what purpose does this serve in 'development'.

They are open equally to anyone, regardless of gender, ethnic origin or age. Yes, but only to the extent that the employer is non-discriminatory

1.3   Investing in People

Investors in People is a national UK quality standard developed in 1990, incorporating the views of employer, trades union and practitioner organisations. It assists organisations to develop a strategic framework for future goals and targets, identifying the steps necessary to achieve them. It sets a standard of good practice aimed at improving organisational performance through its people that can be integrated into overall business planning and HR development policies. It gives a specific focus to training and development. Feedback and reviews are an essential part of the process.

Investors in People UK, established in 1993, is the national and international guarantor of the standard. The organisation conducts its work in partnership with training agencies throughout the UK. It is designed to complement other initiatives, such as SVQs/NVQs, and works closely with professional, educational and industry bodies.

Thousands of employers have worked towards the standard. The assessment process takes from 6 to 18 months depending on the nature of changes required and the attitudes of staff at all levels in the organisation. Operational, human resource, training or quality managers may take specific responsibility with support from higher management. Assessors liaise with participating organisations throughout the Investors in People accreditation process. They check evidence, interview a sample of employees and forward the final submission to a recognition panel made up of senior local business executives. If unsuccessful, feedback will indicate what improvements the organisation should make to meet the standards.

To achieve recognition as an Investor in People, organisations must to follow this sequence of actions:

- understand the standard and its strategic implications
- audit the organisation against the standard, identifying any gaps in current practice
- make a commitment to meeting the standard that is communicated to all employees
- make planned changes to meet the standard
- collate evidence for assessment against the standard
- achieve recognition as an Investor in People
- maintain and reinforce a culture of continuous improvement.

There are four key principles underlying the cyclical process of continuous improvement:

- commitment to invest in people to achieve business goals
- planned development of skills, individuals and teams
- creation of a well-defined and continuing training and development programme directly tied to business objectives
- evaluation of outcomes in respect of individual progress towards goals, value achieved and future needs.

Organisations are assessed against 23 indicators in order to receive recognition, of which six relate to induction and subsequent training. For example it is required that 'all new employees are introduced effectively to the organisation and all employees new to a job are given the training and development they need to do that job' (Alberga et al., 1997).

It is therefore expected that all employees will:

- understand and agree what is required to perform their jobs
- be able to do those jobs effectively and understand why they are important
- be given the essential materials, tools, training and information to do the job well
- know how well they are doing
- understand what to do when things go wrong
- be motivated to do a good job
- have systems and guidelines which help rather than hinder
- be given clear leadership and support.

Effective two-way communication within the organisation serves a number of purposes and is a crucial element in the process. The mechanisms selected depend on the characteristics of the organisation. Examples include team briefings for senior managers and all employees, newsletters and staff meetings. Employees are encouraged to put forward ideas at any time. However, more structured approaches may be adopted such as formal suggestion schemes, quality circles and action teams.

Performance reviews provide a channel of communication. They also serve to identify individual training and development needs that are regularly reviewed against organisational objectives. Alternative approaches include job appraisals, skills audit, staff attitude surveys or career planning meetings. Identified training and development needs similarly may be met through a variety of approaches: on-the-job or in-service training, correspondence or distance learning, day release or evening classes.

In general, employees have been found to have positive attitudes towards the initiative. A survey of more than one thousand employees carried out for Investors in People indicated that 75 per cent had experienced boredom or frustration in their jobs, implying that effective human resource development could offer a solution. Half suggested that this resulted in stress and was a significant factor in staff turnover. The total cost of employing someone has been estimated to be at least double the basic salary paid.

Walton (1999) argues that the limitations of Investors in People arise from its formalised nature, focusing on planned training and development in order to achieve already determined business targets rather than being a source of competitive advantage in its own right. It is also restricted to training for individual employees and does not encompass wider HRD issues or the relationship between training and other human resource activities. You might like to evaluate the proclaimed benefits of Investors in People shown in table 1 in the light of these criticisms.

Employees	Employers
Good quality training when needed	Externally recognised standard
Greater job satisfaction	Provides framework for future strategy
Improved communication	More targeted training initiatives
Skill and career development opportunities	Motivated and loyal workers
Greater responsibility and recognition	Reduced staff wastage and absenteeism
More involvement	Greater acceptance of change
Better working environment	Attracts better recruits
Pride in belonging to a successful organisation	Improved competitiveness
Improved earnings	Higher profit and output
	Greater customer loyalty
	Improved quality standards

Table 1: Benefits of Investors in People

ACTIVITY 5

We observed earlier that Collin and Holden believe that there is a 'systematic self-reinforcing framework' of training emerging in the UK. It would be helpful if you could show this as a diagram. Try to include driving forces such as the government, business organisations, TECs as well as outcomes in the form of training targets.

We suggested that it would be helpful to represent the view of Collin and Holden diagrammatically. One reason for this is that by representing ideas in a different way you sometimes get a deeper insight into the views being expressed. Another, is that a diagram can sum up a great deal of information succinctly and memorably. There is no one right answer to the activity, but here is one approach.

The key phrase is 'a systematic self-reinforcing development of training'. So we need to ask what can be self-reinforcing? Usually this implies some kind of feedback loop, in which the stimulus to a process is heightened by the outcomes. We will look at this in one moment.

We can think of training and development as a process of converting untrained personnel into skilled employees. A process can be thought of as consisting of three main elements: inputs, a conversion activity and an output. If it is to be self-reinforcing, then we also need a fourth item, the feedback loop. Each of these elements may consist of many parts, and these parts may interact, but we will approach it simply. So we start the diagram from these three elements, plus the feedback, then elaborate as required.

First, let's begin by listing some of the inputs to the process. They include government pressure – persuasion, carrots (such as awards, tax incentives), sticks (such as disapproval, fewer contracts), employer commitment to training, etc.

Now we list the outputs. These include improved job satisfaction for staff, greater retention of staff leading to cost reductions, better trained and more productive staff leading to cost reductions, etc.

Next we identify the process we are concerned with – training, staff development, planned experience.

Finally, to be self-reinforcing there must be some positive feedback: that is, outcomes that encourage the process to continue. So in the diagram, there must be a feedback loop from outcome to input.

Now we construct a diagram using the three elements and a feedback loop. In our diagram, we have included the bare minimum of detail; you may amplify this as you feel right.

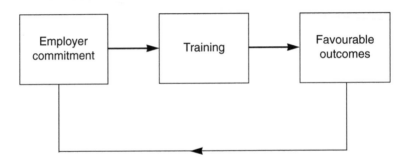

Figure 1: Simplified diagram of the training framework

Each of the main boxes could contain many items, and you might have written them in. But there is an advantage in keeping things simple; a broad general representation won't be wrong in detail, and it is easier to remember.

We have stated the advantages of a simple solution to the question but you might feel you'd like to see something more complex. Here is a fuller solution.

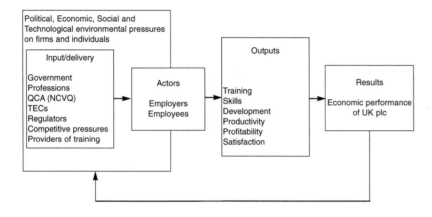

Figure 2: The self-reinforcing system of training in the UK

The second diagram focuses more clearly on the context of training, but again, the self-sustaining nature of the process is indicated by the feedback loop. This shows feedback from the general performance of the UK economy to the environment of the firm; in figure 1 we only considered feedback in the specific context of the employer. Both approaches are correct, but neither is complete.

Summary

In this section we considered the relationship of training and human resource development to human capital and national competitiveness. The poor state of training in the UK throughout the last century has often been criticised. There have been numerous government initiatives with little evidence of success. Recently, however, schemes to encourage vocational training and bring unemployed people back to work have been introduced, including National and Scottish Vocational Qualifications and the Investors in People scheme, which appear to offer more potential for improving human capital.

SECTION 2

Human Resource Development at the Organisational Level

Introduction

In this section we outline the purpose and function of human resource development at the organisational level. We discuss the attitudes of key areas of industry towards training and other forms of development, focusing on small and medium-sized enterprises (SMEs) which constitute the main sources of growth in employment. We also evaluate methods of assessing and addressing employee development needs within organisations. A broad overview is given of methods by which development may take place.

Development programmes involve more than training. They begin with induction and integration of new employees. Recruits need constant accurate assessment, counselling and personal challenge. Development also involves socialisation of employees to fit the cultural requirements of the company. A much-publicised modern approach places development within the learning organisation. HRD also focuses strongly on management development, emphasising career plans, performance objective-setting, and self-managed learning.

The aim of this section is to help you to:

- assess the purpose and functions of human resource development
- evaluate the reasons why training does or does not occur in small and medium-sized enterprises
- explain the concepts of knowledge management and the learning organisation
- outline the process of strategic human resource development at an organisational level.

2.1   Strategic HRD

Human resource development is a process involving a combination of some or all of:

- formal and informal training
- planned and unplanned experience
- career planning
- education and personal development.

The broad objective of HRD is to enhance individual (and, therefore, organisational) development and performance but there is no unanimity on how this should be done (El-Sawad, 1998). However, there is an underlying assumption that learning should not be an accidental process but one that is deliberately planned by business strategists. Consequently, strategic HRD should demonstrate some cohesiveness in policy and practice (Walton, 1999). Thompson and Mabey (1994) put forward these elements of a strategic approach to HRD:

- recruiting and inducting employees of the highest possible quality and then deploying them effectively within the organisation
- identifying and improving employees' skills and hence motivation
- conducting regular analyses of job content in relation to the organisation's objectives and individual skills
- reviewing available technology and its potential for automating routine tasks
- drawing on information from performance management and measurement
- identifying training needs
- training with a view to improving present performance and enhancing individual careers
- encouraging employees to accept change as normal and as an opportunity.

As you can probably see, this is an extremely wide range of activities, encompassing a number of elements from other HR and non-HR perspectives. It goes beyond training to bring in a range of possible interventions. But El-Sawad (1998) points out that 'much current HRD practice is still confined to training in its narrowest sense'. However, as we shall see later in this section, there is an emerging trend away from training towards learning, and away from a reliance on training or learning as the only approach to strategic HRD.

Walton (1999) argues that there is an increasing strategic significance in 'inculcating and embedding collective learning processes that enable people to be more customer responsive, team oriented, creative, innovative, business focused and strategically aware'.

Mabey and Salaman (1995) go on to define six conditions which must be met before training and development can be regarded as strategic:

- **alignment with organisation objectives** – training and development must be demonstrably linked to business objectives
- **senior management support** – senior management actively promotes learning so that training and development become part of the culture

- **involvement of line managers** – they are actively involved in planning, coaching and monitoring training and development
- **quality of programme design and delivery** – high-quality development programmes, training courses that match learning objectives
- **motivation of trainees** – sharing in the assessment of training needs and relevance of training and development activities
- **integration with HRM policy** – HRD is continuous with, and mutually reinforced by, other human resource policies covering recruitment and selection, performance assessment, reward, recognition and career development.

Even though these six conditions may appear to be quite restrictive, Walton (1999) contends that this model is incomplete in that it is highly focused on training and development and does not take a sufficiently wide-ranging view of strategic HRD.

ACTIVITY 6

Review Mabey and Salaman's model in the light of Walton's criticisms. Do you agree that it is 'too closely focused on training and development as an activity' as he claims?

Referring to the earlier text, and to your own ideas, develop Mabey and Salaman's model by adding more wide-ranging issues or extending the objectives they provided.

You might have suggested a number of ways in which Mabey and Salaman's model could be developed, but it seems to us that the key features which should be included are these:

- strategic human resource development should include a reference to an individual's personal learning and commitment, and should make more of a point of individual career development
- strategic HRD within an organisation should surely indicate its relationship to the current context of the national framework of qualifications (NVQs/SVQs)
- similarly, its relationship to IiP should be stated
- while the list does refer to the need for HRD to be related to business objectives, it might have been more explicit about the need to focus on innovation and customer needs
- reference should be made to the key factors that all organisations are trying to develop such as innovativeness, commitment, and customer service.

ATTITUDES TOWARDS TRAINING AND HRD

We have considered what we mean by strategic HRD and we will now see what employers think of this approach. Briefly, not a great deal, it seems.

At enterprise level, there has been a tradition of employer reluctance towards involvement in training initiatives. A number of reasons have been put forward to explain this (Stevens and Walsh, 1991)

Poaching

When some companies train and others do not, the non-trainers are likely to try and poach trained staff. According to Stevens and Walsh, fear of poaching may be a greater deterrent than the poaching itself. But fear of poaching is not universal. In Germany, for example, the social market tradition (discussed in the last unit) encourages businesses to train as a contribution to the common good. In other words, training is perceived as being beneficial to the country as a whole.

Cost

British organisations pay more attention to short-term profits than overseas competitors. The cost of training today counts more than the potential of future profits.

Individual lack of interest

Historically, young people in the UK have tended not to see a link between training and higher levels of pay. There is a basis of truth in this belief since British companies have not paid as large a differential for skills as some of their overseas competitors. This attitude may be changing in respect to education, however, as significantly greater numbers go on to higher education.

Weak links between training and performance

It is extremely difficult to prove a direct connection between training and performance. Westhead and Storey (1997) consider that there is no evidence for the connection in small and medium-sized enterprises (SMEs), arguing that the studies that appear to suggest a link are methodologically flawed. SMEs are defined by the European Commission as organisations with fewer than 500 employees, but the vast majority are small companies with fewer than 50 staff.

Internationally, however, there is evidence for a strong connection in larger businesses. An American Management Association (AMA) survey of 1,000 large and medium-sized US businesses indicated a significant correlation between increased training budgets and increased profits and productivity. The survey showed that over the long term, when organisations increased their training budgets after reductions in the workforce, they were 75 per cent more likely to show increased profitability and almost twice as likely to improve employee productivity than companies which had cut training expenses (Gollan, 1997).

A study by the Boston Consulting Group compared 100 German companies and showed a strong link between investment in employees and their stock market performance. The study found that companies which made human resource development a priority gave higher long-term returns to shareholders than the industry average (Gollan, 1997).

TRAINING IN SMALL AND MEDIUM-SIZED ENTERPRISES

The Westhead and Storey (1997) study of training in SMEs concludes that 'a manager or an employee is less likely to be in receipt of training (particularly, job-related formal training) if he or she works in a small rather than a large firm'. However, they reach this conclusion without firm evidence, arguing that because small firms are more likely to use informal on-the-job training than externally validated schemes, it is difficult to measure training levels accurately.

Why is formal training in SMEs a matter of concern? Walton (1999) summarises the argument along these lines.

1. The UK is losing its competitive position in tables of global performance.
2. The country's future competitiveness lies in creating a strong base of highly skilled, knowledge-based employees.
3. SMEs are increasingly important in terms of their contribution to the economy, employing a growing proportion of the workforce.
4. We must therefore upgrade the capacity of SMEs to develop proactive and creative workers.
5. The solution will come from training, particularly planned, formal instruction in skills necessary to achieve an organisation's business objectives.
6. But SMEs do not send their employees on formal, planned training courses.
7. How can SMEs be levered into providing this training?

ACTIVITY 7

Write a short comment on each of the steps in the argument presented by Walton. Think about the views of Stevens and Walsh and also those of Westhead and Storey. You could also bring in some ideas from our discussion in the first part of this unit.

The UK is losing its competitive position in tables of global performance. Historically this is true but there are signs of a possible reversal in the last few years of the twentieth century. Whether this reversal is due to better training or other factors remains to be established.

The country's future competitiveness lies in creating a strong base of highly skilled, knowledge-based employees. We saw in the previous section that this has been the prevailing view for decades, but little has been done (until recently?) to provide a national framework to encourage the creation of such a base.

SMEs are increasingly important in terms of their contribution to the economy, employing a growing proportion of the workforce. Labour Force Statistics appear to support this contention.

We must therefore upgrade the capacity of SMEs to develop proactive and creative workers. We cannot really argue with this point.

The solution will come from training, particularly planned, formal instruction in skills necessary to achieve an organisation's business objectives. This is a very contentious statement. You might have argued against the validity of this statement on at least two grounds. First, that you have not been given any evidence of benefits to SME business performance resulting from training. Second, there are strong arguments in favour of the suitability of informal rather than formal training in SMEs.

But SMEs do not send their employees on formal, planned training courses. It is difficult to measure overall training levels in SMEs because of the relative importance of informal training. However, SMEs do seem reluctant to use external training courses. You may like to think about this in relation to our next discussion.

How can SMEs be levered into providing this training? You could have considered the roles of TECs, LECs and Investors in People as agents of change in this respect.

You might consider doing this activity again after reading Westhead and Storey's further analysis (1997), They provide a deeper analysis of the lower provision of job-related formal training in SMEs when compared with large firms.

Ignorance

This implies that small firms are less likely to provide training for their staff because owners and managers are not aware of the benefits of training. About a third of SME owners do not have any formal educational qualifications and show an antipathy towards educational institutions providing the training. Westhead and Storey argue that one way of tackling this antipathy would be for the state to intervene by cutting the costs of training and by providing direct or indirect subsidies to businesses that provide job-related formal training. If SMEs can be persuaded to try such schemes once, they may experience benefits from training that will encourage them to continue.

Market forces

There are a number of supply and demand issues that we have already suggested may be more significant than ignorance. Westhead and Storey (1997) favour the market forces explanation. Demand issues include:

- SME owners/managers are primarily concerned with the short-term survival of the business – the benefits of training benefits are often long-term
- there is a high probability of trainees in small businesses being poached by other (usually large) employers who can offer higher pay
- career opportunities are limited in small companies, so there is no obvious point in providing training for promotion
- training costs are higher for each individual employee in small businesses
- there is no evidence that training is effective in ensuring that SMEs survive.

On the other hand, supply issues also apply:

- it is expensive for small businesses to fill courses
- training course content should be customised for each firm but this is disproportionately expensive for small businesses
- small firms are in various stages of growth and require different forms of training at each stage, so putting employees from a number of companies on the same course may not be effective.

It would be worth while bearing in mind our discussion of training in SMEs in the discussion of knowledge management that follows.

2.2   HRD and knowledge management

One of the critical ways in which HRM can improve an organisation's competitiveness comes through its impact on the **knowledge base** of a business: the skills and expertise of its employees. Theorists of knowledge management argue that knowledge has two forms: explicit and tacit. **Explicit knowledge** is knowledge that can be documented in manuals, lists of instructions, research papers, and so on. **Tacit knowledge**, on the other hand, becomes obvious only when it is applied and is not so easy to transfer to someone else. According to Grant (1997) knowledge management provides competitive advantage when tacit knowledge can be replicated within an organisation without allowing it to replicate outside. From this perspective, organisations should:

- accept that knowledge is a vital source for value to be added to a business' products and services and a key to gaining competitive advantage
- distinguish explicit and tacit knowledge
- acknowledge that tacit knowledge rests inside individuals and is learned in an unstructured and informal way.
- identify and tap this tacit knowledge and make it part of the 'structural capital' of the business, so that it can be made available to others.

Walton (1999) contends that despite the evident logic of this argument, the orientation of 'seeing the individual as only a source of net worth, has such an instrumental orientation that it fails to pick up how and why individuals learn'. He argues that HRD should be about developing means by which individuals can gain new skills and knowledge rather than concentrate all our time and effort into circulating old ideas.

However, the knowledge management perspective has been useful in highlighting a hitherto ignored aspect of HRD – informal training. This is learning through experience, informal coaching and watching others. Some authors have described it as accidental learning. As we saw earlier, SMEs have been criticised for neglecting formal training, but it has become clear that much and, perhaps, most of the training involved in gaining tacit skills is informal. Moreover, since tacit skills supposedly are the key to strategic advantage, it may be that the value of formal training has been overstressed.

ACTIVITY 8

Read the article on *Share strength* (see Resource 15 in the Resources section). This describes the efforts made by some firms to capture tacit knowledge and make it available throughout the organisation. Write 40–50 words in response to each of these questions:

- to what extent are firms really capturing 'tacit knowledge'?
- is it possible to present such knowledge to other workers in an effective way?

You might have concluded that, in reality, much of the effort going into knowledge management has little to do with HRD, and typically it can be viewed merely as a vast IT exercise in database management. Certainly, making telephone numbers and other contact information available throughout an organisation is more to do with effectiveness in dealing with explicit knowledge. However, by tying these initiatives to innovation and new ideas and then using incentives to encourage staff to come forward, it does seem that some organisations have made limited moves towards capturing tacit knowledge.

The most effective means of conveying tacit knowledge to other workers seems to require 'knowledge sharing', often informally. IT systems can act as pointers so that staff know where to go to tap the organisation's store of knowledge. It is worth noting that the article emphasises the widespread disinterest and general weaknesses of HR professionals when it comes to IT. This makes it likely that knowledge management will founder because the main drivers of IT systems, on the one hand, and people issues, on the other, seem unable to share each other's knowledge.

LEARNING ORGANISATIONS

If we accept that knowledge management is more than a fad, it seems that the role of knowledge is paramount to the way an HRM approach can help create competitive advantage. That knowledge has both technical and social components. What becomes critical is the extent to which a company's knowledge base matches changing competitive conditions through learning. Businesses that actively set out to achieve this are termed learning organisations.

Characteristic	Description
Learning approaches to strategy	Organisational policy and strategy, and their implementation, evaluation and improvement, are consciously structured as a learning process.
Participative policy making	Participation and identification are encouraged in debating policy and strategy. Differences are accepted, disagreements aired, conflicts tolerated and worked with in order to reach decisions.
Informating	Information systems 'informate' as well as automate. Systems allow staff to question operating assumptions and seek information in order to learn about the organisation's goals, norms and processes.
Formative accounting and control	Management systems for accounting, budgeting and reporting are organised in such a way that they assist learning from the consequences of decisions.
Internal exchange	All departments and internal units view themselves as customers and suppliers, constantly in dialogue with each other.
Reward flexibility	Assumptions which underlie reward systems should be made public and alternatives investigated.
Enabling structures	The organisation needs to give space and headroom to meet present needs and respond to future changes.

Boundary workers as environmental scanners	Employees with external contacts – for example, sales representatives and delivery agents – function as environmental scanners, collecting negative and positive feedback to pass on to other staff.
Inter-company working	Information is deliberately shared so as to learn jointly with significant others outside the organisation, such as key customers and suppliers.
Learning climate	Organisational culture and management style encourages experimentation, in order to learn from successes and failures.
Self-development for all	Resources and facilities are accessible to everyone in order to encourage self-development.

Table 2: Characteristics of a learning company
Source: Adapted from Pedler et al. (1991).

Reviewing the concept of the learning organisation, Walton (1999) notes that 'perhaps more than anything else it has helped to put HRD on the strategic agenda'. Earlier in this unit we observed that a national framework of training and (perhaps) development was emerging through an interlocking system of training targets, vocational qualifications and driving agents such as Investors in People. The concept of the learning organisation suggests another framework at the level of the individual business. However, the concept is evolving and remains fairly abstract or, as a senior consultant engagingly described it, 'quite fluffy' (Prothero, quoted in Walton, 1999). What follows is necessarily a considerably simplified consideration of the concept.

The seminal ideas of the concept come from two main sources: Pedler et al.'s (1991) ideas on the learning company (see table 2) and Senge's (1993) five disciplines. According to Senge (1993) learning organisations are organisations in which:

- the capacity of people to create results they truly desire is continually expanding
- new and open-minded ways of thinking are fostered
- people are given freedom to develop their collective aspirations
- individuals continually learn how to learn together.

This set of goals may seem somewhat ambitious but Senge contends that they can be achieved through the gradual convergence of five 'component technologies', the essential disciplines.

Systems thinking

People in an organisation are part of a system. Systems thinking regards an organisation as consisting of different elements. These elements have their own interests and processes, and act, as it were, as small organisations within the larger one. The output of one element is the input for one or more others. So a change in one part of the organisation can have consequences for other parts. For example, the recruitment process is an important provider for production. Production provides inputs for marketing, sales, and procurement. Because of this interrelationship between elements the 'whole' (organisation) operates more effectively than could be forecast from a look at its parts (people, departments, teams, equipment, and so on).

Personal mastery

This discipline allows people to clarify and focus their personal visions, to focus energy, develop patience and see the world as it really is. Employees who possess a high level of personal mastery can consistently generate results which are important to them through their commitment to lifelong learning.

Mental models

These are internalised frameworks which support our views of the world, beliefs in why and how events happen, and our understanding of how things, people and events are related. Senge advocates bringing these to the surface, discussing them with others in a 'learningful' way and unlearning ways of thinking which are not productive.

Building shared vision

Developing 'shared pictures of the future' together so that people are genuinely committed and engaged rather than compliant.

Team learning

Senge sees teams as a vital element of a learning organisation. Hence there is a great significance in the ability of teams to learn.

ACTIVITY 9

Both Pedler et al. and Senge have attempted to define a similar concept in quite different ways. Compare and contrast the two approaches. Jot down where they seem to be different and how they seem to you to be the same.

You may have observed that, not surprisingly, learning is a key component of both models. Moreover, there is an emphasis on the organisation learning as if it is some kind of living organism. Equally, both models stress open-mindedness, discussion and debate in allowing new thinking to develop and spread. There is also a focus on sharing values, ideas and knowledge.

Senge's model is more psychological and individualistic in its stress on personal mastery and mental models. He places more stress on people as individuals and as members of teams. His systems approach also wraps up the disciplines in his model within an all-embracing systems thinking element. Pedler et al. on the other hand are more concerned with the organisation as an organisation, paying attention to the outside world as well as internal participants. Walton (1999) describes their perspective as being 'much more structural and recipe driven, much more focused on processes and practices'. You might feel that they are simply being more practical in their approach, in comparison to Senge's somewhat visionary concept.

The term learning organisation has become a fashionable label for a general trend towards encouraging lifelong learning. Whether such an entity as a learning organisation really exists is another matter. The models we have presented are exhortations or prescriptions for an ideal situation of continuous improvement. As Walton (1999) observes, no business can be a learning organisation since it is always becoming one.

2.3 Training and learning

Human resource development is not just a matter for the state or the organisation – it is also a matter of individual responsibility. One of the trends we have identified in this unit is a move away from training (something done to trainees) towards lifelong learning (something learners do for themselves). Your study of this unit is an example of the latter process. This change has implications for the way HRD is regarded both by the people being 'developed' and the organisations in which they work. We have to recognise that:

- learners have objectives for their learning which may be different from those of their employing organisation

- learners are responsible for their own development, and are likely to learn more effectively and enthusiastically if they are allowed to exercise that responsibility

- learners may want to carry on learning even when they have achieved the competences required by the organisation – preventing them from doing so acts as a demotivator and may encourage them to leave

- HRD puts a premium on knowledge as a commodity that can provide competitive advantage to an organisation

- HRD is a long-term, ongoing process that has to be managed.

HRD is linked to the soft aspects of human resource planning. It needs to be a planned and systematic programme in itself, using a combination of organised working experiences and formal training. Employee development goes beyond training for the sake of it. Instead, training becomes part of a human resource development programme and ceases to be an activity without any link to business objectives. Armstrong (1992) argues that HRD is an empowering process, providing:

- a signal to staff that the organisation believes them to be important
- motivation to achieve appropriate skills and suitable rewards
- tcommitment to the business derived from understanding its values and learning how to uphold them
- identification with the organisation because its aims and policies are better understood
- two-way communication between employees and managers as a by-product of training activities such as workshops
- needs satisfaction – selection for a development programme is an achievement in itself
- job enrichment enhanced by the additional skills learned that are applicable to other aspects of their work
- change management – people increase in understanding and confidence to cope with change.

Tamkin and Hillage (1997) found that employers who were active in HRD identified three main reasons for providing training and development:

- **vision** – development is seen as a way of investing in people, increasing their skills and making the organisation a better place to work
- **utility** – training creates greater effectiveness and efficiency
- **culture** – learning has a positive impact on loyalty, commitment, self-esteem and motivation.

Organisations committed to training and development saw competitive advantage in the positive impact on added value and higher quality. Employee development was viewed as an important contributor to this process. In line with our previous discussion, Tamkin and Hillage found that less committed organisations were deterred by cost implications including course fees and lost time, difficulties in finding appropriate courses and, in a few cases, by resistance from employees. Actively involved employers tended to focus on development with a clear job focus. Employees, on the other hand, sought to increase their general employability.

Based on the discussion above, you should be able to see that the learning objectives of individual employees can coincide with those of employers or may be entirely different.

> ## *Conflicting objectives*
> A shy and retiring business studies graduate moves into her first job. One of her objectives is to learn more about computing so she can use spreadsheets efficiently when she fulfils her ambition of moving into a more quantitative job. Her employers want her to learn graphics and presentational software so she can become a sales executive.

ACTIVITY 10

Take a few minutes to think of learning objectives for new graduates in their first job from both individual and organisational perspectives. Then draw a Venn diagram to show which objectives are likely to be very important to:

- employees only

- employing organisations only

- both.

You could have tackled this activity in a number of ways. One obvious way would be to use two overlapping circles. One circle would apply to employees, the other to employing organisations. The objectives applying to both employees and the organisation could be placed within the overlap area. You could have written down a wide range of objectives. For example, an employee may want to learn in order to get a better job outside the company – an objective of great personal importance which would not be shared by the employing organisation. Management might want to give extensive training on a fairly boring aspect of work, or in an areas of low personal interest, in order to maximise efficiency. Employees would find this unattractive. However, learning which increased the variety and enjoyment of work is likely to increase productivity and would be important to both employees and employers.

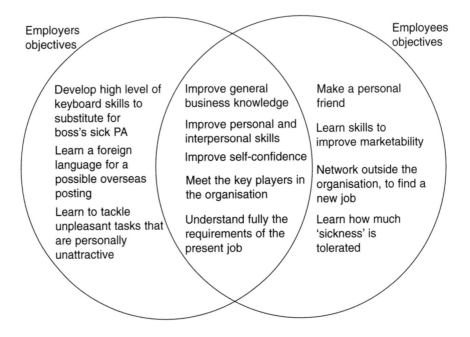

Employers objectives

Develop high level of keyboard skills to substitute for boss's sick PA

Learn a foreign language for a possible overseas posting

Learn to tackle unpleasant tasks that are personally unattractive

Improve general business knowledge

Improve personal and interpersonal skills

Improve self-confidence

Meet the key players in the organisation

Understand fully the requirements of the present job

Employees objectives

Make a personal friend

Learn skills to improve marketability

Network outside the organisation, to find a new job

Learn how much 'sickness' is tolerated

Figure 3: Learning objectives for newly recruited graduates and employing organisations

LINE MANAGERS

Line managers have an important role to play in HRD. Harrison (1992) contends that line managers are primarily responsible for enabling their staff to perform effectively and efficiently. Moreover, she argues that they should give staff continuous learning opportunities in order to develop their abilities and potential. According to Harrison, line managers should:

- establish a working environment with associated systems and policies that act to encourage and support their employees in the acquisition of the skills, knowledge and attitudes they need to perform well in their work

- conduct regular reviews of work targets and assessments of performance and potential to help staff improve and develop in ways that benefit the business and motivate themselves

- monitor and evaluate the results of formal and informal workplace learning on a regular basis.

These may be demanding objectives for busy line managers. In reality, we find that line managers vary considerably in their interest and commitment to HRD. Mabey and Salaman (1995) see this commitment as falling into one of three levels.

Intermittent

There is no genuine commitment to HRD from most line managers with the result that there is little visible training or development.

Institutionalised

There is considerable evidence of training and development activity. However, this may not come from genuine commitment. Instead, it may be due to pressure from senior management or need to spend the training budget.

Internalised

There may be less sign of obvious training and development than in the institutional pattern, but this is due to it becoming part of normal work activities. Highly committed line managers may coach staff, move them between jobs and otherwise create rich learning opportunities.

Megginson et al. (1993) proposed a framework which outlined the roles of line managers and other participants in HRD – senior managers, employees and training specialists.

- Senior managers are responsible for overall establishment of HRD, linking it to other HR activities in ways that clearly support the needs of the organisation now and in the future.

- Line managers must ensure that the policy framework and detailed proposals are compatible with operational requirements. Within that framework they must actively support employee learning with an emphasis on application and utilisation.

- Employees should be committed to their own continuing development and support the management agenda in relating to the organisation's enhanced effectiveness.

- Training specialists (HR practitioners) must work with senior managers to establish the policy framework. They should design and implement the detailed proposals for learning in relation to specified objectives.

ACTIVITY 11

What would be the characteristics of your ideal line manager in terms of employee development? What would he or she need to do in order to develop your potential and increase your ability to perform well in your job? How should your manager relate to staff and other members of the organisation? Write a pen picture of the perfect line manager in about 60–80 words.

You may have characteristics in mind for the kind of manager you would rather work for. Obviously we all have our personal preferences. However, if you drew on the views of the commentators in this section you might have focused on their personal commitment to developing employees: a manager with internalised commitment would be best. Hopefully your ideal line manager would have the opportunity and the ingenuity to give you learning opportunities through project membership, job swaps, and so on. There are also issues to be considered about the ways line managers relate to senior management. Is your ideal line manager able to influence senior managers (and HR practitioners) so that the HRD policy framework is realistic and matches operational requirements?

Summary

Strategic HRD is a more organised and integrated approach to development than piecemeal training. However, there is a particular problem in introducing strategic HRD in small and medium-sized enterprises. Within all organisations, the concepts of knowledge management and the learning organisation offer new approaches to improving HRD. Line managers have a particularly important role in the implementation of HRD objectives.

SECTION 3

Human Resource Development and the Individual

Introduction

In this section we outline the process of human resource management at the individual level. We consider how development needs may be identified and development programmes delivered. The section is concluded with an overview of management development.

The aim of this section is to help you to:

- explain how individual development needs can be established
- outline the range of development methods
- evaluate some basic approaches to management development.

3.1 Identifying development needs

Fowler (1991) advocates a three-pronged approach to identifying individual development needs. First, determine the knowledge that employees need to perform well in their jobs. This knowledge includes job-specific information, such as product or service details, and wider knowledge such as who does what in the organisation.

Then, identify skills or competences required to turn basic knowledge into good performance. They can be developed by formal training, on-the-job coaching, experience or work simulations. Finally, evaluate the attitudes required from good performers.

Much of this information can be generated from other HR processes such as job analysis and performance assessment. But if these are not adequate, Sloman (1993) suggests the following additional mechanisms:

- examine each person's productivity and quality of output
- use assessment centres similar to those we described in the selection process
- use check lists and questionnaires
- use succession plans in identifying future managers
- perform a skills audit in a department or the whole company.

As we have noted earlier, there is an inevitable tension between the development desired by individuals and the development organisations are prepared to offer them. It is useful to distinguish between development needs and wants (Nowack, 1991):

- **development needs** – training needs that would allow an individual employee to perform well on certain tasks or show specific behaviours that the employer considers important
- **development wants** – training for tasks and behaviours which would make employees more marketable but which the organisation considers unimportant.

Nowack observes that traditional training needs analysis techniques are designed to weed out the wants from the needs.

ACTIVITY 12

To what extent will development needs and development wants be revealed from an examination of:

- performance management data
- each person's productivity and quality of output
- assessment centres
- check lists and questionnaires
- succession plans identifying future managers
- a departmental skills audit.

Performance management data – a modern performance management assessment should provide pertinent information on both development needs and wants. This is a major function of performance management in contrast to traditional appraisals.

A person's productivity and quality of output – this will produce information on development needs but not on wants.

Assessment centres could produce both. Exercises are likely to reveal development needs; interviews should allow participants to indicate their development wants.

Job *check lists* will indicate development needs; *questionnaires* may reveal wants, depending on the questions.

Succession plans identifying future managers and *a departmental skills audit* will probably just show needs.

RESPONSIBILITY FOR SELF-DEVELOPMENT

Human resource development puts equal responsibility on both the organisation and the individual employee. Few people expect to spend their whole working life with the same organisation. Equally, few are prepared for a portfolio career. Most underestimate the impact of changes in the employment market on personal training and development needs. Career success involves factors such as:

- acceptance of personal responsibility
- self-knowledge
- systematic career evaluation
- frequent role change.

In particular, selecting a career path depends on a number of factors:

- **self-awareness** – appraising one's own skills, abilities and interests
- **ambition** – self-esteem and motivation
- **opportunity** – education, experience and social contacts.

A survey of 200 graduate recruits to major companies indicated a big gap between their expectations of work and the reality (Price, 1997). Interviewees were committed to their employers but did not intend 'sacrificing their lives' in the interests of career progression. In particular, they did not wish to work long hours even though they considered that this was more likely to gain them recognition within the organisation. Only 26 per cent said they would make their accomplishments known and only 6 per cent that they would try to work with someone viewed as successful.

Graduates seemed poorly prepared for aspects of working life such as inevitable elements of boredom, office politics, or unfair attribution of credit for hard work. It has been suggested that undue attention is given to traditional routes for those seeking rapid career progression. More needs to be done to interest graduates in self-employment or working for small organisations.

ACTIVITY 13

Read through this check list for working managers (adapted from Margerison, 1991). How useful is this type of check list for your own career objectives? Note your own responses.

1. How best can I spend my working time?

2. Who else could do my work?

3. What am I improving and why?

4. What am I for/against?

5. What are my special strengths and weaknesses?

6. What am I doing to develop my effectiveness?

7. What is the likely return versus risk of my objectives?

8. What have I learned in the last month?

9. What motivates me most?

10. How many of my objectives do I achieve on time?

11. What is my action plan for 1 month, 1 year, 5 years?

The greatest value of the questionnaire is apparent when you ask yourself if the activities you are currently engaged in (such as working through this unit) are clearly linked to your deepest aspirations.

Particularly it reminds you of the need to take responsibility for making your own choices of career and then to set your learning goals to match that choice. Many undergraduate students of course, will not yet have decided exactly what they want to do. But remember, goals are there to set you moving, not to chain you forever.

3.2   Development methods

We observed in the previous section, HRD is wider than training. It encompasses an extensive range of development methods and processes. Table 3 shows the prevalence of methods used by 150 major US companies for management development.

Method	Percentage of organisations using method
Job rotation	72%
External executive programme	48%
In-company development programme	47%
Task forces/projects	32%
On-the-job training	28%
Coaching/mentoring	26%
Performance feedback	6%
Teaching/consulting colleagues	1%

Table 3: Development methods used by major US companies
Source: Vicere and Freeman (1990)

You can see from this table that relatively informal and indirect methods such as job rotation, projects and on-the-job training are at least as important as more formal development, whether internal or external. Formal training is even less prevalent for non-managers and this is also the case in the UK (Walton, 1999). In the 1990s, the emphasis of all such methods has tended to be focused on the acquisition of a range of transferable skills, particularly because of the influence of national initiatives such as Investors in People and vocational qualifications.

Mentoring, as we discussed in Unit 6, has become a significant method of encouraging development. Mentors are already established managers able to give support, help and advice to more junior employees. They are not direct line managers but must have an awareness of the junior person's job. Thompson and Mabey (1994) argue that a mentor's job is to help build the junior employee' confidence, awareness of the organisation and its politics, and personal profile in the business.

New technology has reduced the reliance on residential courses and other traditional mechanisms for delivering in-service training. Based on principles of self-managed learning, such programmes can reflect a more co-operative approach to workplace relationships. Employees are encouraged to assimilate new information in a comparatively relaxed and flexible manner. Development is seen as a continuous process with employees viewed as complete people rather than components in a bigger scheme.

Improving customer service at Mecca

Xebec is an interactive learning company providing resources for self-managed programmes in a variety of settings. These range from customer service training for Mecca bingo hall assistants to senior strategic development for Price Waterhouse.

Part of the Rank Organisation, Mecca wished to promote a consistent corporate approach to customer service among 5,500 employees located at 130 sites. CD-ROM programmes combine sophisticated computer graphics with more traditional educational techniques such as question-and-answer sessions. Employees participate in colour-coded thirty-minute sessions designed to be entertaining and challenging. Reactions to service delivery scenarios are networked to a central location.

Mecca's mystery customer monitoring scheme registered a 4 per cent improvement in ratings since inception of this model, which may be expanded to other parts of the organisation.

Source: Adapted from the *Independent on Sunday*, 5 April 1998

The internet is changing the ways in which choices relating to work are made. For the potential employee, it offers a powerful source of information about factors such as career requirements, suitable organisations and selection techniques. It can depersonalise the application and recruitment process and improve the likelihood of equal opportunities, although there may be negative consequences in terms of feedback and motivation.

The UK government currently is considering compiling an electronic profile of each person's education and experience. This is in tune with the ethos of lifelong learning underpinning the proposed University for Industry. This will promote co-ordinated and lifelong education undertaken at home, work or suitable locations in the community. A similar approach has been adopted in regeneration areas responding to long-term unemployment.

Within organisations, intranet systems can deliver training programmes and facilitate efficient, paper-less communication in complex and flexible situations. However this requires consideration of where and how people wish to access and store information. Read the the following description of the Foresite system. Ask yourself how well it illustrates our discussion so far.

The Foresite system

Fife in Scotland traditionally relied on mining and defence-related industries, which are now in decline. Unemployment remains consistently in excess of the Scottish average. The Foresite system was developed in 1991 as part of a strategic regeneration scheme which recognised the need for a highly trained and flexible workforce. It is based on a partnership involving the local authority, Fife Enterprise, the careers service and education colleges. A database integrates details of local employers, types of work, training needs and skills shortages. Major organisations associated with the scheme include Royal Mail, Best of Scotland Holidays and Babcock Rosyth Defence.

Foresite assists agencies to design computer-based training and development programmes, specialising in high-technology engineering employment. Use of the internet, intranets and other distance learning techniques facilitate flexible access. It is recognised that potential participants may lack confidence and have negative experiences of education, compounded by factors such as care responsibilities, lack of money or transport. Motivational courses and practical support are incorporated into the training programmes.

Source: Adapted from *Scotland on Sunday*, 5 April 1998

Computer-based, self-managed learning is increasingly used as a mechanism for delivering training and development programmes. A recent Industrial Society survey of 433 organisations found that 38 per cent used these techniques and 40 per cent thought they would become increasingly important. However, 32 per cent found that work priorities impeded the process (*The Observer*, 29 March 1998).

A 1998 survey into levels of awareness and use of distance learning methods amongst 300 human resource and training managers in large organisations focused on attitudes towards on-line learning using the internet or corporate intranet. Results reflect general concerns that British managers have been very slow to recognise the potential of information technology compared to their equivalents working elsewhere in the world (*HR Network Online*, 17 September 1998). The survey found that:

- 96 per cent acknowledged that on-line learning allowed staff to complete training at their own pace
- over 75 per cent agreed it allowed access to training when people chose
- 44 per cent questioned whether it would be cheaper than traditional methods
- 65 per cent were concerned that it might leave staff isolated
- over 50 per cent felt it was unsuitable for group work, and support and supervision would be difficult
- 81 per cent felt that they needed more information about on-line learning before considering it suitable
- 47 per cent were interested in using the method in the next 12 months increasing to 67 per cent over two years.

ACTIVITY 14

Read over the survey results presented above then jot down your answers to the these questions.

1. What are the HR managers' main arguments against using computer-based systems?

2. What evidence would lead you to think that they are essentially wary of this new development.

3. What positive beliefs did they show in computer-based learning?

4. How keen are HR managers on information technology compared with other managers?

What are the HR managers' main arguments against using computer-based systems? A considerable number questioned whether it would be cheaper than traditional methods, thought that it might isolate trainees and was problematic for group work, team issues and general supervision.

What evidence would lead you to think that they are essentially wary of this new development. A substantial majority wanted more information and, again, a majority pushed their own possible use into the future to some extent.

What positive beliefs did they show in computer-based learning? A majority of respondents felt that the method allowed trainees to control their own learning and work at their own speed.

How keen are HR managers on information technology compared with other managers? Perhaps something of a trick question because the information you are given does not give enough evidence to answer the question. However, you may have read between the lines or noted elsewhere in this unit that many people involved in HRM are lagging behind managers in other disciplines.

3.3 Management development

Many organisations focus their employee development programmes on star performers or 'fast-track' employees. Four categories can be highlighted (Sadler and Milner, 1993):

- highly trained specialists – found in large numbers in high-technology industries such as computing or those with intensive research and development such as pharmaceuticals
- good managers and leaders
- sales and marketing people able to acquire business
- hybrids – individuals with the potential to cross over from a specialism such as human resources into general management.

Sadler and Miller (1993) argue that development programmes must provide promising individuals with:

- **a sense of mission** – they want a satisfying cause more than pay and security
- **an organisation structure** which encourages rather than stifles creativity
- **a performance management system** which identifies and rewards talented individuals – it should give them the chance to develop their skills through challenging work
- **a clear statement** of the link between strategic objectives and the desire of talented people to excel.

Traditionally, people destined for management status were either recruited from the ranks of ordinary employees or brought in on management training programmes. These tended to be focused on graduates and promised a structured development programme followed by steady progression through the management ranks. Flat organisations are likely to offer less scope for these programmes, focusing instead on specialist professional jobs, such as those in IT, finance and HR. Also, there has been a move away from programmes involving lengthy induction periods and work shadowing. Instead new recruits are increasingly being given real jobs in which they earn their money through useful activities (Price, 1997).

The enhanced significance of lateral rather than higher career progression reflects changing employment markets and limited opportunities for promotion. This can represent strategic management of a portfolio career or accumulation of relevant experience prior to applying for more senior positions. Some organisations encourage lateral moves. For example, Volkswagen has introduced broad-banding pay structures reflecting competences not simply seniority. The National Health Service's South Thames Region has a *Skill Swap* programme seen as essential to development of effective partnerships. Critics suggest that employees risk finding themselves trapped with over-specialised, out-of-date skills. However, lateral moves can offer new challenges and greater autonomy .

Concern about the low numbers of women in management has resulted in consideration being given to their particular development needs, both of new female recruits and more experienced staff. Distinctions should be made between structural factors obstructing progress and development of women as people. The former might be addressed by initiatives such as career breaks, refresher training, job-sharing and improved childcare facilities. The latter include programmes directed at such issues as enhancing self-awareness, appreciation of career opportunities and encouraging career management. Women may choose to attend programmes open to women and men or courses specifically designed for women only.

Hammond (1993) identifies three stages in the careers of women managers:

- entering into employment
- establishing and demonstrating competence in managerial work
- developing strategies to progress up the management ladder into more senior jobs.

These tend to be experienced differently from men in otherwise broadly comparable circumstances. Women are said to learn more from others and 'from facing up to hardships'. Conversely, men say they tend to learn from tasks assigned to them. However, those tasks may be of a more challenging nature. Hammond suggests that women make outstanding developers. They appear to have greater 'attending' skills – the ability to work on and care about several tasks simultaneously.

Scase (1998) points out that women lead more than 50 per cent of new small businesses. This trend is partly driven by the adverse experiences of employment in larger organisations. It can be seen as one response to the widespread failure to utilise the talents of women staff 'to the detriment of corporate innovative and competitive advantage'. Data suggest that businesses started by women are less likely to fail in the first year and are more likely to create jobs. This is resulting in changing management styles and new types of business culture. This beneficial effect of diversification reflects badly on the failings of equal opportunity policies that contributed to it.

Scase argues that women link personal growth with their business enterprise. Consequently, the business reflects their personality and aspirations. By contrast, men are said to measure success by promotion and financial reward.

The growth of international business demands that managers are able to function effectively in a range of countries and cultures. Rothwell (1992) concludes that international managers have the following development needs:

- proficiency in their existing task or business specialism
- language training
- experience of living and working abroad
- cultural awareness and interpersonal skills
- knowledge and information.

Volvo

Volvo has introduced a global, fast-track management training scheme based on self-directed learning in centres around the world. Applicants are encouraged to take responsibility for their own development while contributing to organisational objectives. Volvo felt it needed to move away from an almost exclusively Swedish top management layer to develop and promote a broader range of motivated people with a multinational perspective.

With 70,000 staff in 20 different countries, applications were invited for a programme including:

- a two-week introductory session to draw up a personal development plan

- two five-month international placements, relating experience to individual and organisational strategic objectives

- continuous and final assessment

- a presentation.

Participants are allocated to five-person 'learning sets' and choose a mentor from within the organisation. A learning set is a group of individuals who each work on an individual project and report back to the group from time to time. At these meetings, the members discuss the problems they face in their projects, help colleagues to solve problems, and discuss the learning they have achieved.

Staff graduating from the programme apply for new positions within the company.

Source: Thackray (1998).

ACTIVITY 15

To what extent does Volvo's programme seem to deliver appropriate and adequate international management development in terms of our discussion in this section? Identify three elements which you consider to be particularly effective. Explain why in about 15–20 words in each case. Then see if you can jot down three elements which appear to be missing from the Volvo programme. Again, write about 15–20 words to explain each of these missing elements.

On the face of it, Volvo appears to have an excellent development programme. You may have concluded that items such as the personal development plan, self-directed learning and the global nature of the programme are important features. You may have found it more difficult to pinpoint aspects which are missing from the programme but perhaps you included items such as language training, particular attention to women trainees and, particularly, the development of formal knowledge by systematic instruction or education.

MANAGEMENT EDUCATION

Many managers search for professional status backed by business education. Among numerous and diverse qualifications, the principal degree is the Masters in Business Administration. MBA programmes have emphasised rational decision-making and a top-down strategic approach. In 1990, 75,000 MBA degrees were awarded in the USA alone.

Attention has switched to more flexible and continuing processes of development. It has long been argued that faculty-based management education is not adequate. Providing a detached environment in which to study a theoretical framework has a role but risks leaving specific relevant concerns and experiences unaddressed. Equally people may become conditioned to their work environment and unable to learn or adapt. Distance learning, as the next example illustrates, is becoming the most popular way of studying for an MBA.

Distance learning

The Open University Business School provides one example of a rapidly expanding field. The university's administrative base is in Milton Keynes in England but it was founded to provide distance learning opportunities, particularly for people without experience of further education. The prospectus has expanded from short, self-contained courses to an extensive management education programme including an MBA degree, research opportunities and targeted in-house training in partnership with corporate clients.

The majority of students are from the UK or Western Europe, but with increasing numbers from Africa, the Far East and Eastern Europe. A network of 800 associate lecturers supports students in Europe. Various approaches to addressing the needs of more widely dispersed students are being tried. These range from a partnership with the Open Learning Institute in Hong Kong to European tutors travelling to facilitate seminars in East Africa. Research into developments in new technologies to support the distance learning process is ongoing. However, this is not a universal solution.

IBM encourages managers based in Africa, Europe and the Middle East to progress through the Open University certificate and diploma structure to the full MBA degree course. Management training is co-ordinated from IBM's education centre in Belgium. More than 600 staff currently are registered, the majority non-UK residents. IBM is seeking consistency between managerial approaches in multinational centres. In addition, increasing staff mobility requires significant investment in training to be flexible and self-directed.

Source: O'Connor (1998)

ACTIVITY 16

Valerie, aged 22, friendly but slightly nervous, has set her sights on becoming an international manager specialising in production and logistics in East Asia. At the end of her full-time education (including her degree course) she has been offered a well paid job at Wivliscombe Dairies, a small company of 25 employees, owned by her parents. The job is a general management position at its main production plant in the UK where she will oversee production of cheese for the mainly local market. Would you advise her to accept the job? Give reasons for your advice.

Assume that you advised against taking the job in her parents' company. Outline the kind of job and specify in detail the training opportunities she should look for.

From the scenario provided, it looks as if these are Valerie's circumstances:

- she wishes to be in management but not only as a functional expert
- as yet she has had no significant experience of managing
- it is likely that she has a good understanding of her parent's business and the problems of the local economy
- she may be able to speak another foreign language, or even two, but does she have command of any East Asian languages
- she is unlikely to have had experience of working in a different culture, or of East Asian business methods
- Valerie has been offered a job that bears no relation to her career plans.

You may have made some other assumptions as well on which to base your advice, but working with those listed, you might have recommended that she reject the job offer, but keep in touch with parents by e-mail. While it might pay a good salary now, the prospects are limited, the training and experience inadequate, and it bears no relation to her career plans.

Instead you might recommend that Valerie looks for work in a multinational firm with branches in East Asia. It would be unwise to go to a small and possibly unstable company that only traded in that region. Valerie needs a variety of experience and rich development opportunities and facilities. It may be possible to obtain this by frequently moving from firm to firm, but valuable stability is provided if the first employer can provide them within the organisation. Alternatively, she should accept work that requires contact with the staff in East Asia, even if she doesn't get an immediate posting there.

The essential element to look for is good training. It should be broadly based, and offer a range of alternative provisions. A suitable method for gaining experience and knowledge about a range of topics would be action learning. However this lacks systematic development of particular skills and knowledge so suitable

supplementary programmes should be available especially in the area of her chosen specialism.

The company should be willing to support Valerie if she studies on a distance learning programme (such as the Open University MBA), so that she could continue to study as she moved about the world.

A job rotation programme would be very useful, but frequent change might not suit Valerie's 'nervousness', so stability should be provided in some way. A good choice would be a mentoring structure in which a role model would be available to discuss problems, give guidance and introduce Valerie to significant people. The company should make provision for her to study an appropriate language.

While it is unlikely that Valerie will get everything she wants by way of training and development from her first job it makes good sense for her to carefully work out the implications of her career plans, and to try to take some of the responsibility for her own development needs.

Summary

This section highlighted a number of current issues in employee development. The development of managers is a major focus of HRD. Technological change has had a major impact on career development. The purpose and delivery of management education is a matter of concern with a need to emphasise distance learning as a means of lifelong learning.

Unit review activity

Read the article on *Core values shape WL Gore's innovative culture* (see Resource 16 in the Resources section). It is a reasonably long article about a particular company with an unusual non-hierarchical structure. The article covers a lot of HR issues but scarcely mentions human resource development directly. Can you identify the key elements of human resource development that are present within the company and those that are missing? Write 60–80 words giving your interpretation of how HRD might be pursued at WL Gore.

Unit summary

This unit examined fundamental issues in human resource development at national, organisational and individual levels. National initiatives like training and enterprise councils and Investors in People encourage knowledge acquisition through vocational training and provision of training for the unemployed and agencies. Positive attitudes towards training and development in small and medium-sized enterprises need to be encouraged through such schemes. Knowledge management and learning organisations are new concepts which can provide a framework for the processes of strategic human resource development. There are major issues to consider within the area of HRD including the development of managers, changes due to technology and broad aspects of management education.

References

Alberga, T, Tyson, S and Parsons, D (1997) 'An evaluation of the Investors in People Standard' *Human Resource Management Journal*, 7 (2)

Armstrong (1992) *Human Resource Management: Strategy and Action*, Kogan Page

Ashton, D and Felstead, A (1995) 'Training and Development' in Storey, J (ed.) *Human Resource Management: A Critical Text*, Routledge

Beard, J and Breen, E (1998) *IT Labour Market Assessment*, Department for Education and Employment, Research Briefs, Research Report No. 71

Collin, A and Holden, L (1997) 'The National Framework for Vocational Education and Training', in Beardwell, I and Holden, L *Human Resource Management: A Contemporary Perspective*, Pitman Publishing

Corbridge, M and Pilbeam, S (1998) *Employment Resourcing*, Financial Times Pitman Publishing

El-Sawad, A (1998) 'Human Resource Development' in Corbridge, M and Pilbeam, S (1998) *Employment Resourcing*, Financial Times Pitman Publishing

Fowler, A (1991) 'How to identify training needs', *Personnel Management Plus*, November

Gollan, P (1997) 'Training Reveals its Bottom Line Value', *HR Monthly*, May, Australian Human Resources Institute

Grant, R M (1997) 'Strategy at the Leading Edge – The Knowledge-based View of the Firm: Implications for Management Practice', *Long Range Planning*, 30(3), June

Hammond, V (1993) 'Women and Development', *Training and Development*, December

Harrison, R (1992) *Employee Development*, IPM

Mabey, G and Salaman, C (1995) 'Training and Development Strategies', in Salaman, C and Mabey, G (1995) *Strategic Human Resource Management*, Blackwell

Margerison, C (1991) *Making Management Development Work*, McGraw-Hill

NACETT (1996) *Skills for 2000: Report in Progress Towards the National Training Targets for Education and Training*, National Advisory Council for Education and Training

Megginson, D, Joy-Mathews, J and Banfield, P (1993) *Human Resource Development*, Kogan Page

Nadler, L (1970) *Developing Human Resources*, Gulf

O'Connor, M (1998) 'Open for business', *The Independent*, 8 January 1998

Nowack, K M (1991) 'A true training needs analysis', *Training and Development Journal*, April

Payne, J, Payne, C, Lissenburgh, S and Range, M (1999) *Work Based Training and Job Prospects for the Unemployed: An Evaluation of Training for Work*, Department for Education and Employment, Research Briefs, Research Report No. 96

Pedler, M, Burgoyne, J and Boydell, T (1991) *'The Learning Company': A Strategy for Sustainable Development*, McGraw-Hill

Price, A J (1997) *Human Resource Management in a Business Context*, International Thomson Business Press

Rothwell, S (1992) 'The development of the international manager', *Personnel Management*, January

Sadler, P and Milner, K (1993) *The Talent-Intensive Organisation: Optimising Your Company's Human Resource Strategies*, Economist Intelligence Unit

Sapsford, D and Tzannatos, Z (1993) *The Economics of the Labour Market*, Macmillan

Scase, R (1998) 'Women drive the economy', *Independent on Sunday*, 5 April 1998

Senge, P M (1993) *The Fifth Discipline*, Century/Arrow

Sloman, M (1993) 'Training to play a lead role', *Personnel Management*, July

Stevens, J and Walsh, T (1991) 'Training and Competitiveness' in Stevens, J and Mackay, R (eds) *Training and Competitiveness*, NEDO/Kogan Page

Tamkin, P and Hillage, J (1997), 'Individual commitment to learning: Motivation and Rewards', Department for Education and Employment, Research Report No. 11

Thackray , R (1998) 'The car is not the only star', *Independent on Sunday*, 14 June 1998

Thompson, R and Mabey, C (1994) *Developing Human Resources*, Butterworth-Heinemann

Vicere, A and Freeman, V (1990) 'Executive education in major corporations', *Journal of Management Development*

Walton, J (1999) *Strategic Human Resource Development*, Financial Times Prentice Hall

Westhead, P and Storey, D J (1997) *Training Provision and the Development of Small and Medium-sized Enterprises*, Department for Education and Employment, Research Briefs, Research Report No. 26

Recommended Reading

Most basic human resource texts have sections on HRD, the older ones generally emphasising training procedures rather than strategic development. John Walton's (1999) *Strategic Human Resource Development* (Financial Times Prentice Hall) provides an extensive coverage of more strategic issues but also encompasses many of the basic concepts in HRD. You can find a large number of links to articles on training and development-related matters in the HRD section at http://www.hrmguide.com.

Answers to Review Activity

You might have thought that this was a difficult exercise to complete because there is little information to help you. The article talks about various roles and the way staff are hired and paid but what about HRD? Obviously, you have to apply some ingenuity and also speculate about what the real situation might be. You may have concluded that the key lies in the role of sponsor – this role seems to take on some of the functions normally dealt with by a mentor and a line manager.

An important element of the culture and structure of the company is its 'team' focus. By working within teams, newcomers can learn from more experienced staff, learning not just the explicit but also the tacit knowledge and attitudes that underlie the company's success. In effect this reinforces the role of the sponsor.

But what is missing? You could argue that if development needs are being met by the current provision, then nothing is lacking. On the other hand, we would expect that there would be a number of facilities available to supplement the rather informal arrangements already outlined. For example, some systematic appraisal scheme to help in the identification of needs; for example, the provision of appropriate systematic training in say budgeting or IT applications. (These might well exist, but they are not specifically mentioned.)

The essential point of this exercise is to illustrate that while human resource development may be carried out in an organised systematic manner, as indicated in this unit, successful organisations may choose to operate in an entirely different way.

RESOURCES

Resource 1

The credible journey

With people now widely regarded as the most important source of competitive advantage, personnel professionals have an unprecedented opportunity – and responsibility – to contribute to business strategy. But what qualities are needed to ensure credibility with senior directors? *People Management* asked five of HR's finest to reflect on how they influence their top management teams.

Ward Griffiths There are some indications that over the past five years or so, personnel functions have become more closely involved in developing business strategy. Is that the case in your organisations, and what does it mean in practice?

Carmel Flatley Strategy-making is a big opportunity for HR people, because in many organisations the function has responsibility to drive the development of the executive team – and what do top executives need to be better at? So if you are an HR director who knows about the business, appreciates where it should be going and understands the external influences, competitive pressures and so on, then you can be a driver of the whole strategic process. In McDonald's that process – of making sure that strategy is on the agenda at executive meetings – is largely driven by me.

Don Beatie I would certainly expect the HR director of my corporation to be able to contribute as an equal to business strategy. I'm not sure I would go as far as Carmel in seeing business strategy being driven by the HR function, but I do think that it depends on the nature of the business, and I can see how a highly service-orientated business might give more opportunities for HR to be in the driving seat. But this whole issue about having the ability to operate as an equal in the team and to contribute to strategy-making is fundamental.

Ron Collard I agree. It's all about personal credibility. Don's point about being seen as equals is crucial. In our business, despite the fact that everybody recognised it was a people business, for a long time nobody thought HR had a contribution to make. Then there was a growing recognition that in the 1990s people issues were becoming very complex. We have highly talented professionals who can be tempted away at any moment. Suddenly our people were a key part of the strategic agenda, and the need for a credible HR professional to contribute at the top level became more and more important, and therefore accepted.

WG Let's look at what goes into credibility. Is it status, is it relationships with the chief executive or other line managers? Is it to do with delivering a specialised expertise in a particular way in the organisation or environment you find yourself in? How do you as individuals exercise influence?

Nickie Fonda That's a complex question. On the one hand you need a real ability to think like a chief executive. On the other hand, if that is all you do, then the danger is that people won't be paid on time or basic industrial relations will be in a mess. So HR needs not only to be astute in business terms, but also very tidy operationally. This is particularly so with HR, because, except maybe in finance, I'm not sure that there's any other profession where such a wide span of capability is called for.

DB For a start, you've got to have a fundamentally sound relationship with at least the chairman, the chief executive and the finance director. More generally, you've got to be able to meet your line management colleagues on their wavelength – to discuss things in their terms. Then it's all about the relevance of your contributions and your ability to deliver what's needed. And influencing skills are crucial, by which I mean the capacity to listen, absorb and modify other people's positions. All these things together are what builds credibility.

RC Influence also comes from all the individual relationships you have. Each of those people has their own organisational issues, and you need to be seen as somebody who can work rigorously and independently with them, challenge them and help them to understand the issues. You have real influence if and when you're seen as somebody who can help people individually, and the relationship changes from simply an organisational one and also becomes a personal one.

I'll give you an example. One of our board members who ran our biggest business and was responsible for a real breakthrough four or five years ago rang me up and said: "I can't imagine taking any major business decision now without you sitting there." That degree of influence was built over time and was built on helping him as an individual.

CF The relationship you have with key people also depends on how sound your judgement is – on whether the outcomes of the things you recommend over time are seen to be successful. That, of course, depends on professional competence. One of the things that can help to give you credibility is line management experience. You have to prove yourself less in HR if you have that behind you, and I'd recommend all HR people to try to pick this up over time. It gives you the ability to stand up, take the flak and be robust enough to hold up a mirror to the company. Everyone likes to talk about the company's successes, but it's important for someone to point out the issues that must be addressed.

The other thing that has given the HR department credibility in McDonald's is the way that it has taken the people issues and the soft skills and turned them into hard measures: of turnover, training input, legal spend and suchlike. I think that's what Don meant when he talked about the HR function being on the same wavelength as the finance director, the marketing director and the chief executive. It's so important.

RC Perhaps I'm a heretic, but I am not convinced that line management experience is necessary. The fact that we haven't run a factory or whatever is not important if we can show that we understand the business issues. Finance directors don't go around worrying about their lack of line management experience. I think we have to have the confidence to say to people: "We understand your business".

DB I was struck by the phrase that Carmel used – holding a mirror up to the organisation – by which I understand she means challenging conventional thinking. I find that external benchmarking can be useful for this purpose, and can strengthen the credibility factor. Some organisations can be remarkably inward-looking, and the HR department can challenge this by holding up the external reference points and saying: "How is it that those guys over there are managing to do it like that while we're still doing it like this?"

WG That raises another question. Some writers suggest that by closely aligning the personnel function with business management, we find it harder to challenge the conventional thinking and values of the organisation. What you're saying seems to contradict that suggestion.

RC Yes, I completely agree with Don that we need to have the confidence to work with our peers. But at the same time I believe that the personnel role requires us to take a half step back from the close camaraderie that you might get in your senior executive team. And that's a very difficult balance to get right. If you get too chummy, you can't hold the mirror up. But if you don't get chummy enough, then your credibility may be weakened.

DB That's right. One of the tendencies that worries the hell out of me is what I call "The permission-seeking mentality" of some HR functions – the idea that absolutely nothing should be done unless the line management structure says it needs to be done. That's absolute anathema to me. The HR function has to be prepared to walk on stage with a spotlight on it and say: "We believe this because it's fundamentally right for the business for the following reasons." We haven't talked yet about our role as agents of change, but that's also part of the credibility picture. We need to know what needs to change and the skill to make it happen effectively.

WG Nickie, how do you see the role of top personnel specialists as change agents?

NF This issue has been gnawing at me. My experience, working with senior professionals over the past few years, is that a lot of the changes that are needed are big changes, not incremental steps. They are major changes of direction, major changes in capability requirements. But there seems to be a tradition within HR that we want to make a series of little changes. I'm beginning to wonder whether we are gearing ourselves up sufficiently to be able to tackle these big changes.

WG Are you saying there's still a large part of HR that is more concerned with keeping the status quo?

NF I can see why some senior executives might believe that. A good way to illustrate this is to ask what kind of development strategies we have for our people. Do we assume, as Motorola does, that people during their career will go through seven different paradigm changes in the way in which the organisation and their work is construed? Or do we simply assume that we want people to be better at doing today's jobs, with today's responsibilities, in today's organisations? I would guess that in nine out of ten companies the strategy for developing people is stuck in the present. That's not radical.

CF Maybe it doesn't need to be radical. It's important to consider whether people can cope with those big changes. A lot of our people are already dealing with changes in legislation, marketing techniques and the equipment we use. They are flooded with new information from different departments and new expectations in terms of performance. We have to assess how much change they can implement at one time. Also, the rate of change that is needed also depends on how well and organisation is doing. If you're a market leader, perhaps it's a question of gaining inches rather than these big shifts. But if your profits are tumbling, then you are looking for big leaps forward.

NF I'd like to challenge that. Aren't there plenty of examples of companies that were doing well, and which suddenly found the ground taken out from under their feet? Think of the classic business school cases, such as the collapse of Caterpillar's market dominance in earth-moving vehicles, or IBM's in computers. Those companies hadn't been gearing up to face new sources of competition by developing new capabilities.

DB Yes, a lot of people do believe that the point at which you should think about reinventing the business is when you are at your most successful.

RC Doesn't this discussion show the dichotomy in our roles? One aspect is being involved in strategic change – thinking "outside the box". The other is taking operational responsibility for ensuring that the people systems – pay, performance, management, development and so on – support that change. I would be in Carmel's camp here. You cannot change all the people systems overnight, because people don't change that quickly. You have to build things incrementally, and that means deciding what the priorities are.

DB Surely this is where the HR strategy, as opposed to the business strategy, comes in? You are testing for alignment all the time, checking whether your systems, processes, skills and culture are aligned with where the business needs to go. That's the bread and butter of HR, and it raises another question: do we have the HR function and the organisation to deliver?

RC I can quote a specific example. In the recession of the early 1990s we realised we needed much more flexibility in our pay systems. This meant introducing bonuses, despite some belief at the highest level that they were inappropriate for a professional services firm. That was a major business change for us, yet there was no way we could have introduced bonuses overnight across the organisation. So we did it in small steps and now we have a culture that thinks bonuses are a good thing.

WG Let's look more at this issue of alignment. How can we ensure there is a good "fit" between HR practices and wider business goals? The American academic Jeffrey Pfeffer says in his latest book that there is now enough research to enable us to identify the components of best practice in HR. These include employment security, selective recruitment, the presence of self-managed teams in devolved business units, extensive training, comparatively high pay, the reduction of status barriers and the open sharing of information. Of course, he would emphasise that you have to take from this list what's appropriate to your business. So how do you as senior specialists decide what should be in your own bundle of HR policies?

CF Once the company has decided what its competitive strategy is, the HR director has to stand back and see how the people strategy fits. For example, our growth strategy at McDonald's means that we have to give a high priority to recruitment and retention. But I think you also have to look at how the culture of the company, its structure, communications, reward system and training and development underpins the strategy – and that's where you draw from the HR toolkit.

DB I agree with Carmel that you can almost put a template over your business strategy and say this therefore means action points one, two, three, four, five to put the organisation structure, the skills, processes, culture, rewards strategy and communications strategy that we need in place.

RC I would buy the template idea, but I'm conscious that a major change in reward systems, for example, is a significant piece of work, and people both within and outside HR can get caught up in the technical details. You made reference earlier, Nickie, to what line management thinks of our role, and quote often they will look back on a major change programme and think, oh yes, that was all about the new pay system. So the HR leader needs to ensure that his or her colleagues on the top team don't lose sight of the long-term direction.

WG Carmel mentioned measurement systems earlier, but I would ask: how good are we at tracking how what we do impacts on the business? How do you all measure the effectiveness of HR's own contribution.

DB That's an interesting question, because the answer comes at three levels. At a basic level, you can take a measure such as labour turnover, and delve deeper to establish data on, for example, the cost and time taken per recruit. Or we could be a bit more sophisticated and look at the average performance rating of the people who leave the organisation compared to those who stay, which might be reassuring or alarming. The second level concerns line managers and how they rate the effectiveness of the support they are getting from the HR function, and again there are various surveys and structured instruments you can use to measure yourself year on year.

But the really important level is the one not very many of us have got a good grip on – namely, what does HR contribute to bottom-line results? One measure that I would take seriously is the employee opinion survey, where at least you are testing the climate of the organisation. A number of research studies are suggesting that there is a direct correlation between employee satisfaction and customer satisfaction, so an organisational climate survey may be a promising indicator. But any absolute bottom-line measurement of the impact of HR is really difficult.

CF Yes, it's almost blatantly obvious, but we have not been comparing the results of employee opinion surveys and customer satisfaction surveys. Now we're considering how, at the level of individual restaurants, we might poll employees' satisfaction and customer satisfaction at the same time, and come up with an instrument that actually correlates the two.

RC Surely the important thing is that measurement enables you to get into a dialogue on strategic issues. For example, you might set a target that you will retain 90 per cent of your outstanding people. In fact, we thrive on a 20 to 25 per cent turnover. We worry if it's above 25 per cent or below 20 per cent. But the details aren't important. The point is that if you are way off target, that prompts a discussion of the issues and ideas about tackling whatever the problem might be.

WG You seem to be saying that HR must work in a partnership with the line in order to deliver results. What do you do to support and develop line managers to take on their part of the bargain?

CF The HR department's responsibility is to set policy – in consultation with the line, of course – to develop a practical toolkit that line managers can draw from when managing their staff, and to make sure that they have access to all the training they need. We need to use the training to get across the company's philosophy on how to handle people and teach them and motivate them.

NF If HR takes the lead in defining what makes a good manager, then designs the training to enable people to become a good manager and also takes the lead in employee satisfaction surveys to check what people think of their line managers, then in a sense you could say – and I'm being deliberately challenging here – that line management works for HR.

CF Yes, but in McDonald's a lot of people in the HR department are seconded from line management and go back out again. That, of course, sensitises HR professionals to the needs of the line. They don't lose touch.

WG That's a good example of the way that traditional functional distinctions are breaking down and that's a big challenge for people who have studied within a personnel or a marketing or some other professional framework, isn't it?

DB Yes it is. I'm beginning to wonder whether, in the medium term, there's going to be a personnel function as we know it. The possibility exists of defining a much broader role with responsibility for all the capabilities of the organisation, including things that have been kept in separate functional silos up to now – for example IT, core services and facilities – as well as the people side of things. A few organisations have started to do this. For example, I understand that Shell has set up a multi-disciplinary internal consultancy operation. I suspect that this sort of approach will gather pace.

WG When I worked with Kent County Council I was originally the personnel director but ended up managing corporate resources more widely. Our goals were set not in terms of the functional objective that would have characterised our previous operations, but by reference to the overriding goals of the organisation as a whole. And it became evident that people were able to work both within and between functions in flexible ways that hadn't previously been imagined. To that extent, I think that Don is seeing a future in which personnel people will still require effective knowledge and understanding of their specialism, but be able to apply this in a variety of different organisational settings and have their contribution assessed against the goals of the corporation as a whole. So, what do you all see as the implications for how we prepare young people coming into the personnel profession?

RC I foresee that opportunities for the "career generalist", if I can coin that phrase, will be fewer. I think people will need to have a deep specialism – whether it is compensation and benefits, or organisation development, or whatever – because without this they will find it more difficult to gain credibility at the top. But they will also need to have width, in the business sense, to compensate for this deep specialism. The day of being the superstar industrial relations person who more or less "generalised along", is over. That's how I was brought up, so I'm talking about myself in a slightly negative way here. Organisations demand a much greater depth from their individual HR people. So I would encourage any young person wanting to get to the top to combine broad business acumen with a deep specialism within the HR field.

One small point – and you will all say I was bound to say this – is that one way to widen your experience quickly is by doing consultancy work. Whatever the size of the consultancy, your personal credibility is on the front line from a relatively young age, and you are often dealing with quite senior HR people. And if someone says (and I have seen it happen) "sorry, you're the wrong person, I'm not happy working with you", you get an early lesson in what personal credibility is all about.

DB I can't help feeling that there is going to be an enormous convergence – and it's happening already – of the two disciplines of HR and information management. The application of IT and management systems will be crucial to the way that organisations work. So an HR professional's capacity to understand how these can be structured and developed is going to be very important.

CF I agree that we may be moving more towards a "corporate resources" model, and I agree with Ron about the benefits of a deep specialism. But I also think that business management experience is very valuable – where a young person has to take responsibility and actually make a difference and be accountable. It's not important whether this is in a business or in public services or even in the voluntary sector I would also say: get experience of working in different environments.

WG Thank you all.

Ward Griffiths is the IPD's assistant director-general. He was previously deputy chief executive and director of corporate resources at Kent County Council.

Carmel Flatley is a senior vice-president with McDonald's Restaurants and the company's chief executive officer for HR and training in the UK.

Don Beattie is chief executive for personnel at BOC. He is a former IPD vice-president.

Ron Collard is a partner at PricewaterhouseCoopers UK responsible for the firm's HR operations. He is currently the IPD's vice-president for organisation and HR planning.

Nickie Fonda is an organisation strategy consultant. She is working with the IPD on it's relationships with senior personnel practitioners.

People Management, 1 October 1998
Reproduced with permission.

Resource 2

Rewarding a model merger

Lloyds TSB's recent award for best human resource development is hailed in the City, says **Phillip Inman**.

Mergers have a terrible habit of going wrong. The expected cost savings never materialise or the hoped-for combinations of expertise in production or sales and marketing turn out to be a mirage. Worst of all, workers find themselves at war as they jockey for the plum jobs in the new company.

When high street bank Lloyds took over the Trustee Savings Bank in 1995, it created one of the largest banks in the world, with about 90,000 staff. Lloyds Bank was a stock market darling. The ability of its management to create healthy profits without venturing into risky areas like derivatives trading were legendary. Buying the TSB was part of a policy of sticking to its knitting. The fear was that a success story could easily be undermined unless the merger went smoothly.

Today Lloyds is still held in high esteem by the City, in part because of its handling of the merger. According to the judges of the Management Awards, run by the Management Consultancy Association, the decision to overhaul its personnel procedures in conjunction with a firm specialising in human resources not only saved it from a costly bout of internal warfare, but also transformed the way that the new bank communicated with its staff.

The MCA awards have been running for three years and aim to highlight the successes of management consultancy projects.

A spokesman for the association, Will White, says the awards are needed "because firms are often secretive and hold back from publicising their projects or they are bound by client confidentiality".

The newly merged Lloyds TSB group won the award for best human resource development with its partner PA Consulting Group at a low-key awards ceremony held last month in the association's London offices. PA Consulting also picked up the award in the category for the best use of IT with NHS Scotland, while oil giant Shell took the award for best business transformation with consultants Coverdale.

Lloyds wanted PA Consulting to draft proposals that would enhance the reputation of the combined group with its employees. It hoped the plan would mark it out against other blue-chip employers as the preferred destination of graduates and other prospective employees.

A team was set up by human resources director Norman Mitchinson, made up of staff from his department and a PA Consulting team headed by senior consultant Bridget Skelton. The team spent three months designing a new scheme that would integrate the human resource department into the overall strategic aims of the company.

What every company wants from its personnel function is one that looks ahead to the needs of the entire organisation - the skills that will be needed in the future and those soon to become redundant - that will best prepare it for a competitive market place.

Ms Skelton says she sat in on meetings, challenging the schemes put up until the team settled on four models. They studied to what extent personnel decisions should be made in the business or within the human resources function, how many units would provide personnel services (call centres, strategy units, etc) and the degree of risk with each model that they might fail to win enough support and be carried through.

The four models were then whittled down to one. At this point the project team needed to sell the idea to Lloyds' management board before pressing ahead with any implementation. Part of the sell to the board was the prospect of savings amounting to £7.4 million, as well as a more efficient and responsive human resources set-up.

"It was critical to design plans that ensured people engaged, took ownership, and changed their behaviour," says Ms Skelton. "These success factors were all critical to achieving the savings targeted and new working practices."

She says the human resources department now gets involved in the strategic decisions of the bank, has moved to a project culture meeting cost and time constraints and has instilled a greater reliance on "self-help" - increased use of information on PCs, e-mail, manuals, kiosks and call centres to answer enquiries.

Will White says the success of the project was demonstrated by a series of staff surveys that revealed higher satisfaction after the merger. Telephone inquiries by staff were also measurably quicker and there was more information available to the staff. "The point is that companies need to be more open with their staff and Lloyds has shown it is prepared to do that. Communication is the key," he says.

The Guardian, 13 February 1999
Reproduced with permission.

Resource 3

How to determine future work-force needs

HR at the Tennessee Valley Authority has developed an eight-step system for creating and implementing a work-force planning process, by **David E. Ripley**.

Work-force planning is identifying and responding to future HR needs and can be implemented in almost any organization. It can provide a rational basis for developing and funding HR programs needed to support organizational objectives. Initially, the process used should be simple, and should reflect the size and complexity of the organization.

Successful implementation requires strong support from HR, involvement and ownership by line workers, and commitment from senior management. The degree of automated support needed depends on the size and complexity of the organization, as well as the hardware and software currently being used.

Work-force planning involves two major activities. First is developing and analyzing data that identify HR needs. This will include such data as future gaps and surpluses in the work force, diversity statistics, population demographics, health and safety statistics, turnover rates and causes, and employee-opinion survey results. The organization's mission, values, strategic goals and business objectives must also be considered data, as should federal and state laws and regulations.

The second major activity is developing responses to the identified needs. These responses may be action plans (such as recruiting or training plans), or may require developing special programs. Responses normally include both organizationwide activities and programs designed to address the specific needs of various business units.

These activities will add value to any organization. For one, work-force planning contributes to the successful accomplishment of an organization's strategic goals and business objectives. Every strategic goal and business objective has a human element that needs to be identified and provided for in a company's business plan—just as surely as that strategic goal or business objective's financial requirement needs to be identified and provided for.

But most organizations, somewhere in their value statements, also stress creating an environment that enables employees to develop their potential to the fullest, or words to that effect. Work-force planning provides a means to address these employee needs as well as business needs. For example, skill-gap and surplus information projected during the work-force planning process enables any organization to do a better job in such areas as career counselling, training, recruiting, diversity and retraining—both for employees' needs and for tailoring such programs to the specific needs of the organization and its business units. At the Tennessee Valley Authority (TVA), this information has helped the agency implement cross-organizational placement and retraining as alternatives to job cutbacks in the individual business units.

Another way that work-force planning helps add value to the organization is when business plans must be modified to deal with the unexpected. When such circumstances occur, the work-force planning process can provide the knowledge to make intelligent decisions.

Developing a work-force plan requires going through an eight-step process
Before starting into a work-force planning process, an organization should define its desired goal. A goal could be defined as something like: "To develop human resources strategies that respond to identified employee needs and make the necessary HR contributions to the organization's strategic goals and business objectives." This definition addresses both employee and organizational needs, and points clearly to the kind of data that needs to be gathered and analyzed.

Once the desired goal has been determined, process development should begin. If work-force planning is being done for the first time, the process should be kept as simple and as "doable" as possible. Start out walking and run later.

We developed an eight-step methodology. The number of steps isn't particularly important. What is important is that there is an understandable methodology that guides business units through the process.

The steps are:

- lay out a plan and a schedule
- perform a staffing assessment
- develop demand data
- develop supply data
- compare demand and supply data
- develop the work-force plan
- communicate and implement the work-force plan
- evaluate and update the plan.

Laying out a plan and schedule will facilitate accomplishing the next seven steps better. For example, you should create planning teams and management oversight teams for each business unit during this phase that will aid in the implementation process later on.

The staffing assessment involves benchmarking your organization's staff size and skill mix against selected criteria. To do so you must decide on the specific processes or functions to be benchmarked and identify the companies with which to compare. Or, you can focus the staffing assessment internally by examining work drivers, outputs, processes and tasks. Either way, the results can be used to develop a model organization.

This activity may only need to be conducted every few years, but the results need to be continually reviewed as the organization and the business environment change. The larger and more complex the company, the more complex this step will be. Conversely, for a smaller organization – perhaps only dealing with one major function – it may be a relatively quick and simple process.

Next, you need to develop demand data by projecting, over the planning horizon, the numbers of employees and the skills that will be needed to meet business objectives. Although one would expect to move toward the model organization developed in the staffing assessment, it may take some years to get there for any number of reasons. Think of it this way: The staffing assessment model is a destination, while the demand-data projections describe the journey to get there.

Developing supply data is done by projecting the current population over the planning horizon, as if there were no new hires. This requires attrition assumptions concerning resignations, transfers, retirements, deaths, and the number of technical trainees who fail. Assumptions may need to vary by business unit. For example, there may be a unit that has a high number of employees eligible for retirement.

After compiling both the demand data and supply data, you'll need to determine the future gap and/or surplus situation, in both numbers and skills. A gap indicates that the demand will exceed the supply; a surplus indicates that the supply will exceed the demand. Employees in occupations that are projected as surplus are considered to be "at risk." Here, it's important to identify projected gaps in skills critical to the success of the organization and to identify at-risk occupations or employees.

From here, you need to analyze the data to identify issues in three major areas:

- demand and supply data, such as skill gaps and at-risk occupations
- overall corporate issues, such as strategic goals and corporate values related to the work force
- organization-specific issues, such as business objectives or an ageing population in a particular business unit.

You then can develop a work-force plan by identifying future HR needs in these areas and developing strategies and action plans. For example, at TVA, to facilitate cross-organizational placement and retraining of at-risk employees, we developed a system for inputting supply-and-demand data at the department level that's accessible agencywide.

The work-force plan should become a part of the organization's business plan. Communicating it will bring it to life. Effective communication is vital for employees to understand its value. Therefore, you should communicate the basis of the plan, as well as its elements, to all employees. That is, communicate the business-plan strategies and assumptions that the work-force plan is based on, as well as communicating the work-force plan strategies themselves. Make the tie to the organization's business plan clear to all.

Implementation and follow-through will demonstrate your commitment to the plan to employees

Although the logic for work-force planning is sound, that doesn't mean it automatically will be embraced by managers who have many other things to do. No matter how good an idea, it probably will fail unless the organization is ready to accept it.

In addition, moving to a more proactive approach that will get you ahead on the curve involves a shift in thinking and a degree of culture change. The middle of the organization usually drives the implementation of work-force planning, and change driven from the middle – particularly when it involves a shift in culture – normally can't succeed without top-management support.

In our case, work-force planning was viewed as a vehicle to help stabilize employment, so the organization was ready for it. Support was present and has since been reinforced by our new chairman.

As mentioned earlier, a major factor in the successful implementation of work-force planning is how well the organization begins the planning process. Creating a management oversight team for each business unit during that first phase will help drive the process because managers are more likely to take ownership of, and provide support for, a work-force plan that they had a hand in developing. Each of these teams should be headed by a senior manager selected by the organization's senior executive. These teams would be responsible for ensuring that each business unit's planning team develops implementation plans that address such issues as:

- key milestones in plan development
- clarification of accountabilities
- resolution of integration issues associated with the plan, such as discussions with unions
- schedules for completion of activities needed to produce the work-force plan
- the need for a comprehensive communications plan to inform employees of the plan's content, and the business and other assumptions upon which it's based
- organizational critical success factors that the plan must address
- performance indicators to measure work-force action plan progress in addressing critical success factors and meeting business objectives.

The function of management oversight is more important than the particular composition of the teams. In a smaller organization, the chief executive may take this responsibility personally.

There should, however, be planning teams for each business unit, rather than one for the entire company. These teams – also created during the first phase of the process – should be headed by the organization's senior human resources official or designee. Or, some organizations consider this an excellent developmental assignment for other managers. Either way, the teams should have representatives from all key units of the company and should be standing teams, although membership periodically should rotate.

The planning teams' primary responsibility is to manage the actual development of their units' work-force plan and to monitor its implementation. Further, the teams should build ongoing status reporting into the process so that the plans can be modified when necessary.

The planning teams can have subgroups work on particular issues. This is an excellent way to involve a significant number of employees at all levels in the effort. For example, several task teams can be given the job of developing recommended action plans to deal with all identified human resources issues. Another team can deal with integrating action plans with business-plan objectives and the demand forecast with projected budgets. Yet another team might take on development of the communications plan.

The planning teams must stay focused on key issues. Every action plan developed should tie to an identified HR need that in turn ties to strategic goals, organizational values and critical success factors, business objectives, or the like. Action plans should have a clear objective, and progress toward accomplishing the objective should be measurable by an identified performance indicator. It's critical to avoid the activity trap, where the objective can become simply the check-off of activities completed rather than accomplishments.

Implementing work-force plans successfully requires corporate support and automated systems

To be effective, work-force plans need to belong to the business units. The demand forecasts and action plans in particular must be owned by the business units. However, there's a need, particularly in the first few planning cycles, for significant internal consulting support from the corporate staff in developing business unit work-force plans. This support group need not be large, nor should it be doing the business units' work-force planning for them. It should, however, provide the business units with tools and functional support during the process (see "Staffers Support Business Units' Work-force Planning").

One of the tools a corporate support group should supply is a sufficient automated system and the training to use it. Of course, if an organization is small enough, work-force planning can be carried out with a tablet and a hand calculator. As the organization grows, however, it probably will need to go to a PC spreadsheet to input demand data directly and pick up supply data from PC-based human resources information systems (HRIS).

There is an increasing number of good PC-based shelf systems coming available for the small or even midsize organization. However, in a larger and more complex company that needs a number of people at many locations to access the data, an extensive automated support system may be needed. Without it, rolling up data organizationwide, and analyzing it, becomes very cumbersome.

The system an organization installs also may be driven somewhat by its existing hardware and software. In our case, we could see our best option was to go to a mainframe system. Our HRIS existed on mainframe, and although this data could have been downloaded to PCs, many of our potential users didn't have PCs. These users did, however, have access to the mainframe. In addition, we needed to keep the supply data base up-to-date. Because supply is, at all times, current population projected forward, it changes daily.

We developed an SAS mainframe application, which we call WorkForcePlanner, that goes directly to HRIS and extracts supply data as of that moment. Thus, the supply data base is maintained.

Another factor that will impact automated support-system development is the type of data contained in the organization's HRIS. At TVA, our basic planning matrix is job titles and organization codes. Demand data (staffing projections) are entered on this basis and compared to supply data generated from HRIS. The system compares the two and generates gap and surplus data over the planning horizon. We can print and analyze reports on supply and demand or gaps and surpluses on a number of HRIS criteria.

A case can be made that we need more detail on individual skills in our system. Currently, we're working to develop a skills inventory system that will allow us to integrate into our planning system more data on existing population skills and projected position skill needs.

A word of caution on automated support systems: Don't forget that every number the system produces, except for today's actual data, is a guess – a very good guess, perhaps, but still only that. Also, the further out the projection, the more the data degrade. Building an automated system that defines future gaps or surpluses in very specific detail implies a degree of precision that simply doesn't exist.

Having an automated support system does better enable you to update and revise the work-force plan annually. Keep in mind that, above all, the planning process should serve the organization's needs. If, in the middle of the normal cycle, conditions change significantly, there should be no hesitation to modify the work-force plan and its strategies accordingly.

Each action plan should be evaluated frequently. The activities aren't an end in themselves, but are intended as an appropriate response to an identified issue. If they're being properly executed but not generating the desired result, revisit the issue.

There's no reason the process can't be expected to evolve over time as users become more sophisticated in work-force planning. The above steps, for example, have a clear internal bias, with major emphasis on staffing projections. Over time, we expect to put more emphasis on external issues, such as external supply demographics. It's probably wise to start, however, with an internal focus. To repeat, walk before you run. And if you take one step at a time, you should be able to successfully plan for your future HR needs.

Personnel Journal, January 1995
Article by David E Ripley. Copyright January 1995.
Used with permission of ACC Communications Inc./
Personnel Journal (now known as *Workforce*),
Costa Mesa, CA, USA. All rights reserved.

Resource 4

Bonnypark District Council – Human Resources Department

Job Application Form

Full name	
Address	
Town/city	
County	
Post code	
Telephone	
E-mail	
Position applied for	

Personal history

Date of birth	**(dd/mm/yy)**
Marital status	
Nationality	
National insurance number	
Are you related to any Bonnypark District Council staff?	Yes/No
Have you worked for or applied for employment before to Bonnypark District Council?	
Do you hold a full driving licence?	
Detail any endorsements	
How did you learn about this vacancy?	
When would you be able to start?	**(dd/mm/yy)**

Secondary education

Date	School	Qualification	Subject	Grade

Further and higher education

Date	College/ university	Qualification	Subject	Grade

Employment history (commence with most recent position)

Employer	Dates From/ to	Job title	Annual salary	Reason for leaving

Positions of responsibility held outside your employment

Interests and hobbies

Why do you wish to apply for this job?

Any additional information to support your application

References

Two references are required, one of which must be from your current employer or education establishment. Please note that referees will not be approached without your permission. Please give full address, occupation and title of each referee.

1.

2.

Resource 5

Fair chance of a job in IT

The Web is no substitute for a face-to-face meeting when seeking employment, writes **Tim Phillips**.

"Last year we had 46,000 CVs sent to us," admits Janet Knott, head of resource management at Cap Gemini. "After a while one CV can begin to look like another. Meeting those people face to face gives them a better feel for us, and us a better feel for them."

Cap Gemini is one of the first-time exhibitors at ExhibIT 99, the new recruitment fair for IT professionals running today and tomorrow in London's Russell Hotel. Organisers Computer Publishing plan three shows this year, and, if ExhibIT is a success in London, shows in other parts of the UK.

It's an unlikely time to be organising a recruitment fair, as the jobs market is increasingly dominated by online recruitment through searchable Web sites which simply post a list of vacancies with a telephone number. "At the moment I find 95 per cent of my permanent staff through JobSite, and almost 100 per cent of my contractors through JobServe," admits Carl Beetham, managing director of specialist recruiter Unix Connections. So why is he giving up two days to run a stand in the Russell Hotel?

Web-based recruitment, he says, is ideal for lower-skilled jobs in areas like PC support. For Beetham, the highly-qualified permanent staff with practical experience that he calls "gold dust" are those candidates the Web doesn't deliver: "People who make the effort to come through the door of an exhibition are serious about wanting a job. We need to find sharp, astute individuals here."

"We set up ExhibIT because the recruitment agencies and employers that we dealt with wanted a new way to meet IT professionals," explains organiser Simon Bennie. "Over the two days they will each meet hundreds of potential employees."

And the 2000 IT professionals that Bennie is expecting to attend can meet 21 potential employers too. Rubbing shoulders with Cap Gemini are employers like British Gas Trading and recruitment agency Chamberlain Scott.

For Cap Gemini's Knott, who has to find 2,000 permanent IT staff in the next 12 months, ExhibIT 99 is a low- risk way to find high-quality candidates. "If someone joins us as a result of this show, then they have already met the company, and they turn up for work knowing what to expect. They have a chance that they would not otherwise have to meet our people." She adds that inside Cap Gemini there's competition to man the stand from team leaders who want to bag the best new recruits.

Another participant is recruitment agency Computer People, whose marketing manager Tony Ahmet freely admits that he has a "need everywhere" for job candidates. "We get thousands of e-mails a day offering us CVs, but we like to see people before we place them with companies. This event lets us have a more rounded conversation [with them]."

As skill shortages – particularly for permanent positions – continue, exhibitors know they are being interviewed by candidates as well. "Some of our visitors will be window shopping," says Knott.

"Everybody else at ExhibIT is our competition. We have to look good," admits Beetham.

The result: there's more on offer than just jobs. For example, at the Computer People stand, Ahmet will be dispensing more general advice alongside the hard sell. Visitors can get tips on presenting their CVs, or advice on skills training. "Certainly we expect most of the visitors to be there because they want a job," he says, "but we're open to any sort of conversation."

At mortgage broker John Charcol's stand, consultant Andrew Garber will also be making a different sort of pitch. He's not here to recruit contractors, but to help them get mortgages. Traditionally, even the best-paid IT contractors have been unable to get loans, he explains, because they are self-employed, are perceived as having low job security and too few years of trading behind them. "Lenders don't understand them. We help lenders to look at the issue a different way, and the lenders learn to like the contractors." As part of the show, he's giving a seminar on financial planning.

The Web may have changed IT recruitment, but the experience of recruitment fair organisers shows there's still a need for jobseekers and potential employers to look each other in the eye. VisIT, a similar fair that holds regular small shows throughout the year, claims to have found new jobs for more than 1,000 IT staff in 1998.

"The Web is all quantity, and I want quality," says Beetham. "I have 130 e-mailed CVs to go through today, and at least 65 I know now I can't help. With respect, I'm not interested in people e-mailing me job applications from Romania."

The Guardian, 18 February 1999
Reproduced with permission.

Resource 6

Out of the tick box

Encouraging news: performance management is becoming less bureaucratic and more closely focused on development. **Michael Armstrong** and **Angela Baron** report on the findings of a major new IPD research project.

When the former IPM investigated the use of performance management back in 1991, the term was closely associated with performance-related pay (PRP). Ratings were *de rigueur* and appraisal was a top-down process involving unilateral judgements by "superiors" about their "subordinates". Seven years later, the picture is very different.

The latest research from the IPD has found that the process is now much more closely linked to employee development and that many organisations are trying to distance it from pay decisions. Personal development plans, unheard of in 1991, are now used by more than two-thirds of organisations that operate some form of performance management, while a third use competency assessment. Most companies see managing performance as a continuous process involving reviews that focus on the future rather than the past, and where the key words are "dialogue", "shared understanding", "agreement" and "mutual commitment".

Many employers still link pay to performance, but there is a constant search for better methods of doing this than through the appraisal process. As a concept, PRP is fine, but in practice it seems to create as many problems as it does solutions.

Our findings are based on a survey of more than 550 personnel practitioners, visits to 35 organisations and discussions with 12 focus groups of line managers and staff in six organisations. We also undertook six attitude surveys of employees on the receiving end of performance management, and ran two telephone surveys: one on 360-degree feedback and the other on training in performance management processes and skills. In addition, we interviewed a number of management consultants, union officials and commentators.

Nearly 70 per cent of the respondents to our survey have what they described as formal processes for performance management. These are mainly applied to managers and technical, office or administrative staff. Only half of the respondents said that their manual employees are covered. Objective-setting and annual performance reviews are the most popular aspects of performance management process, while fewer than half of those organisations surveyed said that they use PRP. The proportion of organisations using 360-degree feedback is still fairly small (11 per cent). But interest in this technique is growing as the value of gaining feedback from a variety of sources becomes recognised.

Ever since Michael Beer and Robert Ruh coined the term in 1970s, the meaning of performance management has been ambiguous. For the purposes of our study, we developed the following working definition: "A strategic and integrated approach to increasing the effectiveness of organisations by improving the performance of the people who work in them and by developing the capabilities of teams and individual contributors."

But this statement is a generalisation. Performance management processes take many different forms. The approach will depend on the context of the organisation:

its culture, structure and technology, as well as the views of its stakeholders, the work carried out and the type of people involved. Despite this, we were able to spot some trends among the employers we studied.

At the time of the original IPM study, the emphasis was on objective-setting and the appraisal of results against goals. This was a hangover from the discredited system of management by objectives. What is now emerging is a fully rounded view of performance that embraces *how* people get things done as well as *what* they get done. Inputs such as competencies, approaches and understanding have become as important as outputs such as products, goals attained and objectives achieved.

Best-practice organisations recognise that performance management is not simply another means of getting people to comply with objectives cascaded down from on high. They treat it as a joint process requiring managers and team leaders to identify with individuals or teams what support they need. Examples of this can be seen at organisations as diverse as the Victoria and Albert Museum, Bass Brewers and Zeneca Pharmaceuticals. All of these emphasise development in their performance management processes, provide comprehensive training in performance management activities, use an integrated approach and focus on the quality of the management relationship.

In the past, appraisal tended to be a bureaucratic system imposed on line managers by the personnel department. Everyone had to conform to the same procedure and the most important output was a set of ticks on an elaborate form that, once completed, was forgotten unless it was used to determine the size of someone's pay rise.

Since then, there has been a move to cut the red tape. Performance management is now recognised as a tool for managers to use with their team members, but adapted to fit their own circumstances. The emphasis is placed more on how performance is managed than on the outcomes. As one manager put it: "The value is in the quality of the conversations that managers have with their subordinates, not in the sheet filed away in the HR department."

BP Exploration and United Distillers are good examples of companies in which the management of performance is more a way of life than a distinct, stand-alone system. In these organisations, performance is such an essential part of the management ethos that procedures and forms become almost obsolete other than as an *aide-mémoire* or as a way of communicating training requirements to the relevant budget planner. Managers manage performance because it is an essential part of the job.

But problems are likely to arise when performance management is linked with PRP. Many employers believe in paying for performance and/or competence, but they feel that linking them too closely damages the developmental aspects of performance management. The usual solution is to separate performance and pay reviews. Some organisations no longer require overall ratings, but there still has to be a read-across. So how real is the separation? In reality, it is almost impossible to divorce performance management entirely from pay when some form of PRP is in operation. But the consequences of the link can be managed – for example, by ensuring that documents relating to discussions above development are retained by the individual rather than their line manager or the HR department, and that there is openness about the way by which pay decisions are made.

At one time, performance appraisal was synonymous with performance ratings, which were often justified by the need to have a basis for pay decisions. Yet around a quarter of companies operating PRP do not have ratings. Ratings boxes were universally condemned in our survey. Staff deride them, because they see them as inevitably inconsistent and subjective. Managers dislike them, because they feel as if they are writing school reports. And senior managers loathe them, because they see how ludicrous it is to spend time establishing mutual understanding and then to end the process by ticking a box. As one group personnel director said to us: "Ratings denigrate the whole performance management process."

Averse chorus?

It is often assumed that most line managers think that performance management is a waste of time and that, if they do it at all, they do it badly. It is also widely held that employees are hostile to the process and feel demotivated by it. Our focus groups and attitude surveys did reveal a dislike for ratings and for linking the process to pay, but most comments were otherwise favourable.

Professor David Guest of Birkbeck College, London, analysed the results of the survey. He looked at the effectiveness of performance management by examining financial results, skill development, customer care and quality. Against these criteria, more than 90 per cent of managers rated performance management as moderately or highly effective.

These positive responses had caused us to hope that we could establish a link between performance management and organisational effectiveness. The analysis did not detect such a correlation, probably because of the inconsistent application of performance management across organisations and the lack of formal evaluation. Nevertheless, our research has shown that performance management has come a long way, and is now more likely to be part of an integrated approach to people management than it was a few years ago.

We also discovered that there is no room for complacency. Effective performance management requires detailed analysis of the organisational context, better evaluation procedures and a clearer understanding that the methods an organisation uses to measure performance convey important messages about its values. But the overwhelming view of managers and staff is that performance management is a valuable experience and an increasingly important tool for managing people at all levels.

People Management, 23 July 1998
Reproduced with permission.

Resource 7

Companies evaluate employees from all perspectives

The days of traditional supervisor-subordinate performance evaluations are numbered. Companies are turning to 360-degree appraisals – which pool feedback from both internal and external customers – to receive a broader, more accurate perspective on employees. By **John F Milliman**, **Robert A Zawacki**, **Brian Schulz**, **Sally Wiggins** and **Carol A Norman**.

Many supervisors get a little antsy right around performance review time. In the formal performance appraisal system, there's no way for them to know whether an employee is an effective performer in all interactions – or whether the worker is simply an effective performer when the boss is around. What to do if a favored employee receives applause by supervisors but creates an unpleasant buzz among co-workers? How does a supervisor evaluate an employee he or she sees only a few hours each week? Traditional performance appraisals at their worst can be subjective, simplistic and political. Yet the need for accurate, fair performance measurement has increased exponentially as most organizations face increasingly flatter structures, greater internal changes, and more external competitive pressures.

The solution may be provided by 360-degree performance appraisals. Relatively new, they offer an alternative method by which organizations can gain more useful performance information about employees – and make them more accountable to their various customers.

The 360-degree appraisal significantly differs from the traditional supervisor-subordinate performance evaluation
Rather than having a single person play judge, a 360-degree appraisal acts more like a jury: The people who actually deal with the employee each day create a pool of information and perspectives on which the supervisor may act. This group of individuals is made up of both internal and external customers. Internal customers may include supervisors, top management, subordinates, co-workers, and representatives from other departments who interact with the ratee. External customers may include clients, suppliers, consultants and community officials. Anyone who has useful information on how the employee does the job may be a source in the appraisal.

Using 360-degree appraisals provides a broader view of the employee's performance. The most obvious benefit of the 360-degree appraisal is its ability to corral a range of customer feedback. Because each customer offers a new, unique view, it produces a much more complete picture of an employee's performance. Karrie Jerman, HR representative at Colorado Springs, Colorado-based Hamilton Standard Commercial Aircraft, says that 360-degree appraisals are becoming imperative in the lean and mean '90s, where managers have less credibility with their employees due to their larger spans of controls. "The thing we gain the most is input from so many people that know work. Now their peers and customers give feedback," says Jerman. "They feel it's more fair." Carol A. Norman, customer service specialist at Maynard, Massachusetts-based Digital Equipment Corp., agrees that 360-degree appraisals are more fair: "Unlike with supervisors, employees can't hide as easily in 360 appraisals because peers know their behaviours best and insist on giving more valid ratings."

For instance, a manager at Denver-based Johnson & Johnson Advanced Behavioural Technology (JJABT) used a 360-degree appraisal to obtain information about an employee with supervisory responsibilities from that employee's direct reports. The feedback revealed that the direct reports believed the employee was not listening to them and was also being overly critical towards them. This allowed the manager to take corrective action. Prior to the appraisal, she could rely only on grapevine murmurs and her own limited observations of the employee.

In addition to providing broader perspectives, the 360-degree appraisal facilitates greater employee self-development. It enables an employee to compare his or her own perceptions with the perception of others on the employee's skills, styles, and performance. And there's a lot of power in peer feedback. "You can change behaviour more with feedback coming from your peers," says Karen Ripley, materials manager at Digital. "There is often more power there than in managers' feedback." Finally, the 360-degree appraisal provides formalized communication links between employees and their customers. It makes the employee much more accountable to his or her various internal and external customers, because these people now have feedback into the employee's performance rating. Employees who previously might have concentrated a great deal on impressing managers now have a powerful motivation to focus on working well with all individuals inside and outside their department with whom they interact.

At Hamilton Standard, the feedback from a number of employees also helped to clarify job roles and expectations – frequent sources of disagreement between employees from different functional areas. Companies can also use feedback from the various raters to create more customer-oriented goals in the next year.

Companies must resolve a number of issues to use 360-degree appraisals effectively

The first issue employers must solve in implementing 360-degree appraisals is how many raters should be involved, and, more importantly, who should do the rating.

As a rule of thumb, companies generally select between five and 10 raters. Why? Less than five raters unnecessarily limits the perspective on an employee; exceeding 10 raters typically makes the appraisal system too complex and time consuming.

The most important consideration, however, is to choose the right individuals to be raters. One of the first things companies should do is develop a workable definition of what exactly constitutes a peer, an internal customer, etc. Potential raters should be identified as all of those internal and external customers who have significant interactions with the ratee. At JJABT, which has many teams but still retains traditional hierarchical reporting relationships, the ratee develops a list of key internal and external customers that he or she interacts with and then recommends five to 10 individuals to serve as raters. The supervisor still has the ultimate responsibility for the appraisal and ensures that the appropriate raters are selected, thereby preventing the ratee from stacking the deck with supportive customers who will give high ratings.

Unlike JJABT, the Digital Equipment Corporation's and Hamilton Standard's Colorado Springs divisions are organized into self-directed work teams with extremely flat organizational hierarchies. At Digital, the ratee has the primary responsibility for selecting the raters. The Digital ratee works with his or her team leader to select a panel consisting of the coach and three other employees to be objective advocates for the ratee's 360-degree appraisal. Raters are then selected at random from the ratee's team by a computer-generated system and notified by E-mail to participate in the appraisal. The random system ensures that a fair distribution of raters is created.

The most effective 360-degree appraisal elicits feedback from external clients. However, Digital's Ripley warns that companies shouldn't survey external customers excessively. The client may feel uncomfortable with the idea, particularly if it's a new situation. For instance, one Digital client was even concerned about any potential legal issues involved if they gave a bad rating. "Remember that is not the customer's core business," says Ripley. "Providing feedback for our employees should not take away from the profitability. You need to make sure this is a mutually beneficial process." Be strategic in deciding how much information to solicit from clients. When possible, companies may use existing customer satisfaction data or other quantifiable measures of performance in place of a formal appraisal by the client.

Once a company decides who will do the rating, it must create the criteria by which the employee will be judged. The criteria or questions used in 360-degree appraisals should be based on areas with which the rater is familiar. But organizations should fashion the appraisal to fit their unique needs. For instance, in Digital's self-directed teams, each ratee distributes his or her personal-development and work goals to the entire team at the beginning of the appraisal year. Thus, all members of the team have the ability to evaluate each ratee's goals at year end.

With the more traditional hierarchy at JJABT, the supervisor is most aware of the ratee's individual work tasks and goals. Therefore, the various raters ideally evaluate the ratee only on the behaviours or work incidents that they have directly observed.

The JJABT 360-degree appraisal form includes items such as does the employee:

- follow up on problems, decisions, and requests in a timely fashion
- clearly communicate his or her needs/expectations
- share information or help others
- listen to others
- establish plans to meet future needs
- adhere to schedules?

The raters score these items on a scale from 1 (needs improvement) to 5 (outstanding). Space is also provided for the raters to make written comments. The ratee's final performance appraisal consists of a combination of the comments and ratings from the various raters and the supervisor's own feedback on the ratee's performance.

An important consideration involves how many items to include in the appraisal form. A carefully thought out tradeoff must be made between a large number of questions, which provides greater validity, and fewer questions, which require less time. Because each employee is rated by five to 10 other individuals, the appraisal can entail a major time commitment. For this reason, a practical guideline is to keep the appraisal simple by using a one- to two-page form with five to 15 questions taking 10 to 30 minutes to complete.

Effective 360-degree appraisals aren't knee-jerk judgements – they require consideration

Once the data is collected from the various raters, it must be analyzed and summarized for the ratee's final performance appraisal. At JJABT the employee's supervisor is responsible for summarizing the data and determining the final performance rating, which generally includes a mean score and distribution range for each item. Their experience reveals that feedback can't always be taken at face value. For instance, care must be exercised when only one rater has given highly negative or positive feedback. The JJABT managers stress that the key is to look for trends or patterns in the data. If there are questions or ambiguity in the raters' feedback, the supervisor will often solicit additional feedback from the same or new raters. After summarizing the data, the supervisor conducts the formal appraisal interview with the ratee.

At Digital, where self-directed work teams are used, the ratee is responsible for summarizing the feedback from the various raters. The ratee automatically throws out the lowest and highest overall ratings to ensure more objective overall ratings. The ratee then submits a summary analysis of the remaining ratings to his or her panel of advocates. The ratee and the panel of advocates then meet jointly to determine the ratee's final performance rating and development plan.

Another issue all organizations must face is whether the feedback from the various raters should be kept anonymous or be identified openly to the employee being reviewed. Confidentiality can reduce the possibility that the employee will later confront the raters, and thus encourages raters to be more open and honest with their feedback. Jay Kirksey, a member of the leadership team at Hamilton Standard, agrees that it is difficult to ensure completely honest, open feedback when raters are identified: "Organizational maturity is needed to give and receive constructive feedback. Some people had hidden agendas. We found employees were giving lukewarm and fuzzy feedback because of the fear about the feedback coming back to them. The motto was 'Do unto others as they would do unto you.' "

However, confidentiality has its own baggage: Ratees often try to "hunt the ghost down" or figure out which rater provided the negative feedback. It's also sometimes difficult for the supervisor to give clear and specific feedback without giving away the identity of the original source of the feedback.

In an attempt to deal with these issues, JJABT provides raters with the option of being open or anonymous in their feedback. If the rater requests anonymity, then the supervisor must not compromise his or her identity. However, if the rater is willing to be open, then the supervisor may refer the ratee with questions about his or her feedback to the rater.

In keeping with the self-directed team concept, all ratees at Digital have knowledge of the various raters' comments and ratings. To help make this system work, Digital has instituted a rule that no rater can give negative feedback in the appraisal unless the rater has previously given the feedback directly to the ratee. If a ratee challenges the appraisal feedback, then he or she must face the entire team about the issue. Both Hamilton Standard and Digital stress that it takes time to develop open and effective 360-degree appraisals and suggest that most organizations should start with confidentiality until sufficient understanding, maturity and trust is achieved.

Employers must build a bridge over 360-degree appraisals' potential pitfalls
Although 360-degree appraisals can be extremely effective, fair and useful at their best, like any form of performance review, they have their own potential weaknesses and disadvantages. For one thing, receiving a performance feedback from a multitude of sources, including one's peers, can be intimidating. Hamilton Standard's Jerman agrees that 360-degree appraisals don't eliminate the sting of criticism: "Feedback is still hard to take. It's not always fun."

While employees may have trouble receiving feedback, providing feedback is often troublesome for some. Says Sandy Bermester, staffing and training manager for financial services at Palo Alto-based Hewlett Packard: "It's hard for people to give constructive feedback when they have to. People have to have the right mindset and skills to do it well. It takes time to internalize." For these reasons, it's important that the company create a non-threatening atmosphere by emphasizing that the major purpose of 360-degree appraisals is to facilitate the employee's development and performance improvement.

Also, companies that use 360-degree appraisals may find that their biggest disadvantage is the time involved to select raters, fill out forms, and analyze the various information. It's imperative that organizations strike a balance: appraisals must be intricate enough to be meaningful, but simple enough to be completed easily. The time commitment involved is also one reason why many companies conduct formal appraisals only once a year, although semi-annual appraisals may be given to low-performing employees. Hamilton Standard does do informal 360-degree appraisals at mid-year to allow employees to hear feedback and make any necessary adjustments in their work or alter their goals.

There's also the problem of different expectations by the raters. Lynda Powell, regional director of sales at JJABT, says, "Raters tend to have different expectations. Some rate very low while others are lenient and rate very high. For example, one rater wrote in the appraisal that the employee was a very good planner, but then gave that employee only a 3 on a 5-point scale on planning."

Finally, 360-degree appraisals, although potentially more accurate, are still only a means to an end. There will never be a cut-and-dried, objective, final judgment. Another senior-level manager at JJABT has several concerns about feedback: "One, does the employee know enough about the person to rate them? The people doing the ratings do not always understand the situation the employee is in. Two, the inputs of all raters are often treated equally regardless of that raters' position or level of knowledge about the person. The feedback is often summarized overall and is not broken down into different areas to facilitate follow up."

Because of these disadvantages and potential employee concerns, it's essential that organizations develop an effective plan and change process to implement 360-degree appraisals.

First, top management needs to buy in to and clearly communicate the goals of the 360-degree appraisal and how it relates to the company's business strategy and competitiveness. Top management should also appoint a committee of representative managers and employees to develop the appraisal forms and process.

Second, perhaps the single most important key is to provide training to employees on:

- the specific details of the new appraisal process and instrument
- how to give constructive feedback in a productive, noncritical manner. For example, employees at Ford received raining on how to evaluate specific critical incidents and to give feedback before they took part in 360-degree performance appraisals.

Learning to receive feedback is just as important as giving feedback. "What we particularly don't do enough training on is receiving constructive feedback and having to deal with it," says Hamilton Standard's Jerman. "If we don't take it well, people stop giving it. It's a talent that you develop."

The appraisal should first be pilot tested with a select group of employees before it is instituted elsewhere in the organization. Once instituted, it's essential that top management reinforce the goals and responsibilities of employees related to this new appraisal process on an ongoing basis. Tying the appraisal results to the company's reward and recognition systems can also provide added motivation for employees.

An organization must develop an effective change process and orient the appraisal to its particular needs and culture. It takes time and much effort, but when implemented properly, a 360-degree performance appraisal system can enable companies to obtain better performance information and increase employee development and accountability.

Personnel Journal, November 1994
Article by John F Milliman, Robert A Zawacki, Brian Schulz,
Sally Wiggins and Carol A Norman. Copyright November 1994.
Used with permission of ACC Communications Inc./
Personnel Journal (now known as *Workforce*),
Costa Mesa, CA, USA. All rights reserved.

Resource 8

In the classroom, pride and passion mean more than performance pay

Is it often the case that educated people enter a profession assuming they will be incompetent? Not really. Professionals usually imagine they will be good at their job – including the ones who turn out to be terrible. Do many medical students think to themselves, I intend to be a truly lamentable doctor? Probably not.

So it is odd that a major part of the government's strategy for attracting better teachers is to keep repeating that it doesn't want bad ones. Tony Blair wants only first class teachers, which is an impeccable attitude, and he also knows that the profession is facing problems recruiting them. His determination to help matters is beyond doubt and above reproach. It's just that his solutions appear at times confused, suggesting a surprising idea of why teaching is in trouble.

This week, he told a gathering of teachers that the days of 'muddling along' were over, and that we have 'got to make it easier to get rid of teachers who simply can't teach.'

As half of all the teachers in England and Wales will have retired in 10-15 years time, his main task is to attract high quality recruits and keep them from quitting for a nice job in sales. Merely announcing that second rate ones are no longer welcome will be unlikely to do the trick. Rather, the profession has to be made more attractive – which the government obviously knows, because it has now found almost £1 billion in extra pay for teachers over two years . Large pay rises are also proposed in Scotland.

This will be a more effective method of raising standards than the ritual scoldings of lazy teachers. But the question is how to distribute that money, and the proposal Blair was promoting in his ministerial roadshow is performance related pay. At present, two thirds of teachers never earn more than £22,023 a year, a fact not unrelated to the recruitment crisis. Under new proposals, teachers could be paid up to £35,000, without having to take on managerial duties; head teachers, together with external assessors, would evaluate their performance, and award bonuses accordingly.

It is a superficially enchanting solution, for why shouldn't good teachers be paid more than bad ones? The difficulty comes when you try to put it into practice. Teachers' unions complain about the divisiveness of competition, but the flaws are more fundamental. The question is not, is performance related pay fair, but would it actually work?

By definition, if bonuses are to be made big enough to act as a radical incentive, only a small number can be awarded. If more than a small minority deserve one, then this is palpably unfair, in which case a lot of people will feel resentful. Alternatively, if it is right that only a small number of teachers deserve a bonus, you have to wonder why we are employing thousands and thousands who aren't even worth more than £20 odd grand. There is the danger that just because, in theory, a teacher 'could' earn £35,000, it will become the 'fault' of 99 per cent of teachers to in fact be earning half of that. But if the majority of teachers are given bonuses, the sums will be too small to function as an incentive, which was supposed to be the whole point. The government is charmed by performance related pay because it promises another opportunity to get business practices into the classroom. The irony is, after a lengthy infatuation, the business world itself is now rather less enthusiastic about the practice, with many companies preferring to build teams, trust and security instead. Research into performance related pay has found that in an average company, the vast majority of employees think they perform better than everyone else.

They cannot be right, but that isn't the point; the fact that they believe it means performance linked bonuses, far from motivating staff, leave most of them feeling insulted and demotivated. The few who get big bonuses are too pleased with themselves to pay attention to any suggestions for improvement. The many who get nothing, but think they deserved something, are too aggrieved to pay attention either. It does work in some businesses. Stockbroker, say, can see exactly how well they are doing - and as money is the only motive for becoming a stockbroker, they will want a purely financial reward. But teachers are not stockbrokers, and their skills can be as subtle and various as their motivations. I asked a group of trainees in Brighton why they had chosen teaching. Their answers might sound idealistic, even sweetly naive, and may be very different after five years in the job, but they are worth reflecting on. All talked about the idea of changing pupils' lives, and the rewards of doing a job they believed in; they talked very little of salaries, but much of school resources. Most had turned down more lucrative alternative careers, and one talked about 'the difference between being a faceless paper pusher and having a role in society. You carry yourself differently. I wanted to be able to say to myself, I like you. I couldn't do that in my old job, and that counts for something. It doesn't mean that money doesn't count, but this pride counts for something.' They also talked about the relentless pressure, criticism and upheaval. 'You get no support,' complained one, 'everyone blames you for everything. And maybe, when there's no paper for the photocopier again, eventually you'll say, sod it.'

If performance related bonuses have to be introduced, they should go to as many teachers as possible, based on a highly elastic set of criteria, evaluated by the widest range of assessors. The elusive subtlety of good teaching should be accommodated at every stage, and if the system attracts quality, it will be a valuable improvement. But the best teachers will be people who who care little for the fantasy of a lottery salary prize, and want to be paid properly and left alone to teach. For the profession to flower, it will need fewer insults, less interference, less pressure, more respect and, above all, greater freedom.

There is a long history of governments hoping teachers will love their job so much they won't mind earning nothing. There is nothing noble about exploiting a vocation. But if this government won't pay them all properly, we should at least ask that it has the sense to cherish their vocation.

Decca Aitkenhead, *The Guardian*, 22 January 1999
Reproduced with permission.

Resource 9

Missed a motivator?

It is an irony that performance management often fails to perform. **Chris Hendry**, **Paola Bradley** and **Stephen Perkins** discuss why, and suggest a new system for avoiding some of the more common snags.

Towards the end of the 1980s, performance management was bound up in the developing ethos of performance-related pay (PRP). The prevailing wisdom was to fix behaviour to targets and to attach financial rewards to these. As a joint survey in 1992 by the Institute of Personnel Management and the Institute of Manpower Studies revealed, PRP was not always introduced for the best of reasons. There was a preoccupation with defining measures that could be attached to individual rewards, and the connection with organisational performance was often tenuous.

Thinking has moved on, and many people now believe that performance management covers a raft of cultural, communications and development issues, which may or may not lend themselves to measurement. It can mean different things to different organisations, or even to different groups within the same enterprise. For sales staff, it might be performance-related pay; for professionals, it might mean a system of development unrelated to incentive pay. Even among those who still see measurement as a priority, many believe it is a holy grail that is difficult to achieve satisfactorily.

There have been many lengthy definitions of performance management. Our definition for the purposes of this article is that it is a systematic approach to improving individual and team performance in order to achieve organisational goals. We believe the approach you take should depend on your organisation: its culture, its relationship with employees and the types of job they do.

But many line managers, if asked what performance management means to them, would still dwell on individual appraisal and on the negative aspects of this process. It is often seen as time-consuming, bureaucratic and top-down. Any reference to organisational performance and goals would be extremely rare.

The Strategic Remuneration Research Centre (SRRC) has been using its privileged relationship with its membership, a consortium of 30 blue-chip companies, to work with a dozen HR practitioners from large organisations who are trying to bring clarity to this topic. The result is a performance management diagnostic designed to help firms in thinking systematically through the issues involved in developing a new approach to performance management, or in changing aspects of existing reward systems that have a bearing on performance.

There are, of course, other performance management systems and a number of books that also present the subject as a systematic process. But our work concentrates on questions about the nature of the organisation and the process of evaluating the system: does it actually improve the performance of your organisation? If not, why not?

First, let's examine in more detail some of the problems. How do we establish a link between individual behaviour and business objectives? We know that PRP is becoming increasingly popular. A survey of 544 firms carried out by the Industrial Society last year found that two-thirds used monetary incentives, and a slightly lower number (57 per cent) operated PRP. Two-thirds of the personnel managers who responded saw monetary incentives as a good way to motivate employees. A similar proportion also rated non-monetary incentives as a good motivator.

But a survey of 519 HR executives in 1995 by the American Management Association and Hewitt Associates revealed that 80 per cent felt their staff had a poor grasp of the connection between business strategy and their compensation, benefits and HR programmes. In other words, employees may be financially motivated, but are they motivated to do the things that contribute to business strategy?

We believe the reason for this lack of alignment results in part from the way in which most performance management systems are devised: top management decides it is a good idea and hands the job to the personnel department, which has not been privy to the original discussion about the board's strategic performance objectives. As the process cascades down the line, people lose sight of its original objectives.

There is also the problem of what performance improvement is achievable. An Incomes Data Services review of performance pay in the public sector in 1995 said: "If you go down the performance pay road, and people take it seriously, you must continue to pay out. But with the emphasis being on performance pay for all, the money is almost bound to be spread very thinly. More profoundly, where is this improved performance going to come from to justify a larger pot? Public-sector organisations do not, in general, have the advantages of dynamic markets and expanding business opportunities."

As one member of our professional group observed: "We operate in a highly prescribed environment. Our organisation doesn't want initiative except in times of crisis. The objective is to increase reliability and regularity. Reward for performance, defined as doing something over and above the job, is for crisis management and customer commendations. It is not about doing the job better, rather about promoting a better employee-customer interface."

Equally, how do you measure performance and grant rewards where a company is fortunate enough to be in a growing market and enjoying windfall profits? Recent research from Pims, a company performance index, noted that what works as an incentive depends on where a company is on the business cycle. There are external business contingencies that should govern the design of any system.

If you are clear about what performance improvement you are aiming at, you still need to question what motivates people. All reward systems embody assumptions about attracting, retaining and motivating people, and are based on an implicit mix of economic theory and social values, including beliefs about equity and what kind of differentials are acceptable. Performance pay is an obvious attempt to restructure these assumptions. But, in many organisations, senior managers' assumptions about what motivates people will differ widely.

Our expert group of HR professionals acknowledged this. One of them said: "If you had a meeting of 12 managers in our company, there would be a complete spectrum of opinions: from the view that a performance target linked to money is the sole motivator, to the view that motivation is purely intrinsic and you should never introduce money."

These assumptions have a powerful impact on reward systems (whether sophisticated or crude). But as Derek Robinson, an Oxford University economist, reminded us at a recent workshop: "It is the fish who decide what is bait, not the fisherman. We need to ask the fish what they would prefer to nibble."

What of motivation theory itself? Most commentators would probably accept that expectancy theory offers the most robust guide to motivation. Management guru Ed Lawler calls this concept the "line of sight", meaning that people can see the results of their efforts and the rewards they produce.

Here, a problem arises with complex projects that may take a long time to work through. These sorts of tasks are often critical to an organisation's success and are likely to be what senior managers (and groups) spend most of their time addressing. As the link between the task and its outcome becomes more remote, and as it becomes more difficult to predict success, what happens to motivation, especially when performance evaluation systems have a habit of replacing long-term objectives with short-term goals that are easier to measure?

Our group of HR professionals were concerned about this problem. "Does a bonus function as an incentive or as a historic reward for what has been achieved?" asked Mike Redhouse, director of employment policy at Guinness. "Or is it purely symbolic of status?"

If we conclude that the incentive effect is negligible, it may lead us to take a much broader, non-monetary view of motivation. We may also find that many so-called incentives are actually less powerful than a retrospective reward.

If, after all this, you still think you can introduce appropriate incentives, you must identify suitable objectives for relevant individuals and groups. Fully fledged performance management systems view the organisation as a chain of operational goals and external measures on which it is ultimately judged.

The value of such a system is twofold. First, it can highlight the range of goals that have to be achieved. Second, it highlights the contribution that people at all levels can make to both internal and external effectiveness – for instance, to the external measure of customer satisfaction.

A system of objectives and measures, however neat, has a number of inherent problems. It needs to be constructed within a framework of goals and values. Without this, there is a great risk that the different HR processes contributing to overall performance in the short and long term will be misaligned.

"Most organisations have appraisal systems, incentive programmes – in some cases, management-by-objectives processes – and personal development programmes," says Phil Wills, group director of international compensation at GrandMet. But the question remains unanswered as to how, and even whether, these processes should knit together. Does the application of all these disparate processes add up to more than the sum of the parts?

"The big word is alignment," he says. "Organisations don't seem to understand whether their HR processes are aligned, or whether they are pulling in different directions. In practice, each process operates in a vacuum, with different functions and different parts of the same function supporting the operation of individual HR processes. People don't talk, so there's no management process actively co-ordinating and focusing each of the elements on overall performance enhancement."

Alongside this is the problem of the line manager. The line manager is invariably seen as the weak link in the systems we have designed. Goals may be defined at the organisational and individual level but, in practice, the system gets subverted by individual managers or appraisees focusing too much on what matters to them.

If line managers are key to making a performance management system work, how can the system respond to their needs and make their task easier? Too often, it is more about exercising control, when performance management is meant to be about development and improvement. While the line manager may be an important part of the chain, the most crucial link is the workforce as a whole. Rewards are one of the main ways in which organisations structure their relationship with employees, and PRP is an overt attempt to realign this association.

Performance management is not, then, just a narrow question of motivation; it has an effect on an organisation's culture and subcultures. This means that anyone designing and implementing a system must talk through their assumptions and values, plus those of the people it targets. This is the only way to persuade employees to buy into it.

Developing and operating a performance management process is, therefore, fraught with pitfalls. We devised our performance management diagnostic, comprising a series of questions under seven main headings, to help HR managers and their colleagues through the minefield.

The headings follow a logical order. In most organisations, the questions (if they are addressed at all) are answered by different people and are not approached systematically. The personnel manager is responsible for the middle of the process – designing the reward structure and aligning the HR systems – while reasons, objectives and questions about the context are addressed by other parties, often inadequately. The following exchange reflects the way things are in many organisations.

Q: Who owns performance management?
A: It's a 75 per cent: 25 per cent split. Business planning drives quantitative measures; HR drives the competency profiles.
Q: What about the role of the line, and how far have they bought in?
A: They have no choice. Their role is to negotiate around the hard targets and achieve acceptability.

Far from being in the spotlight, the techniques of reward system design should become the focus only at an advanced stage in the process. Too often, this becomes the end in itself. Subsequent monitoring of the performance management process and assessing outcomes is invariably neglected, too.

The diagnostic is designed to get managers to think through the development of performance management systematically: first, to check that they are asking the relevant questions, and second, to consider their answers. But we also think of this as a ripple effect. Answers to one question will affect responses to other questions and the process of thinking issues through should be iterative.

It is clear that performance management gives HR professionals an unrivalled opportunity to lead a debate, currently fragmented, that is at the heart of business. According to Phil Wills, this debate is being conducted in a superficial way, and its significance to the HR role is not fully appreciated. "If you asked a cross-section of senior business-unit leaders what they understood performance management to be, it would result in extremely shallow comment," he says. "Performance management is not a term they are exposed to, or one that they think about. It is not a designated

HR process – there is no piece of paper that says "do performance management" – so there is no spur to action.

"We also lack a common understanding of what we mean by an integrated approach to performance management. It is unclear as to whether anyone has achieved this. For example, do companies see performance management as part of strategic planning and strategy implementation?

"The three parties involved in these processes – HR, finance and strategic planning – do not collaborate at all in the development of their various processes. There is a need to bring these into sync. One of the things HR professionals can do is to become part and parcel of the strategic planning process at the earliest stage, highlighting the issues that the incentive plan might stimulate, derived from the strategic planning process itself."

Mike Redhouse sees the introduction of a management bonus scheme as a valuable catalyst for a strategic debate. This, he says, gives HR professionals the chance to get to the heart of the business.

"A special role for HR is to be able to turn to the guardians of commercial information – in particular, the finance people – and say: 'Tell us what to measure, because we can't introduce an incentive scheme without this.' The debate can then centre around, for example, whether economic value-added or revenue growth is as good as growing contribution."

Martin Days, of BT's group personnel department, takes a similar attitude. "We must encourage the organisation to look at performance in the round, rather than through partial messages," he says. "A fundamental problem is the existence of personnel as a separate discipline. Businesses are organised so as to prompt interventions in the management process by a 'money bunch' of professionals, a 'people bunch', and so on. The truth is, performance is indivisible.

The strategic debate about performance management can therefore offer opportunities and threats to the HR function. "In the past, we have put in so-called incentive and recognition plans, and they have not fulfilled the expectations because we have failed to engage at the heart of the business debate," Redhouse says. "Unless we get smarter at challenging, at providing coherent counsel and at prompting intelligent responses to the question of measuring short-, medium- and long-term objectives, the organisation may question whether it needs HR at all."

The SRRC performance management diagnostic

1 **Reasons**

What has triggered a reappraisal of the performance management system or rewards at this time?

2 **Objectives**

What are our strategic business goals?

Who or what delivers critical performance with respect to the business goals?

What kind of performance contract do we want with employees?

What is the performance system designed to do (e.g., attract, retain, motivate, control)?

3 **Environment**
External contingencies
What stage of the business cycle are we in?
What are the effects of the national/societal culture we operate in on attitudes to performance and differentials?
Internal contingencies
What are the motivational assumptions of the relevant group(s) or employees?
What are the relevant internal employee reference groups and how do they affect attitudes to differentials?

4 **Systems**
What is the range of things we have to do to support the performance/business goals that affect employees' knowledge, capability and motivation?

5 **Design**
Content
How do we define rewards?
How do we define incentives?
What measures are appropriate (e.g., in terms of the short, medium and long term, financial versus non-financial measures, individual versus group)?
Can we measure performance in the ways we want to, and design rewards appropriately?
Can people see this connection?
Process
Are there links or disconnections through the whole reward structure?
Do other managers involved in the design and management of the performance system buy into it?
Is the process manageable?
How do we communicate about performance and rewards, including feedback?

6 **Outcomes**
What is the impact on behaviour (e.g., does the system reinforce the old or motivate new behaviours)?
Retrospectively, what is the pay-off or success criteria?
Is it possible to define or develop return on investment criteria, taking into account the costs of designing and administering the scheme, and of paying for rewards?

7 **Monitoring**
What review process is in place or needs to be created?

People Management, 15 May 1997
Reproduced with permission.

Resource 10

The low down: work and family

Not all changes in employment law take place in the glare of publicity. Comparatively few sex discrimination cases actually have to be fought out at the tribunal and the silliest capture media imagination. Meanwhile the real progress is in out of court settlements.

Recently Catherine Thomasson was awarded £22,500 compensation for having to resign after 12 years with the Royal & Sun Alliance when the company refused to allow her to return to a job-share after maternity leave. Royal & Sun Alliance have agreed to implement a revised job-share policy within 12 months. Many organisations will have to rethink their attitudes to the parents of small children over the next year, because the UK is committed to comply with European directives on parental leave. Legislation is now on its way through Parliament as part of the Fairness At Work Bill will put paternity leave on a statutory footing.

But employment law tends to be decided on case law rather than statute – cases are resolved on the basis of previous decisions rather than what Parliament thinks we should do. So it is significant that Thomasson is not an isolated case. Last year Melanie Diamond, a lawyer, accepted a settlement of £45,000 of an indirect sex discrimination claim against the Solicitors Indemnity Fund. As the mother of three children under five she had not been allowed to reduce or even vary her hours. Both women brought their cases with the support of the Equal Opportunities Commission and an organisation called New Ways To Work, which campaigns to for the introduction of family-friendly working patterns.

As the law is at present, maternity leave must be taken in one chunk and immediately. The Parental Leave Directive allows it to be taken at any time between the birth of a child and his or her eighth birthday. It also compels employers to make provision for leave for family emergencies.

These two cases show employers should be prepared to accept flexible working practices now.

Bill Saunders, *The Guardian*, 25 January 1999
Reproduced with permission.

Resource 11

Flexibility scheduling comes out of flux

No longer are alternative work arrangements the exclusive domain of mothers. Today, companies such as Bank of Montreal and Price Waterhouse are beginning to accommodate all types of workers with assorted needs. A recent study by Catalyst, "Making Work Flexible: Policy to Practice," provides clues to their success. By **Charlene Marmer Solomon**.

A decade ago, flexible work schedules were about as common as e-mail. In other words, not very. Progressive companies were touted for their broad-minded policies of part-time and flextime work, and some experimented with telecommuting. Driving these management practices was the magnanimous attitude that women with young children needed greater flexibility if they were to stay in the workforce. It was a benevolent philosophy, not necessarily a business-driven one.

How times have changed

Today with increasing numbers of organizations offering flexible work arrangements of some type, flexibility is as widely anticipated as a computer with a functioning modem and e-mail capabilities. Although most people continue to work in traditional ways during traditional hours, the idea of flexibility is as common as the sound of a dial tone whirring through a computer. The most sweeping change? No longer are flexible hours and a flexible workplace the domain of young mothers. All types of workers want these options. And, a variety of companies are offering them because they make good business sense.

Flexibility enhances productivity

However dramatic the changes may seem when compared with 10 years ago, the changes within the last few years are evolutionary, not revolutionary. More and more companies continue to experiment with different types of options, accommodating a greater variety of employees through these options. More and more are discovering that in specific cases, these arrangements help with productivity, decrease turnover and reduce employee stress. There are several companies who have offered flexible work arrangements for so long they've moved the effort from a programmatic solution to a more fundamental endeavor that has affected corporate policy and culture.

To measure and propagate the success of such forward-looking companies, Catalyst the New York City-based workplace think tank unveiled its most recent report in February of this year, "Making Work Flexible: Policy to Practice." The report is based on a study it initiated in the Fall of 1994 in which the group identified 31 corporations and professional firms nationally recognized as having exemplary flexible workplace policies and whose motivation wasn't altruistic but business-driven. From confidential telephone interviews and several roundtable discussions, the organization developed guidelines to help other companies create and manage flexibility (see "Making Work Flexible: A Summary"). Among these companies are the Bank of Montreal, Price Waterhouse LLP, KPMG Peat Marwick,

Deloitte & Touche LLP, NationsBank, Aetna Life & Casualty, Corning, Steelcase Inc. and Pillsbury.

As Marcia Brumit Kropf, vice president of the Research and Advisory Services division for Catalyst points out, until recently, flexibility was viewed as an issue for women phasing back into full-time work after a maternity leave. Now anyone male or female may find work needs affected by obligations outside of work: the care of young children, the needs of school-age children, the care of elderly parents, personal development or community work. And American workers of both genders currently face pressure to work long hours and to put in the face time at the office. From the employer's side, flexibility aids in retaining and recruiting valuable employees. It responds to demographic changes in the workforce, reduces turnover, services people in different time zones, meets cyclical or seasonal business demands, provides continuity on projects and in client service, allows operation of a round-the-clock business, and helps maintain morale and performance after reengineering or downsizing.

"The bottom line is to try to recognize and accommodate the needs of a diverse population," says Michael V. Littlejohn, managing director at New York City-based Price Waterhouse LLP. "Flexibility now carries with it a much larger connotation than some of the traditional definitions such as flextime or part-time. It's trying to recognize flexible work arrangements that are more far-reaching."

As if to underscore Catalyst's findings, New York City-based Hewitt Associates LLC unveiled a recent report, "Work and Family Benefits Provided by Major U.S. Employers in 1994," which shows that 66% of the 1,035 organizations surveyed offered flexible scheduling (up 6% from the year before). Of those, 71% offered flextime, 65% offered part-time, 34% offered job sharing, 21% offered compressed work schedules, 14% offered summer hours and 5% provide other options. Flexible arrangements include two types of options: full-time and reduced-time. Full-time options include flextime (workday begins/ends when employee and manager decide), flexible week (fewer but longer days, shorter days in six-day weeks), or flex place (branch offices, telecommuting). Reduced time options include part-time or job sharing.

But creating company policy is one thing; implementing workable practices can be quite another. Consequently, a key component of the Catalyst report is to highlight organizations that put these principles to work.

Provide a variety of flex options.
Toronto-based Bank of Montreal brings together Catalyst's four goals: It builds organizational support for flexibility; it supports managers and users of the practice; it internalizes (or incorporates) the practice, and it sustains the momentum.

The Bank of Montreal has long been a proponent of advancing women throughout its ranks. One example of this is the 1991 Task Force on the Advancement of Women, which was a year-long project sponsored by the bank's president and chief operating officer, Tony Comper. The task force undertook the largest survey of the bank's employees ever. Not only did it uncover myths about women and why they weren't progressing through the organization, but it also provided the basis for developing action plans. The entire flexible work arrangement initiative was an outgrowth of its findings.

"It created an understanding that one of the key things we need to do is to formally support employees men and women who are balancing their multiple commitments to work and family, education and community," says Diane Ashton, vice president of employee programs and the office of work place equality. "The connection to the business case is apparent when we look at demographics and understand our workforce and become concerned we don't have enough women making their way through to our senior jobs (policy-, program-, and product-development type of jobs). We realized we were neglecting the talents of half the working population."

As a result, the company developed a policy called Balancing Multiple Commitments that incorporates flexibility in many ways: through flextime, flexible workweek, part-time on a permanent basis, job sharing and flex place. Flex place allows employees to work two or three days a week in another bank branch that's either closer to home or in a more convenient location. The bank provides this flex space by setting up several workstations at different locations, each with phones, PCs, and other necessities that allow people to work outside of their normal workplace. This also is convenient when someone has appointments with clients that aren't conveniently located to their usual place of work.

The policies are working. At least, they're having the desired effect with regard to encouraging women in their upward movement. For example, the number of female executive officers grew significantly: In 1990, the number increased 6%; in 1991, 9%; and in 1995, 19%.

Furthermore, of the 2,125 positions in the Senior Management Group in October 1991, only 13% were women; exactly four years later the figure had risen to 20.4%.

Ashton herself benefited from the policy when she created an arrangement whereby she worked full time but was paid only for 90% of it. It gave her one half-day a week she saved up. "I used that time to be able to spend more time with my children because they get a lot more time off than our standard four weeks of vacation," she says. "It just enabled me to carry on when there was an emergency. When somebody got chickenpox, I didn't feel like I had to scramble for arrangements." This safety valve relieved the burden.

Build organizational support.
The bank combines all of the important factors cited in the Catalyst report. One of the most important features of Bank of Montreal's flexibility approach is that the policy's spirit is incorporated into the strategic development plan and the business plan. Executive-level managers and all other managers create objectives for hiring, promoting and retaining people and decide how flexibility will fit into those target plans. These create a baseline. Performance appraisals also include attention to flexibility, with each manager remaining accountable for meeting individual goals.

In other words, both employees and managers are responsible for translating these work arrangements into viable options. For example, employees initiate a proposal that explains why the flex arrangement would make their lives easier and present it to local management. The onus of responsibility, though, lies with the manager to be flexible and open-minded. As a protection for both of them, they define a trial period after which time, they sit down and evaluate it.

This shared responsibility and trial period allows employees to generate extraordinary creativity because they can try out different options. For example, a compressed workweek of three days may sound liberating. The bank's operating hours allow this type of work option since many of the branches are open six days a week from 8 a.m. to 8 p.m., allowing employees the option of a Monday, Tuesday, Wednesday shift or a Thursday, Friday, Saturday shift. However, although many employees say they would appreciate it, and believe they've discovered the perfect solution, others may find it an exhausting schedule after trying it for a month.

Since the solutions are employee-generated, employees write a letter to their manager and, once approved, they send a copy to the office of Work Place Equality. This not only establishes the Work Place Equality department as a resource center, it also allows the center to track and understand what people are doing. "The spirit of this policy is that it's employee- initiated," says Ashton. "They come up with the proposal, and it's worked out at a local level between the employee and the manager. This has been one of the strengths of the policy."

Support managers and employees.
One way in which the Bank of Montreal propagated its views was through a 100-page book, "Flexing Your Options." It describes the philosophy, policies and procedures of the bank's commitment to flexible work, including a detailed checklist for a basic employee-initiated proposal. It also includes items such as commonly asked questions by managers, sample manager replies and phone numbers for obtaining further information.

To set the tone, before introducing the five flexible options (flextime, flexible workweek, permanent part-time, job sharing, flex place), the first paragraph of the document states, "While such arrangements aren't for everyone, there is compelling evidence that increased self-management translates into increased productivity. The bank is committed to flex arrangements because they make good business sense. The corporate policy, Balancing Multiple Commitments, outlines the direct relationship between helping employees balance their commitments to work, family, education and community, and improved employee morale, increased productivity and superior customer service."

Internalize the practice; sustain the commitment.
The bank also reinforced its philosophy by accepting these flexible arrangements and by assessing employees' experiences. It believes this practice is important so the arrangements can be tracked for their impact and benefit to the organization. This is one reason the office of Work Place Equality requests a copy of the approved work-arrangement proposal.

Clearly, the bank sustains the commitment by including goals and expectations regarding flexibility in its performance reviews. In fact, employees even rate their managers on this dimension. Each manager's scores (by his or her subordinates) are averaged, and the employees give their boss feedback about the scores.

This integral respect for the concept of flexibility permeates the organization. Therefore, programs are used by individuals in many different situations. For instance, the original intent was to help women advance by relieving some of the family burden (child care time pressures), but others are using it as well: single fathers, for example, or one man who works 40 hours in four days to enable him to spend one day a week leading Boy Scout activities. And, these kinds of arrangements are being used throughout the organization, not just with junior people. Flexibility is permeating the culture. "I know we have senior managers who are either working on a part-time arrangement, compressed workweek or flex place. These aren't people who have been sidelined. They're individuals with important jobs, which is key. We've been able to make flexibility part of the culture. It isn't just seen as something for our most junior people," says Ashton.

Make flexibility a bottom-line issue.
Accounting firm Price Waterhouse LLP (PW) also is lauded in the Catalyst study as a company that integrates flexibility companywide. Indeed, PW is redefining its organization because of an increasingly diverse workforce. Fundamental to that is embracing flexibility. Littlejohn, who heads the Office of Diversity Programs as well as national recruitment, says the effort is twofold: both philosophical and concrete. "The effort recognizes and accommodates the needs of a diverse population (a broader definition than women and minorities, it includes single parents, people who have issues with elder care, child care, and others who want more balance between their personal and work lives).

"Flexibility in the firm goes beyond the concrete part-time and flex-work arrangements. It also involves a philosophical perspective." According to Littlejohn, "We're trying to change the mindset of the firm.

"Traditionally, of course, the mindset was that you give 110% to the firm, and if that means a 60- or 70-hour week, so be it. I've seen a distinctive shift over the past couple of years, recognizing the fact we can no longer expect that of our people."

As in the case of the Bank of Montreal, demographics are fueling the changes. "We have to recognize that as the demographics of society change, so do the firms. For us not only to be productive, but also to be competitive, we have to meet head-on the reality that people have different needs."

Although part-time work options may not seem like such a spectacular innovation at first glance, they're indeed challenging for intensely client-focused firms for which on-the-spot service and attention are synonymous with revenue. Consequently, for PW to adapt its philosophy toward traditional ways of working, it had to reconsider the entire notion of work styles and how to service customers effectively while being responsive to employees. In fact, there were two forces at play simultaneously. One was the needs of the employees. The other was the changing needs of the clients, who have become quite diverse in their profiles. The firm also believes that its clients want professionals who reflect their population and, thereby, their concerns.

Technology can support managers and users.
One of the tools in PW's network is the company's sophisticated technological infrastructure that allows partners and associates to establish virtual offices. With Lotus Notes and voicemail, laptop computers become phones, meeting planners and fax machines, allowing employees to support their clients not only in the client's location, but from anywhere. Technology also has diminished the need for individuals to come into Price Waterhouse offices to transfer information. For example, they previously had to be in the office to have access to files, perform research and provide colleagues with information. No more. Now, most of that can be done remotely via technology.

Given these changes, which facilitate responsiveness to both clients and employees, the company is attempting to extend flexibility in formal and informal ways. PW believes flexible work policies are a powerful tool for attracting and retaining people a competitive necessity. "Big Six professional services firms face a big challenge because people look at them as a mill a sweat shop where people work 60- and 80- hour weeks for three or four or five years and we throw them away if we don't make them a partner," says Littlejohn. "We had to create the mindset that we're becoming a kinder place to work; that we'll try our best to accommodate employees' needs."

And, fundamental to that, the firm is changing some of its values and implementing a new career model. Historically, individuals joined the company shortly after college and worked for eight to 10 years. If they made partner, great. If not, they left the company. It was a rigid career path that allowed no leeway for other options. According to Littlejohn, several problems prompted PW to change the situation. Number one, the firm was losing very good people because they hadn't made partner within the allotted time; number two, employees were saying that partnership wasn't for everyone and alternatives to the partner track would be valued; and number three, clients were expressing the need to have professional service providers who were not only good consultants but also had a depth of knowledge in their specialty. Consequently, the idea of success broadened to include deep technical specialists as well as individuals who wanted a career on the macro level (wanted partnership). Expected time frames also were changed dramatically. Now, there are several career tracks based on the achievement of milestones rather than on the length of time to complete those milestones. Compensation is based accordingly.

Enter the notion of part-time and flextime arrangements. With these essential changes in the structure of the firm, the flex alternatives become viable. No small thing. This is a fundamental shift in the way Price Waterhouse approaches business and thinks about its employees. It relates to changing the culture of PW.

"Because relationships are such a key in a professional services environment, and our clients are paying us a fee, they have certain expectations," says Littlejohn. We can't just say unequivocally we're going to implement something irrespective of our clients' wishes. It requires us to not only sell our employees on this, but we also have to sell our clients. We have to sell our clients on the fact it's good business for them to have someone onsite four days a week versus five days. It's really in the client's best interest to work for a balance so our people are happy and they're happy."

Communication serves managers and employees.
One of the most helpful ways PW communicates its policies is through its newsletters and other organization-wide communication vehicles. It uses these methods to show how flexibility can work and achieve business results as well as satisfy individual needs. Via its communication channels, it relates information such as the fact more than 400 people are working flexibly, including 90 managers and two partners. It also encourages the use of these flexible work possibilities by stating the names of people employees can speak with if they're interested in discussing flexibility.

Price Waterhouse's essential commitment to flexibility comes through as a business imperative. Indeed, the firm appointed its first woman to the top management team whose responsibilities include building the organization's workforce for the next century. Her highly visible task is to develop and evaluate the new career-development paths and service-delivery approaches that will shape PW's future workplace.

Flexible work arrangements are a business imperative.
More and more frequently, as evidenced by Price Waterhouse and the Bank of Montreal, organizations achieve several business advantages when they adopt flex work practices. Paralleling society's changing demographics and expectations about leading a more balanced life, companies find that allowing employees to direct some of their work where, when and how they get the job done not only yields benefits in productivity and retention, but in customer responsiveness as well. By applying technology and many of the changes that already have occurred in the current workplace, they find satisfied, productive, efficient employees translate into revenue.

Personnel Journal, June 1996
Article by Charlene Marmer Solomon. Copyright June 1996.
Used with permission of ACC Communications Inc./
Personnel Journal (now known as *Workforce*),
Costa Mesa, CA, USA. All rights reserved.

Resource 12

Looking for a colour blind employer?

It is a truism admitted among graduate recruiters that they make their minds up about you within 20 seconds of you walking through the interview room door. Scary, huh? Just think – your hairstyle, your eye-contact and the warmth of your handshake can all count for more than your degree.

Add to that your Birmingham accent, your 'female-ness', the fact you're only 21 and you're wearing a nose ring. Handshake getting cooler? Now factor in a wheelchair or the fact that you're black. I'm sorry, but your 20 seconds are up.

Ask any medium or large employer in the UK what their reaction would be and they will tell you that none of these things would make any difference to their decision. They would tell you that in fact to do so would be illegal. Yet the figures seem to tell a different tale.

Equally-qualified black workers earn less and occupy lower positions in firms. They are twice as likely to be out of work than their white counterparts. Women still earn 75p for every £1 earned by men at similar levels, and only 5 per cent of boardroom directors are women.

One in thirty of those with disabilities cannot find work. Job hunters at both ends of the age spectrum are routinely discriminated against in job advertisements and in redundancy rounds. Last month, an Irish call centre worker alleged his call centre employer sacked him for having a 'grating' accent.

How can this still be happening when race, sex and equal pay legislation have been in force for 20 years, and UK disability and ageism legislation has just recently been brought into effect? How can firms proudly state they are equal opportunities employers at the bottom of their job ads, having stood in the employment tribunal dock? Thousands of column inches have been filled on the ramifications of the death of Stephen Lawrence. Campaigners for equality hope the teenager's death will continue to create waves in all areas of life – including employment.

But the question of institutionalised racism is not just one for the police. The British Medical Association and several local authorities as well as some police forces have admitted deeply embedded prejudices to minorities.

According to employers' organisations, companies are doing everything they should be to ensure they treat workers fairly. Nearly three quarters have an equality policy and many monitor recruitment by category. Yet often it is not the intake of women, black or Asian people or other 'minorities' which is weak, but their subsequent rise though the ranks – a more subtle form of discrimination to tackle, according to the Equal Opportunities Commission.

'I always believed that my talent would make everything else irrelevant,' Michael Abutje, a Kenyan Oxbridge graduate, says of his career in the chemicals industry. 'And I thought that if I ignored my suspicions about certain managers, the problems would go away. But I've had to admit to myself I have been blocked from making certain moves – some people just weren't comfortable working with me.' The women who trade in the cut-throat environment of the City also revealed in a survey this month that despite the shoulderpads and the long hours, they are still battered by institutionalised sexism. With promotion prospects bleak, offensive banter rife and pregnancy viewed as career suicide, they argue that from where they stand, the glass ceiling feels more like reinforced concrete.

Paul Gama, the equal opportunities manager of HSBC bank, admits that it takes decades to check the progress of equal opportunities. Gama says that 13 per cent of the bank's graduate intake in 1998 was from ethnic minorities, yet in the early nineties only 1 per cent of Midland's managers were Asian or black. This figure has now risen to just over 3 per cent.

So, in the wake of the Stephen Lawrence inquiry, what are companies doing to respond to the groundswell of feeling against discrimination? A significant number of firms surveyed in the latest issue of People Management magazine say they are 'reconsidering' their own policies in the light of the Lawrence report.

One employer painfully aware of its own poor track record of preferring male, pale and stale civil servants, is Whitehall's Civil Service, which is running radio ads, a billboard campaign and a careers fair in July to target black applicants. 'There's not much recruiting of minorities actually going on now,' admits Limbert Spencer, equal opportunities champion at the Foreign and Commonwealth Office. 'But our priorities are in place.' He, like most other UK employers, rejects the argument for 'positive discrimination' – actively recruiting and promoting those currently under-represented in working life. Yet, he admits it will be a slow battle to change attitudes.

Abutje agrees: 'I hope the Stephen Lawrence report sinks in, somewhere, to change the unwitting discrimination I know goes on. Until then, I have to continue believing my best is good enough.'

Jilly Welch, *The Guardian*, 20 March 1999
Reproduced with permission.

Resource 13

Phone workers' brain strain

Women at telephone call centres suffer 'burnout' after six months and leave their jobs after a year with 'repetitive brain strain', according to research for the European Commission presented yesterday to the Geographers' conference at Leicester university.

Continuously receiving telephone calls through a headset on an automatic system saps women's motivation and eventually forces them to quit, said researcher Vicki Belt of Newcastle university.

The women employed to 'smile down the phone' for telephone banking, booking holidays or selling bathrooms and double glazing often work in huge computerised centres, with up to 2,000 in one room.

"It would be wrong to call them sweat shops because that implies dirty, cramped conditions," said Ms Belt. "These are often comfy and luxurious, but that does not make them good places to work." Britain has the biggest tele-sales force of any country in Europe, with 3,560 call centres employing 163,000 workers, mostly women aged between 20 and 30. Many enjoyed the job, particularly at first, Ms Belt said. Employers often paid for staff nights out every three months. But the work was repetitive, continuous and intense. "After a few months women talked about the need to get off the phone. They call it burn-out - a sort of repetitive strain injury of the brain."

Turnover of staff was enormous. Most left after a year. Some had a few months off before taking a job with another call centre until burn-out occurred again. There were few opportunities for promotion, because the number of supervisors was small.

Many of the jobs are in the north. Barclays and British Airways have call centres in Newcastle and Sunderland. Leeds is known as 'call centre city' and is the home of First Direct bank. These venues are favoured because the women have 'appealing' northern accents.

The researchers, from Newcastle university and the Tavistock Institute, also looked at centres in Ireland and the Netherlands. Ten years ago there were no call centres in Europe, and the EC wanted to explore this new employment area.

Pay is around £10,000 a year basic outside London, and between £14,000 and £19,000 for more skilled IT workers or those with language skills. The number of such jobs is expected to rise for at least another five years.

Paul Brown, *The Guardian*, 6 January 1999
Reproduced with permission.

Resource 14

Unattractive contracts

Lecturers could be forced to accept new pay deals as universities come under pressure from paying students, says **John Carvel.**

Brian Roper, vice-chancellor of North London University, has sparked an industrial relations crisis by pushing through changes in his lecturers' contracts to introduce performance-related pay and flexible working arrangements that echo David Blunkett's plans for schoolteachers.

His approach was condemned as 'stone age management' by Natfhe, the university and college lecturers' union which has called an academic boycott to stop staff at other institutions having further contact with North London. Exam boards will be disrupted this week if external examiners withdraw their services. The university's trades union studies centre could be an early casualty. The dispute has national significance because it could be a foretaste of turmoil ahead as other universities move towards a more customer-oriented business philosophy to satisfy the increasingly demanding requirements of fee-paying students.

Roper is the last vice-chancellor anyone would expect to be in a fight with the unions. He shared platforms with them in the campaign against tuition fees and made no secret of his view that academic salaries are woefully inadequate.

He says his current actions stem from the slogan: 'Modernise or die'. Universities can no longer provide the services they think the students need. They must deliver what the students want at the time and place they want it. 'What's pivotal now is the university's contract with the student. We are moving into a time of demand-side higher education, whereas all the history has been about the supply side.' Roper says there is no hope that national pay agreements can deliver sufficient rewards for lecturers. Over the 10 years of the current negotiating arrangements, academic staff have improved productivity by 50 per cent, but their salaries have not even kept up with inflation.

At North London, between a third and half of staff have reached a point in the pay scale where there are no further increments. That tight system is unlikely to change because the university employers will not want to pay more than their poorest members can afford.

'We want to create a high-wage, high-productivity economy in this university. We want the best and we are prepared to pay high salaries to recruit and retain them. And we are going to invest in their development,' says Roper.

The problem came when he tried to impose a particular version of this approach without Natfhe's agreement. Roper says he lost patience after three and a half years of local negotiations.

From the start of this year he has been hiring staff on new performance-linked contracts that can boost their salaries by up to 10 per cent above the nationally-agreed rate. But their annual holiday drops from seven weeks to six, and their entitlement to an additional six weeks of self-managed scholarly activity will be a lot more strictly monitored. The dispute with Natfhe grew serious when he gave notice just before Christmas that he aimed to introduce the contract for existing staff.

Tom Wilson, head of the union's university department, said Roper was trying to tear up a national agreement and replace it with a local contract that: threatened academic autonomy; required lecturers to be available for work at weekends with no compensation; cut sick leave and sick pay by two thirds; and prohibited industrial action.

'Why seek a no strike clause?' he asked. 'Why attack the very group of staff who have done most to deliver lifelong learning to UNL students? Natfhe members will not accept the dumbing down of their jobs.' Natfhe's view is that North London should have followed other universities such as Brighton, East London, Kingston and Greenwich, which agreed local deals within the national framework to gain the flexible working arrangements they wanted. The dispute's outcome could affect industrial relations across the sector.

'There is massive pent-up demand for this, 'says Roper. 'When it becomes more public, other institutions preparing strategies will go public with them.'

The Guardian, 2 February 1999
Reproduced with permission.

Resource 15

Share strength

Much of the debate in knowledge management so far has centred around technology, yet organisations are finding that the real issue is how to encourage employees to participate. **Geraint John** looks at what some companies are doing to develop a culture of knowledge sharing.

Given the hype surrounding it, there can surely be few managers who have not encountered the term knowledge management – even if, like many, they aren't quite sure what it means. In the past year, the number of books, reports, conferences and web sites devoted to the subject has spiralled, leaving little doubt that this is the biggest thing to hit the world of management since business process re-engineering.

As with previous "big ideas", the IT industry and large management consultancies have not been slow to spot the possibilities for earning a buck or two. Despite the relative infancy of knowledge-sharing initiatives, they already offer all manner of "solutions" to companies that feel they should hop on the bangwagon before their competitors steal a lead. While IT firms push groupware, databases, intranets and "intelligent" search agents, the consultants promise to help turn elusive intellectual assets into tangible business results.

The consultancies cannot lose. As knowledge-based businesses, they were among the first to use new technology to manage information. Now, having made progress internally, they are in a position to sell their expertise to grateful clients. For example, Coopers & Lybrand's UK management consulting arm, which began developing its in-house information and knowledge exchange (Ike) three years ago, launched its knowledge management practice in June, just prior to its merger with Price Waterhouse. Its promotional literature boasts that Ike is saving the firm an estimated £3 million a year simply by reducing the amount of time consultants spend looking for information.

Perhaps not surprisingly, given the legacy of disappointment associated with many re-engineering projects, consultancies are quick to discount the view that knowledge management is merely the latest fad. A recent survey by KPMG Management Consulting led with the finding that only two of the 100 large UK companies polled agreed with this view – in contrast with research last year by Cranfield School of Management in which almost a third did.

Even so, there are signs that disillusionment is creeping in, as stories circulate of expensive technology lying idle and some of the early enthusiasts for knowledge management admit that many of their attempts to capture and share expertise have failed. This feeling that all is not rosy is reflected in the current issue of *Information Strategy* magazine. Under the cover line "the knowledge backlash", it carried a clutch of articles that are highly critical of consultants, IT people and academics for making knowledge management sound more complicated than it really is and for failing to focus sufficiently on practical business issues. "A backlash could be the best thing to happen to the knowledge movement so far," it concludes.

But away from the hard sell and, at times, esoteric arguments about what knowledge actually consists of, many companies are quietly trying to benefit from improved organisational learning. While it may be too soon to point to clear examples of best practice, some early lessons are beginning to filter through. It should come as no surprise to HR professionals that chief among these is the realisation that too much faith has been invested in technology at the expense of people issues.

As Elizabeth Lank, who heads up ICL's knowledge management programme, says: "The organisations that are best at knowledge sharing are not necessarily those with the best technology infrastructure. But they do have a culture of teamwork and trust. If you have that culture, and put in tools to help knowledge flow quickly around the organisation, you have a hugely powerful combination. But if you put all of your investment into the technology and ignore the culture, you've wasted your money."

Data basic
Despite all the talk about capturing "tacit" knowledge (expertise stored in people's heads), much activity thus far has focused on improving access to basic information, such as internal telephone numbers, product and customer details, and "explicit" knowledge – presentations, proposals, memos and so on. Technologies such as Lotus Notes and intranets have undoubtedly made collecting, presenting and sharing this kind of material much easier. But, as many companies have found to their cost, simply implementing the IT does not guarantee that staff will use the information stored, let alone take time out to contribute to it themselves.

In any case, good information management, though essential in improving efficiency and reducing day-to-day frustration, is unlikely in the long run to give companies any significant competitive advantage. What really matters is getting employees to share their insights and experience so that projects can be completed faster and more cost-effectively – in other words, avoiding having constantly to reinvent the wheel.

This is not only a more challenging proposition, but one in which technology seems to have less to offer. But some companies appear to have been seduced by the idea, peddled by certain software vendors, that what they need to do is go round extracting useful knowledge from employees and then store it all in a vast database. Even assuming this were possible, it is unlikely to be very productive.

"If you go and ask people what they know, they will never give you a complete picture," says Dave Snowden, director of the knowledge and differentiation programme at IBM Global Services. "You only know what you know when you need to know it." In any case, he adds, employees would have little incentive to co-operate. "If you bring in a bunch of consultants to try to find out what people know, in the post-re-engineering generation they will think they're about to be downsized."

For organisations, much of the logic behind knowledge management undoubtedly lies in trying to ensure that when valuable employees walk out the door they leave some of that value behind. But increasingly there is a realisation that this somewhat one-sided perspective does little to answer employees' main question: what's in it for me?

Companies with a more sophisticated view of knowledge management are therefore putting a lot of effort into persuading staff that effective knowledge sharing can make their jobs easier and more satisfying, and can enhance their reputation. Rather than trying to capture what they think people might want to know, the emphasis is on finding ways to connect people within "communities of practice" and promoting collaboration between them.

One way of doing this is to build up a "yellow pages" of skills and experience as part of an information management system. Another, often complementary, option is to employ specialist staff to act as knowledge facilitators or brokers – an approach now being pursued at ICL. Either way, the idea is to make it quicker and easier for employees to find someone who might be able to provide help on a particular issue.

If such exchanges are to have more widespread and longer-term value, they still need to be recorded. Yet organisations seem to have enough trouble persuading busy employees to keep their CVs up to date, let alone get them to make a note of lessons learnt. So how can they encourage this kind of behaviour?

Firms such as McKinsey and Andersen Consulting, renowned for their distinctive cultures, seem to have taken a big stick approach, making knowledge sharing part of their work processes and requiring staff to conform. Another trend in the consultancy sector is the development of specific knowledge-sharing competencies for use during recruitment and appraisal processes. Ernst & Young and Pricewaterhouse Coopers are among those that have recently gone down this route, again with the implication that if you don't participate, you are unlikely to get on.

But not all organisations are taking such a prescriptive line. BP's skills database, BP Connect, which has been up and running since late last year, is voluntary. Around 4,000 employees have signed up so far. And the company won't undertake any knowledge-sharing initiative unless there is a clearly defined business or technical issue that needs to be solved. It estimates that the 15 initiatives currently in progress will save around $60 million.

Speaking at the recent Ikon conference in London, Kent Greenes, BP's head of knowledge management, quoted the example of a manager in Colombia charged with making 50 per cent of his workforce redundant. He wanted to know how fellow managers in other countries had approached the issue. As a result, part of BP's intranet, Tap Web, now contains a section on what the company knows about downsizing, including a video interview describing the Colombian experience.

Yet, as Greenes told delegates: "I had been to this guy a year before and said: 'You're doing some great work in drilling, can we help you to capture that so we can share it with everyone else?' His response was: 'Get out of here, we don't have time for that.' But the history of what they did in Colombia [in drilling] is now captured, and they spent time and effort to do that. We're finding that reciprocity is a big driver for us."

Another key motivator, according to Greenes, is the status that goes with being seen as an expert. The biggest benefit of capturing on video an oil rig worker talking about the handover process from one shift to another, for example, has been that "operators, people working in the trenches, all of a sudden realise that BP cares about what they know. The recognition factor is unbelievable." Yet trust between management and employees is clearly essential for this to work.

As yet, few companies seem to be offering explicit financial rewards to employees who make a point of sharing information and knowledge with colleagues. But small inducements, such as bottles of champagne, are being used widely in a bid to raise awareness and encourage staff to put work into the system. Earlier this year Ernst & Young took this a stage further by offering prizes of £1,000 to 10 staff whose submissions were picked at random over a three-month period. According to Tina Mason, a senior knowledge manager at the firm, the number of submissions rose from about 50 a month prior to the "bribe" being offered to around 500 by the end of it, and has now settled down at between 200 and 300 a month.

Bumper start

Mason accepts that this approach emphasises quantity over quality, but insists it is an effective way of getting busy employees used to sharing their work. "Until you've made it part of their everyday life, you need these kinds of incentives to get activity going," she says.

More longer term, the dominant view at present seems to be that special rewards for knowledge sharing should be obsolete in a teamworking environment. Not only that but they are undesirable because they imply that knowledge sharing is an additional task rather than an integral part of people's jobs – and hence more likely to be seen as a fad.

The debate about reward structures is set to intensify as more companies begin to assess the results of their initial forays into knowledge management. This, like other "softer" issues, should be natural ground for personnel and development professionals. But what evidence there is suggests that few as yet are playing a significant role. Harris's research for KPMG found that only 7 per cent of knowledge initiatives were led by HR – half the number driven by the IT department. Separate research among 200 European companies by Cranfield University found that, of all functions, HR was the least likely to say that knowledge management was something it relied on.

Hardly surprising then that eligible respondents for the KPMG survey included chief executives, finance directors and marketing directors – but not HR directors. "Knowledge management just doesn't seem to be on their agendas," says Elizabeth Lank. A notable exception is BT Global (see panel) where a small, strategic HR function is leading a series of initiatives company-wide.

The most common explanation for the profession's lack of involvement is its lack of comfort with technology. But although IT has an important role to play in improving access to information and moving it around organisations quickly, the vast bulk of energy and resources still needs to be devoted to people and process issues. And the investment in IT could help HR in other ways. There is an obvious overlap, for instance, between skills databases that point people in the direction of help and advice and those packaged as part of HR information systems as a way of identifying skills shortages, planning career development, and so on.

Judging by the experience of the pioneers, there seems little doubt that if knowledge management is not to suffer the fate of previous initiatives, HR professionals will need to ensure that the cultural issues are tackled head on.

People Management, 13 August 1998
Reproduced with permission.

Resource 16

Core values shape W. L. Gore's innovative culture

W. L. Gore & Associates Inc., associates (not employees) don't have bosses, they have sponsors. They also don't have titles. Instead, they make commitments.

So what? As Gertrude Stein once said, "A rose is a rose is a rose is a rose." And lots of companies today come up with euphemisms for titles, departments and functions. It has become so trendy that *Fast Company* magazine dedicates space each month to highlight "Job Titles of the Future."

The difference is that at Gore, the manufacturer of Gore-Tex® fabric and other materials, the words they use really do mean something different than the words they re replacing. And they haven't been conjured up in the face of current trends, either. Rather, they've been a part of Gore's history since its beginning more than 40 years ago.

Gore's unique, flat, "lattice" culture stems from the four core values put in place by founder Bill Gore that were meant to foster a creative and energizing work environment. It's a culture that, without HR's commitment to those values, would be doomed for failure.

Innovation is the foundation of Gore

In 1958, Bill Gore left DuPont after 17 years as a research chemist to pursue market opportunities for PTFE (polytetrafluoroethylene), one of the most versatile polymers known to man. Bill and his wife, Vieve, began this new business venture in the basement of their home. Their son, Bob, then a chemical engineering student (and today the president and CEO), suggested the idea that resulted in Gore's first patent for a new PTFE insulated wire and cable product. Within two years, W. L. Gore & Associates moved into its first plant in Newark, Delaware, the company's headquarters.

Today, nearly 6,500 associates in 45 locations around the world continue to expand PTFE's applications in four product areas: electronic products, fabrics, industrial products and medical products. Growth has come to the company because of continual innovation by Gore associates. And innovation has come as a result of Gore's culture.

Because there are no bosses, there are no hierarchies that push decision making through the organization. Because there are no hierarchies, there are no pre-determined channels of communication, thus prompting associates to communicate with each other. And because associates don't have titles, they aren't locked into particular tasks, which encourages them to take on new and challenging assignments.

Sound like chaos? It could be, if it weren't for HR's deep integration in the company and its complete commitment to the company s values:

1. Fairness to each other and everyone with whom we come in contact.

2. Freedom to encourage, help and allow other associates to grow in knowledge, skill and scope of responsibility.
3. The ability to make one's own commitments and keep them.
4. Consultation with other associates before undertaking actions that could impact the reputation of the company by hitting it "below the waterline."

Says HR leader Sally Gore of the people with HR commitments: "Day in and day out, we're champions of the culture, guaranteeing that consideration for people plays into business decisions." HR's structure facilitates this task.

HR is integrated into the business

Gore has a small plant approach, meaning it limits each facility to approximately 200 people. Most plants are self-sufficient, with manufacturing, finance, research and development contained within the facility. That means there's also at least one HR generalist at each plant.

Those generalists are part of the plant leadership team. "They understand the business needs so they can help support them," says Terri Kelly, a business leader in the fabrics division of Gore. (By the way, the philosophy at Gore is that you're only a leader if you have followers. In annual surveys HR conducts, more than 50 percent of associates answer yes to the question, "Are you a leader?")

The generalists co-ordinate the plants people issues, which include hiring, conflict resolution, associate development, strategic planning and associate resource allocation. But they also contribute as members of the businesses leadership teams, keeping everyone focused on the values, the people issues and how they translate to the bottom line. Says Kelly: "In many ways, they're the ones who make sure we're being fair (value #1) and are creating an environment that people want to work in, which is critical to getting business results."

The plant generalists are supported by specialists in corporate headquarters. These include people who specialize in recruiting, training and development, compensation, benefits, relocation and communication. However, that isn't to say that any of these HR people – specialists or generalists – are limited by their location or specialty.

For example, Jackie Brinton, who has been with Gore for 22 years in areas related to HR, has a current specialty focus on corporate recruitment. But right now, she's also serving on a broader HR team, on a divisional HR team and on multiple teams that are putting together different programs within the corporation. A recent project she worked on, for example, was developing a Myers-Briggs module for a training and development team she's part of.

The HR structure has developed over time, changing as the company grows to facilitate maintaining the culture. Likewise, the innovative HR practices the company has in place have developed over time to ensure continual adherence to the values and culture.

It's not business as usual at Gore

Take a look at recruitment. Because of the unique culture at Gore, the interviewing process becomes even more vital. Brinton says the company views hiring as one of its "waterline" decisions – decisions of such critical importance to the company that one person can't make them without consulting others (value #4). Therefore, Gore involves numerous people in the interviewing process. For an HR generalist position at a plant, for example, members of the leadership team at the plant as well as HR specialists who know what competencies are needed would participate.

But HR recruiters like Brinton own the process. "The business defines the business need. I work with the business team to define what the expectations are, and what the skills required to accomplish those expectations are," says Brinton. She also sources candidates and is part of the interviewing and decision-making team.

Interview questions to candidates target not just technical skills but other skills that lead to success in the culture – such as team skills ("Give me an example of a time when you had a conflict with a team member"), communication skills and problem-solving skills ("Tell me how you solved a problem that was impeding your project").

Once a candidate has been identified, recruiters conduct a minimum of two and oftentimes many more reference checks, inquiring not just about title, time and grade but about the traits the company needs. Gore has learned that people who want to just come to work and do the same job day in and day out don't last long. "The needs of the business are changing and we need people who are agile, who can increase their skills," says Brinton. "Continuous learning is an expectation of all our associates" (value #2).

When a person is hired, it s for a particular commitment, not a job (value #3). That commitment might be to run a particular machine, do recruiting or crunch numbers in finance. "We don't have narrowly defined job titles that limit people, but instead, we have general expectations within functional areas," says Brinton. The reason, she says, is because people take greater ownership of something they've volunteered for and committed to than something they are told to do.

The new hire is assigned a sponsor – an associate who has made a commitment to help the newcomer get to what Brinton refers to as "the quick win" (value #2). That is, a sponsor gives the person a basic understanding of his or her commitments and what it will take to be successful in those commitments. As associates commitments and needs change, they and their sponsors may decide they need something different from a sponsor, and that role may also change.

One of the primary responsibilities of a sponsor is to be a positive advocate. As such, the sponsors collect information and feedback regarding personal development from peers and leaders. That information is then shared with a compensation committee. Currently, there are approximately 15 compensation committees within the organization, serving the numerous functional areas of the business. For example, there s a compensation committee for human resources, one for manufacturing, one for engineers, and so on.

The committees are comprised of leaders within the company that understand the value someone in that functional area has, and what technical excellence looks like. HR s role is to ensure the process is fair, and plant generalists are on most of the local committees.

The committees take the feedback they get on associates and come up with a ranking of the people doing that function. The ranking is based on associates' contribution to the success of the business, not just their personal skills. For example, when evaluating an HR professional, a compensation committee would take all the input from other HR associates and plant and corporate leaders, and rank the individual with the other HR associates from highest contributor to lower ones. Then using guidelines based on external salary data, the top of the list will be paid more than the bottom. The objective is to be internally fair and externally competitive. To aid in this goal, compensation specialists at Gore compare the company's compensation levels and benefits periodically to companies such as IBM, 3M, DuPont and Hewlett-Packard.

"Our compensation practice is a good example of our principles in action day to day," says Brinton. "It's our goal to pay people based on the success of the business, and that's fair (value #1). People make their own commitments (value #3), and that affects their level of contribution." Also in fairness, Gore takes into consideration that it's possible that an associate can make a significant contribution to the corporation in a business that is not successful.

Part of Gore s compensation practice is to offer associates stock ownership and profit sharing plans (there's #1 again). In fact, associates own 25 percent of this privately held company – the Gore family owns the rest.

It works for Gore
There's no doubt that Gore's organizational structure and lattice culture wouldn't succeed without the support of these HR practices. And the structure and culture have worked well for Gore, which currently reports worldwide sales of $1.4 billion. However, the picture isn't all rosy. "People have a misconception that this is a soft corporate culture," says Brinton, "but this is a pretty tough environment for people to be in. We put a lot of responsibility on individuals to be personally successful and to work toward business success."

Sally Gore agrees. "I often compare our organizational structure to a democracy to explain the tradeoffs in a structure like ours," she says. "When you look at it from a purely objective standpoint, a democratic government may not be the most time- or cost-effective way to run a country. In the end, however, the quality of life is far better than what you'll find in a dictatorship. We believe the associate satisfaction and spirit of innovation that result from our culture more than compensate for its challenges."

Sometimes a rose is just a rose. But as W. L. Gore demonstrates, sometimes, it's much, much more.

Workforce, March 1999
Article by Dawn Anfuso. Copyright March 1999.
Used with permission of ACC Communications Inc./
Workforce, Costa Mesa, CA, USA.
Website at http://www.workforceonline.com
All rights reserved.

Learning Resources
Centre